Corporate Social Responsibility and Regulatory Governance

International Political Economy Series

General Editor: Timothy M. Shaw, Professor and Director, Institute of International Relations, The University of the West Indies, Trinidad & Tobago

Titles include:

Andrew F. Cooper and Timothy W. Shaw *(editors)*
THE DIPLOMACIES OF SMALL STATES
Between Vulnerability and Resilience

Anthony Leysens
THE CRITICAL THEORY OF ROBERT W.COX
Fugitive or Guru?

Mireya Solís, Barbara Stallings and Saori N. Katada *(editors)*
COMPETITIVE REGIONALISM
FTA Diffusion in the Pacific Rim

Peter Utting and José Carlos Marques *(editors)*
CORPORATE SOCIAL RESPONSIBILITY AND REGULATORY GOVERNANCE
Towards Inclusive Development?

International Political Economy Series
Series Standing Order ISBN 978–0–333–71708–0   hardcover
Series Standing Order ISBN 978–0–333–71110–1   paperback
(outside North America only)

You can receive future titles in this series as they are published by placing a standing order. Please contact your bookseller or, in case of difficulty, write to us at the address below with your name and address, the title of the series and one of the ISBNs quoted above.

Customer Services Department, Macmillan Distribution Ltd, Houndmills, Basingstoke, Hampshire RG21 6XS, England

Corporate Social Responsibility and Regulatory Governance

Towards Inclusive Development?

Edited by

Peter Utting

José Carlos Marques

palgrave
macmillan

UNRISD
United Nations
Research Institute
for Social Development

First published 2010 by
PALGRAVE MACMILLAN

Palgrave Macmillan in the UK is an imprint of Macmillan Publishers Limited, registered in England, company number 785998, of Houndmills, Basingstoke, Hampshire RG21 6XS.

Palgrave Macmillan in the US is a division of St Martin's Press LLC, 175 Fifth Avenue, New York, NY 10010.

Palgrave Macmillan is the global academic imprint of the above companies and has companies and representatives throughout the world.

Palgrave® and Macmillan® are registered trademarks in the United States, the United Kingdom, Europe and other countries

ISBN 978–0–230–57644–5   hardback

This book is printed on paper suitable for recycling and made from fully managed and sustained forest sources. Logging, pulping and manufacturing processes are expected to conform to the environmental regulations of the country of origin.

A catalogue record for this book is available from the British Library.

A catalog record for this book is available from the Library of Congress.

10   9   8   7   6   5   4   3   2   1
19   18   17   16   15   14   13   12   11   10

Printed and bound in Great Britain by
CPI Antony Rowe, Chippenham and Eastbourne

Contents

List of Tables, Figures and Box

Tables

Figures

Box

Preface

One of the most vibrant movements for institutional reform to have emerged during the past two decades is one that attempts to recast the role of business in society and development. The 'corporate social responsibility' (CSR) movement is backed by a powerful coalition of forces, including the senior management of many large companies, business associations, non-governmental organizations (NGOs), trade unions, consumer groups, 'shareholder activists', governments and international organizations. Its underlying principle is that companies, with some prodding and support from their 'stakeholders', can do much on their own accord to improve their social, environmental and human rights record. Indeed, they can become active partners in crafting patterns of development that are socially inclusive, environmentally sustainable and respectful of human rights. But surrounding CSR is a polemic that remains as vibrant today as when the concept first entered the mainstream.

Despite major variations in the response to CSR by companies, sectors and 'varieties of capitalism', it is possible to draw up a rough balance sheet of achievements and failures. CSR discourse has become ubiquitous and has been instrumental in raising awareness that firms have responsibilities other than to their owners and 'the bottom line'. Over time more and more issues have become part of the CSR portfolio, and there has been a gradual shift in emphasis from 'talking the talk' to 'walking the walk'. But the promise of CSR has not materialized. Indeed, the multiple crises that the world is currently facing provide stark evidence of just how inadequate it is. Despite all the talk about responsiveness to stakeholder issues, transparency and participation, and about being concerned with the long-term or sustainable development, CSR has failed to make much of a dent in those sectors, structures and institutions associated with crisis, inequality and unsustainable development. In fact, CSR may have done more to reinforce rather than correct imbalances in power relations between states, business and civil society actors.

In this volume we suggest that understanding both the potential and the limitations of CSR requires recognition of the fact that much of CSR thinking is itself in crisis. This manifests itself in four respects: it tends to be ahistorical, failing to draw on the lessons of history regarding the conditions and contexts that encouraged business to be an effective partner in development; it is empirically weak, focusing narrowly on 'best practice' cases and providing little systematic evidence of outcomes and impacts; it is conceptually thin, excluding certain theoretical perspectives that are key for understanding the potential and limits of CSR; and it is politically naïve, failing to interrogate sufficiently the complex ways in which multiple actors and interests, operating on various scales, shape policy and practice. This volume brings together authors from different disciplinary fields in order to address these shortcomings, recognizing that part of the explanation for the intellectual crisis of CSR relates not only to the compartmentalization of academic inquiry, but also the tendency for mainstream thinking to be dominated by particular disciplines and schools of thought. The chapter authors are associated with critical management studies, international relations, development studies, law, human geography and political science. The chapters are based on papers that were originally prepared for a conference on Business, Social Policy and Corporate Political Influence in Developing Countries organized by the United Nations Research Institute for Social Development (UNRISD) in Geneva in November 2007, and for an UNRISD project that examined the role of business, state and civil society actors in developmental processes conducive to poverty reduction.

On behalf of UNRISD we would like to thank the United Kingdom Department for International Development (DFID) for having provided financial support for the above conference where the original drafts of several of the chapters in this volume were presented. As is the case with all UNRISD research, this work would not have been possible without the core funding provided by the governments of Denmark, Finland, Mexico, Norway, Sweden, Switzerland and the United Kingdom. We are particularly grateful to Rebecca Buchholz for editorial assistance, as well as to Anita Tombez and Katrien De Moor for copy-editing the manuscript.

Peter Utting and José Carlos Marques
Geneva and Montreal, 6 April 2009

Notes on the Contributors

Michael Blowfield is a Senior Research Fellow at the University of Oxford Smith School for Enterprise and the Environment. His recent publications include *Corporate Responsibility: A Critical Introduction* (with Alan Murray, 2008); 'Stewards of virtue? The ethical dilemma of CSR in African agriculture', with Catherine Dolan (*Development & Change*, 2008), and 'Reasons to be cheerful? What we know about CSR's impact' (*Third World Quarterly*, 2007). He is also a Teaching Fellow at the London Business School and a Visiting Professor at Middlesex Business School.

Colin Crouch is Professor of Governance and Public Management at the Business School of Warwick University. He is also an External Scientific Member of the Max Planck Institute for the Study of Societies. His most recent books include *Post-Democracy* (2004) and *Capitalist Diversity and Change: Recombinant Governance and Institutional Entrepreneurs* (2005).

Ruth Findlay-Brooks is a Development Director with the University of Cambridge Programme for Sustainability Leadership. She has contributed to a number of journals and publications, most recently as a contributing author to *The A to Z of Corporate Social Responsibility* (2007).

Doris Fuchs is Professor of International Relations and Development Politics at the University of Münster. She is co-editor (with Jennifer Clapp) of *Corporate Power in Global Agrifood Governance* (2009) and author of *Business Power in Global Governance* (2007) as well as *Institutions for Environmental Stewardship* (2003). Her primary areas of research are private governance, sustainable development and consumption, food politics and policy, and corporate structural and discursive power.

Catia Gregoratti is a PhD candidate (Politics) at the University of Manchester and a Research Associate at Newcastle University. She has co-edited a special issue of the graduate journal *Political Perspectives* entitled 'New Perspectives on Africa', and her research has also been disseminated through the University of Manchester Centre for International Politics (CIP) Working Papers Series.

Paddy Ireland is Professor of Law at the University of Kent Law School. Among his most recent publications are 'Shareholder primacy and the distribution of wealth' (*Modern Law Review*, 2005), and 'Limited liability, shareholder rights and the problem of corporate irresponsibility' (*Cambridge Journal of Economics*, 2008).

Agni Kalfagianni is a Researcher at the University of Stuttgart, Department of International Relations and European Integration. She is the author of the monograph *Transparency in the Food Chain: Policies and Politics* (2006) and *Corporate Social Responsibility in the Aquaculture Chains in the Netherlands and the EU* (2006).

José Carlos Marques is a former Research Analyst in the Markets, Business and Regulation Programme at the United Nations Research Institute for Social Development (UNRISD). He holds an MSc in Development Management from the London School of Economics and Political Science, and is currently pursuing a PhD in Strategy and Organization at McGill University.

Ndangwa Noyoo is a Senior Social Policy Analyst in the Social Policy Programme of the National Department of Social Development in South Africa. His publications include *Social Policy and Human Development in Zambia* (2008) and *Social Welfare in Zambia* (2000).

Florence Palpacuer is Professor in Management Studies at the University of Montpellier. She has published numerous articles and book chapters on global production and its social consequences in terms of jobs and local development. Recently, she has co-authored a book on changing layoff patterns in large multinationals in France, titled *Sortie(s) de cadres: Le licenciement pour motif personnel comme outil de gestion de la firme mondialisée* (2007).

Renginee Pillay is a Lecturer in Law at the University of Surrey and a PhD candidate at the University of Kent, where her doctoral research focuses on the role of CSR in developing countries. Her most recent publication is *CSR and Development: The Mauritian Experience* (Conference Proceedings of the 7th Annual International Academy of African Business and Development Conference, Accra, Ghana, 2006).

Ngai-Ling Sum is a Senior Lecturer in the Department of Politics and International Relations at Lancaster University. She is co-author (with Bob Jessop) of *Beyond the Regulation Approach* (2006) and (with Pun Ngai) of 'Paradoxes of ethical transnational production: Code of conduct in a Chinese workplace' (*Competition and Change*, 2005).

Peter Utting is Deputy Director of the United Nations Research Institute for Social Development (UNRISD), where he also coordinates the Markets, Business and Regulation Programme. His publications include the edited volumes *Corporate Accountability and Sustainable Development* (with Jennifer Clapp, 2008) and *The Greening of Business in Developing Countries: Rhetoric, Reality and Prospects* (2002).

James Van Alstine is a Lecturer in Environmental Policy at the University of Leeds Sustainability Research Institute. His publications include 'Governance from below: Contesting corporate environmentalism in Durban, South Africa' (*Business, Strategy and the Environment*, 2009), and the co-authored report, *Managing Risk and Maintaining License to Operate: Participatory Planning and Monitoring in the Extractive Industries* (2008).

Rob van Tulder is Professor of International Business–Society Management, Erasmus University Rotterdam/Rotterdam School of Management and coordinator of the SCOPE databank project. His recent books include *Reputations at Stake* (Het Spectrum, 2003), *International Business–Society Management: Linking Corporate Responsibility and Globalization* (2006), and *Skill Sheets: An Integrated Approach to Research, Study and Management* (2007).

Wayne Visser is Founder and CEO of CSR International; he is also a Visiting Professor in CSR at Mannheim University, and Senior Associate and Internal Examiner at the University of Cambridge Programme for Industry. His recent books include *Landmarks for Sustainability* (2009), *Making A Difference: Purpose-Inspired Leadership for Corporate Sustainability and Responsibility (CSR)* (2008) and *The A to Z of Corporate Social Responsibility: A Complete Reference Guide to Concepts, Codes and Organisations* (co-edited with D. Matten, M. Pohl and N. Tolhurst, 2007).

Thurstan Wright is an Analyst at The Climate Group, an international NGO, where he supports the Corporate Engagement and Policy teams in projects that aim to build high-level political and business support for an ambitious post-2012 climate change agreement. Prior to joining The Climate Group, he was at the University of Cambridge Programme for Industry, where he coordinated The Prince of Wales Corporate Leaders Group on Climate Change and Business and the Environment Programme.

List of Abbreviations and Acronyms

AAC	Anglo-American Corporation
ACFTU	All-China Federation of Trade Unions
AFL–CIO	American Federation of Labor–Congress of Industrial Organizations
ALMPs	active labour market policies
ANC	African National Congress
AQMA	Air Quality Management Act
BASD	Business Action for Sustainable Development
BEE	Black Economic Empowerment
BITs	bilateral trade treaties
BOP	bottom of the pyramid
BP	British Petroleum
BRC	British Retail Consortium
BSAC	British South Africa Company
C.A.F.E.	Starbucks' Coffee and Farmer Equity Practices
CAT	Centro de Apoyo al Trabajador (*Workers Support Centre*)
CCC	Clean Clothes Campaign
CEO	chief executive officer
CLR	Campaign for Labor Rights
CORE	Corporate Responsibility Coalition
CSO	civil society organization
CSR	corporate social responsibility
Danida	Danish International Development Assistance
DEAT	Department of Environmental Affairs and Tourism (South Africa)
EIA	environmental impact assessment
ETI	Ethical Trading Initiative
EU	European Union
Eurep	Euro-Retailers Produce Working Group
FDI	foreign direct investment
FLA	Fair Labor Association
FoEI	Friends of the Earth International
FSC	Forest Stewardship Council
FWF	Fair Wear Foundation
GATS	General Agreement on Trade in Services

GATT	General Agreement on Tariffs and Trade
GCCs	Global Commodity Chains
GDP	gross domestic product
GEAR	Growth, Employment and Redistribution
GFSI	Global Food Safety Initiative
Global-Gap	Global Partnership for Good Agricultural Practice
GNA	good neighbour agreement
GPNs	global production networks
GRI	Global Reporting Initiative
GSB	Growing Sustainable Business
GTZ	Deutsche Gesellschaft für Technische Zusammenarbeit (*German Technical Cooperation*)
HIV/AIDS	human immunodeficiency virus/acquired immunodeficiency syndrome
HLL	Hindustan Lever Ltd.
HSE	health, safety and environment
IFIs	international financial institutions
IFS	International Food Standard
ILO	International Labour Organization
IMF	International Monetary Fund
INGOs	international NGOs
ISO	International Organization for Standardization
ITGLWF	International Textile, Garment and Leather Workers Federation
JANUN	Jugend Aktion für Natur- und Umweltschutz Niedersachsen (*Youth Action Network for Nature Conservation and Environmental Protection*)
KCM	Konkola Copper Mines
KGT	Kenya Gatsby Trust
LDCs	least developed countries
MDGs	Millennium Development Goals
MFA	Multi-Fibre Agreement
MMD	Movement for Multiparty Democracy
MOU	Memorandum of Understanding
MPP	Multi-Point Plan
MSIs	multistakeholder initiatives
MSN	Maquila Solidarity Network
NAFTA	North American Free Trade Agreement
NGOs	non-governmental organizations
NORAD	Norwegian Agency for Development Cooperation
OECD	Organisation for Economic Co-operation and Development
PAT	Partnerships Assessment Tool
PCCP	Postgraduate Certificate in Cross-Sector Partnership

PPPs	public–private partnerships
PR	public relations
RMB	Renminbi (currency of the People's Republic of China)
ROI	return on investment
ROSCs	Reports on the Observance of Standards and Codes
RST	Rhodesian Selection Trust
SACOM	Students and Scholars Against Corporate Misbehaviour
SAPIA	South African Petroleum Industry Association
SCI	Sustainable Communities Initiative
SDCEA	South Durban Community Environmental Alliance
SEA	Strategic Environmental Assessment
SITEMAG	Sindicato Independiente de Trabajadores de la Empresa Matamoros Garment (*Independent Union of Matamoros Garment Workers*)
SMEs	small and medium-sized enterprises
SMOs	social movement organizations
SO_2	sulphur dioxide
SROI	social return on investment
SZITIC	Shenzhen International Trusts and Investment Company
SZITIC-CP	SZITIC Commercial Property Development Co., Ltd.
TNCs	transnational corporations
TRIPS	Trade-Related Aspects of Intellectual Property Rights
UK	United Kingdom
UN	United Nations
UNCTAD	United Nations Conference on Trade and Development
UNDP	United Nations Development Programme
UNFIP	United Nations Fund for International Partnerships
UNIP	United National Independence Party
UNRISD	United Nations Research Institute for Social Development
UR	Uruguay Round
USA	United States of America
USAS	United Students against Sweatshops
VoC	varieties of capitalism
VOC	volatile organic compound
WFP	World Food Programme
WSSD	World Summit on Sustainable Development
WTO	World Trade Organization
ZCCM	Zambia Consolidated Copper Mines

Introduction: The Intellectual Crisis of CSR

Peter Utting and José Carlos Marques[1]

Turbulent events in the world's financial, food and energy markets, global recession, as well as the urgency of climate change, growing inequality and persistent poverty, suggest that various features of globalization and economic liberalization are fundamentally flawed. They also starkly contradict the development scenarios of those who had been touting the virtues of self-regulating markets, minimalist states and the capacity of large firms to recast their role in society through 'corporate social responsibility' (CSR). An offshoot of the free market ideology that took hold in the 1980s, CSR matured within the context of the 'institutional turn'[2] of the 1990s, which had both an analytical and a constructivist or normative dimension. The former sought to better understand how institutions affect society and economic performance, as well as how large firms – as organizations – enjoy some autonomy from market forces to pursue their strategic interests. The constructivist dimension was concerned with filling governance gaps and fine-tuning institutions, in particular through so-called voluntary initiatives and 'private regulation', in an attempt to minimize certain perverse effects of economic liberalization that affected workers, communities, consumers and the environment. Such effects increasingly threatened the legitimacy of big business as well as the dominant ideology underpinning the rise of corporate power, namely neoliberalism. CSR, then, sought to address new challenges for business associated with risk, uncertainty and complexity. However, it did so in a way that was as much about sustaining core features of contemporary, corporate-led capitalism as improving corporations' social and environmental performance.

Mainstream perspectives on CSR held out the promise that corporate self-regulation and voluntary initiatives could be harnessed to address many social and environmental problems – where the state had failed, private enterprise and non-state actors could succeed. Although a variety of non-state actors, notably business associations, non-governmental organizations (NGOs) and various company stakeholders, played a role in this new approach, in practice, it was large firms, in particular transnational corporations (TNCs), that engaged more directly with the discourse and instruments of CSR. The literature on the topic suggests that, potentially at least, CSR has profound implications for developing countries. The scope for win–win possibilities or the so-called 'business case' – whereby CSR would translate into conventional pro-business benefits such as competitive advantage, profitability, productivity and market share – was thought to be considerable.[3] Economic actors should, and could, broaden their strategic focus beyond 'the bottom line' and be guided by a 'triple-bottom line' associated with financial, social and environmental performance (Elkington 1997). As a result, business could contribute to a pattern of 'inclusive development' where goals of social development and environmental protection are not dwarfed by those of economic growth and macroeconomic stabilization. Such reasoning characterized CSR as a focal component in the transformation of the traditional roles of the state and business in development. Indeed, big business was wooed by the international development community to engage with the global effort to reduce poverty through the Millennium Development Goals (MDGs) and public–private partnerships (PPPs). The expectation was that companies and business associations would become developmental agents, often assuming functions typically associated with the state in relation to the provisioning of basic – or public – goods and services, standard setting and inspection.

Not only have tangible achievements paled in comparison to the promise but, in some respects, the mainstream CSR agenda[4] has also missed the mark in terms of the issues it has prioritized. A conception of the role of business in society that contrasted sharply with Milton Friedman's notion that 'the business of business is business' (albeit within a context of state regulation), CSR was typically defined in terms of greater responsiveness on the part of companies to societal and stakeholder concerns; integration of social and environmental considerations in business operations; voluntary initiatives that go beyond both philanthropy and standards embodied in law; and 'doing no harm'. Although the CSR agenda gradually broadened over time, taking on board more issues related to social, sustainable and rights-based development, major blind spots remained. The current financial crisis, its economic and social fall-out, and all that has been revealed of corporate practices that underpinned the crisis, provides clear evidence that critical issues were left off the mainstream agenda.[5] Not only did the CSR 'movement' pay scant attention to the financial sector,[6] it also displayed somewhat of a narrow focus on aspects of development related to particularly visible forms of environmental degradation, eco-efficiency, occupational health and safety in TNC affiliates and top-tier suppliers, child labour in the supply chain, and community assistance. Another major component of social development, namely rights, gradually came to figure more prominently in CSR discourse and standard-setting. In practice, however, concrete measures and progress to address both labour rights and the broader category of human rights were limited.

However, the major blind spot in both CSR discourse and practice is related to a third crucial dimension of social development, namely distributional justice and equity (Utting 2007). Just how gaping a hole this was on the CSR agenda has become strikingly clear in the context of the current financial crisis where issues of executive pay, dividends to shareholders and tax avoidance/evasion, as well as the relationship between a debt-driven consumption model and the compression of real wages or inequities in the functional distribution of income loom large. Another dimension of distributional injustice, namely the gross inequities in the distribution of value within global commodity or supply chains, also partly explains a curious paradox – how three decades of economic globalization and growth of foreign direct investment (FDI) not only resulted in chronic North–South imbalances but also failed to make a significant dent in poverty levels, with malnutrition actually increasing in many countries. Furthermore, while CSR purported to address certain governance gaps and imbalances between corporate rights and responsibilities that characterized globalization and liberalization, in some contexts it served to reinforce distributional inequities by fostering a certain anti-state bias in the regulatory domain, while enhancing the power and authority of TNCs in global supply chains and global governance.

How did this situation come about? Why did an approach with so much promise achieve so little? And why did so much of the burgeoning literature on CSR fail to take stock of such failings? These are the central questions addressed in this volume. In this introduction we distill insights from the various chapters and some other writings in an attempt to understand what went wrong and what might be done to correct the outcomes. We suggest that what was at fault was not simply a number of strategic and operational limitations but indeed the intellectual project surrounding CSR itself. We focus on four analytical and empirical limitations that point to an intellectual crisis of CSR. These concern the fact that CSR thinking is largely ahistorical, empirically weak, theoretically thin and politically naïve. Each of the chapters that follows this introduction deals with some combination of these aspects.

Analytical and empirical gaps

A quarter of a century has passed since the publication of *Strategic Management: A Stakeholder Approach*, the book by R. Edward Freeman (1984) that was instrumental in catapulting 'corporate social responsibility' (CSR) into the field of management studies. And nearly two decades have passed since preparations for the United Nations Earth Summit drew global corporations into the international sustainable development agenda. In the aftermath of these ideational and institutional developments, expectations about the role of the private sector, TNCs in particular, in development have changed considerably. Numerous international organizations, governments, NGOs and business associations are urging big business to play a more proactive role in social and sustainable development via a range of voluntary initiatives intended to improve their social and environmental performance. Corporations are actively participating in private regulatory initiatives that both set standards and oversee their application. Furthermore, they are increasingly engaged in PPPs or so-called 'bottom of the pyramid' (BOP) business models that supply goods and services to low-income groups or consumers or engage them as producers in supply chains.

As a result, CSR discourse has become ubiquitous. Indeed, a movement of considerable ideological and political weight, involving a broad coalition of social actors and institutions, has emerged (Bendell 2004; Utting 2008a, 2005a). The upshot has been a significant expansion of the CSR agenda. But what does all this imply for the central issue addressed in this volume, namely how to craft development models that are more inclusive?[7] The global reach of CSR discourse and practice has generated a vast literature that attempts to assess the potential and limits of CSR and identify the so-called drivers underpinning contemporary business–state and business–society relations. Much of the literature is characterized by a fairly myopic take on the dynamics of institutional change and somewhat polarized positions on the status and future of CSR. This has resulted in an exciting debate surrounding the question of whether big business helps or hinders the task of promoting inclusive development via CSR, PPPs and private regulation, but the analytical foundations on which the debate is grounded are somewhat shaky. Both academic and activist inquiry often suffers from disciplinary compartmentalization, ideological turf battles and relatively simplistic or uni-modal institutional solutions for dealing with the social and environmental downside to corporate globalization. The analysis of what works, what does not and what needs to change is often constrained by the tendency to ignore key conceptual, historical, empirical, political and institutional dimensions.

The early literature on CSR often situated itself in one of two camps. One highlighted the potential of CSR, drew heavily on 'best practice' examples to suggest that the transition from 'business-as-usual' to 'corporate citizenship' was feasible or well underway, and assumed that 'learning by doing', awareness of win–win possibilities, stakeholder dialogue and admonitions from 'the court of public opinion' were key to replication and scaling-up. Power asymmetries, structural constraints, the role of the state, and inter-group conflict and bargaining were downplayed if not altogether ignored in such explanations.[8] Business then was part of the solution. If it was not quite there yet, the potential was considerable once certain institutional fine-tuning took place (Zadek 2001).

Another camp tended to dismiss CSR as 'greenwash' or window-dressing aimed at diverting public attention, countering threats of regulation and legitimizing what was fundamentally 'business-as-usual'. Such perspectives tended to emphasize the structural conditions of contemporary capitalism that posed fundamental obstacles to voluntaristic approaches.[9] This critical literature played a key role in interrogating and demystifying CSR discourse, pointing out the limits of corporate self-regulation, keeping the spotlight on the perverse effects of corporate capitalism and neoliberalism, and focusing attention on the need for alternative regulatory approaches and patterns of consumption and production (Kitazawa 2007; International Forum on Globalization 2002). It also informed activist campaigns that kept the pressure on big business to improve its social, environmental and human rights performance.

However, the 'greenwash' perspective suffered from three major problems. First, by dismissing CSR reforms as 'business-as-usual' it seemed to downplay the possibility that institutional reform (that was progressive from the perspective of social development) could develop from activism and contestation. Second, it failed to grasp the mix of institutional and political conditions that historically rendered capitalism, or particular sectors or industries, more palatable under certain models of development. These conditions had to do with so-called varieties of capitalism, business preferences, path dependency, the nature of the state and its regulatory and welfare orientation, the interplay and complementarity of 'voluntary' and 'legalistic' regulation, the correlation of social forces, the role of struggle, participatory forms of governance and social pacts involving non-state actors (Hall and Soskice 2001; Evans 2005b). Third, attention to the goal of regulating corporations by hook or by crook could crowd out consideration of certain trade-offs and unexpected consequences for enterprises and workers in developing countries. Furthermore, regulation in and of itself would not necessarily address certain key issues of concern to 'the global justice movement' to do with unequal power relations and the nature of the economy (Newell 2008).

While much of the literature is still associated with one or other of these camps, there is greater recognition of the need for a more nuanced, empirically and theoretically grounded understanding of the contemporary role of corporations in governance and development and the potential and limits of CSR.[10] More in-depth inquiries into the impacts of specific CSR initiatives and developing country experiences are emerging.[11] And increasing attention is now being focused on a more comprehensive notion of 'corporate accountability', which implies moving beyond ad hoc voluntary initiatives, top-down 'do-gooding' and very selective forms of stakeholder engagement. Instead, this approach emphasizes the need for mechanisms that oblige corporations to answer to various stakeholders, allow victims of corporate bad practice to channel grievances and seek redress, and entail consequences for companies that do not comply with agreed standards (Bendell 2004; Newell 2002). Such mechanisms often involve more meaningful forms of participation, reconnecting CSR and public policy or law, and finding ways in which voluntary and legalistic approaches can be mutually reinforcing (McBarnet et al. 2007; Utting 2008b, 2005b). It also means resurrecting the role of the state as a key actor in regulatory governance and questioning the implicit or explicit anti-state bias that has infused mainstream thinking about CSR.

This volume deals with these issues. It does so by addressing what we believe are four fundamental limitations of the mainstream literature, some of which are also shared by more critical perspectives:

- ignoring the lessons of history that shed light on why and how business contributed to inclusive development at different times, in different countries;
- emphasizing empirical approaches that thrive on anecdotal evidence and the analysis of how CSR affects business, with limited systemic understanding of corporate responses and development impacts;
- disregarding certain theoretical perspectives that help to illuminate the potential and limits of CSR; and
- failing to grasp the complexity of institutional settings and power relations that drive progressive reform and deepen CSR.

Learning from history

The first limitation relates to the ahistorical nature of much of the literature. If history is alluded to, the starting point is often the reality or perception of inefficient and corrupt government, or 'state failure', as well as the notion that globalization renders past forms of regulation and governance ineffective. From this perspective, traditional approaches to business regulation are seen as fundamentally flawed. So-called 'command and control' regulation is considered a blunt instrument that stifles innovation. Numerous labour and environmental laws exist but are rarely enforced. At the international level, governments are often unable to agree on 'hard' regulatory instruments as, for example, in the case of the United Nations (UN) Code of Conduct for TNCs some two decades ago.[12]

Missing from these accounts is the body of empirical evidence describing the circumstances that shaped the role of business in social development during different time periods. It is important to situate CSR on a historical trajectory in order to reveal the conditions, strategies and contexts that were conducive to socially responsible business in the past; to consider which elements are relevant to today's circumstances; and to determine whether they are being considered in current strategies to promote CSR. The perspective provided by several of the chapters in this volume (see, in particular, Colin Crouch, Paddy Ireland and Renginee Pillay, and Ndangwa Noyoo),[13] as well as a forthcoming companion volume, reveal the complex set of economic, political and institutional conditions, or governance arrangements, required to ensure the sustainable contribution of business to social development. Examples of these include:

- relatively strong states with a developmental vision and welfare orientation;
- social pacts whereby business, the state (and in some contexts, labour groups) engaged in extensive national-level dialogue and negotiation concerning how to reach national social and economic objectives;
- labour movements and/or other social groups that acted as countervailing social forces;
- corporate elites that were 'socially embedded' through their relations with local communities; and
- the rise of 'managerialism' in the early decades of the twentieth century, which not only provided a certain autonomy from shareholder interests but cultivated a degree of responsiveness to societal concerns in contexts where there was a strong ethos about corporations acting in the public good.

In such contexts the notion of what constituted socially responsible business was generally quite different to contemporary CSR. Paying taxes, generating employment, employing workers for the long term, upholding labour rights and giving back to the community through philanthropy were routine expectations. The mix and relative weight of elements, however, could vary substantially under different 'varieties of capitalism' and policy regimes. This analysis suggests that the drivers of contemporary CSR, in particular those associated with reputation and risk management, and various forms of interaction with NGOs, differ from, and seem considerably weaker than, those underpinning business activities and strategies associated with inclusive development in the past.

The contrasts provided by historical analysis highlight how the changing context of state–market relations and the configuration of social forces are key to understanding the substance and trajectory of CSR. While the Freemanesque language of 'stakeholder responsiveness', 'stakeholder dialogue' and 'stakeholder capitalism' is commonly spoken, the concept of shareholder primacy, incentives for senior management and appropriate signalling of the market have dominated capitalist logic over the past quarter century (Boyer 2005). This period has also witnessed major changes in the configuration of social and institutional forces. We see the rise of finance and retail capital, and the so-called structural power of business, the decline of organized labour and certain institutions of mainstream democracy, the weakening of corporatist social pacts, the rolling back of certain state regulatory functions and capacities, and the rise of the business-friendly or FDI-friendly competition state (Reich 2007; Stiglitz 2004). A key change has been the restructuring of industrial production and the integration of suppliers and distributors, from both the North and South, into global value chains (Gereffi and Korzeniewicz 1994). Dominated by TNCs that control production, marketing and research and development (R&D), the nature, local embeddedness and developmental impact of such chains varies considerably.[14]

Empirical analysis

The second limitation addressed in this volume relates to the gap between CSR discourse and reality, that is, the failure to measure and evaluate real progress in CSR performance and its impacts on small enterprises, people and the environment in developing countries. The corporate social performance (CSP) – corporate financial performance (CFP) literature in the management discipline, for example, defines CSP quite narrowly and only in the developed country context.[15] Moreover, it focuses upon the financial outcomes of CSP for the firm with little consideration of the social consequences. In this volume we are particularly concerned with the limited attention to outcomes and impacts associated with inclusive development. Several chapters (see contributions by Michael Blowfield; Rob van Tulder; Ruth Findlay-Brooks, Wayne Visser and Thurstan Wright; Doris Fuchs and Agni Kalfagianni; and Catia Gregoratti) address these aspects. They show that:

- the CSR agenda has been promoted with a considerable rhetorical zeal that emphasizes stated objectives or intentions as opposed to concrete evidence of performance and impacts; far more attention has been paid to assessing what CSR does for business and the 'bottom line' than for people and the environment;
- the level of engagement of the world's largest 100 corporations with CSR and issues of poverty reduction varies considerably, and is more 'inactive' or 'reactive' than 'active' or 'proactive', although such engagement varies to some extent according to different industries and regional 'varieties of capitalism'; and
- the objectives of certain types of PPPs and private standard-setting initiatives are often not realized in practice, the distribution of benefits may be heavily skewed towards more powerful stakeholders, and PPPs often fare poorly in relation to participation and accountability.

Theoretical perspectives

The third limitation of mainstream writing is its inability to adequately assess its potential and limits of CSR from a developmental perspective because it is conceptually shallow. Considerable attention has been paid to management and organizational theory, as well as some strands of governance theory, in explaining why the modern-day corporation – in contexts of globalization and liberalization – should, and does, engage with CSR.[16] Moreover, Polanyian analysis has enriched our understanding of the political economy of CSR. Particularly important in this regard are analyses that draw on Polanyi's concepts of embeddedness and the 'double movement' in order to show both why CSR is necessary in a normative sense, as well as its political and economic underpinnings. This notion of 'embedded liberalism' (Ruggie 1982) accepts the reality of economic globalization and liberalization but insists on the need for institutions that can mitigate perverse social effects. In the words of the UN Secretary-General's Special Representative for Business and Human Rights, John Ruggie, what is needed is 'principled pragmatism' (United Nations 2006). While this approach has advanced our understanding of the role of CSR, it runs the risk of associating almost any institutional reform or 'thickening' with progressivity. As several chapters in this volume point out, different agendas or logics are at play in the field of CSR, often with quite different implications from the perspective of inclusive development. The particular role of institutions, therefore, is to some extent up for grabs or shaped by contestation. Furthermore, what matters is not simply institution building or reform per se but the mix and relative weights of different institutions associated with the state, the market, the firm, civil society and communities.

Also important is the nature of the structural changes that are occurring as well as institutional path dependence. Both establish important boundaries as to what is possible in terms of CSR and why certain firms, industries and societies may be more or less amenable to CSR reforms. Several chapters examine such contexts drawing on certain variants of governance theory, varieties of capitalism analysis, neo-Gramscian and neo-Foucauldian perspectives, as well as French regulation theory (see in particular, Colin Crouch; Ngai-Ling Sum; Doris Fuchs and Agni Kalfagianni; James Van Alstine; and Florence Palpacuer).

This analysis reveals a number of important limitations of contemporary approaches associated with 'voluntarism' and private regulation, and provides pointers to regulatory frameworks and modes of governance potentially more conducive to inclusive development. Two key conceptual themes running through the volume relate to *power* and *institutional complementarity*. The former highlights:

- the need to factor in the changing nature of the state in contexts of globalization, state–market relations and societal and elite perceptions of the role of the state, in order to understand why regulatory authority is delegated to, or assumed by, non-state actors;
- the importance of power relations between different social actors and stakeholders, and their role in framing the CSR agenda, as well as how costs and benefits of CSR are negotiated and distributed among stakeholders and within value chains;

- the various ways 'corporate power' manifests itself – structurally, instrumentally and discursively (Fuchs 2005);
- how the potential to improve labour standards through CSR confronts contradictory processes associated with changes in systems of industrial organization and regulation linked to both labour market flexibilization and new technologies that facilitate cost-cutting and corporate control of value chains;
- whether aspects of economic governance associated with 'corporate hierarchy', that is, the relative autonomy from competitive pressures that large corporations enjoy, can provide certain spaces for top-down CSR and voluntary corporate action;
- the extent to which CSR serves an important legitimizing role for corporate elites and that it is exercised not only through co-optation and 'window dressing' but also through their exercising moral, intellectual and cultural leadership;
- how the broadening and deepening of CSR depends crucially on 'counter-hegemonic' struggles, 'countervailing' (state and civil society) forces, and changes in the configuration of social forces; and
- that the depth and sustainability of contestation and 'pressure from below' may be limited due to fragmentation, resource constraints, co-optation and the dynamics of issue management and policy influence.

The analysis of institutional complementarity in this volume, which draws in particular on neo-Gramscian and 'the regulation approach',[17] sheds considerable light on the potential and limits of CSR. From the perspective of inclusive development, institutional complementarity manifests itself in different guises and has very different implications. At a systemic level, CSR – or what Ngai-Ling Sum refers to as 'the new ethicalism' – can be viewed as a response on the part of elites to craft a 'social fix' and 'institutionalized compromise' or regulatory regime more conducive to the long-term reproduction or 'sustainability' of capitalist relations. In this regard it reinforces an approach to development centred on economic liberalization that could not be secured solely on the basis of legal and regulatory changes associated with free trade, deregulation, intellectual property rights and so forth – or what has been called 'new constitutionalism' (Gill 2008). At the micro-level of the firm or supply chain a dual dynamic may also occur with large retail corporations exerting unjustifiable pressures on suppliers to lower costs and margins, and increase the intensity of labour, while simultaneously engaging in some aspects of CSR for reasons of legitimacy. However, institutional complementarity is also evident in various hybrid forms of regulation that combine elements of both voluntary and legalistic regulation in ways that can deepen CSR policy and practice from the perspective of inclusive development (Utting 2008b).

The politics of corporate accountability

The fourth limitation relates to analysis of institutional change that is politically naïve or expedient. In a context where perspectives on appropriate forms of business regulation remain fairly polarized between those who are critical of state regulation and favour voluntary initiatives, and those who are sceptical of the latter and call for binding regulation, several chapters point to the need to move beyond this dichotomy (see, in particular, Colin Crouch; Paddy Ireland and Renginee Pillay; Ndangwa Noyoo; Catia Gregoratti; James Van Alstine; and Florence Palpacuer). They consider how different types of institutions and actors – private, civil and state – operating at multiple scales – locally, nationally, regionally and internationally – interact and cohere in ways that generate regulatory frameworks more conducive to inclusive development. Shifting the focus beyond 'voluntarism', important elements of a different approach are examined and proposed; one that reconnects CSR and public policy, voluntary initiatives and law, contestation and policy change, 'participation' in project design, and 'old' and 'new' social movements. The concept of corporate accountability, referred to above, emerges as an alternative to mainstream CSR, which often disregards such aspects.[18]

To understand, then, the political underpinnings of institutional reform, in general, and of a transition from CSR to corporate accountability, in particular, attention is focused on actual or potential shifts in the correlation of social and institutional forces, the changing nature of activism and the strengthening of countervailing centres of power associated with the state and civil society.[19] Inter-group bargaining and the reality of conflict between different interests remain important in agendas of progressive institutional change (Mouffe 2005). However, such modes of contestation and governance are frequently deemed to be ineffective and passé – instead partnership and dialogue are portrayed as contemporary, more desirable alternatives (SustainAbility 2003; Tesner 2000). Although they may play a constructive role, partnership and dialogue are not panaceas. Their effectiveness depends upon specific conditions that control for power asymmetries, respect core precepts and institutions of democracy, promote genuine participation, and guard against the risk of transferring regulatory authority to unaccountable actors.

An important starting point in understanding the politics of corporate accountability is the recognition that as corporations assume both a more overt presence in the public domain and take on functions hitherto associated with the state, their role as political actors is augmented and they become legitimate targets of contestation. In addition to conventional roles associated with lobbying and political financing, the politicization of the corporation manifests itself in other ways, for example, taking on state functions of basic service provisioning, standard setting, monitoring and inspection (Crane et al. 2008). Rightly or wrongly, some civil society actors and local communities perceive global corporations as highly implicated in global injustice. Such connections derive, for example, from the so-called 'race to the bottom' or the ability of corporations to relocate to take advantage of de-regulation; their structural power and threats of capital flight and capital 'strikes'; their dominant role in global value chains associated with sub-standard working conditions and threats to small enterprises, livelihoods and the environment; the 'unfair' distribution of value within value chains; and various ways in which global corporations, or the business associations to which they belong, aid and abet the spread of neoliberal policies and associated externalities detrimental to the social and environmental conditions in developing countries (Utting 2008a).

In several chapters particular attention is paid to the role of new forms of activism, participation, networks and alliances. 'Multi-scalar' governance and regulation emerge as a key element of institutional and political arrangements and contexts conducive to taming corporate capitalism in contexts of globalization. In some countries and industries there are signs that a certain 'thickening' of the institutional environment is taking place that combines softer and harder regulation and politics in ways conducive to ratcheting up CSR and corporate social and environmental performance. In the context of globalization, and the current global crises, this process, however, remains incipient and, as Palpacuer points out (Chapter 11), the sustainability of institutional initiatives and modes of contestation that have, or could potentially result in, 'progressive' outcomes is also in doubt.

Chapter outlines

The 11 chapters that follow this introduction all address some combination of the historical, empirical, conceptual, political and institutional gaps referred to above.

In Chapter 1, Colin Crouch critiques the simplistic 'state versus market' dichotomy that infuses much of the literature and develops an analytical framework for understanding changing modes of governance associated with CSR. These modes comprise a political dimension, consisting of government and law; an economic dimension, consisting of markets and 'corporate hierarchy'; and a social or associative dimension, consisting of civil society, networks and the community. He demonstrates how specific modes, notably those associated with markets and a particular strand of law that reinforces the rights of global corporations and investors, have become ascendant during the neoliberal era. At the same time, however, global oligopolistic corporations enjoy some autonomy from competitive pressures and freedom of action to engage in CSR. A range of social pressures and relations, associated with civil society activism and community-based networks and governance, also influence how firms will respond. Whether CSR is, or becomes, a meaningful institutional response from the perspective of inclusive development depends to a large extent on the nature of such pressures and relations, as well as political governance. Variations in the relative roles of political, economic and associative governance explain differences in the content and trajectory of the CSR agenda by firm, industry and society. At present, however, TNCs and global capitalist elites are often 'disembedded' from local societal networks and relatively unfettered by political governance. For this reason contemporary CSR often resembles a modern equivalent of *noblesse oblige* where the social obligations of elites are largely defined and implemented by the elites themselves.

Drawing on theoretical perspectives that derive from Gramsci and Foucault, in Chapter 2 Ngai-Ling Sum provides a novel conceptual analysis that facilitates the understanding of how the contemporary CSR agenda relates to, and reinforces, a particular pattern of capitalist development and industrial restructuring. She examines the implications of CSR for power relations within global value chains and how CSR and other mechanisms enable global corporations to reinforce their control over suppliers. Building from a neo-Gramscian approach, especially Stephen Gill's concept of 'new constitutionalism', she examines the ways in which international agreements under the World Trade Organization (WTO) 'unlock' countries for international trade and investment. Focusing on the rise and role of Wal-Mart in China, the chapter reveals how Wal-Mart has entered joint-venture partnerships with state-owned investment trusts and global financial companies in order to establish local economic governance regimes that serve to consolidate Wal-Mart's sourcing and retailing activities. This growing 'Wal-Martization' trend indicates the shift in power from manufacturers to retailers (and financiers) and indicates how the corporation has been able to impose 'everyday low prices' and wages on its suppliers, local competitors and workers. This form of 'trickle-down economics' has prompted the formation of Wal-Mart monitoring groups that investigate and report its uneven distributive impact in the transnational arenas. The idea of 'CSR-ization' is introduced to describe how CSR is implemented at the factory level and constitutes an important component of 'new ethicalism' – an ethico-managerial strategy that serves to supplement the juridico-political focus of 'new constitutionalism' and thereby reinforce global capitalism. By situating CSR in the context of structural change and ongoing struggles by civil society actors, important elements of a 'cultural political economy' approach to the study of CSR emerge.

Paddy Ireland and Renginee Pillay (Chapter 3) adopt a historical lens to assess the potential of CSR as an instrument of economic and social development. Ideas about the social responsibilities of corporations, they argue, are far from new and can be traced back at least as far as the 1920s and 1930s when the idea of the 'socially responsible corporation' began to emerge. The chapter examines the context in which these earlier and more substantive ideas about the social responsibilities of corporations developed and how this context has changed. The authors highlight two crucial differences in today's structural and institutional context that seriously constrain CSR: shareholder primacy and legal arrangements associated with new constitutionalism. The chapter goes on to examine the prospects for pushing beyond contemporary 'ameliorative CSR' towards 'transformative CSR' that can enhance the contribution of corporations to inclusive development. Key in this regard are legal and regulatory reforms associated with the corporate accountability movement.

The relevance of both history and the role of the state are also emphasized by Ndangwa Noyoo who examines in Chapter 4 the historical evolution of CSR in Zambia. He identifies the contributions and limitations of CSR during the colonial, post-independence, neoliberal and post-structural adjustment periods. During previous eras, CSR was linked to public policy. During the colonial era, mining companies were expected to substitute for the European welfare state, providing welfare benefits for the white settler population to the exclusion of the local population. In the post-independence period, a nationalized mining industry was urged by the state to expand significantly its CSR activities not only to African employees but also beyond the enterprise to the community. During the contemporary era, CSR tends to consist of ad hoc initiatives, largely disconnected from public policy and development strategy. The chapter concludes by arguing that a stronger regulatory framework is needed to improve the social and environmental performance of companies, and that CSR needs to be linked to the government's social development agenda. The author argues that the community development approach, which seeks to empower local communities and enhance people's capabilities, could provide a framework for benchmarking, monitoring and evaluating CSR.

Chapter 5 by Michael Blowfield addresses both conceptual and empirical flaws in CSR thinking, specifically the analysis of how business relates to poverty and poverty reduction. He lays out a conceptual framework that facilitates a more nuanced understanding of whether business can be expected to go beyond its conventional economic roles to become a more active agent of inclusive development, the role of CSR in this process, and how companies might be held to account for their development outcomes. The starting point is to uncover the very different ways that business relates to poverty – as a 'cause', 'victim' and 'solution'. A framework that explains how business relates to poverty and under what conditions it chooses to act as a development agent could provide a more solid base both for measuring progress and impacts and for holding companies to account. The experience of CSR and business as a development agent suggests that development ends can best be served when there is genuine collaboration whereby various actors pursue shared or complementary poverty objectives. But such collaboration needs to move beyond the current notion and reality of 'partnerships'. It may involve, for example, different ways of connecting business with local needs and capabilities, voluntary initiatives and mandatory regulation, and, as in the case of social entrepreneurship, social and commercial objectives. It would also require dealing with asymmetrical power relations that distort the distribution of costs and benefits, as well as holding companies accountable for development outcomes. So-called countervailing forces, including government and civil society agents, appear to have had more success in getting companies to commit to development objectives than in holding them to account for delivery and outcomes. Without such accountability, randomness and unpredictability are likely to characterize CSR, 'leaving open the possibility that for all of the justification for business to be a development agent, it will remain a development maverick'.

In Chapter 6, Rob van Tulder assesses efforts in recent years to engage big business in poverty reduction and to forge an 'entrepreneurial way' out of the poverty trap through such means as PPPs, issue management, microcredits, supply chain management, the BOP and new business models. He examines how the issue of poverty alleviation by corporations has developed over time and the very different responses and levels of engagement adopted by the world's 100 largest corporations. Such variations suggest significant limits to what could be considered a 'sustainable corporate story' involving a proactive strategic and operational response. Responses are found to vary by regional varieties of capitalism from which the firm originates and types of industry. The chapter also assesses whether current forms of engagement of big business with the contemporary international poverty reduction agenda provide grounds for optimism or pessimism. While rather narrow approaches to poverty reduction are found to prevail, the experience of some European firms suggests the possibility of more meaningful partnerships, broader approaches to the BOP and novel business models. This partly reflects different regulatory frameworks with which corporations in different countries and regions must interact but also implies sectoral dynamics. Indeed, van Tulder suggests that NGOs and international organizations involved in promoting CSR may be better advised to adopt a sectoral approach, rather than one that targets individual corporations. The dynamics of issue management raises questions for the future, in particular, the fact that the degree of urgency surrounding issues such as poverty reduction tends to fluctuate not because of any significant change in the objective reality but because the issue may be crowded out in the public (mediatized) arena by other issues (for example, climate change), or because, rightly or wrongly, signs of incipient progress in dealing with the issue emerge. This cautions against an excessive reliance on firms and self-regulation, or faith in best practice examples, to address poverty, and an enhanced role for governments, new combinations of self- and mandatory regulation, as well as partnerships and transparency-increasing measures and benchmarks.

The next two chapters examine the potential and limits of PPPs, which are increasingly seen as a key component of global governance conducive to inclusive development. Many governments, international agencies, corporations and NGOs view them as an effective way to deal with complex development problems that cannot be resolved through interventions by single actors and institutions. Chapter 7, by Ruth Findlay-Brooks, Wayne Visser and Thurstan Wright, draws on several years of research on partnerships conducted at the University of Cambridge Programme for Sustainable Leadership (CPSL). Exploring the experiences of partnership practitioners, along with current thinking on the topic, the analysis suggests that partnerships are not a straightforward option. Some see them as merely a short-term response to rapid global change. There can also be issues of accountability and power imbalance, when unelected businesses and NGOs have influence in states where governments are either weak or failing. Even where they are the best solution, there can be real obstacles in both the development and management of partnerships, which are too easily ignored. The authors of this chapter conclude that, if partnerships are to bring about structural change and long-term development impacts, they need to be firmly tied into genuinely inclusive consultation processes, operate within accountability frameworks, be properly supported and evaluated, and, where appropriate, lead ultimately to policy change.

Chapter 8 by Catia Gregoratti reflects on the contribution of PPPs involving business and the United Nations. It provides an empirical and conceptual assessment of one of the largest UN programmes, the Growing Sustainable Business (GSB) Initiative, promoted by the United Nations Development Programme (UNDP). The chapter first sketches a framework for understanding the political economy of partnerships for development, and then assesses the GSB programme. Drawing on extensive empirical research conducted in Eastern Africa, the chapter examines the participatory nature of the programme, its degree of inclusiveness and other development outcomes. In contrast to the programme's stated objectives, GSB structures are found to be elitist and top-down, resulting in limited developmental outcomes. Key actors involved in designing projects have a narrow economic understanding of development. The outcome is 'a form of technocratic governance that remains largely silent about equity aspects of development'. A key point to emerge from the analysis is not only the gap between objectives and performance, but the crucial need to interrogate the political nature of partnerships, the power relations involved, and the possibility that partnerships act as a vehicle for replacing government as a provider of public goods and services. Various policy implications emerge from this assessment: more meaningful participation of intended beneficiaries in project design and implementation, public reporting and monitoring, and aligning commercial interests and project design with national development plans.

In Chapter 9, Doris Fuchs and Agni Kalfagianni examine the role of CSR and private regulation in the governance of the global food system, which has important implications for the question of social development and sustainability. They seek to better understand how business actors, and specifically TNCs, impact social aspects of sustainable development in developing countries through the creation of private institutions of food governance. The analysis involves a power-theoretic approach: actors draw power from structural and material as well as ideational and normative sources. Their power is, therefore, structural, instrumental and discursive. The authors consider both the social impacts of private food governance and the democratic implications of private governance institutions. They examine both input-oriented arguments for procedural democracy and output-oriented arguments, that is, whether private institutions contribute to, or constrain, the creation of the conditions necessary for social protection and reducing inequality in the long term. Moreover, they discuss the concept of deliberative democracy as an alternative approach for the legitimation of food governance beyond state regulation. Through this analysis Fuchs and Kalfagianni show that large retailers have acquired rule-setting power as a result of their material position within the global economy and their control of networks and resources. This power is reinforced by their lobbying activities, in particular those concerned with the content of food standards. Their greater political legitimacy reflects their discursive power, which feeds off notions or perceptions of their alleged expertise and efficiency vis-à-vis public actors. Despite considerable limitations in terms of the issues addressed and the crowding-out effects on smaller producers, the social implications of private food governance have received little attention. The fact that power imbalances and other factors constrain the level and effectiveness of 'participation' in both design and evaluation of food standards points to serious concerns regarding input and output legitimacy.

In Chapter 10, James Van Alstine examines the complex ways in which actors, institutions and ideas intervene and interact to promote CSR. After presenting a theoretical framework that draws on concepts from institutional and organizational theory, the author examines the dynamics of change that has resulted in improvements in the performance of fuel oil refineries in South Africa related to the environment and public health. Particular attention is focused on the role of parent company influence, civil society contestation and governance structures. But to understand the dynamics of change it is essential to refer to 'multi-scalar' governance and activism, which involves actors, institutions, ideas and events operating at different levels. These include the host locality, host country, home country, and regional and international levels. It is found that in the post-apartheid context of democratic transition, new countervailing centres of civil society and state power have emerged to discipline business and promote social pacts and innovative multistakeholder initiatives (MSIs) conducive to inclusive development. A progression has occurred from discursive struggles to normative and, subsequently, regulative institutions as an internationally networked civil society has demanded accountability from both the private and public sectors, and government has begun to build capacity. Variations in the role of parent companies, influenced by different institutional, organizational and activist contexts, can also be significant in shaping company performance at the local level.

In Chapter 11, Florence Palpacuer analyses the ways in which transnational networks of 'counterpowers' are contributing to the emergence of new forms of social dialogue in the global apparel industry. The globalization of the apparel industry grew at a rapid pace during the 1990s. Over the same decade, a number of activist organizations were established by various civil society movements in Europe and North America, with the aim of promoting developing countries' workers' rights by diffusing knowledge of abusive conditions and promoting solidarity in developed countries' markets, as well as by pressuring brands to take on greater responsibility vis-à-vis employment conditions at their overseas suppliers' factories. A number of MSIs, such as the Fair Labor Association (FLA) in the United States or the Ethical Trading Initiative (ETI) in the United Kingdom, were established on the principle of involving corporations, civil society movements and labour unions in their governance system. Building on the notion of corporate accountability and on recent advances in regulation theory, the chapter suggests the recent emergence of these institutions and innovative forms of social dialogue and interaction between transnational activist networks, involving both old and new counterpowers and global corporations can contribute to new modes of regulation in the global economy. What is less clear is whether conditions for an institutional stabilization of these forms of interaction exist. It is argued that from the perspective of regulation theory, such stabilization is a necessary condition for these institutional forms to contribute to effectively regulating the global economy.

Whither CSR?

The contemporary global crises referred to at the beginning of this chapter suggest a somewhat uncertain picture of the future of CSR. The weakening of finance capital and neoliberal orthodoxy; an opening for the state to reassert its role as a developmental and regulatory agent; and the legitimacy bestowed upon the global justice movement that may now claim 'I told you so', suggest the possibility of a shift in the configuration of social forces that may favour processes of institutional reform conducive to inclusive development. Indeed, global corporations that hitherto bought into voluntarism may themselves call for a level of clarity and new rules of the game that only regulation can provide. The current crisis and its regulatory fall-out appears to have undermined the strand of mainstream CSR that instrumentalized voluntarism as part of a political project to legitimize 'business-as-usual', justify minimalist states, and stabilize a variety of capitalism associated with gross inequalities.

How will all this affect CSR? Karl Polanyi's (1944) historical analysis of the diverse routes out of capitalist crisis – fascism, communism and New

Deal social democracy – provides a cautionary tale for projecting the future of state–business–society relations in times of crisis. The buzzwords of the current crisis – regulation and responsibility – appear to bode well for an alternative approach to mainstream CSR emphasized in this volume, namely corporate accountability. But much will hinge on the emergence and character of countervailing forces. The regulatory state may be reasserting itself but the role of social movements and citizenship remains less clear, as does the capacity of nation states to reach strong international agreements that are effective throughout the global economy.[20]

In the short term the financial crisis and its recessionary consequences could easily lead big business to batten down the hatches and refocus on the single – as opposed to the triple – bottom line. The imperative to reduce costs may also lead to even greater reliance on sub-contracting and labour flexibilization.[21] And the performance of Wal-Mart in the midst of the crisis suggests that the preferences of some consumers may shift from 'ethical' considerations to 'everyday low prices'. Furthermore, the framing of CSR or what constitutes socially responsible enterprise may change as trade unions and others shift their priorities from working conditions and labour rights to the terms of retrenchment, retraining and employment creation.

While the trajectory of CSR remains uncertain, it is usually the case that crises provoke a search for alternatives that involves rethinking mainstream approaches and conventional wisdom. The intellectual crisis of CSR described in this chapter makes such a rethink all the more imperative. The chapters that follow provide key pointers as to how it might be addressed. To recap, this requires addressing four limitations of the mainstream CSR agenda and some critical perspectives, namely their propensity to be ahistorical, empirically weak, theoretically thin, as well as politically and institutionally naïve. More specifically, it is crucial to:

- learn from the history of state–business–society relations in contexts where embedded liberalism and developmentalism in particular countries and regions resulted in more inclusive patterns of structural change and socially responsible business;
- move beyond rhetoric and best practice illustrations to examine more systematically corporate responses and real developmental outcomes, as well as the distribution of costs and benefits among different stakeholders;
- draw more broadly on theoretical perspectives and concepts that shed light on what is possible in contexts of contemporary capitalism, and the potential, limits and drivers of institutional change; and
- understand power relations, the politics of institutional change, and the complex interactions of actors, institutions and ideas operating at multiple scales.

All of the above suggest profound limits to voluntarism as an approach to inclusive development. However, under certain institutional and political economy conditions firms will, and do, act in a socially responsible manner. This volume identifies various historical and contemporary contexts where business relates to workers, communities and the environment in this way. There is, however, another dimension of socially responsible business that has not been examined in any depth. Both in this volume and in the CSR literature more generally, relatively little attention has been paid to the question of whether organized business interests support or undermine what the United Nations Research Institute for Social Development (UNRISD) has called 'transformative social policy', that is, diverse aspects of state policy that impact social development and inclusive growth.[22] What are the social policy preferences of firms and business associations? Are they necessarily at odds with progressive aspects of social policy? How do governments and regulatory institutions respond and adapt to the increasing structural and lobbying power of business? These aspects are addressed in a companion volume to this book entitled *Business, Politics and Public Policy* (Marques and Utting forthcoming).

Notes

1. The preparation of this chapter benefited from comments from various participants at the symposium on The Responsible Corporation in a Global Economy, organized by the Warwick Business School and the Social Trends Institute, 21–2 March 2009. Special thanks go to Peter Newell and Colin Crouch for their feedback, as well as to Rebecca Buchholz and Karla Utting for comments and editorial assistance.
2. The term has been used by Peter Evans (2005a) to refer to the increasing attention within development theory and analysis to the role of organizations, culture, norms and perceptions.
3. Holliday et al. (2002); Porter and van der Linde (1995); Schmidheiny (1992).
4. While CSR discourse and practice are constantly evolving and vary in different institutional and societal contexts, much of the mainstream literature, which emphasizes the considerable advances already achieved in CSR or its inherent potential, tends to focus on a fairly standardized set of issues and instruments, which are referred to below. It is in this sense that we refer to 'a mainstream CSR agenda'.
5. The conditions that underpinned the current crises emerged over several decades. They included, for example, the rolling back of some of the state's regulatory functions, as well as industrial and social policy; the decline and neglect of small enterprises, infant industries, farmers and domestic agriculture; speculative financial activities; unsustainable consumption patterns, energy use and carbon emissions; and the political disempowerment of organized labour and some other subaltern groups.
6. Although several banks promoted 'ethical investment' funds and the International Finance Corporation (IFC) launched the Equator Principles related to project financing in 2003, it was not until 2006 that a comprehensive set of CSR guidelines and promotional instruments emerged in the shape and form of the Principles for Responsible Investment (PRI).

7. The term inclusive development is used here to refer to policy regimes, governance arrangements and patterns of growth and structural change that are conducive to social protection, equity, participation and environmental sustainability.
8. Hopkins (2003); Holliday et al. (2002); Porter and van der Linde (1995); Sustain-Ability (2003).
9. See, for example, Cutler (2008); Greer and Bruno (1996); Klein (2000); International Forum on Globalization (2002); Richter (2001); Rowell (1996).
10. See, for example, Blowfield and Murray (2008); Braithwaite and Drahos (2000); Crane et al. (2008); Eade and Sayer (2006); Gibbon (2008); Levy (2008); Newell and Frynas (2007); Rittberger and Nettesheim (2008); Utting and Zammit (2006); Zammit (2003).
11. Barrientos and Smith (2006); Bekefi (2006); Clay (2005); Fig (2007); Locke et al. (2007); O'Rourke (2003).
12. More recently, the United Nations Norms on the Responsibilities of TNCs and Other Business Enterprises with Regard to Human Rights experienced a similar fate.
13. José Carlos Marques and Peter Utting (eds), *Business, Politics and Public Policy* (Basingstoke: UNRISD/Palgrave Macmillan, forthcoming).
14. The degree to which these production chains are embedded in the local context is a major concern for developing countries. This may range from enclave operations like the mining corporations in Africa (UNCTAD 2005) and high-tech firms in India and Mexico (Gallagher and Zarsky 2008) to companies, like Unilever in Indonesia, that are more tightly integrated (upstream and downstream) into domestic market networks and social relations (Clay 2005).
15. This stream of research has also resulted in ambiguous conclusions regarding the relationship between CSP and CFP with some authors calling for a redirection of this research to broader social concerns. See Orlitzky et al. (2003); Margolis et al. (2007); and Margolis and Walsh (2003).
16. DiMaggio and Powell (1991); Keohane (2002); Porter and van der Linde (1995).
17. For a comprehensive analysis of this body of theory, see Jessop and Sum (2006).
18. Regarding the definition and analysis of corporate accountability from this perspective, see also Bendell (2004); Newell (2002); Utting (2008a, 2008b, 2007, 2005b).
19. See also Peter Evans (2005b).
20. The G-20 communiqué, *The Global Plan for Recovery and Reform* of 2 April 2009, suggests, however, some movement in this direction.
21. See Maquila Solidarity Network (2009).
22. UNRISD defines transformative social policy as state intervention that aims to improve social welfare, social institutions and social relations. It involves overarching concerns with redistribution, production, reproduction and protection, and works in tandem with economic policy in pursuit of national social and economic goals. An important feature of transformative social policy is also the establishment and enforcement of standards and regulations that shape the role of non-state actors and markets in social provisioning and protection.

References

Barrientos, Stephanie and Sally Smith, *The ETI Code of Labour Practice: Do Workers Really Benefit? Report on the ETI Impact Assessment* (Brighton: Institute of Development Studies, University of Sussex, 2006).

Bekefi, T., *Viet Nam: Lessons in Building Linkages for Competitive and Responsible Entrepreneurship* (Boston, MA: UNIDO and Kennedy School of Government, Harvard University, 2006).

Bendell, Jem, *Barricades and Boardrooms: A Contemporary History of the Corporate Accountability Movement*, Programme on Technology, Business and Society, Paper No. 13 (Geneva: UNRISD, 2004).

Blowfield, M.E. and A. Murray, *Corporate Responsibility: A Critical Introduction* (Oxford: Oxford University Press, 2008).

Boyer, Robert, 'From shareholder value to CEO power: The paradox of the 1990s', *Competition and Change*, Vol. 9, No. 1, March (2005) 7–48.

Braithwaite, John and Peter Drahos, *Global Business Regulation* (Cambridge: Cambridge University Press, 2000).

Clay, Jason, *Exploring the Links between International Business and Poverty Reduction: A Case Study of Unilever in Indonesia* (Oxford: Oxfam GB, Novib [Oxfam Netherlands], and Unilever, 2005).

Crane, Andrew, Dirk Matten and Jeremy Moon, *Corporations and Citizenship* (Cambridge: Cambridge University Press, 2008).

Cutler, A. Claire, 'Problematizing corporate social responsibility under conditions of late capitalism and postmodernity'. In Volker Rittberger and Martin Nettesheim (eds), *Authority in the Global Political Economy* (Basingstoke: Palgrave Macmillan, 2008).

DiMaggio, Paul J. and Walter W. Powell, 'Introduction'. In Walter W. Powell and Paul J. DiMaggio (eds), *The New Institutionalism in Organizational Analysis* (Chicago: University of Chicago Press, 1991).

Eade Deborah and John Sayer (eds), *Development and the Private Sector: Consuming Interests* (Bloomfield, CT: Kumarian Press, Inc., 2006).

Elkington, John, *Cannibals with Forks: The Triple Bottom Line of 21st Century Business* (Oxford: Capstone Publishing, 1997).

Evans, Peter, 'The challenges of the "institutional turn": Interdisciplinary opportunities in development theory'. In Victor Nee and Richard Swedberg (eds), *The Economic Sociology of Capitalist Institutions* (Princeton, NJ: Princeton University Press, 2005a).

———, 'Counter-hegemonic globalization: Transnational social movements in the contemporary global political economy'. In Thomas Janoski, Robert R. Alford, Alexander Hicks M. and Mildred A. Schwartz (eds), *Handbook of Political Sociology: States, Civil Societies, and Globalization* (Cambridge: Cambridge University Press, 2005b).

Fig, David (ed.), *Staking Their Claims: Corporate Social and Environmental Responsibility in South Africa* (Scottsville: UNRISD/University of Kwa-Zulu Natal Press, 2007).

Freeman, R. Edward, *Strategic Management: A Stakeholder Approach* (Boston, MA: Pitman Publishing, 1984).

Fuchs, Doris A., *Understanding Business Power in Global Governance* (Baden-Baden: Nomos, 2005).

G-20 (Group of Twenty), *The Global Plan for Recovery and Reform*, Communiqué of 2 April 2009 (2009). www.londonsummit.gov.uk/resources/en/news/15766232/communique-020409 (accessed on 13 April 2009).

Gallagher, Kevin P. and Lyuba Zarsky, *The Enclave Economy: Foreign Investment and Sustainable Development in Mexico's Silicon Valley* (Cambridge, MA: The MIT Press, 2008).

Gereffi, Gary and Miguel Korzeniewicz (eds), *Commodity Chains and Global Capitalism* (Westport, CT: Praeger Publishers, 1994).

Gibbon, Peter, 'An analysis of standards-based regulation in the EU organic sector, 1991–2007', *Journal of Agrarian Change*, Vol. 8, No. 4, October (2008) 553–82.

Gill, Stephen, *Power and Resistance in the New World Order* (Basingstoke: Palgrave MacMillan, 2008).

Greer, Jed and Kenny Bruno, *Greenwash: The Reality behind Corporate Environmentalism* (Penang: Third World Network, 1996).

Hall, Peter A. and David Soskice (eds), *Varieties of Capitalism: The Institutional Foundations of Comparative Advantage* (Oxford: Oxford University Press, 2001).

Holliday, Charles O., Stephan Schmidheiny and Philip Watts, *Walking the Talk: The Business Case for Sustainable Development* (Sheffield: Greenleaf Publishing, and San Francisco: Berrett-Koeler Publishers, 2002).

Hopkins, Michael, *The Planetary Bargain: Corporate Social Responsibility Matters* (London: Earthscan, 2003).

Internationalization Forum on Globalization, *Alternatives to Economic Globalization: A Better World Is Possible* (San Francisco, CA: Berrett-Koehler Publishers, Inc., 2002).

Jessop, Bob and Ngai-Ling Sum, *Beyond the Regulation Approach: Putting Capitalist Economies in Their Place* (Cheltenham, UK and Northampton, MA: Edward Elgar, 2006).

Keohane, Robert, *Power and Governance in a Partially Globalized World* (London: Routledge, 2002).

Kitazawa, Yoko (ed.), *How to Regulate and Control Neo-Liberal Globalization*, Workshop on International Regulations, 2003–2006 (Tokyo: Pacific Asia Resource Center, and Paris: Fondation Charles Leopold Mayer for the Progress of Humanity, 2007).

Klein, Naomi, *No Logo* (London: Flamingo, 2000).

Levy, David, 'Political contestation in global production networks', *Academy of Management Review*, Vol. 33, No. 4 (2008) 943–63.

Locke, Richard M., Fei Qin and Alberto Brause, 'Does monitoring improve labor standards? Lessons from Nike', *Industrial & Labor Relations Review*, Vol. 61, No. 1 (2007) 3–31.

Maquila Solidarity Network, *How Will the Global Financial Crisis Affect the Garment Industry and Garment Workers?* (2009). http://en.maquilasolidarity.org/ sites/maquilasolidarity.org/files/2009-02-25%20MSN-FinancialCrisis-Feb09-ENG.pdf (accessed on 25 February 2009).

Margolis, Joshua D. and James P. Walsh, 'Misery loves company: Rethinking social initiatives by business', *Administrative Sciences Quarterly*, Vol. 48, No. 2 (2003) 268–305.

Margolis, Joshua D., Hillary Anger Elfenbein and James P. Walsh, *Does It Pay to Be Good? A Meta-Analysis and Redirection of Research on the Relationship between Corporate Social and Financial Performance* (Cambridge, MA: The Mossavar-Rahmani Center for Business and Government, John F. Kennedy School of Government, Harvard University, 2007).

Marques, José Carlos and Peter Utting (eds), *Business, Politics and Public Policy* (Basingstoke: Palgrave Macmillan, forthcoming).

McBarnet, Doreen, Aurora Voiculescu and Tom Campbell, *The New Corporate Accountability: Corporate Social Responsibility and the Law* (Cambridge: Cambridge University Press, 2007).

Mouffe, Chantal, *On the Political: Thinking in Action* (London: Routledge, 2005).

Newell, Peter, 'CSR and the limits of capital', *Development and Change*, Vol. 39, No. 6, November (2008) 1063–78.

——, 'From responsibility to citizenship: Corporate accountability for development', *IDS Bulletin*, 33(2) (2002) 91–100.

Newell, Peter and Jedrzej George Frynas, 'Beyond CSR? Business, poverty and social justice', *Third World Quarterly*, Vol. 28, No. 4 (2007) 669–81.

Orlitzky, Marc, Frank L. Schmidt and Sara L. Rynes, 'Corporate social and financial performance: A meta-analysis', *Organization Studies*, Vol. 24, No. 3 (2003) 403.

O'Rourke, Dara, 'Outsourcing regulation: Analyzing non-governmental systems of labor standards and monitoring', *Policy Studies Journal*, Vol. 31, No. 1 (2003) 1–29.

Polanyi, Karl, *The Great Transformation: The Political and Economic Origins of Our Time* (Boston: Beacon Press by arrangement with Rinehart & Company, Inc., 1944).

Porter, M.E. and C. van der Linde, 'Green and competitive: Ending the stalemate', *Harvard Business Review*, September-October (1995) 120–34.

Reich, Robert, *Supercapitalism: The Transformation of Business, and Everyday Life* (New York: Knopf, 2007).

Richter, Judith, *Holding Corporations Accountable: Corporate Conduct, International Codes and Citizen Action* (London: Zed Books, 2001).

Rittberger, Volker and Martin Nettesheim (eds), *Changing Patterns of Authority in the Global Political Economy* (Basingstoke: Palgrave Macmillan, 2008).

Rowell, Andrew, *Green Backlash: Global Subversion of the Environment Movement* (London and New York: Routledge 1996).

Ruggie, John G., 'International regimes, transactions, and change: Embedded liberalism in the postwar economic order', *International Organization*, Vol. 36, No. 2, Spring (1982) 379–415.

Schmidheiny, Stephan, *Changing Course: A Global Business Perspective on Business and the Environment* (Cambridge, MA: MIT Press, 1992).

Stiglitz, Joseph E., *The Roaring Nineties: Why We're Paying the Price for the Greediest Decade in History* (London: Penguin Books, 2004).

SustainAbility, *The 21st Century NGO: In the Market for Change* (London: SustainAbility, 2003).

Tesner, Sandrine, *The United Nations and Business. A Partnership Recovered* (New York: St. Martin's Press, 2000).

UNCTAD (United Nations Conference on Trade and Development), *Economic Development in Africa: Rethinking the Role of Foreign Direct Investment* (Geneva: United Nations, 2005).

United Nations, *Promotion and Protection of Human Rights: Interim Report of the Special Representative of the Secretary-General on the Issue of Human Rights and Transnational Corporations and Other Business Enterprises*, UN document No. E/CN.4/2006/97), Commission on Human Rights, 22 February (New York: United Nations Economic and Social Council, 2006).

Utting, Peter, 'The struggle for corporate accountability', *Development and Change*, Vol. 39, No. 6, November (2008a) 959–75.

——, 'Social and environmental liabilities of transnational corporations: New directions, opportunities and constraints'. In Peter Utting and Jennifer Clapp (eds), *Corporate Accountability and Sustainable Development* (New Delhi: Oxford University Press India, 2008b).

——, 'CSR and equality', *Third World Quarterly*, Vol. 28, Issue 4 (2007) 697–712.

——, 'Corporate responsibility and the movement of business', *Development in Practice*, 15(3/4), June (2005a) 375–88.

——, *Rethinking Business Regulation: From Self-Regulation to Social Control*, Programme on Technology, Business and Society, Paper No. 15 (Geneva: UNRISD, 2005b).

Utting, Peter and Ann Zammit, *Beyond Pragmatism: Appraising UN–Business Partnerships*, Programme on Markets, Business and Regulation, Paper No. 1, (Geneva: UNRISD, 2006).

Zadek, Simon, *The Civil Corporation: The New Economy of Corporate Citizenship* (London: Earthscan, 2001).

Zammit, Ann, *Development at Risk: Rethinking UN-Business Partnerships* (Geneva: The South Centre/UNRISD, 2003).

1
CSR and Changing Modes of Governance: Towards Corporate *Noblesse Oblige?*

Colin Crouch

The governing ideology of both the global and most national economic policy regimes today is normally described as 'neoliberal'. By this is meant primarily a reliance on 'the market' as the main mechanism of socioeconomic governance, with government intervention being withdrawn to its basic role in a capitalist economy of supporting the market regime itself. Such a generalization, however, can be challenged as too sweeping. Several authors have pointed out the considerable diversity of approaches that can be and are called 'neoliberal'.[1] Moreover, the extreme libertarian wing of neoliberal thinkers would argue that the state is not even necessary to the maintenance of the market, as left to themselves free human individuals would construct markets.[2]

In this chapter I shall not re-enter these existing debates, but rather challenge the argument that the new prevailing regime can be best characterized in terms of 'the market'. It will be argued instead that the role of the individual transnational corporation (TNC) as an actor in socioeconomic governance has been neglected, not only in accounts of the present but also of the past. It is essential that analysis of the policy and politics of development takes full account of the giant corporation as a form of governance in its own right, and not subsume it within concepts of 'lobbying' states or 'distorting' markets. While such approaches might preserve the state/market dualism that is used by the majority of analyses, they direct our attention away from a fundamental institution. Once large firms are seen in this way, it is possible to investigate how they behave, not just as market actors, but generally within society. This opens the possibility of studying corporate social responsibility (CSR) in relation to theories of governance.

In what follows, I begin by outlining a general approach to the analysis of different forms of socioeconomic governance which incorporates the corporate hierarchy alongside others. The analysis goes on to examine changes in governance systems that have occurred in previous decades, commencing with those that immediately preceded the neoliberal era, before providing a general account of contemporary socioeconomic governance in developing societies. Consideration is then given to the specific role of corporate hierarchy, the scope for CSR and the role of associational forms of governance in shaping business behaviour.

Conceptualizing socioecononomic governance

Boyer, along with Hollingsworth and others,[3] has developed a general approach to the analysis of different forms of socioeconomic governance which incorporates the corporate hierarchy:

> If the first mechanism [the market] relies upon interest and horizontal interactions among actors, at the opposite, the second [the state] is built upon obligation and an asymmetric exercise of power. Therefore, if one takes into account both the motive of action (either interest or obligation) and the distribution of power among actors (either symmetric or typically hierarchical) four other coordinating mechanisms emerge: the private hierarchy of organizations and firms, the community, the association, and finally network. Hence societies and economies exhibit a multiplicity of institutional arrangements, more or less imperfect, that have to be compared one with another and not with a mythical pure market economy.
>
> (Boyer 2007)

'The private hierarchy of organizations and firms' relates to the distinction made in the theory of the firm between the firm as a nexus of markets and as an organization (Coase 1937; Williamson 1975). It can best be illustrated with reference to the labour market. A large firm can acquire labour by making a series of contracts with external suppliers of labour services, or it can hire workers directly as its employees, paying them a regular wage in exchange for their placing themselves under the control of the firm's management. While they remain in its employment, the firm does not relate to these workers as an equal partner in a market contract, but becomes an authority over them. In fact, even in its contracts a large transnational enterprise dealing with a large number of small, local contractors – as in a supply chain – acquires something of an authority role. These contracts are asymmetrical, with the large customer firm having many more options than the local suppliers. This enables the firm to impose conditions on the suppliers and therefore to act in a hierarchical relationship to them. This will be especially the case where, as is usually the case with TNCs, competition is imperfect, giving firms enough protection from immediate market pressure to develop strategy and exercise discretion in how they manage their relationships.

A word is needed on the other forms of governance mentioned.[4] 'Associations' are formally constituted organizations of members sharing certain common interests, which they seek to advance by devoting resources to the association and allowing it to work for them. Major examples in the economy are business associations and trade unions, but they also exist in many other walks of life. 'Networks' are less formal than associations; they are unlikely to have a formal constitution or organization, and may not even have a name. Their members cooperate on an informal basis, and may derive strength from a capacity to pool strength for certain tasks. Major examples are found in the strong, but informal collaborative links often found among firms in the same or related industries within specific geographical areas. 'Communities' are similar to networks in their informality, but whereas it is relatively easy for persons to join or leave a network, communities typically have difficult entry and exit, defined by geographical isolation, ethnic specificity or other tight defining criteria.

Varieties of the developmental state

Following the state/market dichotomy that will later be criticized, we can depict the pre-neoliberal regimes that existed in many developing societies as having been various forms of the 'developmental state' (Evans 1995; Weiss and Hobson 1995). The stylized facts that characterize this model of development usually include the following: at a certain point (some time from the 1950s to the 1970s, often after colonial liberation) the state committed itself to advancing economic development. Broadly following Prebischian late developer theory (Love 1980), it did this by encouraging domestic industrial production behind a wall of protection. This kept out imports from more developed economies, giving local firms a chance to equip themselves to compete. Export activity was restricted. There was often a concentration on heavy industry (steel, basic chemicals). There was little attempt to build up mass domestic demand, which was considered too weak to drive growth. Both production and consumption were therefore concentrated among state and corporate actors. There was a distinction within this model between those economies largely owned by the state (for example, China and the Soviet Union), and those in which private capital operated, sometimes alongside state industries (for example, Brazil and India).

A variant of the developmental state departed from the heavy industry and protectionist implications of the pure model. Here development was concentrated on (or at least included) light industrial production (such as clothing and electrical appliances – for example, Malaysia). This approach, like the heavy industry model, also saw little role for domestic mass consumption, but was necessarily more export-oriented than the heavy-industry model. It was based primarily on private ownership, but there was still a strong role for government in supporting the development projects of firms within a national development programme. Because light industry firms were often small and medium-sized enterprises (SMEs), this approach accommodated a larger social category than could be fully incorporated within national elites, as in the heavy industry model. Some countries were hybrids of this and the heavy industry model (for example, Singapore and South Korea). A final type of economy cannot really be called 'developmental', as it concerned countries with primarily commodity-based economies, while the main thrust of modernization strategies was to get out of commodity production and into manufacturing of various kinds (for example, Botswana, Kenya and Peru). In addition, there had typically long been foreign involvement in the sectors concerned. These have therefore not been examples of autarchic development, even if governments were sometimes concerned with the level of foreign involvement.

Broadly speaking, the overall pattern of governance modes in these different forms of developmental state can be depicted as in Table 1.1.

Government was clearly the overwhelming force in the state-owned heavy industry model: rule of law was rarely allowed to impede government action. The market played very little part; associational governance was largely an extension of the state within a framework of authoritarian corporatism. Networks and communities actually functioned strongly as the informal economy on which much day-to-day economic activity, but not the state's modernization strategy, depended. In the privately owned heavy industry model, corporate hierarchy played a clear role, although it was often strongly connected to the state.

Under authoritarian corporatism (Crouch 1993; Schmitter 1974), leaders of interest organizations (primarily those of capital and labour) constitute part of the governing elite and do not offer open challenges to the state. Business associations subordinate their member firms to the state plan, while union leaders attempted to minimize labour discontent. The developmental state was likely to make considerable use of this model. Such a state required a mobilization of national resources around its economic project; it therefore preferred to work with ostensibly representative interests rather than press on alone and have to deal with individual firms. It also aimed to mobilize the population around its growth project, and found 'tame' unions helpful for establishing links with the working population. On the other hand, tight political control was exercised over union leaders, as the developmental state did not tolerate open conflict. Labour organizations which would not collaborate with such a system would be confronted and subject to sanctions as occurred, for example, in Singapore (Chua 2007).

This was far less the case where there were elements of democracy and civil society. For example, India was not an authoritarian system and unions were active. However, given the vast labour surpluses of the country, they were not powerful and their incorporation was therefore cheaply acquired during the Nehru developmentalist period (Chibber 2007). Depending on the kind of regime, therefore, organized labour might play some part in governance alongside private employers in a more bargained form of corporatism made

Table 1.1   Developmental states and forms of socioeconomic governance

Forms of developmental state	Types of economic governance						
	Government	Law	Market	Corporate hierarchy	Association	Network	Community
1. *Heavy industry, state-owned firms*	Fundamental to economic and welfare model	Imposed on population; not necessarily followed by government	Minor	Important, in both economic and welfare governance	Some role within state dominance	Important in shadow economy as counter to state in economic governance	Important to shadow economy and to welfare governance
2. *Heavy industry, private (and some state) firms*	Fundamental to economic and welfare model, alongside private firms		More than in 1., but still minor because of protectionism and weak mass consumption	Important in economic governance; rarely involved in welfare	Occasionally some role		Important for linking political and economic elites. Among mass of population, fundamental for welfare
3. *Light industry, private firms*			More than in 2., because of insertion in international trade				
4. *Commodity production*	Important		As 3				

possible by the existence of private owners. This would be restricted to the modern, industrializing sector and would usually exclude the mass of the rural population. In the light-industry, export-based model, external market forces acquired a stronger governance position in a model that otherwise resembled the previous one.

Networks and, in traditional economies, actual communities have been fundamental in sustaining and advancing productive activity in a number of different circumstances. They are particularly important in sustaining the informal and even shadow sectors, within which, in practice, a large majority of the working population in developing societies operates. By definition, the shadow sector was not part of a developmental state's strategy, and in the case of a heavy-industry-based strategy its small enterprise base would place it outside the scope of official policy. However, it would play an important *de facto* role in sustaining a more flexible form of economic activity than the formal economy could embrace. Where strategy was based on light industry, an informally supported industry might eventually become an important part of a national economy, as in Taiwan, Province of China (Chang 2007). Ethnic minorities (or suppressed majorities) often used their tight community networks to sustain informal economies outside the scope of a central state system. In addition, the family (as a core community institution) is fundamental in traditional societies in maintaining social welfare among poor people. It has therefore often played a background role in development in 'enabling' government not to focus on welfare.

However, none of these minor forms of socioeconomic governance were as important to the developmental state itself as the hierarchy of the large corporation. Even in the state-owned, Soviet form, there was usually a distinction between political and administrative actions of the state, on the one hand, and managerial actions of the corporation, on the other. Where private interests owned the firms that were of strategic importance to the development plan, they became major extractors of rent and providers of corporate social welfare. There was mutual interest-serving between firms and government, as the former needed a continuing supply of privileges (protectionist policies and resources) from the latter, while government needed the firms to fulfil its plans and enhance social cohesion. Often the same elite families were engaged in both spheres. Political power could be used to sustain the firms from which the families drew their wealth; and this wealth in turn sustained the families' political dominance.

The elites of rent-seeking corporations in developmental states were *embedded* elites. The protectionist national strategy, as well as their family and social links to the political elites, tied their interests to the nation-state and its territory. Among these elites, community and network governance came very strongly into play. Especially if there were elements of democracy in the political system (as particularly in the Indian case), they also thereby had ties to the population and some organized popular groups, and needed to respond to some of their needs. This explains the simultaneous association of some developmental states with powerful, wealthy, rent-seeking elites and a certain level of welfare state development. This combination of an economically active state and basic welfare produces a superficial resemblance between the developmental state and social democracy. However, the presence of very wealthy families owning the corporations through which the state operated, and the persistence of extreme poverty despite the existence of welfare policy, suggests a different political model. This was particularly the case when the state was non-democratic and associated with repression of civil dissent or autonomous trade unions. Social policy more often resembled aristocratic *noblesse oblige* than modern concepts of welfare citizenship.

From developmentalism to neoliberalism

At various moments from the late 1970s onwards the different orthodoxies that had governed economic development in the decades immediately after the Second World War – Keynesianism, the developmental state, the social market, state socialism – came under strong challenge from neoliberal thinking advocating a stronger role for markets and a reduced role for the state. In the eyes of international agencies like the World Bank and the International Monetary Fund (IMF), state-directed economic development was associated with inefficiency and corruption among unhealthily mixed economic and political elites. In Eastern and Central Europe the command economy was clearly stagnating, and a desire to shift to a different system was among the pressures that produced a collapse of those systems at the end of the 1980s.

But behind these changes in ideology lay important shifts in global economic structure, in particular, sectoral shifts and a general commitment to participation in international trade. Partly as a result of changes in technology, it was becoming feasible for major corporations to arrange their sourcing, production, distribution and management systems on a transnational scale in order to maximize economies of different commodity, labour and product markets. To realize the gains of such a scale of organization, firms required a deregulation of national financial regimes, so that they could move money around the world in line with their production activities. This was forthcoming in a series of changes during the 1980s, which quite quickly produced an almost global financial market. This, in turn, made possible the rise of a global financial sector.

A further technical development that lay behind the changes was the growth of several high value-added, sometimes manufacturing but mainly services sectors that had before been either restricted to national bases by regulation (such as banking and finance itself) or barely existed (information technology). The desire of corporations in the already rich countries to shift from standard manufacturing into these newly growing fields meant more scope for developmental states to operate internationally in their accustomed basic and heavy manufacturing sectors, or low-wage, low-skill light indus- tries. However, an increasing number of developmental states also saw opportunities for themselves to develop in the new sectors, which were con- siderably more profitable than both the heavy and light industry specialisms in which they had earlier been working.

These changes profoundly altered the behaviour of states and economic elites, with consequences across a broad range of policies, including social policy. The changes are often summarized as involving a move towards the market, but examination of the full range of governance modes suggests that individual large corporations play a role not strictly anticipated by such a shift. What differs from the developmental state is the kind of corpor- ation concerned and its role within the society. In addition, the state has not disappeared from prominence in the new model as the simple label of neoliberalism might suggest. Again, however, it plays a different role.

For those countries that had depended on the import substitution model of development, the shift to economic openness produced greater shocks than in those with a light industry export model. For both, the internation- alization of finance and production by TNCs opened the possibility of new sources of investment and sales in international markets, in exchange for dropping the protection enjoyed by domestic producers. In several countries economic dynamism is today increasingly powered by up-market services sec- tors. This has considerable attractions in terms of bringing high value-added activities into a poor country. On the other hand, it can lead to increasing gaps between those working in such sectors and the mass of the population still in traditional agriculture or the low-productivity sectors of the informal urban economy. As Boyer (2007) concludes:

> More precisely, the impact of internal and external liberalization has been reassessed. In some cases, the strengthening of *market forces* and price mechanisms has been quite helpful in reducing poverty, if not inequal- ities: it seems to be the case for China and other Asian countries. In other instances, the *full liberalization* of product, labour and financial markets has been quite detrimental to macroeconomic stability since the bursting out of major financial crises has exacerbated poverty creation in the very same countries that represented themselves as dominated by a large mid- dle class: one recognizes the dramatic transformation of the Argentinean economy.

Social policy under the competition state

Whereas social policy in many developmental states often addressed multiple concerns related to social protection, production and redistribution (UNRISD 2006), there has now been a considerable increase in a productivist approach that uses social policy to upgrade the quality of the workforce in terms of basic health as well as skills and capacities. As in the advanced economies, parts of the working population come to be seen as a resource worthy of investment. A key example is the move from passive to active labour market policies (ALMPs). The former had been concerned mainly with guaranteeing income security during times of employment instability; ALMP was concerned with improving the individual workers' chances of gaining better and more highly skilled employment. Similar approaches developed in other fields, including the improvement of social infrastructure in order to improve national or city-level competitiveness (OECD 2006).

These kinds of policies implied a state that was actively engaged in promoting national economic strength, not through autarchy and centralized national plans as in the 1960s, but by strengthening the basis on which firms could compete in global markets. This is a distinct agenda from a true neoliberal one, in which ALMP means the provision of negative and positive incentives to individuals to enter the labour market. The two can, however, become mixed as a productivist strategy for labour-market activization. The governments of countries seeking to enter dynamic new sectors of the high-tech economy became increasingly interested in aspects of this model.

The competition state, as the new form of active but neoliberal state is often described, can, and often does, imply bearing down on labour costs, welfare spending and social infrastructure to give free rein to market forces and TNCs to pursue development goals in the context of profit maximization. In these cases, poverty, poor health and low educational levels are not seen as a problem and may even be a condition of the growth model. The type of social partnership approach that has emerged in countries like Brazil and South Africa can potentially mitigate this tendency. In practice, however, as Farnsworth explains (see companion volume), power relations are often skewed towards business. Referring to South Africa, Kaggwa (see companion volume) describes how the competitiveness challenge created by reintegration into the global economy in 1994 motivated a partnership between government, industry and labour to map out the country's policy for the automotive industry. The policy framework formulated was successful in enabling local industry to participate in the global automotive value chain, but social outcomes were relegated in the process, leading to subsequent policy concern among organized labour and government.

There is, however, also the possibility of a stronger emphasis on social policies. As Boyer (2007) explains:

> by providing some basic collective goods related to health, education and security, the corresponding [welfare] expenditures should be classified as investment, since they contribute to social capital formation. Its volume and composition are therefore factors of production and contributors to growth. . . . Within these new analytical frameworks, some *welfare policies* aiming at the development of workers' and citizens' securities may have

favourable productive impact and positively affect the dynamic efficiency of the economic regime.

Farnsworth (2005; and see companion volume) tracks the development of this position in the stance of international organizations. For example, by 2005, the Organisation for Economic Co-operation and Development (OECD) was promoting active social policy that might help change the conditions in which individuals develop, rather than limiting themselves to ameliorating the distress these conditions cause (OECD 2005). Its 2005 report promoted employment-centred social policy, and defended the private financing of social policy as a way of helping individuals to 'face the true price of social protection, and thereby reduce the risk of excess provision' (OECD 2005: 43). Farnsworth shows a similar shift in the position of the World Bank, which in the same year (2005) spoke of the need to create opportunities for people to escape from poverty and improve their living standards.

Experience has been so varied that it is difficult to provide a coherent overarching account of the impact on welfare and poverty reduction policies across developing economies, or even to group them in meaningful clusters. The analysis above does suggest, however, the following conclusions:

- Some sections of the mass population have gained from increasingly sophisticated productivist social policies, although these have left out of consideration large swathes of the population, as indeed had been the case with the earlier developmental state models.
- There has been some trickle-down effect of reduced poverty as overall levels of growth have risen in the dynamic sectors of several economies.
- The welfare obligations sometimes recognized by embedded (usually protectionist) local elites are not necessarily followed by the largely ex-patriot elites of TNC managements. Hypothetically, this tendency can be offset by corporate hierarchy and CSR strategies on the part of such elites; a question to which we return below.

Analysing governance in the competition state

Table 1.2 shows the kinds of governance modes associated with the changing sectors of production and growing orientation towards international markets. Before moving on to consider the institutions of key interest – the state, market and corporate hierarchy – it is important to note that the two governance modes that one might have expected to decline with modernization are in fact growing in importance. These are networks and, particularly surprising, community. Networks are, of course, important to firms in the advanced countries in the high-tech and innovative sectors of the kind that many developing countries are trying to encourage. Whether inward investors are interested in developing networks in the latter is not clear. Networks, and

Table 1.2 Developmental models and socioeconomic governance since the 1980s' 'neoliberal turn'

Forms of developmental state	Types of economic governance						
	Government	Law	Market	Corporate hierarchy	Association	Network	Community
1. Advanced services and high-tech products, private firms	Provides infrastructure and encourages foreign direct investment (FDI)	No necessary change from earlier model	International markets guide production; mass domestic markets sometimes still weak	Fundamental, particularly of inwardly investing TNCs; no necessary welfare role	Declining	Sometimes important among SMEs; important in shadow economy, which is often growing in importance	Important to shadow economy and to welfare governance; increasing if shadow economy growing and welfare state shrinking
2. Light industry, state and private firms	Provides infrastructure and encourages FDI; also maintains overall control		International markets guide production subject to overall government control; mass domestic markets still weak	Fundamental, of both domestic firms and inwardly investing TNCs; welfare role in domestic firms	Not important		
3. Light industry, private firms	As 1		As 1	As 1	Declining		
4. Commodity production	Important		As 3	Important in economic governance; rarely involved in welfare	Declining		Important for linking political and economic elites. Among mass of population, fundamental for welfare

traditional communities, are, however, important for the sustenance of workers in the informal and shadow economies that are probably increasing in these countries as stable work in agriculture and formal employment in manufacturing decline as part of the flexibilization of work. This often appears in employment statistics as a rise in self-employment, but it is more accurately seen as informalization rather than entrepreneurial company formation. More relevant for the present concern with poverty strategies, traditional communities (mainly families) are playing a growing welfare role in those societies where a general decline in state welfare support is required by the neoliberal modernization model.

On the other hand, associational governance, never as strong in developing economies as in the advanced economies, has weakened under the impact of the transnational economy. (It has done the same in many advanced economies.) Associational governance suffers from two handicaps in a changing, globalizing economy (Crouch 2005). First, business associations are usually based on defined industries, and in a time of change the identity of industries shifts and new ones are created. Second, associations usually form at the national level, which becomes less important in a global economy: in particular, large inward investors are unlikely to make use of national associations in the countries in which they invest, preferring to lobby effectively for themselves in relations with government.

Nowhere has government become inactive. However, it now plays the role of the competitive state in relation to the encouragement of FDI, and also in the adaptation of welfare and infrastructure policy to national economic plans. Whereas many developmental states tried to equip their economies by *protecting them from* international competitive pressures, the competition state *equips its firms for* competition – or welcomes direct inward investment from international enterprises considered more efficient than local firms. This is achieved partly by the establishment of a strong infrastructure, which firms then use as support when finding their own way in the market – as opposed to fulfilling a government plan. A major example is Viet Nam (Dinh 2007), which rapidly shifted its strategy after 1986 to infrastructure construction rather than intervention.

There is no necessary change in the general role of the rule of law where the mass of the population is concerned; however, guarantees of stable law do have to be offered to inward investing firms. These may more generally enjoy a different legal regime from the rest of the country, with enterprise zones and special fiscal arrangements. The competition developmental state is not therefore necessarily characterized by a general growth in the rule of law, but more likely by a compartmentalization of legal systems operating within the country.

Individual large corporations continue to play a major role, and continue to do so through strong links with local political elites. Except in very large states, individual TNCs often occupy strategic roles within these economies.

As part of this, they are usually able to negotiate deals with governments that do not conform to the abstentionist concept of the neoliberal political economy. Firms are frequently offered inducements to invest, privileged tax positions and exemptions from local labour and environmental laws.[5] The new model therefore resembles the old in that key firms continue to enjoy a partnership with the political elite. For example, in India, while the coalition of capitalists around the previous import substitution path has lost influence, the new export-oriented elite retains close political links (Chibber 2007). Stronger examples of state capture by economically powerful groups are apparent in Peru (see companion volume) and Costa Rica (Cortes and León 2007). These developments are quite inconsistent with the neoliberal model, as are the 'cronyism' and privileges, bordering on or actually becoming corruption, that have been associated with privatization programmes from Ireland to Russia.

Governance by corporate hierarchy and CSR

Consideration of the economic and political role of TNCs raises the question of their role in welfare and poverty issues, which involves discussion of the part being played by CSR. Do TNCs play a different role in developing societies from the locally embedded elites characteristic of the old developmental state? In theory, the combined ascendancy of markets and corporate hierarchies – that is, the rise of economic against political and social modes of governance – marks the rise of those modes least able to cope with negative externalities, including various forms of social distress. These will possibly be tackled only if oligopolistic firms use their relative freedom from market constraint to develop private social policy as a part of their business strategy and the governance role of their corporate hierarchies. How likely is this?

Firms subject to intense competition will find it difficult to do, as anything that prevents them from setting prices as low as possible will be an important disadvantage (Van de Ven and Jeurissen 2005). It has, however, been argued from the perspectives of both neoclassical and evolutionary economics that firms might use CSR as a strategy for achieving market niches that protect them – at least temporarily – from competition. Amalric and Hauser (2005) argue from a neoclassical perspective that firms can use socially responsible behaviour to differentiate their products, attracting customers who are concerned about such issues. They even claim that it is possible to construct the whole organization around social responsibility, making it less easy for rivals to compete on these grounds. They also point to the usefulness of CSR for 'reputation management' and – moving outside the neoclassical frame – for anticipating and warding off government regulation. For Maxfield (2008), working explicitly from an evolutionary perspective, firms are constantly learning and trying out new possibilities in a highly uncertain world; CSR strategies may emerge as one of the results of this. Such drivers of CSR, which relate to strategy and practices at the level of the firm, yield wide variations in response, from more meaningful changes in social and environmental performance to firms merely presenting images of themselves as socially responsible.

In this chapter the issue of CSR is raised, not through economics, but through the sociopolitical concept of governance. The key question is what changes, if any, have taken place in the form taken by relationships between economic elites and social policy in the transition from embedded state-centred modernizing elites to internationally-oriented and inward-investing ones? Reference was made above to the way in which welfare policies in developmental elites often appeared as a kind of *noblesse oblige* on the part of elites. The old French aristocratic concept of *noblesse oblige* was that aristocracies were supposed to take upon themselves certain social obligations in recognition of the privileged position they occupied in society. But they decided for themselves what constituted their obligations and accepted no wider scrutiny or debate around these, let alone democratic influence. Is CSR the *noblesse oblige* of transnational corporate elites? Here we address this question, primarily drawing on empirical studies referred to in this and its companion volume,[6] as well as other studies carried out by the United Nations Research Institute for Social Development (UNRISD). This analysis not only shows the major variations that exist, thereby cautioning against broad generalizations about the substance and quality of CSR, but also reveals that the extent of public scrutiny of business elites and corporate accountability varies considerably under different governance systems.

Referring to the contemporary era of economic liberalization in India, Sood (2007) argues that in the new paradigm, the identification of needs, accountability of services and transparency in implementation are increasingly performed by civil society institutions, while business provides the resources for investment and is increasingly engaging with voluntary CSR initiatives. The role of government is largely reduced to coordination and facilitation. The business–social policy linkage is currently more evident in decisions on the direction of social policy (target oriented, debating the legitimacy of needs and restricting transfer payments) and in the choice of instruments to deliver social policy goals, such as public private partnership.

In another UNRISD study, Sood and Arora (2006) examine the scale and quality of CSR in India, suggesting that it has been driven primarily by a long history of corporate philanthropy, new imperatives of international competition and market access, and peer pressure from business organizations. Such factors have resulted in a growing number of CSR initiatives and an array of institutions promoting this approach. Its uptake, however, is limited to a relatively small group of companies linked to the international market, while initiatives consist primarily of 'returning to society' rather than realizing workers' or citizens' rights. Such limitations reflect both weaknesses in civil society activism as well as state regulation.

In Latin America, Schneider (2007) mainly sees business interests moving *away* from proactive support for, and participation in, social policy, to big business favouring enhanced social policies only where its activities are concentrated in high skill, high quality sectors – which is not usually the case in the subcontinent. In Brazil, we see business elites pursuing a dual strategy of promoting CSR (Cappellin and Giuliani 2004) and lobbying to reduce the so-called 'Brazil cost' (Mancuso, see companion volume) – the supposed extra burden of social costs incurred by firms doing business in Brazil rather than in certain competitor nations. With considerable success, industrial entrepreneurs have undertaken extensive collective work to identify congressional bills with a greater potential impact on their costs; define a unified response to the most relevant bills; and make their opinion known during the decision-making process. CSR discourse and practices have also proliferated in Brazil. Driven by international competitive pressures, civil society activism, and some socially-conscious business associations, the CSR agenda has gathered momentum and also engaged with some government programmes, notably Zero Hunger, but has tended to focus primarily on issues external to the workplace, including community assistance and the environment (Cappellin and Giuliani 2004).

The contradictions between CSR and lobbying are highlighted by Slob and Weyzig (see companion volume). They reveal how powerful TNCs have supported lobbying efforts that were not in line with their own public policy statements or CSR policies. Moreover, most companies did not disclose public policy positions at all and lacked a comprehensive system to align lobbying practices with CSR policies. As a consequence, firms have lobbied successfully for policies that have had negative impacts for developing countries, including occasions when the direct target of corporate lobbying has not been the legislation in a developing country itself, but an international trade agreement. The disclosure of information on donations, which forms the main activity where CSR practices lead firms to be transparent about lobbying activities, turns out not to have been an important aspect of this lobbying activity. Direct lobbying and constituency building by individual companies as well as various collective strategies tend to have a much larger influence and account for a far greater share of lobbying budgets.

CSR not only sits uncomfortably with certain lobbying practices, it can also be used as a tool to discipline suppliers and workers in ways that imply benefits for global corporations that dominate the value chain and costs of other stakeholders. Focusing on the case of Wal-Mart in China, Sum (chapter 2) claims that the techniques of CSR are used to depoliticize labour issues by narrowing the range of points of leverage. The struggle over labour and environmental conditions is thereby translated into, and confined to, codes, auditing standards, programmes, projects, and documentation systems promoted by private and public actors at different levels. For the TNCs, codes of conduct and CSR help to legitimize the privatization of labour and environment standards. These are then 'traded' as moral resources that are an integral part of their overall corporate response to challenges.

In some neoliberal contexts CSR might be seen as a *replacement* for a state that is retreating from its engagement with economy and, also, society. Wall (2007) has considered the case of Kazakhstan, a large post-Soviet republic in Central Asia, with extensive natural resources but also high levels of rural poverty, as the earnings of the mineral extraction industries flow to the cities and beyond Kazakhstan itself. Foreign energy firms have invested heavily in the country since independence in 1991. These firms have adopted CSR strategies in fields like health care that were traditionally seen as the realm of the state. In health care provision this is particularly prevalent. Wall found that in the early years the state encouraged outside investors to take over responsibility for health care, but this has been associated with corruption, weakening existing institutions and a lack of control or ownership of the spending. There is now a decline in the government's use of this as part of the criteria for winning contracts and securing production sharing agreements (PSAs).

An increasingly important aspect of the privatization to individual corporations of transnational economic governance concerns the development of private standards (Schepel 2005; Sum, chapter 2). These have also become involved in CSR policies, an important case being the position of farmers in poor countries in the food production industry, where the making of standards is often dominated by retail corporations in the advanced countries. In a study of these standards, Fuchs and Kalfagianni (chapter 9) found little attention being paid to the social implications of sustainability, and many small farmers and small retailers being driven out of the market, though they acknowledge that standards providing for good working conditions have also been developed. They question the democratic legitimacy of the increasing privatization of food governance, there being considerable inequality in access to the development of private standards, as well as lack of transparency and accountability in most cases.

Similar questions concerning the adequacy of private governance are raised by Gregoratti (chapter 8) in a study of the Growing Sustainable Business (GSB) Initiative in Kenya and Tanzania. She found that corporate interests and economic ideas shaped the GSB's deliberation processes; and that these have encouraged the emergence of a form of elitist governance that remains largely indifferent to the needs of local communities. She also evaluated the partnership projects being carried out in Kenya and Tanzania, and asserts that 'the private sector's efforts to be portrayed as an integral actor in development activities is nothing more than a "business as usual" approach'. On the basis of this evidence, Gregoratti calls for a rethink by the GSB and the United Nations Development Programme (UNDP) concerning the implications and operationalization of partnership for development, arguing that such 'supply-driven' interventions compound the political power of business, replace the role of governments as a provider of public goods and the corollary creation of elitist mode of governance. They could, however, be perceived as more legitimate and even prove to be more effective, she argues, if the concerns of poorer groups were to be prioritized over the commercial gains of the business sector and if 'sustainable business' initiatives were selected to reinforce state-led developmental policies to amplify the impact of existing initiatives (see also Newell and Frynas 2007).

If corporations increasingly take on roles normally associated with the provision of public goods, whether these be tackling social problems or engaging in regulation or standard-setting, they are entering the polity and cannot expect to be as relatively unchallenged there as when they simply engage in the provision of goods and services in relatively free markets. The immediate expectation, entertained for example by several of the writers cited above, is that governments will challenge them and reclaim sovereignty over public space. However, as we have seen, many governments have historically been responsive primarily to various business and political elites and have not necessarily been exemplary guardians of the interests of a general public or of the socially excluded poor. Today they are in addition very dependent on inward investors for the real wealth and opportunities that they bring. It is possible that those concerned at the neglect of social issues need to broaden their analysis of the social forces that might be brought to bear. In particular, attention is moving to consider the role of civil society groups and social movements. These increasingly address corporations as well as, or even instead of, governments. Sometimes this is because of the obvious power that corporations wield, especially as they mark out a clearly political agenda. Sometimes it is because a corporation, sensitive to customers and activists in the advanced world, may be more likely to respond to pressure than a government in a developing country with weak civil society.

Various authors in this volume call for a corporate *accountability* approach to CSR, rather than a corporate *sovereignty* one, with civil society actors building pressure for meaningful involvement of business on social issues. This might be seen as a move away from *noblesse oblige* to a system involving challenge and scrutiny – measures that are associated with democratization, though hardly democracy itself.

As an example of these developments, Sood (2007) claims that, while the history of corporate paternalism has played an important part in shaping community expectations and CSR practices in India, in more recent years civil society, consumers and other actors have increased the pressure on companies to adhere to social and environmental standards, and that this new 'civil regulatory' environment has had impacts on business. Issues of CSR and stakeholder engagement were debated in India as early as the 1960s, and there is evidence available of businesses going beyond compliance and setting best practice standards in labour relations and community development even before India's independence in 1947.

Van Alstine (chapter 10) shows how new countervailing centres of power emerged to discipline business and promote social pacts conducive to inclusive development in South Africa. There, the governmental priority given to economic growth and international competitiveness had set up a potential conflict between environmental health, social policy and inclusive development goals. Within this context he explored how the fuel oil industry articulated its contribution to society, and how and why the issue areas of environmental and public health had been contested and constructed relating to two oil refineries in Durban. He found that innovative multistakeholder initiatives (MSIs) had emerged, and a progression had occurred from normative to regulative institutions as an internationally networked civil society demanded accountability from both the private and public sectors, and as government began to build capacity. Initiatives for strategic environmental assessment and the government's attempt to implement policies failed to produce the desired results. However, an MSI in South Durban emerged as a successful example that gained the levels of trust needed to become legitimate in the eyes of both industry and communities.

Noyoo (chapter 4) argues similarly for a more collective approach to CSR in Zambia. Many of the professed CSR activities in that country and elsewhere are hortatory in nature and at times resemble a wishlist. A strong intellectual orientation to CSR is needed, he argues, and in at least the Zambian case advocates the Community Development tradition. This seeks the empowerment of local communities and strengthening of the capacity of people as active citizens, on the one hand, and the capacity of institutions and agencies (public, private and non-governmental organizations/NGOs), on the other.

However, local civil societies are often weak. In a review of corporate lobbying and CSR in India, Slob and Weyzig (see companion volume) find that, even where trade unions existed, they were not very effective in advocating the rights of workers beyond issues related to wages and could not, therefore, contribute much to the larger corporate responsibility debate. To some extent, this shortcoming was offset by the emergence of other civil society actors. However, their activism in the early phase was limited by government policies to the role of service delivery agents; it was only in the 1990s, when this role broadened, that NGOs started to have greater effect. They tended to influence state policies rather than confronting business head-on.

To recall an earlier discussion above, there may be differences depending on whether individual corporations, or associations of them, play the key role. The combined effect of neoliberalism and the rise of strong TNCs has been to diminish the role of associations. However, the latter, being collective actors, can sometimes be more likely to take account of the externalities of economic activity than individual firms. Schneider (2007), in research on a number of Latin American cases, finds that the role of associations could be rescued: the more state actors draw business associations into policy making and the more government officials delegates responsibility for policy implementation to associations, the greater are business incentives to invest in the institutional capacity of these associations. Although policy makers rarely have strengthening associations as a policy priority, the fact that these state actions affect business organization and participation in policy makes clear that these outcomes could in fact be objects of policy.

A difference between individual company and more collective approaches to social issues was also found by Palpacuer (chapter 11) and Merk (2007) in their studies of TNCs exposed to anti-sweatshop campaigns that attacked substandard working conditions. Individual companies would take many steps, but those engaging in an industry-wide approach would go further, developing sectoral framework agreements, and engaging in international social dialogue with relevant stakeholders.

Today, in industries like textiles, clothing and footwear, a large number of ethical codes have been adopted, and CSR has turned into what Miller has called a 'routine management function' (Miller 2004: 220). However, both Palpacuer and Merk argue that the overall influence of the anti-sweatshop movement must not be overstated. Global production practices continue to worsen in many parts of the developing world, and governments still fail to enact or enforce labour laws. The redirection of orders towards countries such as China that outlaw or restrict freedom of association among workers further reinforces the exclusion or marginalization of them and their organizations from the mechanisms set up to implement, monitor or verify code compliance. At the heart of this crisis, Merk claims, lies a regulatory vacuum created through the shift from nationally-oriented production systems to globally organized production networks.

Cappellin and Giuliani (2004) similarly describe the engagement of civil society in CSR issues in Brazil. They show that interest in improving the social and environmental performance of firms increased significantly in the 1980s, and was driven to a large extent by domestic concerns, actors and contexts. A crucial element was the diffusion of certain values and ethical principles related to democratization and progressive religious thinking. Democratization also paved the way for the expansion of civil society organizations and social movements concerned with the social and environmental impacts of business. Again, business associations, that not only represented the economic interests of their members but also addressed philosophical and cultural issues, including the relationship of business to society, took an important role. Critical of traditional corporate behaviour, this network tried to raise the social awareness of firms and promote philanthropic activities. In the 1990s the actors and institutions promoting CSR expanded considerably. Political parties, NGOs, trade unions, the media, local government, consumers and shareholders all became involved, along with some business associations and proactive managers and firms. The momentum behind CSR was also reinforced by international influences and pressures associated with cross-border management of TNCs, global civil society activism, environmental certification, and international social, environmental and human rights norms and law.

The authors point to another important change occurring in the 1990s. As companies sought to restructure and become more competitive internationally, some managers – and business management scholars – recognized the potential of using CSR initiatives as a way of reducing costs, increasing competitive advantage and managing risks and reputation. The international repercussions of Brazil's unfavourable business image pushed them to prioritize a few specific areas, including poverty, violence, child labour, education and environmental protection. Segments of business, particularly the largest firms in more dynamic sectors, assumed leadership roles in social actions, seeking to fill some of the gaps that resulted from the perception or reality of a weak public sector. CSR became part of a broader strategy to gain legitimacy; a way of cleaning up the soiled image of entrepreneurs and companies that were regarded by many as responsible for the concentration of wealth and growing speculation in financial investment.

Another approach to a kind of 'collectivization' of CSR are the cross-sector partnerships described by Findlay-Brooks et al. (chapter 7) as being seen by many governments, international agencies and corporations as the most effective way to deal with complex and intractable development problems that have defeated single-sector interventions. However, they argue, they raise issues of accountability and power imbalance, when unelected businesses and NGOs have influence in states where governments are weak or failing. Even where they are the best solution, there can be real obstacles in both the development and management of partnerships which are too easily ignored. They conclude that, if we are relying on partnerships to bring about structural change and long-term development impacts, then they need to be firmly tied into genuinely inclusive consultation processes, operate within accountability frameworks, be properly supported and evaluated, and, where appropriate, lead ultimately to policy change.

Conclusions

Relations among states, corporations, civil societies and poor populations in the earlier form of developmental state were more complex than often presented by the stylized facts of the literature. The new, ostensibly neoliberal, regime is at least equally complex. Once one takes account of both the level of intervention still available to the competition state and the full range of governance modes identified by Hollingsworth and Boyer (1997) (and not just the over-simple antithesis between state and market), one has a potentially rich and varied range of different forms of neoliberalism. Particular attention needs to be focused on the role of inwardly investing TNCs within developing societies that have either replaced or, more likely, moved in alongside domestic elites as the key decision makers over major socioeconomic issues.

The key question then becomes – and the same question is equally salient at the present time in the advanced countries – in what ways can the social power of these corporations be constitutionalized so that they contribute effectively to the wide range of neglected externalities and social questions at stake in the contemporary world?

In the late nineteenth and twentieth centuries, the main answer that emerged in the then industrializing parts of the world concerned with economic growth, social protection or cohesion was for the state, itself gradually becoming democratic, to take various powers within the economy. In both those countries and in the developing world, that answer is not so obviously available today. First, the choices of location offered to many TNCs by the increasingly global economic playing field restrict the capacity of individual states to regulate their economies. Second, governments face difficult choices between providing fiscal and regulatory regimes for inward investors which improve the rate of growth for their economies which might eventually benefit their populations; but which meanwhile may mean increasing inequality and reduced social policy provision. Third, many political elites do not have track records that suggest that they would seriously pursue such a role even if it were available.

Finally, if in this context the corporate hierarchies of TNCs are becoming major sources of governance, rivalling states and markets, attention turns to the role of these firms as political actors themselves, rather than as entities that could easily be regulated by public policy. Existing research on the role of CSR in social policy in developing societies, some of which has been summarized above, presents a highly ambiguous picture. Clearly, there are important examples of firms playing this kind of role and contributing to health, education and environmental quality, not only among their workforces, but within the wider local communities around their plants. And there are cases, for example, in parts of Africa where the CSR of a foreign TNC constitutes the main source of welfare. But there are also many cases where CSR is more a part of public relations than of social policy. Even where it is more serious, firms rarely possess true expertise in the policy fields in which they become engaged. Particularly problematic is the fact that CSR is within the sole control of the headquarters of the enterprises concerned: there is no democratic control, and managing elites of the corporations are not 'embedded elites', themselves responsive to local communities. This is why it has been described here as constituting a modern equivalent of *noblesse oblige*. The social obligations of pre-democratic aristocracies were defined and implemented by the aristocracies themselves, with no external monitoring or challenge.

This fact directs our attention in turn to the groups in civil society that might emerge as political counterparts to these corporations in an emerging politics of corporate accountability, and to what implications such an emerging polity would have for the world's poor. Very frequently the groups concerned in this new form of activism are just as disembedded as the corporate elites themselves, being based in the home countries of the corporations and operating mainly by trying to influence the product markets of the firms in the rich countries where the bulk of consumers live. In the absence of active and robust civil society organizations in many countries of the developing world, this is often the best that can be achieved. In general, however, one can conclude that the quality and value of TNCs' contribution to social policy in developing societies will be as strong as the campaigns for trying to ensure wider public debate, scrutiny, challenge and transparency in their activities.

Notes

1. See, for example, the contrast between Danish and United States (US) neoliberalism, described by Campbell and Pedersen (2001).
2. The classic source for this account of the market as being somehow 'natural' is Hayek (1973). Among important critiques of the position are North (1990) and Greif (2006).
3. See Boyer (2007); Hollingsworth and Boyer (1997); Hollingsworth et al. (2002).
4. Strictly speaking, the state should be separated into 'government' and 'law'; this is done in the graphical representation of the argument below, but it is not discussed in the text as our attention is focused on the role of firms and their corporate hierarchy.
5. Exemption from taxation and restrictive laws might seem to be pure expressions of neoliberalism. However, if they exist in a context where other firms in other jurisdictions are not enjoying the same conditions, they become privileges.
6. Peter Utting and José Carlos Marques (eds), *Business Politics and Public Policy* (Basingstoke: UNRISD/Palgrave Macmillan, forthcoming).

References

Amalric, F. and J. Hauser, 'Economic drivers of corporate responsibility activities', *The Journal of Corporate Citizenship*, No. 20 (2005) 27–38.

Boyer, R., *Growth Strategies and Poverty Reduction: The Institutional Complementarity Hypothesis*, mimeo (Paris: Paris-Jourdan Sciences Economiques, 2007).

Campbell, J. and O.K. Pedersen (eds), *The Rise of Neoliberalism and Institutional Analysis* (Princeton, NJ: Princeton University Press, 2001).

Cappellin, P. and G.M. Giuliani, *The Political Economy of Corporate Responsibility in Brazil: Social and Environmental Dimensions*, Programme on Technology, Business and Society, Paper No. 14 (Geneva: UNRISD, 2004).

Chang, Y.-F., *Wealth and Income Inequalities in Taiwan*, mimeo (Geneva: UNRISD, 2007).

Chibber, V., *Organized Interests, Development Strategies and Social Policies*, mimeo (Geneva: UNRISD, 2007).

Chua, B.H., *Singapore: Growing Wealth, Poverty Avoidance and Management*, mimeo (Geneva: UNRISD, 2007).

Coase, R., 'The nature of the firm', *Economica*, No. 4 (1937) 127–53.

Cortes, A. and A. León, *Costa Rica: Conflictividad Social y Distribución, 1950–2005*, mimeo (Geneva: UNRISD, 2007).

Crouch, C., 'Neo-corporatism and democracy'. In C. Crouch and W. Streeck (eds), *The Diversity of Democracy* (Cheltenham: Edward Elgar, 2005).

——, *Industrial Relations and State Traditions* (Oxford: Oxford University Press, 1993).

Dinh, D.D., *Growth with Equity: Double Click for High Economic Growth and Quick Poverty Reduction: The Case of Vietnam*, mimeo (Geneva: UNRISD, 2007).

Evans, P.B., *Embedded Autonomy: States and Industrial Transformation* (Princeton, NJ: Princeton University Press, 1995).

Farnsworth, K., 'International class conflict and social policy', *Social Policy and Society*, Vol. 4, No. 2 (2005) 217–26.

Greif, A., *Institutions and the Path to the Modern Economy: Lessons from Medieval Trade* (Cambridge: Cambridge University Press, 2006).

Hayek, F.A., *Rules and Order* (London: RKP, 1973).

Hollingsworth, J.R. and R. Boyer (eds), *Contemporary Capitalism: The Embeddedness of Institutions* (Cambridge: Cambridge University Press, 1997).

Hollingsworth, J.R., K.H. Müller and E.J. Hollingsworth (eds), *Advancing Socio-Economics: An Institutionalist Perspective* (Lanham, MD: Rowman and Littlefield, 2002).

Love, J.L., 'Raúl Prebisch and the origins of the doctrine of unequal exchange', *Latin American Research Review*, No. 15 (1980) 45–72.

Maxfield, S., 'Reconciling corporate citizenship and competitive strategy: Insights from economic theory', *Journal of Business Ethics*, Vol. 80, No. 2 (2008) 367–77.

Merk, J., *The Structural Crisis of Labour Flexibility: Strategies and Prospects for Transnational Labour Organising in the Garment and Sportswear Industry*, paper presented at the Conference on Business, Social Policy and Corporate Influence in Developing Countries, UNRISD, Geneva, 12–13 November (2007).

Miller, D., 'Negotiating international framework agreements in the global textile, garment and footwear sector', *Global Social Policy*, Vol. 4, No. 2 (2004) 215–39.

Newell, P. and G. Frynas, 'Beyond CSR? Business, poverty and social justice: An introduction', *Third World Quarterly*, Vol. 28, No. 4 (2007) 669–81.

North, D.C., *Institutions, Institutional Change, and Economic Performance* (Cambridge: Cambridge University Press, 1990).

OECD (Organisation for Economic Co-operation and Development), *Competitive Cities in the Global* Economy (Paris: OECD, 2006).

——, *Extending Opportunities: How Active Social Policy Can Benefit Us All* (Paris: OECD, 2005).

Schepel, H., *The Constitution of Private Governance: Standards in the Regulation of Integrating Markets* (Oxford: Hart Publishing, 2005).

Schmitter, P.C., 'Still the century of corporatism?', *Review of Politics*, Vol. 36, No. 1 (1974) 85–131.

Schneider, Ben Ross, *Business and Social Policy in Latin America: Sources of Disconnect*, paper presented at the Conference on Business, Social Policy and Corporate Political Influence in Developing Countries, Geneva, 12–13 November (Geneva: UNRISD, 2007).

Sood, A., *Changing Nature of State–Business Relations in India: Implications for Social and Labour Market Policies*, paper presented at the Conference on Business, Social Policy and Corporate Influence in Developing Countries, UNRISD, Geneva, 12–13 November (2007).

Sood, A. and B. Arora, *The Political Economy of Corporate Responsibility in India*, Programme on Technology, Business and Society, Paper No. 18 (Geneva: UNRISD, 2006).

UNRISD (United Nations Research Institute for Social Development), *Transformative Social Policy: Lessons from UNRISD Research*. UNRISD Research and Policy Brief, No. 5 (Geneva: UNRISD, 2006).

Utting, Peter and José Carlos Marques (eds), *Business Politics and Public Policy* (Basingstoke: UNRISD/Palgrave Macmillan, forthcoming).

Van de Ven, B. and R. Jeurissen, 'Competing responsibly', *Business Ethics Quarterly*, Vol. 15, No. 2 (2005) 299–317.

Wall, C.R.L., *Kazakh Public Policy and Corporate Social Responsibility: An Analysis of Health Care Provision in an Era of CSR and Kazakh Nationalism*, paper presented at the Conference on Business, Social Policy and Corporate Influence in Developing Countries, UNRISD, Geneva, 12–13 November (2007).

Weiss, L. and J.M. Hobson, *States and Economic Development* (Cambridge: Polity Press, 1995).

Williamson, O.E., *Markets and Hierarchies: Analysis and Antitrust Implications: A Study in the Economics of Internal Organization* (New York: Free Press, 1975).

2
Wal-Martization and CSR-ization in Developing Countries

Ngai-Ling Sum

Introduction

This chapter explores the rise of multinational retail and sourcing chains in the context of neoliberal capitalism promoted by the World Trade Organization (WTO) and other institutions as part of the post-Washington Consensus. Focusing in particular on Wal-Mart and its operations in China, it examines the changing social relations between different types of capital along supply chains, as well as between capital and workers at different points in these chains. These changes have led to political challenges from a range of national and transnational groups and have prompted some to ask whether the adoption of corporate social responsibility (CSR) is leading to the 'marketization of the social' and/or 'socialization of the market'.

This chapter addresses such issues in four sections, drawing on neo-Gramscian[1] and neo-Foucauldian[2] perspectives and, indeed, showing how they can be combined in productive ways. The first section deploys the neo-Gramscian approach, especially Gill's (1995, 1998, 2002) concept of 'new constitutionalism', to examine how international agreements under the WTO, such as the General Agreement on Trade in Services (GATS), 'unlock' countries for international trade and investment and also facilitate the rise of multinational chains in the developed and developing countries. The second section focuses on developing countries, especially China, examining how Wal-Mart has reshaped its corporate culture and entered into local joint-venture partnerships to consolidate its retailing and sourcing activities. The third section explores how this growing 'Wal-Martization' trend shifts power from suppliers-manufacturers to retailers (and financiers). In particular, it indicates how, based on its control over the supplier system, Wal-Mart has been able to impose 'Everyday Low Prices' and low wages on its suppliers, local competitors and workers. This is a form of trickle-down economic poverty that has prompted Wal-Mart watching groups across different scales. In response to criticisms and monitoring, state institutions, trade unions and non-governmental organizations (NGOs) have attempted to bring CSR to Wal-Mart in developing countries, including China. I introduce the concept of CSR-ization to describe how CSR is implemented at the factory level. The fourth section returns to Gill's idea of 'new constitutionalism' but supplements it by introducing the notion of 'new ethicalism' to rethink the logic of certain novel features of global capitalism. This general mapping of the CSR terrain would be incomplete without noting continuing struggles by movement-oriented NGOs. The chapter ends by suggesting the need for a 'cultural political economy' research agenda to study these tensions in the making of a social economy.

'New constitutionalism' and the rise of multinational chains

The WTO's GATS is a multilateral trade agreement[3] that promotes the gradual liberalization of international trade in services (for example, banking, education, accounting, retailing). When national governments originally signed up to the GATS in 1994, they undertook to ensure that all levels of government conformed to the agreement. Even though there was little consultation with national or local governments about the implications of the GATS for domestic regulatory authorities, it is law that applies to authorities at all levels of government. Its mandate is based on the rule of anti-discrimination of foreign traders and the removal of 'non-tariff barriers'. These allow the WTO to limit national laws/regulations that favour domestic actors. For example, in the case of retail and wholesale service (under Mode 3 on commercial presence abroad), the GATS rules give global supermarket chains the right to set up shops in local sites. Any local rules (for example, opening hours and land use laws) can be challenged as barriers to trade.

From a neo-Gramscian perspective, the WTO-GATS helps to tilt the global economic order towards neoliberal accumulation by creating a political-legal trade and investment framework that reconfigures power relations in favour of (trans-)national capital and against domestic government and citizens. This fits into a political strategy for which Gill (1995) coined the term 'new constitutionalism'. This involves 'the politico-juridical locking in of commitments to a disciplinary neoliberal framework of accumulation on the world scale' (Gill 2002: 2). In contrast with old/democratic constitutionalism, which provides citizens with rights and freedom by limiting the power of the government, 'new constitutionalism': (1) locks in (or confers) privileged rights of (trans-)national capital by anchoring them in a cross-cutting web of (trans-)national laws and regulations; and (2) locks out (or insulates) democratic scrutiny on marketized issues. This form of (global) new constitutionalism partly underpins and complements what Gill has termed 'disciplinary neoliberalism'. This combines the structural power of capital with the 'capillary power' of panopticism (à la Foucault)[4] (1975), which will be examined in the second section.

GATS can certainly be seen as a form of new (global) constitutionalism and, in the retail trade arena, it locks in the rights of 'big box' retailers like Wal-Mart to set up stores in local sites by easing the local rules on the number of stores, their locations and size limitations.[5] This 'softening' of the local facilitates the expansion of multinational chains such as Wal-Mart in the markets of developed and developing countries. According to *Fortune 500*, Wal-Mart was the world's largest private company, amassing revenues of \$351[6] billion in 2007. It is more than three times the size of the world's next largest retail company – Carrefour. Established in Arkansas in 1962, by 2008 it had more than 7,000 stores in 14 countries. Its growth is mediated by the use of different commercial and cultural practices. For example, while its entry into the United Kingdom (UK) market occurred through its takeover of another supermarket chain (Asda); it has entered China as a retailer through joint ventures with a state-owned company.

Wal-Mart entered Mexico in 1991 and became the largest private employer, operating 889 stores in 2007 that generated \$278 million – more than the country's entire tourism sector. Wal-Mart was also prominent in Brazil where it had 299 stores in 2007, and in Puerto Rico where it had 54 stores (Wal-Mart 2007). In Asia, Wal-Mart entered Shenzhen (China) in 1996 and the Republic of Korea in 1998. China's opening in response to the WTO since 2002 has seen Wal-Mart expand its operations to 67 stores in key cities and regions, generating revenues of more than RMB[7] 8.6 billion in 2006 (\$1.08 billion at the prevailing exchange rate). This expansion in China has been facilitated by forming joint-venture partnerships and adapting the Wal-Mart culture to a Chinese context (which will be termed recontextualization below).

Wal-Martization and developing countries: the disciplining of retailing and sourcing arenas

Wal-Mart has formed partnerships with the state-owned Shenzhen International Trusts and Investment Company (SZITIC). The first of these glocal (global–local) partnerships was the Wal-Mart SZITIC Department Store Co., Ltd, in which SZITIC holds a 35 per cent stake (see Figure 2.1). Its formation was complemented by the transfer and recontextualization of 'Wal-Mart' corporate culture into the Chinese environment. This process is nicely captured by Davies's (2007: 1–27) term 'Wal-Mao'.

Wal-Mart as Wal-Mao in China: disciplining of retailing

To understand this hybridized identity we can begin with Wal-Mart's own brand of corporate culture. Moreton (2007a: 102–23) argued that, emerging in the shadow of the 'Washington Consensus', we find a Wal-Mart-led 'Bentonville Consensus'.[8] It grew out of a 'particular ecology of the Sunbelt service sector in an era of Christian revival. Its popular orthodoxy of

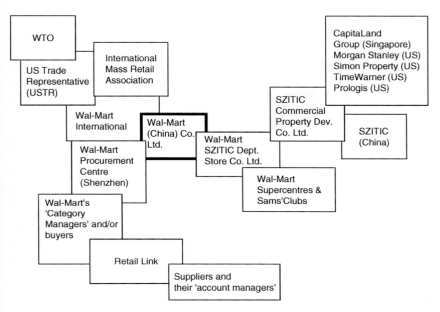

Figure 2.1 Key transnational forces and the Wal-Mart-SZITIC partnership in China
Source: Compiled by author.

"servant leadership" circulated between the overlapping spheres of white-collar vocational training and evangelical theory' (Moreton 2007a: 104). It epitomized an amalgam of the cultures of business and Pentecostalist Bible schools that drew on discourses of servant leadership and Christian free enterprise. Moreton (2007b: 777) further suggests that this united 'southwestern entrepreneurs, service providers, middle managers, students, missionaries, and even waged employees in the ethos of Christian free enterprise'. This Christianization and 'southernization' of American corporate-societal culture expressed itself in the service economy as a 'how-may-I-help-you' Wal-Mart founded upon the imagined charisma of Sam Walton (Boje and Rosile 2008: 178). The latter promoted the slogan of *Everyday Low Prices* and the values of 'respect for the individual', 'respect for the customers', and 'striving for excellence'.

This framing of Wal-Mart's corporate culture in a religion-community paradigm was recontextualized in China through its articulation with the cult of Mao. For Davies (2007), the Sam Walton 'servant leadership' ideology is translated as Mao's 'serving the people' (now 'people' probably means 'consumers'). Thus 'Wal-Mao' circulates among Wal-Mart management and supermarket workers in China. The resulting 'Wal-Mao' culture is grounded in the disciplining of everyday supermarket work-life, with posters of Sam Walton waving like Mao and calling for workers to take 'pride in outstanding performance' (Davies 2007: 9–10) as well as for workers to join the Wal-Mart family (for example, wearing a 'My-Wal-Mart' lapel pin and adopting English names at work). This 'Wal-Mao' style of acculturation and subjectivation also offers workers (and even shoppers) the clichéd experience of working (shopping) in an urban-Americanized environment and, for some, is even seen as part of the 'pedagogy for success' for modernization and the dream of living in post-revolutionary cosmopolitan China.

This dovetailing of service ideology with China's modernization drive relies on a process of cultural re-imagination that renders Wal-Mart not only acceptable in a Chinese context but even worth imitating by local Chinese companies. For example, local supermarkets have integrated the 'Mart' suffix into their own names, for example, RT Mart, Trust Mart, WuMart. Building on this Wal-Mao story, the Mart fashion, and the entrance of Tesco and Carrefour into the transnational supermarket onslaught in China, SZITIC widened its Wal-Mart partnership by entering shopping mall development during the recent property boom. It set up the SZITIC Commercial Property Development Co., Ltd. (SZITIC-CP) in 2003 and provides shopping centre spaces for Wal-Mart. This is achieved by entering joint ventures with regional-global financial capital coming variously from CapitaLand Group (Singapore property development consortium), Morgan Stanley (United States/US corporate finance firm), Simon Property (US real estate group), TimeWarner (US film and media corporation), and Prologis (US distribution-facility provider). Such joint ventures between SZITIC-CP and transnational capitals have facilitated Wal-Mart's expansion in China through the construction of shopping centres at 67 sites up to and including 2006.[9] This combination of global-regional-local commercial, financial and media capital helped to establish a particular transnational governance regime that facilitates retailing by Wal-Mart and its partners in China (see Figure 2.1).

Wal-Mart's sourcing in China: disciplining costs and margins

Wal-Mart does not just retail in China; it also sources from South and North parts of coastal China. *Wake Up Wal-Mart.com* called this the 'ultimate joint venture'.[10] In statistical terms, this 'joint venture' means that Wal-Mart is the 'Number One Importer of Chinese Goods' into the United States. More than 70 per cent of the goods sold in Wal-Mart stores are made in China, with Chinese exports to Wal-Mart estimated at approximately $25 billion for 2006 (Gereffi and Ong 2007: 48). Between 2001 and 2006, Wal-Mart accounted for approximately 9.6 per cent of total US imports from China (Scott 2007). These data indicate not only China's importance for the expansion of Wal-Mart but also the role of the arrangements between Wal-Mart and its suppliers in competing on 'Everyday Low Prices'.

Underlying this stress on price-value competitiveness is the use of information technology that integrates retailing with the global supply chain.

Wal-Mart has developed its own communication-logistical-inventory system that enables it to link the retailer with its suppliers worldwide. Since 1983 Wal-Mart has installed bar-code readers in all its distribution centres; it followed this up in 2005 with radio-frequency identification.[11] It also introduced a software programme in 1991 called *Retail Link* that bridges Wal-Mart with its suppliers. This innovation has made Wal-Mart the largest private satellite communication operator in the world. It operates a four-petabyte data warehouse that collects point-of-sale (POS) data (for example, store number, item number, selling amount, selling cost, and so on) and keeps track of inventory down to item level. These capacities have allowed Wal-Mart and its suppliers to examine and forecast consumer demand patterns as well as to coordinate product sales and inventory data through the *Retail Link* system since 1996. Mainstream economic and management studies argue that this technological prowess enables Wal-Mart to manage its supply chain by 'sharing information' with its suppliers and gain cost advantages related to automation, joint demand forecasting, and the 'just-in-time' supply system (for example, bar-code triggered replenishment, vendor-managed inventory and faster inventory turnover time) (Holmes 2001; Basker 2007). However, this kind of 'information sharing' in lean retailing (Bonacich and Wilson 2006: 234–5) can also be employed coercively (Free 2006: 14–16; 2007: 900). Given that price-value and cost competitiveness drive supply chains of this kind (Christopher 2005: 123), the everyday operations of mega-retailers are based on particular calculating practices that manage costs and margins. More specifically, these practices include 'category management' and 'activity-based costing'.

First, 'category management', which began in the supermarket business, allows giant retailers to improve sales and profits by managing product categories (for example, apparel, toys) as separate business units. For Spector (2005: 77), this practice allows supermarkets 'to oversee the store not as aggregation of products, but rather as an amalgam of categories, with each category unique in how it is priced and how it is expected to perform over time'. Wal-Mart began its own category management in the food sector and then extended it to other products. This practice allows a retailer to work with its supplier(s) to develop category plan(s) that 'determine its place within the store, evaluate its performance by setting goals, identify target consumer, divine ways to merchandise stock, and display the category' (Spector 2005: 77–8). Category captains (formerly called 'buyers') and category managers are appointed to facilitate these routine retailer-supplier contacts and, in the case of Wal-Mart, via the Retail Link.

Second, underlying 'category management' is a range of calculating practices of 'activity-based costing' concerned with monitoring the profitability of each product category (Christopher 2005: 111). To improve profitability and efficiency, suppliers are required to open their accounts to retailers (called 'open book accounting'), with the aim of coordinating activities to reduce costs and/or maximize margins. In the case of Wal-mart, suppliers' managers are trained through a help desk and classes (organized in-house or outsourced) to submit reports to its Retail Link on areas such as inventory, pricing, performance, sales and promotion.

Supplier scorecards have a key role in managing the mass of information that is assembled. As a form of selective knowing, they capture the financial details of a demand-pull supply chain (Christopher 2005). Scorecards allow Wal-Mart category managers (and their assistants) keyhole views into suppliers' 'sales', 'markdown', 'margins', 'inventory' and 'return' (see Table 2.1). This produces a new knowledge space that renders suppliers' financial conditions visible in order to identify cause-and-effect relations bearing on the chain's efficiency and profitability (Edenius and Hasselbladh 2002: 249–57; Norreklit 2003: 601). Under constant pressure to review product categories, the identification of these cause-and-effect relations provides the everyday bases of calculation, intervention, hard-nosed negotiation and control. Mechanisms of control enable category managers to perform the following routine activities: (1) evaluating the change of each supplier's costs and margins and requiring it to match its lowest price or even cut it; (2) comparing each supplier's costs and margins with the average; (3) introdu- cing a form of coordinated competition among suppliers (for example, asking a specific supplier to match lower prices of competing suppliers); (4) asking for alternatives based on a panoramic view of the suppliers' costs and margins; and (5) clawing back funds (or in Wal-Mart's term 'payment from suppliers') in the forms of 'volume incentives, warehouse allowances, and reimbursements for specific programs such as markdowns, margin protection and advertising' (Wal-Mart 2007: 44).

Seen through the micro-accounting practice of scorecards, this 'information-sharing' in the supply chain also sustains a kind of organizational control based on informational 'supervision'. The visibility and benchmarking of suppliers enable Wal-Mart's 'category managers' to demand lower prices, benchmark the average, and demand refunds from suppliers. Such monitoring practices highlight the unequal power relation between retailer and suppliers – an asymmetry revealed in a report in *Frontline* in which a former manager, named Lehman, recounts:

> And the buyers at Wal-Mart — my understanding is that the buyer said: 'No way. You're not going to raise your cost. If you can't sell it to us for the same price or less than you did last year, we'll find somebody else. We'll go to another company.' And that's what Wal-Mart tried to do, and it really hurt (the supplier).
>
> The communication is one way: It's our way or the highway. You do it our way, or you hit the highway. We'll find somebody else. (Frontline 2004)

Table 2.1 Knowledge produced in Wal-Mart supplier scorecards

Measurement criteria	Elements of measure
Sales measurements	• Overall % increase • Comparable-store sales • Average sales/store • Sales at full prices vs. markdown
Markdown measurements	• Markups and markdowns ($, units and %) • Prior and current retail price
Margin measurements	• Initial margin • Average retail price • Average cost • Gross profit at item level • Gross profit/item/store • Margin mix
Inventory measurements	• Replenishable store inventory • Non-replenishable store delivery • Warehouse inventory • Lost sales from out-of-stock • Excess inventory • Distribution centres outs • Total owned inventory
Return measurements	• Customer defective returns • Store claims

Source: American Logistics Association (2005: 16).

This way of disciplining suppliers can be seen, in neo-Foucauldian terms, as a virtual panopticon.[12] Computerized corporate 'wardens' conduct organizational surveillance of suppliers who are also enrolled in their own disciplinary gaze. In short, the use of scorecards and similar micro accounting practices enable Wal-Mart to expropriate margins from suppliers (see below on the factory rating system as another example of organizational surveillance). This seemingly 'managerial-logistical-information fix' is not only techno-economic but also political. In the latter regard, it exhibits asymmetrical power relations that assist the transformation of capital-to-capital social relations, in particular by tilting the balance in favour of the retailers than the suppliers-manufacturers in the buyer-driven commodity chains (Gereffi and Korseniewicz 1994; French 2006).

This asymmetry between retailer and suppliers-manufacturers was further intensified when Wal-Mart sought to further lower costs by scaling back its middleman arrangements. In China, it set up its own Global Procurement Centres in Shenzhen (and Shanghai) in 2002. This centre is both a localized training and negotiations centre with local suppliers-manufacturers. As a training centre, Wal-Mart requires suppliers to send managers to be trained in a Wal-Mart Procurement Centre. Hedrick Smith (2004) reported this process as follows:

> Chinese entrepreneurs describe how Wal-Mart presses them to integrate their operations into Wal-Mart's business plans and supply chain. Frank Ng, a partner in Force Electronics, which makes radio-controlled toys and other high-tech gadgets for Japanese toy firms to sell to Wal-Mart, told me Wal-Mart requires his firm to send managers for training to Wal-Mart's center in Shenzhen, makes the firm use Wal-Mart's computer software, and then monitors its production.

With this informational supervision, Wal-Mart's procurement staff members are constantly making deals with hundreds of Chinese manufacturers to produce goods tailored to Wal-Mart's own stringent specifications, including pricing, quality assurance, sales, efficiency and delivery. For many Wal-Mart suppliers entering the negotiations centre, the experience is a tough one. If their goods do not match Wal-Mart's specified sales/price level, suppliers are immediately shown the door. In the negotiation centre, supply deals are made 'in a heartbeat' (Bonacich and Wilson 2006: 239).

This firm grip over suppliers-manufacturers and the unrelenting push for cost and price-value competitiveness means that manufacturers, in turn, must pass on their costs and production insecurity (for example, termination of orders) to their workers. Workers in Wal-Mart's supplier factories, which the International Labour Rights Fund (ILRF) terms 'Wal-Mart Sweatshops', may see their wages cut and safety and welfare measures ignored. This was evident in a report produced by *Students and Scholars Against Corporate Misbehaviour* (SACOM 2007), a Hong Kong-based NGO that monitored Wal-Mart activities. This report identified labour abuses (for example, wage and hour violations, unsafe working conditions, deprivation of labour contract protection) in five toy factories in China that manufactured for Wal-Mart.[13] As for its own workers, the familiar practice of Wal-Mart in the United States of paying a 'minimized minimum wage' (Lichtenstein 2006) applies even more vigorously in developing countries. It pays the same low wage as other main retailers in developing countries but its workers receive even lower social benefits (Durand 2007). Indeed, while some local retailers try to prevent turnover by offering some social benefits, Wal-Mart prefers to stabilize its workforce by selling shares to its employees (assuming they have money to buy them).

This overall process can be summarized as Wal-Martization. Building on the definition provided by SACOM (2007) and concentrating on the production side, this chapter treats Wal-Martization as a change in the social relations of production where power shifts from suppliers-manufacturers to big retailers with downward pressure being exerted upon a flexible workforce in their search for low-cost strategies and price-value competitiveness. This process is mediated by changes in technological-logistical and managerial-calculative practices that enable the retailers to more effectively conduct organizational surveillance of suppliers and for the latter, in turn, to engage in self-monitoring, as well as, to some extent, tactical manoeuvres in the buyer-supplier game.

Contestation and CSR-ization

Rejecting Paul Krugman's (1997) neo-modernization argument that 'bad jobs at bad wages are better than no jobs at all', unions, NGOs and community groups have mobilized at local, national and transnational scales against Wal-Martization and its associated cost-reduction practices. *The American Federation of Labor–Congress of Industrial Organizations* (AFL-CIO's) *Eye on Wal-Mart, CorpWatch, Wal-Mart Watch, Wake-Up Wal-Mart, Sprawl-Busters, Frontline, Wal-Mart Class Web Site*, and Students and Scholars against Corporate Misbehaviour (SACOM) are some of the initiatives that target the activities of the corporation. The website of *ReclaimDemocracy.org* recorded 94 anti-Wal-Mart groups in the United States alone in 2006. It classified them into three categories: (1) eight anti-big box chain and pro-local business groups; (2) 15 national anti-Wal-Mart or neutral information sources; and (3) 71 community organizations fighting Wal-Mart or other big box chains.[14] In general, groups within and beyond the United States are challenging Wal-Mart's non-union strategy, sexual discrimination, unpaid overtime, threats to local small retailers, aggressive land-use policies and destruction of US jobs.

These corporate-watch efforts deploy the Internet (for example, websites and blogs) to bring together alternative voices, campaigns, exposure of abuses, and networking against the corporation (for examples, see Table 2.2). Some groups (for example, *Wal-Mart Watch*) have even hired political public relations (PR) firms to help organize their campaigns (Featherstone 2005). Others use 'name and shame' strategies to expose its shortcomings (for example, use of prison labour by Wal-Mart suppliers in China, use of child labour in Honduran sweatshops, and the removal of Wal-Mart from the *Domini 400 Social Index* in 2001) (Appelbaum and Lichtenstein 2006: 119).[15] In response, Wal-Mart has increasingly appropriated the image of 'good corporate citizenship' and adopted, directly or indirectly, CSR in and across different sites.

In pursuit of better reputational and brand capital, Wal-Mart is adopting CSR as part of its business strategy to boost investor and consumer confidence. It has set up an *Ethical Standards Programme* with elaborate factory certification protocols. This programme was established following the 1992 National Broadcasting Company (NBC) exposé on child labour abuse in Bangladesh and has since extended to other developing countries. The programme includes certification of labour standards and training components and, since 2006, audits have also verified environmental standards (see Table 2.3). By early 2005, there were 23 Ethical Standards offices covering

Table 2.2 Examples of anti-Wal-Mart groups involved in corporate watching

Name of union/NGO/ community group	Nature of the group
AFL-CIO	• Largest union in the United States • Runs the 'Paying the Price at Wal-Mart' website • News and specialized topics on Wal-Mart (for example, job exports, environment)
CorpWatch	• A research group based in Oakland, CA • Campaigns against sweatshops (for example, Wal-Mart and Nike) and private military contractors
Wal-Mart Watch	• A US-wide public education campaign • Sponsored by the Service Employees International Union (SEIU) • A watchdog on Wal-Mart business practices
Wake Up Wal-Mart	• Sponsored by the Union of Food and Commercial Workers (US) • Critic of Wal-Mart and its business practices (for example, substandard wages)
Sprawl-Busters	• Consultancy group to design and implement campaigns against megastores • Pro-local business and community
Frontline: Is Wal-Mart Good for America?	• A foundation-funded group • Specialized interviews with Wal-Mart insiders • Anti-Wal-Mart news from America and China
Wal-Mart Class website	• Female workers in Wal-Mart and their class lawsuit
SACOM	• A Hong Kong-based NGO • Campaigner for workers' rights and monitor of workers' conditions in China (for example, Wal-Mart subcontractors)

Source: Author's compilation from information obtained from http://reclaimdemocracy. org/walmart/links.php (accessed on 4 December 2007).

several regions (Americas, Far East, Indian subcontinent, Southeast Asia and Europe, Middle East and Africa). Audits are performed by Wal-Mart trained Global Procurement auditors and/or Wal-Mart approved third party audit firms. All factories are audited at least once and up to four times a year.

Each year, Wal-Mart produces an ethical sourcing report. In its 2006 report, it stated that its Ethical Standards team is responsible for:

verifying that suppliers comply with the Standards for Suppliers. The standards include provisions for the following: health and safety, environment, compensation, hours of labor, seventh day of rest, forced or prison labor, underage labor, discrimination, compliance with applicable

Table 2.3 Wal-Mart Ethical Standards Programme, 1992–2006

Year	Wal-Mart Ethical Standards Programmes
1992	• Wal-Mart's Factory Certification programme • Includes Standards for Suppliers according to local employment and labour laws • Focus on Bangladesh and China
1993–1996	• First Factory Certificate programme manual • Pacific Resources Exports Ltd. auditing factories directly producing for Wal-Mart • PriceWaterhouseCoopers was involved auditing at a later stage
1997–2001	• Factories in Egypt, Pakistan, India and Nicaragua were added
2002	• Assumes its own global procurement and directly manages its Factory Certificate programme
2003	• Wal-Mart Ethical Standards associates train buyers, suppliers and factory managers on Wal-Mart Supplier Standard • A product quality assurance programme (including reviews and internal audit)
2006–2008	• Environmental elements also included in the audit process (for example, packaging scorecard)

Source: Mutuc 2006.

local laws and regulations, freedom of association and collective bargaining, rights concerning foreign contract workers, and right of audit by Wal-Mart. (Wal-Mart 2006: 10)

In 2007, *Wal-Mart Watch* criticized its 2006 report for glossing over the serious problems with its supply chain (Roner 2007). Some of these problems were highlighted by a SACOM report (2007), which described Wal-Mart's auditing process as being 'self-policing'. According to this report, *Wal-Mart's Sweatshop Monitoring Fails to Catch Violations: The Story of Toys Made in China for Wal-Mart*, factory inspections were announced in advance and managers coached workers to give the 'correct answers'.[16] Workers were encouraged to become 'voluntary liars' through a material incentive of RMB50 (approximately $8 at the prevailing exchange rate) and were also told the little capitalist tale that a factory's loss of orders would translate directly into workers' loss of future employment opportunities. In addition, factory owners manufactured 'wage documents' and 'time cards' that indicated that workers were sufficiently paid in terms of base and overtime wages without exceeding the maximum working hours. In reality, workers' monthly wages shrank significantly and overtime was not recorded (2007: 15).

Comparing mass retailers such as Wal-Mart and brand-name firms, Liu (2003: 18–19), from the Institute of Contemporary Observation in Shenzhen, reported the following comments by a manager on Wal-Mart's auditing practices:

> Wal-Mart's social responsibility inspection team only spend about three hours at the factories, during which they verify wages, working hours and personal records, make a brief inspection tour of the factory, and meet three or four workers in the factory office's reception room. They also said that Wal-Mart inspections were generally quite easy to bluff, and that because Wal-Mart's unit prices for order are extremely low, their inspection teams were not likely to seriously demand that the factory adhere to the code of practice.

All these criticisms point to the pro-corporate and pro-management nature of the auditing practices in the implementation of CSR programmes.[17] Its 'self-policing' practices also allowed for 'self-serving' calculations in which the corporation and its suppliers alike appropriated CSR as part of business strategies – to secure reputation and stock market value for the former and certificates and future orders for the latter.

As part of its overall business strategy, Wal-Mart needs to secure its reputation and thereby its stock market value in the financial markets via its ability to manage its CSR. Given that investors tend to be reactive rather than proactive, the control of CSR information is critical for the market. One particular knowledge apparatus that is deployed in the 2006 *Report on Ethical Sourcing* was the benchmarking of factories in the supply chains. A factory rating system in four colours (green, yellow, orange and red) was deployed. Drawing loosely on a traffic light metaphor, it classifies, categorizes and excludes/includes suppliers according to their compliance with labour standards (see Table 2.4). As a discursive tool, it helps to showcase Wal-Mart's CSR performance (see Table 2.4 on audit results), if not its efficiency and competence, to the consumer and investor publics via the business media. This way of constructing suppliers as objects of Wal-Mart's ethicalism also allows the factories to become objects of intervention. By defining some of them as problems via the elaborate colour-coded system, Wal-Mart instituted a 'three strikes' approach to ensure compliance. This means: (1) if a factory owned and/or utilized by a supplier is deemed 'failed', it will not accept any merchandise from that particular factory and the supplier receives a 'first strike'; (2) if another factory owned and/or utilized by that supplier fails, it will not accept merchandise from that second factory and supplier receives a 'second strike'; and (3) if a third factory owned and/or utilized by the same supplier fails, or if it concludes at any time that the supplier has a pattern of non-compliance, the supplier receives a 'third strike' and Wal-Mart will cease doing business permanently with the supplier (Wal-Mart 2003: 10–11).[18]

Table 2.4 Wal-Mart's system of factory ratings and results

Factory Ratings	Degree of violations/risk	Conditions of order	Audit validity	Audit Results (in %)		
				2006	2005	2004
Green	No/minor violations	Orders can be placed	Re-audit after two years	5.4	9.6	19.1
Yellow	Medium risk violations	Orders can be placed	Re-audit after 120 days	51.6	37.0	38.8
Orange	High risk violations	Orders can be placed	Re-audit after 120 days	40.7	52.3	32.5
Orange-age	One or two underaged workers found		Re-audit after 30 days	0.4	0.8	8.8
(Grey)			Four orange ratings in a two-year period result in a factory being disapproved	2.10	0.1	8.8
Red/failed	Most serious	Existing orders are cancelled No future orders	Permanently barred	0.2	0.2	0.8

Source: Wal-Mart 2006.

Such discipline-and-punishment mechanisms displace the costs of clearing up 'sweatshops' downward onto suppliers, and those found to be in serious non-compliance with its codes are struck off the Wal-Mart supply chain permanently (SACOM 2007: 15). This panoptic system of factory-rating that places suppliers in green, yellow, orange and red categories is coupled with Wal-Mart's *Retail Link* system, which requires suppliers to open their accounts and submit scorecards, as discussed under 'Wal-Mart's Sourcing in China: Disciplining Costs and Margins'. This dual panoptic system produces calculating practices, constant surveillance and even fear that disciplines suppliers-manufacturers to: (1) communicate their costs and margins; (2) review delivery dates, costs, and prices of their products under the constant gaze of demand data; (3) enter into hard-nosed negotiations with Wal-Mart's category managers; and (4) prevent their factories from being struck off the certification system and losing orders. These micropolitics of control along the supply chain affect the workers in terms of job insecurities, longer working hours, welfare cuts and the spread of market logics. In this regard, the institutionalization of CSR procedures and systems produces the paradoxical result that more effort goes into preparing reports, auditing factories, obtaining certificates, ensuring orders and keeping jobs than actual advancement of labour rights protection. This tendency towards the managerialization and commodification of CSR has led to CSR-ization in which auditing and managerial practices of securing certificates/orders take priority over the social-moral elements in corporate responsibility. In this regard, the 'S' in CSR is taken over by 'A' as in corporate 'audit' responsibility.

In theoretical terms and drawing from Foucault (1975), CSR-ization can be seen as a technology of control in which the audit and certification discourses, practices and procedures are used to ward off dangers and gain mastery over social activism. More specifically, this technology of control involves a 'procedure of rarefaction', based on a selective thinning of the moral elements in corporate responsibility and its accompanying thickening of managerial practices (for example, standards, audits, time cards, reports and certificates) in the name of CSR. These processes are mediated by ethical standards, departments of big corporations, audit firms, consultancy firms, lawyers, service-oriented NGOs, and so on. Apparatuses, such as mission statements, programmes, standards, sourcing reports, audit reports and certificates, are used. These are supported by managerial logics of inspection, auditing, form-filling, filing, ratings, certifications and indexes. These microtechnologies of control normalize and discipline thoughts and common sense under the managerial-performance gaze of the CSR experts and their 'report and certification order'. They act as a kind of paper panopticon[19] in which subjects refashion subjectivities by reflecting on (and internalizing) these auditing and rating mechanisms so that their conduct becomes and remains congruent with this order. This mechanism seeks to activate and 'responsibilize' suppliers and their managers to become calculative/entrepreneurial subjects accepting the standards. They become self-monitoring, self-motivating persons aligned with the latest development in enhanced neoliberalism (see the fourth section). Agencies perform and repeat these subjectivities through mundane institutional events (for example, training, inspecting, reporting, meetings and planning on factory floors) and routine practices (for example, working, managing, and recruiting) of everyday life. These knowledging technologies normalize and discipline through principles of observability, monitoring, reporting, categorizing and rating. The dominance of the managerial-audit gaze through rational instrumentalities such as 'scorecards', 'costs', 'inventory', 'codes of conducts', 'certificates', 'reports', 'time cards', and so on, remake a more complex round of neoliberal hegemony.

Such criticisms have led more recently to the further reinvention of CSR so that it has become a kind of 'strategic corporate philanthropy'. Influenced by Porter and Kramer's (2002, 2006) arguments that 'corporate philanthropy' can become a source of 'competitive advantage', philanthropy moves from 'just about charity' towards being a part of a broader and more strategic approach to business investment. This strategic CSR, as it is labelled in the business management literature, is recommended as a source of 'opportunity, innovation and competitive advantage' (Porter and Kramer 2002: 76). Such thinking is the intellectual basis of recent corporate ventures into a reinvented approach to CSR. For example, under its Ethical Standards Department, Wal-Mart has formulated an International Giving Programme. Together with an NGO called the Hope Foundation in 2007, they co-launched a $1.2 million three-year grant to build Industrial Centres of Hope in five Indian communities (Bangalore, Chennai, Mumbai, Panipat and Moradbad) where the factories of its suppliers are located. This grant provides quality education and will equip 1,000 young people in the first year with life skills through vocational training, computer skills, English language education and social skills (Chatterjee 2007). This kind of charitable giving concerned to improve education and technological know-how will benefit the company in two ways: (1) promoting community goodwill and helping to smooth progress of retailing activities; and (2) educating and enskilling future employees. Porter and Kramer (2002: 66–7) describe such benefits in terms of 'improvement in competitive context'.

This kind of corporate–NGO programme has been criticized as self-serving (Jones 2006) and hinges on the thin line between 'donations' that increase the social welfare of the communities and those that enhance the economic performance of corporations. Nonetheless, these schemes, together with the financing of university research centres on retailing, continue to spread to different parts of the world. In the case in China, Wal-Mart donated RMB666,000 ($82,000 at the prevailing exchange rate) to the Hope Foundation to work with the quasi-state China Youth Development Federation on the *Hope Project* in 2004. According to the Wal-Mart web site on China, this project, which it described as a 'donation' and not an 'investment in human capital', involved:

> help[ing] 1,000 farmer children in Beijing, Tianjin and Shenzhen to continue their elementary education. Wal-Mart respectively made a donation of RMB 200,000 in Harbin, Helongjiang Province and Changchun, Jining Province to build a primary school. Wal-Mart also made a donation of RMB 200,000 to help building ten Project Hope community centers in Nanjing (Wal-Mart, 2008).

These strategic 'donation' schemes can often be the most cost-effective way to improve competitiveness contexts and create entrepreneur-students who seek to improve their opportunities on the market. The case of Wal-Mart in China does not stop here. Apart from cooperating with the above-mentioned quasi-state youth organization, CSR has been institutionalized through a top-down strategy. This involves targeting of Wal-Mart by the

Chinese government and the official union (the All-China Federation of Trade Unions) (ACFTU) because of the retail firm's size and profile as a giant foreign company in the context of the politics of economic opening in China. The latter began in 1979 and involves the People's Republic of China's (PRC) government in continuously juggling the desire to attract foreign direct investment (FDI) from corporations like Wal-Mart, the drive for national protectionism, and the risk of social and labour unrest. The manoeuvring of this delicate balance, especially in the face of increasing labour protests and 'instability' in foreign-invested companies, led President Hu Jintao on 14 March 2006 to order the ACFTU to do a better job in establishing trade unions in foreign-invested enterprises. This reinforces the move to take on high-profile giants such as Wal-Mart, in the hope of encouraging other foreign companies (for example, Eastman Kodak and Dell) to fall in line.

For the ACFTU, engagement with, and endorsement of, unionization of Wal-Mart outlets is part of its 'anti-independent union' strategy and its discomfort at China being seen as a 'big sweatshop'. In addition, the ACFTU has been trying to build its membership in the foreign-owned sector since 1999. After years of negotiation and under threats of lawsuits, this top-down state–union alliance had managed to 'persuade' Wal-Mart – the corporation – and its store workers to set up branch unions (Chan 2005). By October 2006, unions had been set up in 66 stores. Some question whether these localized setups guided by the ACFTU are actually promoting the rights of workers or merely helping to boost its declining membership and to service and support the government, especially in its control of the private-sector workforce (Chan 2007). According to one report, six months after they were introduced, 'Wal-Mart union branches have done little more than organize social events and run employee clubs' (Ruwitch 2007).

Articulation between 'new constitutionalism' and 'new ethicalism': enhanced neoliberalism

This examination of the corporate–state–union–NGO efforts at CSR-ization in China illustrates the more general rush to adopt 'codes' and 'philanthropy' in the remaking of neoliberalism. The articulation of institutional icons and key symbols such as the WTO, trade liberalization, FDI, CSR, codes of conduct, and corporate philanthropy raises the question why such competitive-ethical discourses are being combined and circulated among (trans-)national elites in this way. Inspired by the neo-Gramscian approach (Cox 1987; Gill 1995), this chapter argues that, by emphasizing and adopting CSR programmes, corporations can not only avoid legal regulation but also respond to civic activism in self-interested ways through 'risk management', building 'reputational capital' and enhancing 'responsible competitiveness'. These efforts represent, in part, a 'passive revolution'[20] insofar as the corporate–state–consultancy–NGO actors adjust their discourses and practices in the process of adapting and reproducing neoliberal hegemony. In the present case we observe the enhancement of neoliberalism to the CSR field where new coalitions are formed and critics are co-opted. Such flanking mechanisms may offer temporary moral leadership under the rubric of CSR/corporate philanthropy and, more generally, through the engagement of private business in the 'social' dimension of globalization. This marketing of moral-social claims (albeit in narrow terms) and related managerial practices are institutionalized and serve to rebalance the unstable equilibrium of forces in favour of the dominant coalition of retail, finance, state and professional actors. But they are the product of resistance and cannot suspend struggles. They also reproduce the deep social tensions between capital, labour and the environment in transnational production.

This new development in neoliberalism suggests that Gill's 'new constitutionalism' needs to be complemented by recognition of the emerging role of the 'new ethicalism'. 'New constitutionalism' involves international juridico-political strategies and mechanisms (for example, WTO/GATS) that emphasize the locking in of the right of (trans-)national capital and the locking out of domestic scrutiny of marketized policies/practices. To secure the unstable equilibrium of compromise to sustain economic expansion, dominant social forces such as transnational corporations (TNCs), state managers, service-oriented NGOs, accountancy-consultancy firms, state-regulated trade unions, and some international organizations try to develop and support new flanking mechanisms that can reshape hegemony via governance tools such as CSR and 'corporate philanthropy'. This development reveals the need to add to Gill's juridico-political focus by introducing the role of the socio-ethico-managerial dimensions. The concept of 'new ethicalism' does this by capturing these strategies that seek to reconnect economic policies with (new) socio-moral norms that are dominated by technicalized and managerialized practices. While 'new constitutionalism' highlights the disconnection/locking out of marketized policies from domestic political scrutiny, 'new ethicalism' highlights the reconnection of economic strategies with socio-ethico-managerial elements in corporate responsibility. However, this reconnection involves a procedure of rarefaction whereby social-ethical elements are thinned out selectively and there is thickening of managerial practices through CSR-ization (see Figure 2.2).[21]

It is through this articulation between 'new constitutionalism' and 'new ethicalism' that global capitalism is passively revolutionized and thereby embarks on a further, albeit more complex, round of production of enhanced neoliberalism (Jessop 2002: 265–6).[22] 'New ethicalism' not only helps to co-constitute 'new constitutionalism' but also provides the latter with a body of knowledge and regulatory instruments that can strengthen its micro-governing capacities (for example, on factory levels). This helps to re-engineer temporary leadership by providing neoliberal common sense

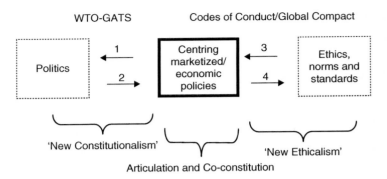

Figure 2.2 Articulation of 'new constitutionalism' and 'new ethicalism'
Source: Adapted from Sum (2005).

with a soft moral spin; but this is not so moral or so binding that it overwhelms neoliberalism's economic imperatives. Ethical-managerial practices in CSR and corporate philanthropy, rather than exclusively moral projects, are selectively interpreted in neoliberal and neo-utilitarian terms in which actions are judged by their outcomes (for example, risks, reputational performance and profit) and not social justice or the greatest good for the greatest number. This way of 'managerializing the ethical' is uniquely suited to modern management techniques and the well-established grammars and languages of corporate auditing and self-monitoring.

This conjunctural articulation and constitution of 'new constitutionalism' and 'new ethicalism' on the macro level is being normalized, on the micro level, by knowledging technologies based on and reinforcing CSR discourses, apparatuses (programmes, manuals, reports and certificates) and techniques (for example, categorization, judgment and rarefaction). These mundane practices have contributed to the emergence of ethicalized factories and corporations but not without contestation. Exploring these issues in their complex articulation can contribute to the development of a 'cultural political economy' of CSR (Sum 2004). Inspired by Gramsci and Foucault, this examines the macro- and micro-level dialectics of cultural hegemony. Specifically, it explores the articulation/co-constitution of 'new constitutionalism' with 'new ethicalism', the micro bases of macro-cultural hegemonies, and, in this case, the discourses, apparatuses and techniques of CSR-ization.

Likewise, on the micro level, it investigates the microphysics of managerial power related to code and donation practices, such as code/guideline writing, corporate reporting, evaluation mechanisms, grant writing, funding agreements, project assessments, and 'self-responsibilizing' factory managers, service-oriented NGOs, workers, students. These assemblages of CSR-related practices contribute to the emergence of 'new ethicalism', which can be defined as an ethicalized-managerial regime that seeks to stabilize neoliberal capitalism through 'managerialization' and 'technification' of CSR.

The macro-micro articulation of 'new constitutionalism' and 'new ethicalism' exists alongside 'progressive' workers' attempts and glocal movement-oriented NGOs' attempts to resist this CSR-ization trend through various forms of action, negotiation, and resistance. A wave of transnational initiatives that focuses on corporate accountability and coalition building emerged (Bendell 2004). More specifically and under this banner SACOM was founded by labour activists/academics and students in collaboration with the US National Labour Committee and with labour organizations in southern China. It has transnational linkages with NGOs such as Wal-Mart Watch and Sweatshop Watch, and so on. It adopts a three-pronged strategy: (1) monitor corporations such as Wal-Mart through public campaigns; (2) enhance global–local networking activities between workers, NGOs, student groups, trade unions, human rights activists, lawyers, academics, environmentalists and ethical consumers in efforts to regulate corporate power; and (3) empower the labour force as active agents in promoting rights in the workplace. Local and transnational groups of this kind have sporadic success, especially on case-specific bases, in launching complaints, redressing unfair dismissals and setting up workers' training courses and committees. Nonetheless, these transnational bottom-up efforts face constant struggles to find a suitable balance between the need to secure funding from large unions and foundations, the problems generated by issue drift as these NGOs move from one target to the next, the fatigue that sets in through repeated writing of 'name-and-shame' reports, and the difficulties of selecting partners with whom to form counter-hegemonic alliances without entirely being co-opted into CSR-ization and analogous processes of passive revolution.

Conclusion

This chapter deploys a cultural political economy approach[23] to examine the role of socioeconomic imaginaries such as 'cost competitiveness' and 'CSR' in remaking of social relations. Cultural political economy is a distinctive approach that combines neo-Gramscian and neo-Foucauldian theoretical tools to explore political economy and its semiotic dimensions. It pays particular attention to the importance of the interaction between the discursive-material as well as the macro-micro power relations. Drawing

mainly on the case of Wal-Mart in China and its emphases on 'cost competitiveness' and 'CSR', this chapter highlights the changing power of retail
capital, especially the ways it deploys information technologies and account-
ing/auditing practices in disciplining suppliers via its informational and
standard supervision. Its grip over suppliers means that manufacturers,
in turn, must pass on their costs of production and production insecurities to workers. This 'Wal-Martization' trend represents a change in social
relations where power shifts from suppliers-manufacturers to big retailers
with downward pressure being exerted upon a flexible workforce in their
search for low-cost strategies and price-value competitiveness. This prompted
the emergence of Wal-Mart watching groups that investigate and report
its uneven distribution impact in the transnational arena. In pursuit of
better 'reputational capital', Wal-Mart is adopting CSR in which managerial logics and practices, such as benchmarking, auditing, certification and
reporting, dominate. This chapter describes this as CSR-ization in which
these flanking mechanisms roll out neoliberalism under the guise of a 'new
ethicalism'.

This enhancement of neoliberalism suggests that Gill's 'new constitutionalism' needs to be complemented by recognition of the emerging role of
the 'new ethicalism'. At this stage of global capitalist development, their
articulation is grounded in the locking in of rights of capital supported by
the legal infrastructure such as WTO-GATS. This allows retail giants such as
Wal-Mart to enter into partnerships with local concerns. The Wal-Martization
trend and related micropractices of control over the suppliers generate labour
and environmental concerns across different sites. These social concerns
gave rise to the privileging of CSR discourses and the emergence of related
microtechnologies of power, such as reporting, benchmarking, auditing and
certification. In this regard, CSR, ethical standards and even social donations are managerialized and technicalized to become corporate commodities
and are 'traded' as moral resources that are an integral part of their overall
corporate response to challenges. For the CSR professionals and their industry, auditing standards, factory rating, and record writing are developed as
part of their knowledge products in the so-called knowledge-based economy.
They become part of the toolkit of 'responsible competitiveness' under the
post-Washington consensus. The crucial question to be explored in further
theoretical, empirical, and political work is whether CSR and its related practices involve attempts to 'marketize the social' or 'socialize the market'. At first
sight, CSR would seem to involve the socialization of the market, that is, the
taming of the market through its subordination to ethical standards. But, as
we have seen in the ways CSR has been managerialized and technicalized,
it may also be seen as an attempt to draw on the legitimacy of extra-
economic norms and practices to reinforce, flank, and support the continuing
dominance of market relations. This tension and ambiguity within social
economy remains a site of struggles and negotiations between hegemonic and

counter-hegemonic forces as efforts are made to promote the latest round of enhanced neoliberalism. Re-socialization of the market is called for to counteract the 'CSR-ization' of global capitalism.

Notes

1. The neo-Gramscian perspective for the study of international political economy is promoted by Cox (1987). Drawing on Gramsci's idea of hegemony, Cox sought to understand how the world order was established and maintained by a transnational managerial class in three interrelated ways: its association with a dominant mode of production, the formation of a state/society complex that is relatively coherent with the economic structure, and hegemony based on a mix of coercion and consent that secures conformity with the requirements of economic and political domination. For Cox, elements of historical structures are the reciprocal interacting combination of ideas, material capabilities and institutions. This notion of hegemony and historical structures have been utilized by Cox (1987) and Gill (1995, 2002). Here, international institutions such as the International Monetary Fund (IMF), World Bank and WTO operate as mechanisms through which universal norms of a world hegemony is expressed. Gill's concept of 'new constitutionalism' sought to map the neoliberal norms of market opening under neoliberalism. For a critique from a cultural political economy perspective, see Jessop and Sum (2006a, 2006b).
2. Neo-Foucauldian perspective is a development of Foucault's work in specific fields such as organization studies (McKinlay and Starkey 1998), critical accounting (Miller and Rose 1990) and educational research (Besley and Peters 2007), and so on. In these various fields, neo-Foucauldians work on disciplinary technologies, models of panopticon and governmentality (governmental rationality) (Dean 1999), and so on, to examine specific mechanisms, technologies, procedures and tactics that are assembled and deployed in neoliberal governance (see also notes 4 and 12).
3. GATS is one of 17 major WTO 'Uruguay Round' agreements.
4. According to Foucault (1975), the primary difference between Bentham's panopticon and the 'disciplinary mechanism' of panopticism is that the panopticon is a physical architectural design in which discipline is enforced and panopticism enforces discipline invisibly, for example, via databases, closed-circuit television (CCTV) cameras and best practice manuals (see also note 14). This chapter will examine two kinds of panopticism as microtechnologies of control. The first is a 'virtual panopticon' (see the discussion under 'Wal-Mart's Sourcing in China: Disciplining Costs and Margins') that rests on the disciplinary use of database information such as Wal-Mart's *RetailLink* and calculating practices in the scorecards. The second is a 'paper panopticon' (see the discussion under 'Contestation and CSR-ization') in which mission statements, programmes, standards, audit reports, and certificates are used to discipline factory managers and workers to be more in line with the managerial-ethical order under CSR.
5. This easing of the local is evident in a letter from Wal-Mart Executive Vice-President, Michael Duke, to United States (US) Trade Representative, Robert Zoellick, on 1 May 2002. Wal-Mart stated its policy preference in terms of: 'Countries also should be encouraged to remove any size limitations on individual stores,

      numeric limits on the number of stores in country and geographic limitations on store locations in the country' (Wal-Mart 2002: 4).

6. All references to $ are to US dollars.

7. RMB = renminbi (Chinese currency of the People's Republic of China).

8. Wal-Mart is headquartered in Bentonville, Arkansas. Moreton (2007a: 104) thus termed Wal-Mart's corporate culture as 'Bentonville Consensus' by analogy with the 'Washington Consensus' in the public sphere.

9. SZITIC sold 65 per cent of 14 ongoing projects stake to CapitaLand, and 65 per cent of five ongoing projects' stake to Morgan Stanley and Simon Property in 2005.

10. For details on this 'ultimate joint venture', see www.wakeupwalmart.com (accessed on 25 September 2007).

11. Wal-Mart is also upgrading its technology from barcodes to radio-frequency identification/RFID (that is, tag tracking).

12. Panopticon was first proposed by Jeremy Bentham as an architectural prison design. He envisioned a prison space that included an observation tower housing wardens with a ring of cell of inmates surrounding it. This 'all-seeing-place' was designed to enclose and discipline any group that requires supervision. Foucault (1971) seized this idea of a controlling space and applied it as a metaphor to examine the oppressive use of information and knowledge in modern disciplinary society (see also note 4 on virtual panopticon).

13. For more general studies on Chinese labour conditions not specifically related to Wal-Mart, see Chan (2001) and Pun (2005).

14. See http://reclaimdemocracy.org/walmart/links.php (accessed on 7 July 2007).

15. For a discussion of the wider debate of Wal-Mart and its partnership with China, see Martin (2004).

16. Similar results were reported by the NGO War on Want. In its report entitled *Fashion Victims: The True Cost of Cheap Clothes at Primark, Asda and Tesco* (War on Want 2006), a worker from a Bangladeshi Wal-Mart supplier recorded that: 'Every month there are two to three visits to the factory by buyers, and the visitors basically talk with the management. Workers get prior notice for such visits and sometimes visitors also talk with 10–15 workers who are selected by the management. These workers are instructed by the management on what to say to the auditors, and if there are any workers who are unable to follow the instructions they are asked not to come until the auditors' visit ends.'

17. See also O'Rourke (2000, 2002, 2003); Sum and Pun (2005); CCC (2005); Barrientos and Smith (2006).

18. Document on Wal-Mart website in 2003, since removed; copy on file with author.

19. See note 4 on 'paper panopticon'.

20. 'Passive revolution' is a term used by Gramsci (1971) to examine the ways in which a social class maintains its hegemony through gradual, molecular changes that operate through passive consent, the decapitation of resistance movements, and absorption of opposition through compromise and concession.

21. Given that this chapter is an attempt to Gramscianize Foucault, the term 'ethics' is not defined in a Foucauldian manner. It means values and customs for a good life.

22. Articulation connects two independent entities and co-constitution involves the interactive development or co-evolution of two otherwise relatively independent entities.

23. Sum (2004); Jessop and Sum (2006a); Sum and Jessop (forthcoming).

References

American Logistics Association, Exchange Roundtable, *What's Leading Edge with Today's Leading Mass Volume Retailers?* (Dallas, TX: 8 March 2005). www.hoytnet.com/HTMLobj-315/ALA2005R3-FINAL_with_Pics_March_8_2005.ppt (accessed on 12 May 2008).

Appelbaum, Richard P. and Nelson Lichtenstein, 'The new world of retail supremacy: Supply chains and workers' chains in the age of Wal-Mart', *International Labour and Working-Class History*, Vol. 70, Fall (2006) 106–25.

Barrientos, Stephanie and Sally Smith, *The ETI Code of Labour Practice: Do Workers Really Benefit?, Report on the ETI Impact Assessment 2006, Part 1: Main Findings* (2006). www.eti2.org.uk/Z/lib/2006/09/impact-report/ETI-impact-1-main-get.pdf (accessed on 10 June 2008).

Basker, Emek, 'The causes and consequences of Wal-Mart's growth', *Journal of Economic Perspectives*, Vol. 21, No. 3 (2007) 177–98.

Bendell, Jem, *Barricades and Boardrooms: A Contemporary History of Corporate Accountability Movement*, Programme on Technology, Business and Society, Paper No. 3 (Geneva: UNRISD, 2004).

Besley, Tina and Michael A. Peters, *Subjectivity and Truth* (New York: Peter Lang, 2007).

Boje, David M. and Grace A. Rosile, 'Specters of Wal-Mart: A critical discourse analysis of stories of Sam Walton's ghost', *Critical Discourse Studies*, Vol. 5, No. 2 (2008) 153–80.

Bonacich, Edna and Jake B. Wilson, 'Global Production and Distribution: Wal-Mart's Global Logistic Empire'. In S.D. Brunn (ed.), *Wal-Mart World: The World's Biggest Corporation in the Global Economy* (New York: Routledge, 2006).

CCC (Clean Clothes Campaign), *Looking for a Quick Fix: How Weak Social Auditing Is Keeping Workers in Sweatshops* (2005). http://www.cleanclothes.org/ftp/05-quick_fix.pdf (accessed on 10 June 2008).

Chan, Anita, 'Organizing Wal-Mart: Two steps forward, one step backward for China's unions', *New Labour Forum*, Vol. 16, No. 2 (2007) 87–96.

——, 'Recent trends in Chinese labour issues: Signs of change', *China Perspectives*, No. 57, January–February (2005). http://rspas.anu.edu.au/ccc/publications/ChinaPerspectives57.pdf (accessed on 10 June 2008).

——, *China's Workers under Assault: The Exploitation of Labour in a Globalizing Economy* (Armonk, NY: M.E. Sharpe, 2001).

Chatterjee, Surojit, 'Wal-Mart grants $1.2 million to Hope Foundation to educate underserved', *International Business Times*, 4 September (2007). http://in.ibtimes.com/articles/20070903/wal-mart-grants-1.2-million (accessed on 7 October 2007).

Christopher, Martin, *Logistics and Supply Chain Management* (Harlow, Essex: Pearson Education, 2005).

Cox, Robert, *Production, Power and World Order* (New York: Columbia University Press, 1987).

Davies, David J., 'Wal-Mao: The discipline of corporate culture and studying the success at Wal-Mart China', *The China Journal*, No. 58 (2007) 1–27.

Dean, Mitchell, *Governmentality* (London: Sage, 1999).

Durand, Cédric, 'Externalities from foreign direct investment in Mexican retailing sector', *Cambridge Journal of Economics*, Vol. 31, No. 1 (2007) 1–19.

Edenius, Mats and Hans Hasselbladh, 'The balanced scorecard as an intellectual technology', *Organization*, Vol. 9, No. 2 (2002) 29–73.

Featherstone, Liza, *Wal-Mart's P.R. War*, *Salon.com*, 2 August (2005). www.dsausa. org/lowwwage/walmart/2005/Wal-Mart's%20P.R.%20War.html (accessed on 11 December 2007).

Foucault, Michel, *Discipline and Punish: The Birth of the Prison* (New York: Random House, 1975).

——, 'Order of discourse', *Social Science Information*, Vol. 10, No. 2 (1971) 7–30.

Free, Clinton, 'Supply-chain accounting practices in the UK retail sector: Enabling or coercing collaboration?', *Contemporary Accounting Research*, Vol. 24, No. 2 (2007) 897–933.

——, 'Walking the talk? Supply chain accounting and trust among UK supermarkets and supplies', *Social Science Research Network*, 29 November (2006). www.papers.ssrn.com/sol3/papers.cfm?abstract_id=948245 (accessed on 10 May 2008).

French, John D., 'Wal-Mart, retail supremacy and the relevance of political economy', *Labour Studies in Working-Class History of the Americas*, Vol. 4, No. 1 (2006) 33–40.

Frontline, *Is Wal-Mart Good for America? Interview Jon Lehman*, 16 November (2004). www.pbs.org/wgbh/pages/frontline/shows/walmart/interviews/lehman.html (accessed on 5 September 2007).

Gereffi, Gary and Miguel Korseniewicz, *Commodity Chain and Global Capitalism* (Westport, CT: Greenwoood Press, 1994).

Gereffi, Gary and Ryan Ong, 'Wal-Mart in China: Can the world's largest retailer succeed in the world's most populous market?', *Harvard Asia Pacific Review*, Vol. 9, No. 1 (2007) 46–9.

Gill, Stephen, *Privatization of the State and Social Reproduction? GATS and New Constitutionalism*, paper presented at the Centre for the Study of Globalization and Regionalization Workshop on GATS: Trading Development (University of Warwick, Coventry, 20–21 September 2002).

——, 'New constitutionalism, democratization and global political economy', *Pacifica Review*, Vol. 10, No. 1 (1998) 23–38.

——, 'Globalization, market civilization and disciplinary neoliberalism', *Millennium*, Vol. 24, No. 3 (1995) 399–423.

Gramsci, Antonio, *Selection from the Prison Notebook* (London: Lawrence and Wishart, 1971).

Holmes, Thomas J., 'Bar codes lead to frequent deliveries and superstores', *RAND Journal of Economics*, Vol. 34, No. 4 (2001) 708–25.

Jessop, Bob, *The Future of the Capitalist State* (London: Policy Press, 2002).

Jessop, Bob and Ngai-Ling Sum, *Beyond the Regulation Approach: Putting Capitalist Economies in Their Place* (Cheltenham: Edward Elgar, 2006a).

——, 'Towards a cultural international political economy: Post-structuralism and the Italian school'. In M. de Goede (ed.), *International Political Economy and Poststructural Politics* (Basingstoke: Palgrave Macmillan, 2006b).

Jones, Del, 'Good works, good business', *USA Today*, 25 April (2006) 1B–2B.

Krugman, Paul, 'In praise of cheap labour', *Slate*, 7 March (1997). www.slate.com/id/1918 (accessed on 21 March 2006).

Lichtenstein, Nelson (ed.), *Wal-Mart: The Face of Twenty-First-Century Capitalism* (New York: New Press, 2006).

Liu, Kaiming, *Global Purchasing Practices and Chinese Women Workers* (Shenzhen: Institute for Contemporary Observation, 2003).

Martin, Eric, *The Great Wal-Mart of China: Part II*, 23 November (2004). http://tianews.blogspot.com/2004_11_01_archive.html (accessed on 2 December 2008).

McKinlay, Alan and Ken Starkey (eds), *Foucault, Management and Organizational Theory* (London: Sage, 1998).

Miller, Peter and Rose, Nicholas, 'Governing economic life', *Economy and Society*, Vol. 19, No. 1 (1990) 1–31.

Moreton, Bethany, 'The soul of neoliberalism', *Social Text*, Issue 25, No. 392 (2007a) 103–23.

——, 'The soul of the service economy', *Enterprise and Society*, Vol. 8, No. 4 (2007b) 777–83.

Mutuc, Jose Edgar S., *Standards and Standardization for SMEs and Subcontractors* (2006). www.bworld.com.ph/Downloads/2006/Outsourcing4.ppt (accessed on 4 September 2007).

Norreklit, Hanne, 'The balanced scorecard: What is the score?', *Accounting, Organizations and Society*, Vol. 28, No. 6 (2003) 591–619.

O'Rourke, Dara, 'Outsourcing regulation: Analyzing nongovernmental systems of labour standards and monitoring', *The Policy Studies Journal*, Vol. 31, No. 1 (2003) 1–29.

——, 'Monitoring the monitors: A critique of corporate third-party labour monitoring'. In Rhys Jenkins, Ruth Pearson and Gill Seyfang (eds), *Corporate Responsibility and Labour Rights: Codes of Conduct in the Global Economy* (London: Earthscan, 2002).

——, *Monitoring the Monitor: A Critique of Price Waterhouse Cooper's Labour Monitoring*, White Paper, released 28 September (2000).

Porter, Michael and Mark Kramer, 'Strategy and society: The link between competitive advantage and corporate social philanthropy', *Harvard Business Review*, Vol. 84, No. 12 (2006) 1–14.

——, 'The competitive advantage of corporate philanthropy', *Harvard Business Review*, Vol. 80, No. 12 (2002) 57–68.

Pun, Ngai, *Made in China: Women Factory Workers in a Global Workplace* (Durham, NC: Duke University Press, 2005).

Roner, Lisa. 'North America: Wal-Mart's ethical sourcing – Green does not mean ethical', *Ethical Corporation*, 19 October (2007). www.ethicalcorp.com/content.asp?ContentID=5407&rss=37.xml (accessed on 10 June 2008).

Ruwitch, John, *With Wal-Mart Unionized in China, Now What?* Reuter, 26 March (2007). www.reuters.com/article/featuresNews/idUKHKG27104620070326?pageNumber=4 (accessed on 6 September 2007).

SACOM (Students and Scholars against Corporate Misbehaviour), *Wal-Mart's Sweatshop Monitoring Fails to Catch Violations: The Story of Toys Made in China for Wal-Mart*, June (2007). www.sacom.hk/Uploads/WalMart%20Report(SACOM)Jun2007.pdf (accessed on 15 December 2007).

Scott, Robert E., 'The Wal-Mart effect: Its Chinese imports have displaced nearly 200,000 US jobs', *Economic Policy Institute*, 27 June (2007). www.epi.org/content.cfm/ib235 (accessed on 13 June 2008).

Smith, Hedrick, 'Who calls the shots in the global economy?' *Frontline*, 16 November (2004). www.pbs.org/wgbh/pages/frontline/shows/walmart/secrets/shots.html (accessed on 4 July 2007).

Spector, Robert, *Category Killers: The Retail Revolution and Its Impact on Consumer Culture* (Boston, MA: Harvard Business School, 2005).

Sum, Ngai-Ling, *From 'New Constitutionalism' to 'New Ethicalism': Global Business Governance and the Discourses and Practices of Corporate Social Responsibility*, paper prepared at the European Consortium for Political Research Joint Sessions, Workshop 24 on Transnational Private Governance in the Global Political Economy (Granada, Spain, 14–19 April 2005).

——, *From 'Integral State' to 'Integral World Economic Order': Towards a Neo-Gramscian Cultural International Political Economy*, Working Paper No. 7, Cultural Political Economy Research Cluster, Institute for Advanced Studies, Lancaster University, 2004. www.lancs.ac.uk/ias/polecon/index.htm (accessed on 4 October 2006).

Sum, Ngai-Ling and Bob Jessop, *Towards a Cultural Political Economy* (Cheltenham: Edward Elgar, forthcoming).

Sum, Ngai-Ling and Ngai Pun, 'Globalization and paradoxes of ethical transnational production: Code of conduct in a Chinese workplace', *Competition and Change*, Vol. 9, No. 2 (2005) 181–200.

Wal-Mart, Education Support: Project Hope (2008). www.wal-martchina.com/english/community/3_education.htm (accessed on 6 October 2008).

——, *Wal-Mart 2007 Annual Report* (2007). www.walmartstores.com/Media/Investors/2007_annual_report_pdf (accessed on 9 June 2008).

——, *2006 Report on Ethical Sourcing* (2006). http://walmartfacts.com/reports/2006/ethical_standards/documents/2006ReportonEthicalSourcing.pdf (accessed on 20 October 2007).

——, *Factory Certification Report, March 2003–2004* (2003). www.walmartstores.com/Files/FactoryCertificationReport2003.pdf (accessed on 15 October 2007).

——, Letter from Wal-Mart Executive Vice-President, Michael Duke, to US Trade Representative, Robert Zoellick, 1 May 2002. www.citizen.org/documents/WalMart_GATS_comments.pdf (accessed on 4 July 2007).

War on Want, *Fashion Victims: The True Cost of Cheap Clothes at Primark, Asda and Tesco*, December (2006). www.cleanclothes.org/ftp/06-12-Fashion_Victims.pdf (accessed on 10 April 2008).

3
Corporate Social Responsibility in a Neoliberal Age

Paddy Ireland and Renginee G. Pillay

Introduction

The idea of corporate social responsibility (CSR) has risen to prominence with remarkable rapidity to become, in the words of *The Economist*, 'an industry in itself, with full-time staff, newsletters, professional associations and massed armies of consultants' (*The Economist* 2004). Embraced by corporations, touted by academics, and advanced by non-governmental organizations (NGOs) and policy makers as a potential mechanism for achieving social policy objectives and furthering economic development, CSR has become one of the flavours and hopes of the new Millennium. 'By following socially responsible practices', the United Kingdom's (UK's) Department for International Development (DFID) has claimed, 'the growth generated by the private sector will be more inclusive, equitable and poverty reducing' (DFID 2004).

This chapter assesses contemporary CSR's potential and limits as an instrument of economic and social development by contrasting current conceptions and practices with those of the past. Ideas about the social responsibilities of corporations, it argues, are far from new and can be traced back at least as far as the 1920s and 1930s. At present, these earlier ideas tend to be portrayed as mere precursors of contemporary CSR. In fact, we argue, the ideas about the 'socially responsible corporation' which emerged in the 1930s and rose to prominence in the decades after the Second World War were markedly more radical than contemporary ideas about CSR. The former entailed a fundamental challenge to the principle of shareholder primacy and a radical reconceptualization of the corporation as a *public* institution, suggesting that directors should owe duties to employees, consumers, creditors and society as a whole, as well as to shareholders. By contrast, contemporary ideas about CSR tend to be premised on a shareholder-oriented model of the corporation as a *private* enterprise in which directors owe enforceable duties only to shareholders. While the earlier idea of the socially responsible corporation had a genuinely transformative edge, therefore, contemporary CSR is essentially ameliorative, seeking to temper without unsettling or displacing the idea of the corporation as a private, exclusively shareholder- and profit-oriented enterprise (Pillay 2006). This chapter explores the contexts in which these different ideas about the social responsibilities of corporations developed. Just as the earlier idea of the socially responsible corporation was a product of a particular historical context and part of a wider set of ideas about the nature of the corporation, so too is CSR in its current form.

The key to understanding the relative conservatism of contemporary CSR, we suggest, is to be found in the seismic changes which took place in the corporate world during the neoliberal counter-revolution of the 1980s and 1990s. It is best understood as an *adjunct* to the revived and reinvigorated, shareholder-oriented conception of the corporation, which has an appeal to both corporations and their critics. For corporations ever more obviously prioritizing shareholder interest in a world in which income and wealth inequalities are growing, CSR is a potential source of legitimacy. For those concerned about corporate 'externalities', CSR is a way of trying to temper the effects of the increasingly ruthless corporate pursuit of 'shareholder value' without challenging the seemingly inviolable and common-sense principle of shareholder primacy and the political consensus of which it is part (Crouch 2006). This is reflected in the attempt by many advocates of CSR to build their case on the claim that far from compromising the interests of share-holders, CSR in fact makes good business sense. It is also reflected in the nature and character of contemporary CSR, which, in keeping with neoliberal ideas about the role of the state in economic life, relies very heavily on voluntarism, self-regulation, partnerships and 'soft' law. While the contemporary CSR movement's general acceptance of the central tenets of the neoliberal orthodoxy enhances its political acceptability both to states and corporations, it also limits what it is likely to be able to achieve.

The potential of contemporary CSR is being further constrained, we argue, by the rise of what has been called the 'new constitutionalism' (Gill 1995). At the same time as the advocates of CSR are seeking to persuade corporations to engage in socially responsible self-regulation, a shareholder-oriented model of the corporation is extending its global reach and the legal rights of shareholders are being entrenched and strengthened. Much effort has been made by international agencies, such as the Organisation for Economic Co-operation and Development (OECD) and the World Bank, to export a particular model of the corporation around the world. Equally important, legal and quasi-legal rules are being established that not only secure the rights of transnational capital but are beyond political control. States are increasingly conferring sovereign powers on international organizations, with the result that a 'new constitutionalism' is emerging which seeks to give investors (especially foreign investors) inviolable rights, removing important aspects of policy from state control and diminishing its ability not only to intervene in the market but to regulate corporations. The range of political possibility and the scope for democratic intervention are being narrowed. While contemporary CSR's broad acceptance of the prevailing neoliberal consensus might make it politically palatable, it also limits its potential as a tool of social and economic development. The 'soft' law of CSR is no match for the 'hard(er)' laws protecting shareholder interest. With the emergence, however, of the 'corporate accountability movement', attempts are being made to re-radicalize the concept of CSR. If the corporate accountability movement is to realize its ambitions, we argue, it needs to explore corporate governance reform. In this context, the more radical ideas about CSR which emerged in the 1920s and 1930s are instructive and worth revisiting.

The chapter begins by looking at the circumstances surrounding the emergence of the idea of the 'socially responsible corporation' in the 1920s and 1930s. It moves on to examine the circumstances surrounding the demise of transformative CSR and the rise of the shareholder-value model of the corporation in the wake of the neoliberal counter-revolution. Against this backdrop, it traces the rise of contemporary CSR, noting its general acceptance of shareholder primacy and the key tenets of neoliberalism, as well as its essentially ameliorative aspiration. It then moves on to assess its potential as a tool of economic and social development in a world in which attempts are being made not only to globalize the Anglo-American, 'shareholder value' model of the corporation but to 'constitutionalize' and entrench the rights of shareholders and other investors. It concludes by exploring the rise of the corporate accountability movement, arguing that it needs to focus not only on corporate regulation but also on corporate governance if it is to achieve its ends.

The shareholder and the rise of the corporate economy

The idea that corporations should conduct themselves in a socially responsible manner is far from new. There has, however, been a tendency to treat ideas about CSR as essentially monolithic, with the result that contemporary CSR is treated as little more than a continuation or extension of earlier ideas that emerged in the 1920s and 1930s and became commonplace in the 1950s and 1960s. These, however, were significantly different from those which have risen to prominence in recent years. An examination of the different contexts in which these alternative conceptions of CSR developed and of the wider sets of ideas of which they were part is instructive, for it helps to throw the specific nature of contemporary CSR into sharper relief.

The backdrop to the ideas about CSR which emerged in the inter-war period (1918–1939) was 'the rise of the corporate economy', the process in which the economies of the most industrialized countries of the West came to be dominated by a relatively small number of large joint stock corporations (Hannah 1976). This process was accompanied not only by a declining belief in the capacity and beneficence of free market competition and a growing belief in the need for 'planning' of various sorts (by both private industry and the state), but by an ever wider dispersal of corporate shareholders and their ever greater 'externalization' and detachment from corporations, particularly in countries such as the United States (US) and the United Kingdom. This changed the way that both shareholding and corporations were perceived.

In the eighteenth and early nineteenth centuries the shareholders of the large joint stock companies from which these corporations grew were often involved in management or in the monitoring of management. By the early twentieth century, however, they had for the most part assumed the role of purely passive, *rentier* owners of titles to revenue, uninvolved in, and external to, the process of production. The consequences of this development were highlighted in 1932 by Adolf Berle and Gardiner Means in their famous book, *The Modern Corporation and Private Property* (Berle and Means 1932). On the basis of the findings of their empirical research, Berle and Means concluded that the shareholders of many large US companies had become very widely dispersed and that this, coupled with the fact that most of them took little interest in the day-to-day running of corporations, had led them to lose control of the corporations in which they held shares. Ownership and control were being separated, leaving more and more corporations under the effective control of their managers. This, Berle and Means suggested, was creating a serious problem of managerial accountability.

Berle and Means' findings resonated with earlier work which, recognizing the changes that were taking place in the corporate world, had begun questioning the characterization and status of corporate shareholders. In the United States, in particular, more and more commentators were suggesting that the rise of the modern corporation and of the corporate economy was contributing to fundamental changes in the nature of property and property rights. The sociologist Thorstein Veblen, for example, argued that ownership, which had previously entailed the control of tangible material assets and carried with it various duties and responsibilities, was, with the rise of the modern joint stock corporation, coming to entail mere passive possession of intangible corporate capital. Corporate shareholders, he argued, had been reduced to the status of 'anonymous pensioners'; they were 'absentee owners' possessing claims 'to unearned or free income', 'prescriptive rights to get something for nothing'. He accordingly likened them to corporate bondholders, arguing that the lines between debt and property, credit and capital, and stock and bond were becoming increasingly blurred (Veblen 1904, 1919, 1923).[1] In the United Kingdom, similar views were expressed by the economic historian R.H. Tawney and the political scientist Harold Laski (Tawney 1921; Laski 1925). By the late 1920s more and more commentators were remarking on the resemblance between shareholders and bondholders, suggesting that the former were, like the latter, 'owed' rather than 'owning', thereby implicitly questioning their proprietary status. 'The average stockholder in the large corporation', wrote Franklin Wood, 'regards himself more as a security holder than as in any sense a responsible managing partner in the corporate enterprise'. As a result, he argued, the legal distinction between bondholders and stockholders was 'fast becoming a distinction unwarranted by the actual situation' (Wood 1928: 59; see Frank 1933: 332 for a similar view). When Berle and Means' work appeared, it seemed to offer empirical confirmation of this claim and this led some commentators to begin to reconceptualize not only the corporate shareholder but the corporation itself.

Corporations had, of course, long been recognized as legal entities separate from their shareholders, particularly for liability purposes: shareholders could not be made liable for debts of the corporations as long as their shares were fully paid-up, as they almost invariably were. In certain crucial respects, however, corporations were still identified with their shareholders. Thus, while directors were bound as a matter of law to act in the best interests of 'the company', this was interpreted to mean that they had to act in the best interests of the shareholders. In this crucial respect, therefore, corporations and their shareholders were treated as synonymous, a view which found expression in the principle of shareholder primacy and the common-sense (if legally unsustainable) belief that shareholders 'own' corporations (Ireland 1999a). In the 1930s, however, some commentators began to argue that the idea of separate corporate personality – and the separateness of corporations from their shareholders – needed to be taken *more* seriously. It was this belief that animated the American corporate lawyer E. Merrick Dodd in his famous exchange with Berle in the early 1930s on the purpose of the corporation (see Ireland 1999b).

Concerned about what he saw as the growing unaccountability of managers of many large American corporations, Berle had been pressing since the late 1920s for a strengthening of the fiduciary duties of directors to compel them to pursue the interests of all shareholders. He could see no other way of making managers accountable and preventing them from feathering their own nests or pursuing the interests of a controlling minority group of shareholders (Berle 1926, 1931). Dodd responded by contesting the close identification of corporations with their shareholders that this entailed, arguing that important changes were taking place in 'public opinion' about the corporation. Society, he argued, was coming to see business not as a purely private enterprise but as something with wider social obligations. Moreover, he argued, corporate managers were beginning to respond by accepting that they had 'social responsibilities', a view which Dodd believed was receiving an increasingly sympathetic hearing from the judiciary, notwithstanding the traditional view that charity had no place at meetings of boards of directors.[2] Crucially, according to Dodd, while such an extended view of corporate managerial responsibility was 'difficult to justify if [one] insist[ed] on thinking of the business corporation as merely an aggregate of stockholders', it could easily be reconciled with a view of the corporation as a real entity, 'as an institution which differs in the nature of things from the individuals who compose it'. Once one recognized the corporation as a truly separate 'person', he suggested, there was no reason why it should not operate, through its managerial agents, as a 'good citizen ... with a sense of social responsibility'. Dodd thus began to develop a conception of the corporation as a partially, if not predominantly, public institution with broad social responsibilities (Dodd 1932, 1935; Berle 1932).

By the time *The Modern Corporation and Private Property* was published in late 1932, Berle's own position had begun to shift. The rise of the modern corporation, he argued with Gardiner Means, 'involved an essential alteration in the character of property', giving rise to important questions about both the orientation of public corporations and the allocation of rights within them. Because shareholders were now the owners of 'passive' rather than of 'active' property, the 'traditional logic of property' was no longer applicable to them. Having relinquished so many of the rights traditionally associated with ownership, they could no longer properly, or accurately, be called the corporation's owners. They had 'surrendered the right that the corporation should be operated in their sole interest', 'releas[ing] the community from the obligation to protect them to the full extent implied in the doctrine of strict property rights'. The community was entitled 'to demand that the modern corporation serve ... all society'. Various groups should be 'assign[ed] ... a portion of the income stream on the basis of public policy rather than private cupidity' (Berle and Means 1932: 355–6, 1967; see also Ireland 2000).

The socially responsible corporation: the rise and fall of transformative CSR

After the Second World War, as more and more commentators came to question the idea that shareholders were corporate 'owners' in the traditional sense of the word, sentiments of this sort became commonplace, as did the belief that corporations were becoming more socially responsible. In an influential collection of essays published in 1959, for example, Edward Mason argued that with the 'equity holder ... joining the bond holder as a functionless *rentier*' and having 'only the vaguest idea where 'his property' is or of what it entails', the 'traditional justifications' for private enterprise and private property had 'gone forever'. The old argument that private property ownership was essential to the 'full development of personality [and] to the maintenance of individual freedom' might still be valid in relation to 'individual possessory holdings', Mason argued, but it did not apply to corporations whose 'owners' had been converted into *rentiers* (Mason 1959, 1966: 2–6, 14–15). The perceived erosion in the legitimacy of shareholder corporate rights and the principle of shareholder primacy was manifested in various ways. In the United States, a number of commentators argued that shareholder voting rights should be pared down or even rescinded (Chayes 1959, 1966: 25; Manning 1958: 1490–3). Others called for a wider conception of corporate 'membership' which would embrace other groups, in particular employees. In the United Kingdom, for example, the prominent company lawyer, L.C.B. Gower, asked whether it was 'not time to recognise that share-holder democracy, with its exclusive emphasis on the profit-making element in corporate activity, has a slightly old fashioned ring?' (Gower 1955: 927). In a similar vein, George Goyder called for company law reform aimed at creating 'participating' and 'responsible' companies, membership of which would be extended not only to shareholders but to employees, consumers and the community. He recognized that this required 'a certain subordin-ation of the shareholders interest', but argued that the legitimacy of their claims over corporations and corporate income were limited. In his view, they were entitled, at most, to a fair return on their investment though not necessarily to a perpetual return; perhaps, he suggested, shares should be compulsorily amortized (Goyder 1961). A few years later, K.W. (later Lord) Wedderburn echoed this view, arguing that company law 'should *not* treat the shareholder as a "proprietor" entitled to control' and that there was 'no reason not to equate [the shareholder's] position with that of a well secured creditor' (Wedderburn 1965).

Indeed, during this period it became widely believed not only that cor-porations *should* be run in the wider social interest but that they *were* in fact increasingly being run in this way. This was the era of 'managerialism' (Nichols 1969). Managerialists argued that with corporate managers free from strict shareholder control and free also from the full rigours of market com-petition as a result of the growth in oligopoly and monopoly, they were no longer bound to prioritize shareholder interest and to maximize profits. Initially, some argued that managers were using their newly acquired dis-cretion to pursue their own interests (Burnham 1942), but by the 1950s the general view was that managers were increasingly balancing the interests of different groups. These beliefs were reflected in the rapid rise of the idea of the 'socially responsible' or 'soulful' corporation (Kaysen 1957: 314). By the 1960s, Berle was describing corporate managers as 'administrators of a community system' and arguing that the American corporation 'should not be seen as a business device but as a social institution' (Berle and Means 1967). The implication was that shareholder rights needed to be diminished, corporations reconceptualized and directors' duties redefined.

Unsurprisingly, the growing influence of views of this sort did not pass unnoticed or unchallenged. Some bitterly complained that they posed a threat to capitalism itself (Manne 1956, 1964; Friedman 1962: 133). Others hailed them as indicative of the emergence of a new, more civilized society. By the 1950s and 1960s – the heyday of Bretton Woods and shackled finance, of Keynesianism and social democracy, of trade unions strong enough to mount a serious challenge to the power of capital, and of states thought capable of achieving economic and social policy goals – more and more commenta-tors were arguing that the declining power of corporate shareholders was contributing to the emergence of a new corporate culture and to import-ant changes in the nature not only of corporations but of capitalism. In the United States, for example, Berle began referring to the modern American business system as one of 'People's Capitalism' or 'Collectivism' (Berle 1954: 24), while J.K. Galbraith talked of shareholders as 'vestigial', of the subservience of the corporation to society and the state, and of the supersession of the market (Galbraith 1956). In the United Kingdom, views of this sort were echoed by sociologists like Ralf Dahrendorf and Labour Party intellectuals like Anthony Crosland. Dahrendorf (1959: 46–7) claimed that in the new 'post-capitalist' society 'the imputation of a profit motive' had 'never been further ... from the real motives of men than it is for modern bureaucratic managers'. Crosland agreed, arguing that large corporations were now controlled by managers who were increasingly 'independent not only of the firm's own shareholders, but ... of the capitalist or property owning class as a whole'. As a result they were balancing the interests of shareholders with those of employees, customers and the community at large. For Crosland, so significant were the changes that 'present day society' had to be distinguished from capitalism, whose traditional ruthlessness and aggressive individualism had been replaced by 'a suave and sophisticated sociability'. Using 'a historical definition', it was, he argued, 'manifestly inaccurate' to call contemporary Britain a capitalist society.[3] For Crosland, the pattern of ownership of industry – whether it was nationalized or privately owned – was now largely irrelevant, for it did not determine the extent to which socially responsible goals were pursued. Large corporations 'acted in fundamentally the same way, whether publicly or privately owned'. The key to social change lay in the education of the corporate managers in *de facto* control of industry; or, more radically, in the composition of corporate boards of directors (see Ireland 1996). Should not other groups – employees, consumers, the community – be represented to ensure that all social interests had a voice in corporate decision-making processes? This idea underlay the considerable pressure that was exerted from the mid-1950s for the introduction of 'industrial democracy' or 'worker participation' which would have seen the appointment of workers' representatives on to the boards of directors of large corporations, along the lines of the German co-determination (see, for example, Schregle 1987; Wedderburn 1995).

As embodied in the notion of the 'socially responsible corporation', then, CSR frequently entailed a radical reconceptualization of the nature of the corporation and an explicit rejection of the principle of shareholder primacy: it was underlain by the belief that it was perfectly legitimate to subordinate the interests of shareholders to those of other groups, or of society as a whole. As part of a wider body of ideas about changes which were thought to be taking place in the nature of capitalism, CSR in this form had *transformative* aspirations, looking to bring about radical social changes and a different form of capitalism – or, indeed, in some versions, something other than capitalism. However, from the late 1970s, as finance reasserted its power and neoliberal ideas began to rise to prominence in the personalized form of 'Thatcherism' and 'Reaganomics', transformative CSR hit the rocks. The radical idea of the socially responsible corporation was abandoned and the principle of shareholder primacy was reasserted with a vengeance. When the idea of CSR began to reappear in the 1980s in the context of a new 'shareholder value' conception of the corporation, it took a very different form.

Neoliberalism and the reassertion of shareholder primacy

Neoliberalism began life in the late 1940s as a small anti-collectivist, pro-free-market intellectual movement. By the 1980s, however, it had been transformed from a marginal intellectual movement into an effective and aggressive political force. By the mid-1990s, it had established itself as the new economic orthodoxy, shaping public policy in ways unthinkable only a few decades earlier. Neoliberalism advocates 'new forms of political-economic governance premised on the extension of market relationships' (Larner 2000: 5). What distinguishes it from many other pro-market bodies of thought, however, is its particularly fierce assertion of the existence of a universal, market-based, purely 'economic' logic or rationality – one rooted in human nature and the natural propensity of self-interested human beings 'to truck, barter and exchange' (Smith 1776: vol. I, 25). If it is permitted to operate without impediment, it is argued, this rationality – the rationality of 'the market' – will maximize productivity, wealth and welfare. The key supposition of neoliberalism is, therefore, that free markets – private, contractual economic ordering and the unregulated forces of supply and demand – are the best way to ensure the efficient allocation of resources and the maximization of wealth and welfare. Indeed, so strong is neoliberal theory's belief in the market that non-market institutions tend to be portrayed as artificial, man-made, market substitutes only to be used in situations of 'market failure' (Chang 2002: 90–3, 97–100).

It follows that the state should provide an institutional framework within which the market and its economic logic can operate, but should otherwise seek to minimize its interventions in the economy, including in corporate affairs. This belief underlies the neoliberal push for the 'depoliticization' of economic life (Boycko et al. 1995), for the creation and protection of private property rights ('privatization' and the 'rule of law') and the encouragement of free trade and free markets ('deregulation' and 'liberalization'), for if the natural and beneficent rationality of the market is to function without distortion, market actors (such as corporations) need as far as possible to operate (contract) without constraint. This view has, of course, been forcefully propounded in recent decades by international financial agencies, such as the World Bank and the International Monetary Fund (IMF) when providing financial assistance to developing countries and advising them on the best route to economic and social development. As a result, it has exerted considerable influence over policy formulation and state–business relations.

The rise of neoliberalism has been accompanied by not only a push to extend the sphere of the market and to 'deregulate' but also a fierce reassertion of the principle of shareholder primacy and the shareholder-oriented model of the corporation. The origins of this development are to be found in the growing power and influence of finance and financial interests in recent decades. Indeed, for some, the growing power of finance lies at the heart of neoliberalism as a political project. Neoliberalism, they argue, is the ideological expression of financial power (Harvey 2005; Duménil and Lévy 2004).

As we have seen, in the 1950–1960s heyday of the idea of the 'socially responsible corporation', corporate shareholders in places such as the United States and the United Kingdom were for the most part dispersed and passive. Since then, however, they have gradually reunited in institutions and become collectively much more active. The rise of a wide range of institutional investors and the increase in shareholder activism which has accompanied this development has precipitated a radical shift in the balance of power within corporations and contributed to a dramatic change in corporate culture (Henwood 1997). Maximization of 'shareholder value' – a mixture of dividends and capital (share price) growth – has emerged as the dominant goal of corporations and their executives: share prices rather than production have become the guiding lights of economic activity (Harvey 2005: 32). It is a goal which has been partly imposed on, and partly voluntarily embraced by, corporations. The element of imposition has come from the stock market and the 'market for corporate control' (Manne 1964),[4] in whose constant shadow corporate executives now work. At the same time, however, there have been important changes in the ways in which corporate executives are remunerated – the rise of such things as share options and performance (often share-price) related bonuses – which have realigned their interests and brought them much closer to those of shareholders. By the 1980s academics and policy makers, particularly in the United States, had begun vigorously to reassert the economic superiority of the unequivocally shareholder-oriented model of the corporation,[5] justifying the prioritization of shareholder interest not so much on the (problematic) grounds of shareholder 'ownership' rights as on the consequentialist grounds that shareholder-oriented corporations are more efficient and deliver higher rates of growth than their rivals (Ireland 2000). Indeed, by the end of the century it was being claimed that the debate about corporate governance was over: the exclusively shareholder-oriented, Anglo-American model of the corporation had triumphed over its more stakeholder-friendly German, French and Japanese rivals. 'The recent dominance of a shareholder-centered ideology of corporate law among the business, government, and legal elites in key commercial jurisdictions', Henry Hansmann and Reinier Kraakman argued, has resulted in a world in which 'there is no serious competitor' to this view of the corporation. We had, they concluded, reached the 'end of corporate history' (Hansmann and Kraakman 2001: 439, 468). Even if some are reluctant to endorse this extravagant claim fully, there is little doubt that the more stakeholder-friendly models of corporate governance of Continental Europe and Japan have been undermined (Albert 1993; Dore 2000) and that a ruthlessly shareholder-oriented model of the corporation has spread around the world, promoted by the OECD and the World Bank. The OECD's *Principles on Corporate Governance* (OECD 1999, 2004),[6] for example, are unashamedly shareholder-oriented (Soederberg 2004).

The rise of contemporary CSR

It was against this unpromising backdrop that CSR in its contemporary form emerged. Paradoxically, its origins are to be found in the reassertion of the principle of shareholder primacy and the emergence of a corporate culture dedicated to the maximization of 'shareholder value' and the raising of share prices. In a world in which many multinationals are richer and more powerful than some states and regions,[7] questions have inevitably arisen as to how far the multinational corporation 'has a responsibility to maintain the framework of the society in which it operates and how far it should reflect society's priorities in addition to its own commercial priorities' (Chang and Ha 2001: 33). Business may have gained 'more power', but the consequence of this, Ciulla argues, is to burden it with it 'more social obligations' (Ciulla 1991: 69).

Increasingly well organized and with a growing international membership, NGOs began to put pressure on corporations, particularly those operating in developing countries, to 'clean up their acts' as early as the late 1970s, mounting campaigns to 'name and shame' companies involved in what they considered socially irresponsible behaviour. In 1977, for example, the Infant Formula Action Coalition (INFACT) launched a boycott in the United States on Nestlé's products to protest against the unethical way in which the company was marketing artificial baby milk in Third World countries.[8] The ability of NGOs to adeptly enlist media support in these campaigns was particularly visible in relation to companies trading with, and in, apartheid South Africa, leading to the adoption of the Sullivan Principles by American firms with operations in the country. The Principles provided a set of voluntary labour and anti-discrimination standards, with a focus on the position of the non-white workforce (McCrudden 1999). NGOs also put pressure on firms to adopt Codes of Ethics – by 1986, 75 per cent of all *Fortune 500* companies in the United States had done so (Ciulla 1991: 73) – and organized a number of other campaigns, particularly in the environmental sphere, in the 1990s.[9]

In the 1990s, NGOs also played a key role in drawing public attention to the activities of the Royal Dutch/Shell Group in the Niger Delta of Nigeria, highlighting the demand of Nigeria's Ogoni people that Shell compensate them for extracting oil from their land. The conflict led to the execution of nine Ogoni leaders and activists in 1995, and demands for a boycott of Shell products immediately afterwards.[10] Around the same time, pressure from US and UK groups forced new scrutiny of the way child labour was used in the Asian sporting goods industry, in the production of everything from footwear to soccer balls (Cowell 2000:1). Nike Inc., in particular, bore the brunt of sustained attacks (see Herbert 1997; Toftoy 1998). These developments eventually led United Nations (UN) Secretary-General Kofi Annan to propose a 'Global Compact' in an address to the World Economic Forum in 1999 (United Nations 1999).[11] Its aim was to bring together corporations, governments, UN agencies, workers, NGOs and other civil society actors to foster action and 'partnerships' in the pursuit of 'good corporate citizenship'.[12] The large number of high-profile corporate financial scandals that marked the beginning of the new Millennium (Enron, WorldCom, Global Crossing, Tyco, Adelphia, Parmalat and others) further reinforced the claim that corporations needed to be made more 'socially responsible' (Coffee 2003). Over time, these various strands coalesced around the idea of CSR.

If the pressure for corporations to behave in a more socially responsible manner initially came from NGOs, however, the newly emerging notion of CSR was soon embraced by the corporate world. Within management studies, stakeholder theory gained currency, particularly following the publication by R. Edward Freeman of *Strategic Management: A Stakeholder Approach* (Freeman 1984). Many corporations concluded that for reasons of social and political legitimacy – and also, perhaps, brand image – they needed to be seen as 'socially responsible'. As a result, companies adopted codes of conduct or sets of principles like the Royal Dutch/Shell Group Statement of General Business Principles (Royal Dutch Shell plc. 2005), built, we are told, on the core values of honesty, integrity and respect for people. The Principles recognize that Shell is responsible not only to shareholders, customers and employees, but also to all those with whom they do business and to society as whole. In a similar vein, Nestlé has adopted 'business principles' (Nestlé SA 2004) whereby their corporate objective is to 'manufacture and market the Company's products in such a way as to create value that can be sustained over the long term for shareholders, employees, consumers, business partners'. As this suggests, contemporary CSR has come to be associated with notions such as 'corporate citizenship' ('understanding and managing a company's wider influences on society for the benefit of the company and society as a whole') (Marsden and Andriof 1998); 'the triple bottom line' (corporations should focus not only on the economic value they add but also on the environmental and social value they add and/or destroy);[13] and 'sustainable development' (development that meets the needs of the present without compromising the ability of future generations to meet their own needs [World Commission on Environment and Development 1987]). The revised OECD *Guidelines for Multinational Enterprises* now states that 'enterprises should take fully into account established policies in the countries in which they operate, consider the views of other stakeholders' and 'contribute to economic, social and environmental progress with a view to achieving sustainable development' (OECD 2000).

The potential of ameliorative CSR

Undoubtedly it is mainly because CSR in its contemporary form has been embraced by corporations that it has gained so rapidly in strength in the last decade or so. It is, however, markedly less radical in nature than its earlier, more transformative predecessor. As we have seen, CSR in its original form entailed not only a radical reconceptualization of the corporation as a social institution rather than as a private enterprise, but also a significant relegation of shareholder interest. By contrast, contemporary CSR operates very much within the prevailing neoliberal consensus, leaving unchallenged the shareholder-oriented model of the corporation. As such, it is in many ways most accurately regarded as a mere *adjunct* to the emergence of the shareholder value model of the corporation. Contemporary CSR is not, and does not purport to be, transformative in nature. It is, and purports to be, only *ameliorative*. It makes little effort to displace the view that the goal of business is the pursuit of shareholder interest and maximization of shareholder value. Its objective is the much more modest one of trying to ensure that maximization of shareholder value is not pursued by corporations without their having some regard to the impact of their activities on society at large. It seeks to *induce* more socially responsible behaviour from corporations. Moreover, whereas the idea of CSR originally entailed an open recognition that conflicts of interest between corporate shareholders and other groups were not always reconcilable and argued that they should not always be resolved in favour of the shareholder, contemporary CSR downplays the irreconcilability of these interests, emphasizing the scope for 'partnership'. Its advocates thus commonly seek not only to induce the adoption of an expanded concept of the 'bottom line' – the 'triple bottom line' – but to make a 'business case' for CSR, arguing that engagement in (self-regulatory) CSR is good for the financial bottom line of corporations and that maximization of shareholder value is good for society as a whole.

The prominence of the idea of 'partnership' in contemporary CSR discourse highlights another way in which it operates within the prevailing consensus. In keeping with the neoliberal market-based model of economic and social development, with its emphasis on free trade, freedom of movement for capital and limited state intervention in and regulation of economic affairs, contemporary CSR promotes not the legal regulation of corporations by the state but self-regulation by corporations themselves. Indeed, its emphasis on voluntarism and self-regulation is one of its defining characteristics. Legal or political interventions *by the state* to get corporations to address the interests of non-shareholding groups, Colin Crouch has argued, 'stand outside the CSR frame, the CSR literature being almost exclusively concerned with the actions of firms' (Crouch 2006: 1548). Reflecting this, a European Union (EU) Communication defined CSR as 'a concept whereby companies integrate social and environmental concerns in their business operations and in their interactions with their stakeholders *on a voluntary basis* [emphasis added]' (European Commission 2002). In a similar vein, a United Nations Conference on Trade and Development (UNCTAD) paper on 'Social Responsibility' in transnational corporations (TNCs) indicated that CSR may 'assume economic, social, political and ethical dimensions in that TNCs are expected to conduct their economic affairs in good faith and in accordance with proper standards of economic activity while also observing fundamental principles of good socio-political and ethical conduct' (UNCTAD 2001: 11). The standard mechanisms of contemporary CSR are thus codes of conduct (Jenkins 2001), standards, statements of intent and partnerships,[14] in which maximization of shareholder value – supposedly efficiency and growth enhancing in itself – is implicitly portrayed as a goal that can be reconciled with socially responsible behaviour by corporations and the interests of non-shareholding groups.

Given its essentially ameliorative, voluntary, self-regulatory nature, we should not be surprised that contemporary CSR has gained such widespread corporate acceptance, at least at the level of rhetoric. It is clearly arguable that it is precisely because of its modest impact on actual corporate practices and positive impact on corporate images and reputation – something which can of course itself be marketed – that it has been embraced so warmly by the corporate world. Indeed, some claim that CSR has become a key element in corporate strategies to stave off direct government regulation and public criticism by projecting an image of corporate responsibility and fairness in a world where inequality and social injustice are growing. From this rather cynical perspective, the adoption of codes of conduct by corporations is an effective way of carrying on business as usual – including prioritizing maximization of shareholder value – while claiming to be caring and socially responsible.

The seeming limitations of CSR in its contemporary form have not, however, prevented it from being embraced by more and more development agencies. Nowadays, an increasing number of governments, civil society institutions and corporations see self-regulatory CSR as a potential bridge between business and development, and in the developing world self-regulatory CSR programmes are commonly discussed in terms of their potential contribution to poverty alleviation and the achievement of social and economic objectives (Blowfield and Frynas 2005: 499). For Antonio Vives of the Inter-American Development Bank, for example, 'CSR, by its very nature, is development done by the private sector, and ... perfectly complements the development efforts of governments and multilateral development institutions' (Vives 2004: 46). But is meaningful CSR really reconcilable with the maximization of shareholder value by corporations? Or was the business executive who told a reporter from *Marketing Week* that 'the idea that making a profit can be reconciled with being ethical is nonsense' (Benady 2004) getting closer to the truth? What potential does CSR in its contemporary form really have, not least in fostering economic and social development in the global South?

Soft law meets hard law: Investor rights and the new constitutionalism

There are good reasons for being sceptical about the potential of CSR in its present form, not least because of the growing lack of symmetry between the ways in which the aspirations of investors and shareholders, on the one hand, and non-shareholding social groups, on the other, are currently finding legal (and other) expression. In pressing the case for voluntary self-regulation by corporations, the advocates of CSR generally rely on 'soft law', on quasi- or non-legal instruments which either lack binding force altogether or whose binding force is noticeably weaker than that usually associated with 'hard' law.[15] In sharp contrast to this, the aspirations of investors are finding expression in much 'harder' legal and quasi-legal forms. While the advocates of CSR seek to modify corporate behaviour through voluntarism and self-regulation, a ruthlessly shareholder-oriented, Anglo-American model of the corporation which is antithetical to meaningful CSR is being entrenched around the world by legal and other means. We focus on two aspects of this latter process here: the development and forcible promotion of allegedly 'universal' standards of 'good corporate governance' and the entrenchment, through constitutional and quasi-constitutional mechanisms, of investor rights.

Following the East Asian crisis of 1997–98, international financial institutions (IFIs) began to consider how to quell the growing volatility of the international financial system. This led the World Bank and the IMF to identify 12 areas where standards are said to be important for the institutional underpinning of macroeconomic and financial stability. In each of these areas, international standards were developed, against which the practices of particular countries could be regularly measured and assessed.[16] The 'universal' standards on corporate governance were developed by the OECD and World Bank. The OECD *Principles of Corporate Governance* seek to embed the shareholder-oriented model of the corporation around the world. Although they purport to allow for differences between jurisdictions, on closer inspection it is clear that they in fact seek to promote a specifically Anglo-American model of corporate governance, one characterized by dispersed ownership and a ruthless focus on 'shareholder value'. This is, perhaps, most apparent in the Principles' concern with the protection of outside, minority shareholders, which is essential to the protection of the interests of Western institutional investors, and their focus on the interests of shareholders rather than stakeholders, concern for the latter being much more common in Bank-centred models of corporate governance characterized by 'blockholding' or more concentrated ownership (Soederberg 2004). Compliance with the Principles, as with all the standards, is formally voluntary but the signals that would be sent to the international financial community by non-compliance (and their impact on a country's Standard & Poor debt rating) mean that compliance is, in reality, more or less compulsory if capital flight and investment strikes are to be avoided. With the World Bank promoting the implementation of the standards on a regular basis, the OECD Principles have become a formidable disciplinary mechanism, entrenching a fiercely shareholder-oriented model of corporate governance around the world.

These attempts to entrench a firmly shareholder-oriented, Anglo-American model of corporate governance have been accompanied by further measures aimed at entrenching investor rights through constitutional and quasi-constitutional means. New regulatory frameworks have been established aimed not merely at institutionalizing investor rights but at constitution-alizing them, at giving them 'a level of fixity outside of politics' so that they are immune to political pressures and changes in state policy (Schneiderman 2000a:106). Because of their constraining effects on states of these rules, they have come to be described as representing a new form of (neo)liberal consti-tutionalism. The object of this 'new constitutionalism', as Stephen Gill has called it, is to 'provide political anchorage for capital in the long term ... through political and legal mechanisms that are difficult to change' (Gill 1995, 2000: 2).

This new regulatory framework, which encompasses legal and quasi-legal agreements, the institutionalization of standards, as well as domestic consti-tutional changes of the traditional sort, is most clearly evident in the gradual emergence of a complex transnational legal framework for the promotion and protection of foreign investors. A new 'investment-rules' regime has been actively promoted and developed by the leading OECD countries,[17] with the result that an interlocking network of rules for the liberalization and protec-tion of foreign direct investment (FDI) has emerged, embodied in a variety of legally binding agreements aimed at providing the most stringent possible legal protections for foreign investments: in bilateral trade treaties (Bilateral Investment Treaties/BITs) with common tenets, in regional trade agreements, such as the North American Free Trade Agreement (NAFTA) (and specifically its investment chapter), and, at the multilateral level, in things such as the agreement on Trade-Related Investment Measures (Muchlinski 2007: chap-ters 15–17). States have, in effect, conferred on international organizations powers which, when exercised by states themselves, are usually referred to as 'sovereign powers', with the result that sovereignty itself has become a contestable concept (Sarooshi 2005).

Many of the obligations owed by states under this new 'investment rules' regime are based around the idea of 'non-discrimination' and the principle that states may not distinguish, for regulatory purposes, between foreign and domestic investors. Thus, in accordance with the national treatment rule, foreign investors are to be treated as if they were economic citizens of the host state; most-favoured-nation-status mandates that foreign investors receive treatment no less favourable than that accorded by the host state to investors from any other country. The principle of non-discrimination also rules out performance requirements such as rules calling for the use of local goods, labour or services. Stringent rules concerning 'expropriation' have also been established. Indeed, according to Kenneth Vandevelde, the rule on expropriations is 'the single most important goal of the US BIT Programme' (Schneiderman 2001: 524). These rules place major restrictions on the state, not only prohibiting measures that 'directly or indirectly' expropriate investment interests (such as nationalization) but also measures which are 'tantamount to expropriation'. This covers not only complete 'takings' (Schneiderman 2001: 524), but also so-called 'creeping' expropriations and so-called 'regulatory' expropriations, regulatory measures (such as market or corporate regulation)[18] which so impact on the value of an investment that they are said to be the equivalent of a taking. Measures that involve 'partial' expropriation are also prohibited (Schneiderman 2001: 524). Crucially, third-party investors are increasingly being given standing to sue before domestic courts and international arbitration tribunals should their investments (and their ability to generate revenue) be impaired. As a result, states are constrained not only by fears of capital flight but by the threat of litigation, arising out of their pursuit of economic and social policy objectives that negatively impact on investment interests. The NAFTA's takings rule, and its restatement in BITs has, Schneiderman concludes, 'helped to institutionalize a discourse of limited government that will constrain administrations from pursuing a variety of measures to regulate the marketplace' (Schneiderman 2000b: 772). The goal, he says, is first to establish regimes of rules which protect foreign investments and then to freeze these regimes (and in some cases roll-back measures which do not conform with them): once investors have entered, states cannot impose further or new conditions on them which undermine their investment interests. In this way, established investments are protected far into the future.

The constitutionalization of rights is, of course, widely seen as a positive development – as power-diffusing, as spreading liberal, egalitarian values – not least by lawyers. It has certainly empowered the judiciary: the world, Ran Hirschl has suggested, has 'been seized by a craze for constitutionalization and judicial review' (Hirschl 2004a: 105), a development which has been widely welcomed by both academics and activists. Judicial institutions have been transformed into important political actors at both the national level and supranational level (the European Court of Justice, the European Court of Human Rights, and so on). There are, however, very good reasons for doubting whether the trend towards constitutionalism and the rise of what Hirschl calls juristocracy, is really driven by a genuine commitment to democracy, social justice or universal rights. As Hirschl argues, more likely it is part of a 'broader process whereby political and economic elites, while . . . profess[ing] support for democracy, attempt to insulate policymaking from the vicissitudes of democratic politics' (Hirschl 2004a: 71–3; 2004b). The expansion of the concept of 'expropriation', for example, significantly limits the range of policy and regulatory choices available to states (Muchlinski 2007: 577–620). Indeed, Gill argues, 'by imposing, internally and externally, binding constraints on the conduct of fiscal, monetary, trade and investment policies', the 'new constitutionalism' seeks precisely to insulate key aspects of economic life from majoritarian politics and democracy (Gill 1995: 413). It seeks to limit what states can legally do, narrowing the range of political possibility (Schneiderman 2001: 523). In the struggle between shareholder interest and the wider social interest, the balance of power has shifted. Countries are becoming increasingly locked into a 'rule of investment law' which 'renders foreign investors immune from legislative and administrative action that substantially impairs their investment interests' (Schneiderman 2001: 522). While shareholder interest is protected by the rule of law, however, the wider social interest with which CSR is concerned relies more and more on voluntary codes. When 'soft' law meets 'hard' law, the latter is likely to prevail. We should not be surprised, then, that the reassertion of the principle of shareholder primacy has coincided with a further skewing of the distribution of wealth towards the very wealthy (Ireland 2005).

From responsibility to accountability: re-radicalizing CSR?

One response to the spread of the Anglo-American model of corporate governance and to the rise of the new constitutionalism is to look with even greater urgency to voluntary self-regulation and CSR in its contemporary form. If it is becoming more difficult to compel corporations to act in a more socially responsible manner – in part because states, complicit in their own disempowerment, have rendered themselves less able to regulate business in the traditional way – it is easy to fall back on trying to persuade them to do so, exerting whatever forms of pressure are available.[19] Recently, however, the voluntary, self-regulatory nature of contemporary CSR has begun to meet with more and more criticism.

The origins of these criticisms lie in an increasingly widespread belief that CSR is often treated by corporations as little more than a public relations or window dressing exercise (Utting 2002: 6) and that many of the claims corporations are making, not least in relation to their contribution to social and economic development, are largely empty. The Christian Aid Report, *Behind the Mask: The Real Face of Corporate Social Responsibility*, published in January 2004, for example, lists a string of transgressions by TNCs – such as Shell, British American Tobacco (BAT) and Coca-Cola – that vigorously espouse their commitment to CSR (Christian Aid 2004). This prompted the charity to call for corporate behaviour to be governed and regulated by enforceable rules and to join hands with Action Aid, Amnesty International, Friends of the Earth and Traidcraft, in the guise of the Corporate Responsibility Coalition (CORE),[20] to seek the passing of legislation which would require the Government to complete a 12-month investigation and review into any negative impacts arising out of the activities of UK companies operating abroad, and recommend legal changes on how any problems might be addressed.

In this context, commentators have begun to identify an emerging division between those who are concerned with corporate *responsibility* and those concerned with corporate *accountability*.[21] The growing 'corporate accountability' movement views the corporate self-regulation which characterizes contemporary CSR as insufficient or, in some versions, fundamentally flawed. They do so for two principal reasons. First, it is argued that voluntary action fails to deal with the problem of 'democratic deficit' (Bendell 2004: 17). Thus, Newell claims that the civil groups engaging with business have 'neither the mandate nor the legitimacy to represent broader publics' (Newell 2001: 913); in a similar vein, Bendell argues that 'civil regulation' can never be a substitute for state or international regulation (Bendell 2004: 17). Secondly, it is increasingly being argued by NGOs that the voluntary self-regulation championed by the advocates of contemporary CSR is ineffective and needs to be replaced by regulation. In the words of a recent United Nations Research Institute for Social Development (UNRISD) report, 'international business cannot be expected to author their own regulation: this is the job of good governance' (UNRISD 1995:19). Likewise, the United Nations Development Programme's (UNDP's) *Human Development Report* for 1999 concluded that 'multinational corporations are too dominant a part of the global economy for voluntary codes to be enough. Globally agreed principles and policies are needed' (UNDP 1999). CORE (no date) is even blunter, asserting that 'the voluntary approach to corporate responsibility has failed'.

The idea of corporate accountability seeks to overcome some of the deficiencies of contemporary CSR. It places much greater emphasis on corporate obligations and on the imposition of legal liabilities and penalties for non-compliance (Utting 2008). In the words of Friends of the Earth International (FoEI), it demands 'going beyond voluntary approaches and establishing mechanisms which provide adequate legal and financial incentives for compliance' (FoEI 2002). To this end, the emerging corporate accountability movement has embraced a wide variety of mechanisms for holding corporations to account as an alternative to simply urging them voluntarily to improve standards or report (UNRISD 2004: 3; Utting 2008). Advocates of corporate accountability thus support initiatives which empower 'stakeholders' to challenge corporations (FoEI 2002) and promote everything from complaints procedures to independent monitoring, from compliance with national and international law and other agreed standards to mandatory reporting and redress for malpractice (UNRISD 2004: 3). It encompasses such things as the UN 'Norms on the Responsibilities of TNCs and Other Business Enterprises with Regard to Human Rights',[22] the Aarhus Convention on mandatory environmental reporting (UNECE 2003), the International Right to Know Campaign,[23] the creative use of the US Alien Tort Claims Act (ATCA) and various forms of transnational litigation (Muchlinski 2007). The idea is to make it impossible for corporations to 'pick and mix' bits of voluntary, self-regulatory CSR to 'make themselves look cuddly' (Siegle 2004). One of the principal strategies of the corporate accountability movement has thus been to try to 'ratchet up' voluntarism to such an extent that 'the boundary between voluntary and legalistic institutional arrangements becomes a much greyer area where some soft and some hard approaches or instruments coexist and fuse in ways that [are] complementary' (Utting 2008). It has, to some extent at least, succeeded in that voluntarism has in certain contexts become almost mandatory: law has been used 'to make business adoption of CSR policies much more of a legal obligation that the discourse of voluntarism . . . would suggest' (McBarnet 2007: 12).

Although it is in its infancy and often sets itself against contemporary CSR, the corporate accountability movement is in some ways an attempt to re-engage CSR with its radical roots and to challenge some of the tenets of the neoliberal consensus. In particular, it reasserts the importance of states and intergovernmental institutions positively regulating and wielding authority over corporations. It thus calls for a restructuring and rethinking of the relationship between business and the state, for more *legal* regulation of corporations by the state and other agencies, and for a return to 'hard' (or, at least, 'harder') law. In this way it has begun to challenge not only the belief that CSR can be achieved by voluntary self-regulation by corporations themselves but the prevailing neoliberal consensus about the role of the state. It has also begun implicitly to challenge the idea that the purely 'economic' rationality of the unregulated market operates in the interests of aggregate social welfare; and the related idea that the pursuit by corporations of the interests of their shareholders necessarily serves the interests of society as a whole. As such, its emergence is to be welcomed, for those who wish to see corporations behave in a more socially responsible manner need simultaneously to work within the prevailing consensus and to try to change it. As Doreen McBarnet has pointed out, however, the corporate accountability movement may be asking more of law than law can deliver, for corporations are very adept at circumventing regulatory control and creatively complying with the law. As powerful economic and political actors, they are also very adept at getting any progressive legal changes that are secured diluted or reversed. As Utting says, 'the route to justice through liability is fraught with obstacles' (Utting 2008). Indeed, McBarnet argues that 'the pervasive nature of such an approach to law in business suggests the need for some further, extra-legal driver not only to secure a commitment in business to socially responsible policies *beyond* the law, but to secure business's responsible compliance *with* the law' (McBarnet 2007: 13).

This observation returns us to CSR in its original, transformative form, for what the corporate accountability movement has yet to do is to engage with corporate governance reform and the impact of the emergence of a corporate culture – an 'extra-legal driver' – obsessed with 'shareholder value'. As things stand, with finance in the ascendancy, shareholders in exclusive possession of corporate control rights and managers focused on share prices, the very idea of CSR is in certain crucial respects at odds with contemporary corporate culture, however much corporations express a rhetorical commitment to it. If CSR truly is to become something that comes from *within* corporations, rather than something which is externally imposed upon them using laws which they will constantly be trying to circumvent, dilute or change, corporate culture is in need of radical reform. The key to this is to be found in the structures of corporate governance. Reform needs to move well beyond the conservative agenda of Sarbanes-Oxley, the UK Combined Code on Corporate Governance[24] and the OECD Principles. What is needed is the resurrection of the more radical reform agendas sketched by the originators of the idea of CSR. It means reforming corporate rights structures, the composition and duties of boards of directors and moving towards new conceptions of corporations as social or quasi-social institutions and of managers as members of a profession rather than as the agents of shareholders (Khurana 2007). For some of the reasons explored here, this will not be easy, for it entails confronting the hegemony of finance and the neoliberal ideas which support it. It is, however, difficult to escape the conclusion that without a re-radicalization of this sort, not only will CSR disappoint its proponents, the corporate accountability movement will also achieve far less than its advocates hope.

Notes

1. Both Smith and Marx had long before commented on the *rentier* nature of joint stock company shareholders: Smith 1776: vol. II, 724–58; Marx 1893: chapters 23 and 27.
2. As per the famous American case of *Dodge Brothers* v *Ford Motors* Michigan Supreme Court (1919), 204 Mich. 459, 170 N.W. 668.
3. Crosland (1956, 1962); Dahrendorf (1959); Ireland (1996).
4. The theory of the market for corporate control is that 'inefficient managers, if not responsible to, and subject to displacement by, owners directly, can be removed by stockholders' acceptance of take-over bids induced by poor performance and a consequent reduction in stock value' (see Herman 1981: 10).
5. This found expression in the rapid rise of contractual theories of the corporation (see Easterbrook and Fischel 1991).
6. Initially adopted in 1999, revised in 2004.
7. Citigroup's revenue exceeds the total output of India; Mitsubishi exceeds the gross domestic product (GDP) of South Korea; Microsoft is bigger than the Netherlands;

General Motors (GM) is bigger than Turkey; and the combined revenues of General Motors and Ford exceed the combined GDP for all of sub-Saharan Africa (see Chang and Ha 2001: 33).

8. For a history of the campaign, see IBFAN (no date).
9. See, in general, the website of the Northern Alliance for Sustainability (ANPED): www.anped.org. Corporate environmentalism, as it has been labelled, is seen to have been kick-started by the Rio Earth Summit in 1992 (see Utting 2000) and by a number of 'green business networks' that followed in its wake. For a list of some of these networks, see the EnviroLink Network website: www.envirolink.org. See also the Global Development Research Center website on sustainable business: www.gdrc.org/sustbiz/index.html (accessed on 20 June 2008).
10. Royal Dutch Shell also came under attack in the mid-1990s when it planned to sink the Brent Spar oil platform in the Atlantic Ocean. It had to abandon it subsequently in the face of protests from environmentalists, especially Greenpeace (see Kaptein and Wempe 2002: 6–13).
11. The purpose of the Global Compact is to encourage companies to embrace 10 principles of CSR relating to observance of human rights, the establishment and upholding of labour standards, the protection of the environment and the upholding of anti-corruption practices.
12. Taken from the Global Compact website: www.unglobalcompact.org (accessed on 6 September 2003).
13. From the SustainAbility website: www.sustainability.com/philosophy/triple-bottom/tbl-intro.asp (accessed on 12 May 2004).
14. For the United Nations (UN), a 'partnership is a voluntary and collaborative agreement between one or more partners of the UN system and non-state actors, in which all participants agree to work together to achieve a common purpose of undertaking a specific task and to share risks, responsibilities, resources, competencies and benefits' (see Nelson 2002). For a comprehensive review of CSR in the context of United Nations and Business Partnerships, see Zammit (2003).
15. The concept of 'soft law' originated in the context of international law but has now been transferred to other areas. Some international practitioners are reluctant, however, to accept its existence. For some, soft law is non-law, representing little more than an aspiration without commitment. The hope of its exponents is that soft law will morph into 'hard' law at some point in the future through usage and the passage of time.
16. The international financial institutions (IFIs) refer to these as the Reports on the Observance of Standards and Codes (ROSCs). Participation in the ROSCs is 'voluntary', though refusal to submit to these practices is inevitably seen as sending negative signals to the international financial and investment communities.
17. Extended more recently to include the worldwide constitution and protection of widely defined International Property rights (Trade-Related Aspects of Intellectual Property Rights/TRIPS, and so on).
18. Thus items, such as a public car insurance plan and proposals for the plain packaging of cigarettes, triggered threats of litigation under NAFTA.
19. Colin Crouch, for example, has called for the 'marketization' of CSR. The idea is to get 'so-called stakeholders (especially consumers and employees) [to] express their demands through their normal market transactions'. In this model, interests that are not linked to the firm through the market 'can enter the frame only if the values of consumers, employees or investors develop a taste for caring about them strong enough to generate a market niche' (Crouch 2006: 1548).

20. See www.corporate-responsibility.org (accessed on 20 June 2008). CORE represents over 100 charities, faith-based groups, community organizations, unions, businesses and academic institutions.
21. Bendell (2004); Hamann et al. (2003); Richter (2001); McBarnet (2007).
22. These were drafted in 2003, but have now been shelved. For full text, see ECOSOC (2003).
23. It includes the American Federation of Labor–Congress of Industrial Organizations (AFL-CIO), Amnesty International USA, Earth Rights International, Global Exchange, Oxfam America, and the Sierra Club. Their proposal aims to extend the Emergency Planning and Community Right to Know Act of 1986. The legislation established a US Toxic Release Inventory, which required companies in the United States to register information on their use, storage and release of toxic substances. This had a beneficial impact in reducing emissions by US companies over subsequent years. However, the legislation only applied to activities in the United States, an irony given that the legislation was in part a response to the Indian chemical factory disaster in Bhopal in 1984 that killed thousands. The 200 groups backing the International Right to Know (IRTK) campaign argued that the United States should extend its right to know laws geographically to cover US activities abroad and, qualitatively, to also cover important non-environmental issues (see International Right to Know Campaign 2003).
24. For the newest version of the Code, see FRC (2006).

References

Albert, Michel, *Capitalism vs. Capitalism* (New York: Four Wall Eight Windows, 1993).

Benady, D., 'The light fantasy', *Marketing Week*, 12 February (2004) 21.

Bendell, Jem, *Barricades and Boardrooms: A Contemporary History of the Corporate Accountability Movement*, Programme on Technology, Business and Society, Paper No. 13 (Geneva: UNRISD, 2004).

Berle, Adolf, *The Twentieth Century Capitalist Revolution* (New York: Harcourt Brace, 1954).

——, 'For whom corporate managers are trustees', *Harvard Law Review*, Vol. 45, No. 8, June (1932) 1365–75.

——, 'Corporate powers as powers in trust', *Harvard Law Review*, Vol. 44, No. 7, May (1931) 1049–74.

——, 'Non-voting stock and bankers' control', *Harvard Law Review*, Vol. 39, No. 6 (1926) 673–93.

Berle, Adolf and Gardiner Means, *The Modern Corporation and Private Property* (New York: Macmillan, 1932; New York: Harcourt Brace & World, 1967, revised edition).

Blowfield, Michael and Jedrzej George Frynas, 'Setting new agendas: Critical perspectives on corporate social responsibility in the developing world', *International Affairs*, Vol. 81, No. 3, May (2005) 499–513.

Boycko, Maxim, Andrei Shleifer and Robert Vishny, *Privatizing Russia* (Boston, MA: The MIT Press, 1995).

Burnham, James, *The Managerial Revolution* (London: Putnam, 1942).

Chang, Ha-Joon, *Globalisation, Economic Development and the Role of the State* (London: Zed Books, 2002).

Chang, S.J. and D. Ha, 'Corporate governance in the twenty-first century: New managerial concepts for supranational corporations', *American Business Review*, Vol. 19, No. 2 (2001) 32–44.

Chayes, Abram, 'The modern corporation and the rule of law'. In Edward Mason (ed.), *The Corporation in Modern Society* (Cambridge, MA: Harvard University Press, 1959; New York: Athenaeum, 1966, reprint).

Christian Aid, *Behind the Mask: The Real Face of Corporate Social Responsibility* (London: Christian Aid, 2004). www.corporate-responsibility.org/C2B/document_tree/View-ADocument.asp?ID=26&CatID=16 (accessed in September 2007).

Ciulla, J.B., 'Why is business talking about ethics?: Reflections on foreign conversations', *California Management Review*, Vol. 34, No. 1 (1991) 67–86.

Coffee, J.C., 'What caused Enron? A capsule of social and economic history of the 1990s'. In P.K. Cornelius and B. Kogut (eds), *Corporate Governance and Capital Flows in a Global Economy* (Oxford: Oxford University Press, 2003).

CORE (Corporate Responsibility Coalition), *About Us: Putting People and Planet before Profit* (no date). www.corporate-responsibility.org/C2B/document_tree/ViewACategory.asp?CategoryID=41 (accessed on 20 June 2008).

Cowell, Alan, 'International business: A call to put social issues on corporate agendas', *The New York Times*, 2 April 2000. http://query.nytimes.com/gst/fullpage.html?res=9C02E4D6153FF935A35757C0A9669C8B63 (accessed in September 2008).

Crosland, C.A.R., *The Conservative Enemy* (London: Jonathan Cape, 1962).

——, *The Future of Socialism* (London: Jonathan Cape, 1956).

Crouch, Colin, 'Modelling the firm in its market and organizational environment: Methodologies for studying corporate social responsibility', *Organization Studies*, Vol. 27, No. 10 (2006) 1533–51.

Dahrendorf, Ralf, *Class and Class Conflict in an Industrial Society* (London: RKP, 1959).

DFID (UK Department for International Development), *Socially Responsible Business Team Strategy: April 2001–March 2004* (London: DFID, 2004).

Dodd, E. Merrick, 'Is the effective enforcement of the fiduciary duties of corporate managers practicable?', *University of Chicago Law Review*, Vol. 2 (1935) 194–207.

——, 'For whom are corporate managers trustees?', *Harvard Law Review*, Vol. 45, May (1932) 1147–63.

Dore, Ronald, *Stock Market Capitalism: Welfare Capitalism – Japan and Germany versus the Anglo-Saxons* (Oxford: Oxford University Press, 2000).

Duménil, G. and D. Lévy, *Capital Resurgent: Roots of the Neoliberal Revolution*, D. Jeffers (trans.) (London: Harvard University Press, 2004).

Easterbrook, F.H. and D.R. Fischel, *The Economic Structure of Corporate Law* (London: Harvard University Press, 1991).

The Economist, 'Two-faced capitalism', 24 January 2004.

ECOSOC (United Nations Economic and Social Council), *Responsibilities of Transnational Corporations and Other Business Enterprises with Regard to Human Rights*, UN Doc. No. E/CN.4/Sub.2/2003/L.8 (New York: United Nations High Commission for Human Rights, 7 August 2003). www.eldis.org/static/DOC13036.htm (accessed on 20 June 2008).

European Commission, *Communication from the Commission Concerning Corporate Social Responsibility: A Business Contribution to Sustainable Development*, COM (2002) 347 (01), July (Brussels: European Commission, 2002).

FoEI (Friends of the Earth International), *Towards Binding Corporate Accountability: FoEI Position Paper for the WSSD* (London: FoEI, 2002). www.foe.co.uk/pubsinfo/briefings/html/20020730133722.html (accessed on 30 September 2007).

Frank, Jerome, 'Book review', *Yale Law Journal*, Vol. 43 (1933) 989.

Freeman, R. Edward, *Strategic Management: A Stakeholder Approach* (Boston, MA: Pitman, 1984).

FRC (Financial Reporting Council), *The Combined Code on Corporate Governance* (London: FRC, 2006). www.frc.org.uk/documents/pagemanager/frc/Combined%20Code %20June%202006.pdf (accessed on 20 June 2008).

Friedman, Milton, *Capitalism and Freedom* (Chicago, IL: The University of Chicago Press, 1962).

Galbraith, J.K., *American Capitalism* (Oxford: Blackwell, 1956).

Gill, Stephen, *The Constitution of Global Capitalism*, paper presented at the 41st Annual Convention of the International Studies Association (Los Angeles, 14–18 March 2000).

——, 'Globalisation, market civilisation, and disciplinary neoliberalism', *Millennium: Journal of International Studies*, Vol. 24, No. 3 (1995) 399–423.

Gower, L.C.B. 'Book review of Emerson & Latcham, Shareholder Democracy (1954)', *Harvard Law Review*, Vol. 68 (1955) 922–7.

Goyder, George, *The Responsible Company* (Oxford: Blackwell, 1961).

Hamann, Ralph, Nicola Acutt and Paul Kapelus, 'Responsibility versus accountability? Interpreting the World Summit on Sustainable Development for a synthesis model of corporate citizenship', *Journal of Corporate Citizenship*, No. 9 (2003) 32–48.

Hannah, Leslie, *The Rise of the Corporate Economy* (London: Methuen, 1976).

Hansmann, Henry and Reinier Kraakman, 'The end of history for corporate law', *Georgetown Law Journal*, Vol. 89, No. 2 (2001) 439–68.

Harvey, David, *A Brief History of Neoliberalism* (Oxford: Oxford University Press, 2005).

Henwood, Doug, *Wall Street: How It Works and for Whom* (London: Verso Books, 1997).

Herbert, Bob, 'Mr Young gets it wrong', *The New York Times*, 27 June 1997. http://query.nytimes.com/gst/fullpage.html?res=9B0DEFD81231F934A15755C0A961958-260 (accessed in August 2008).

Herman, E.S., *Corporate Control, Corporate Power* (Cambridge: Cambridge University Press, 1981).

Hirschl, Ran, 'The political origins of the new constitutionalism', *Indiana Journal of Global Legal Studies*, Vol. 11 (2004a) 71–3.

——, *Towards Juristocracy: The Origins and Consequences of the New Constitutionalism* (Boston, MA: Harvard University Press, 2004b).

IBFAN (The International Baby Food Action Network) *The Issue: History of the Campaign* (no date). www.ibfan.org/english/issue/history01.html (accessed on 20 June 2008).

International Right to Know Campaign, *International Right to Know: Empowering Communities through Corporate Transparency* (2003). www.amnestyusa.org/justearth/irtk. pdf (accessed on 20 June 2008).

Ireland, Paddy, 'Shareholder primacy and the distribution of wealth', *The Modern Law Review*, Vol. 68, No. 1 (2005) 49–81.

——, 'Defending the rentier: Corporate theory and the reprivatization of the public company'. In John Parkinson, Andrew Gamble and Gavin Kelly (eds), *The Political Economy of the Company* (Oxford: Hart Publishing, 2000).

——, 'Company law and the myth of shareholder ownership', *The Modern Law Review*, Vol. 62, No. 1 (1999a) 32–57.

——, 'Back to the future: Adolf Berle, the Law Commission and directors' duties', *Company Lawyer*, Vol. 20 (1999b) 203–11.

——, 'Corporate governance, stakeholding, and the company: Towards a less degenerate capitalism?', *Journal of Law and Society*, Vol. 23, No. 3 (1996) 287–320.

Jenkins, Rhys, *Corporate Codes of Conduct: Self-Regulation in a Global Economy*, Programme on Technology, Business and Society, Paper No. 2 (Geneva: UNRISD, 2001).

Kaptein, M. and J. Wempe, *The Balanced Company – A Theory of Corporate Integrity* (Oxford: Oxford University Press, 2002).

Kaysen, C., 'The social significance of the modern corporation', *American Economic Review*, Vol. 47, No. 2 (1957) 311–19.

Khurana, Rakesh, *From Higher Aims to Hired Hands: The Social Transformation of American Business Schools and the Unfulfilled Promise of Management as a Profession* (Princeton, NJ: Princeton University Press, 2007).

Larner, Wendy, 'Neo-liberalism, policy, ideology, governmentality', *Studies in Political Economy*, Vol. 63 (2000) 5–25.

Laski, Harold, *A Grammar of Politics* (London: Allen & Unwin, 1925).

Manne, Henry G., 'Some theoretical aspects of share voting – An essay in honor of Adolf A. Berle', *Columbia Law Review*, Vol. 64(8) (1964) 1427–45.

——, 'Book review of Richard Eells, Corporation Giving in a Free Society', *University of Chicago Law Review*, Vol. 24 (1956) 194–8.

Manning, Bayless, 'Review of J.A. Livingston, the American Stockholder', *Yale Law Journal*, Vol. 67 (1958) 1477–90.

Marsden, C. and J. Andriof, 'Towards an understanding of corporate citizenship and how to influence it', *Citizenship Studies*, Vol. 2(2) (1998) 329–52.

Marx, Karl, *Capital, Vol. III* (London: Lawrence and Wishart, 1893; 1974 edition).

Mason, Edward, 'Introduction'. In Edward Mason (ed.), *The Corporation in Modern Society* (Cambridge, MA: Harvard University Press, 1959; New York: Athenaeum, 1966, reprint).

McBarnet, Doreen, 'Corporate social responsibility beyond law, through law, for law: The new corporate accountability'. In D. McBarnet, A. Voiculescu and T. Campbell, *The New Corporate Accountability: Corporate Social Responsibility and the Law* (Cambridge: Cambridge University Press, 2007).

McCrudden, C., 'Human rights codes for transnational corporations: What can the Sullivan and McBride Principles tell us?', *Oxford Journal of Legal Studies*, Vol. 19, No. 2, Summer (1999) 167–202.

Muchlinski, Peter, *Multinational Enterprises and the Law*, 2nd edition (Oxford: Oxford University Press, 2007, 2nd edition).

Nelson, J., *Building Partnerships. Co-operation between the United Nations System and the Private Sector*, report commissioned by the United Nations Global Compact Office (New York: United Nations, 2002).

Nestlé SA, *Nestlé Corporate Business Principles* (2004, 3rd edition). www.nestle.com/All_About/Business_Principles (accessed on 20 June 2008).

Newell, Peter, 'Managing multinationals: The governance of investment for the environment, *Journal of International Development*, Vol. 13, No 7 (2001) 907–19.

Nichols, T., *Ownership, Control and Ideology: An Inquiry into Certain Aspects of Modern Business Ideology* (London: George Allen and Unwin Ltd, 1969).

OECD (Organisation for Economic Co-operation and Development), *Principles of Corporate Governance* (Paris: OECD, 2004). www.oecd.org/document/49/0,3343,en_2649_34813_31530865_1_1_1_1,00.html (accessed in September 2008).

——, *The OECD Guidelines for Multinational Enterprises* (Paris: OECD, 2000, revised version). www.oecd.org/dataoecd/56/36/1922428.pdf (accessed in September 2007).

——, *Principles of Corporate Governance* (Paris: OECD, 1999). www.ecgi.org/codes/documents/principles_en.pdf (accessed in September 2008).

Pillay, Renginee G., *CSR and Development: The Mauritian Experience*, paper presented at the International Academy of African Business and Development (IAABD) 7th Annual International Conference (Accra, Ghana, 23–27 November 2006).

Richter, J., *Holding Corporations Accountable: Corporate Conduct, International Codes, and Citizen Action* (London: Zed Books, 2001).

Royal Dutch Shell plc, *The Shell General Business Principles* (2005). www.shell.com/sgbp (accessed on 20 June 2008).

Sarooshi, D., *International Organizations and Their Exercise of Sovereign Powers* (Oxford: Oxford University Press, 2005).

Schneiderman, David, 'Investment rules and the rule of law', *Constellations*, Vol. 8, No 4, December (2001) 521–37.

——, 'Constitutional approaches to privatization: An inquiry into the magnitude of neo-liberal constitutionalism', *Law and Contemporary Problems*, Vol. 63, No. 4, Autumn (2000a) 83–109.

——, 'Investment rules and the new constitutionalism', *Law & Social Inquiry*, Vol. 25 (2000b) 757–87.

Schregle, Johannes, 'Workers' participation in the Federal Republic of Germany in an international perspective', *International Labour Review*, Vol. 126 (1987) 317–27.

Siegle, Lucy, 'Faking it', *The Observer*, 31 October 2004. http://observer.guardian.co.uk/ print/0,3858,5049792-110648,00.html (accessed on 20 June 2008).

Smith, Adam, *Wealth of Nations, Vol. 1* (1776, first edition; Oxford: Clarendon Press, 1976, edited by R.H. Campbell, A.S. Skinner and W.B. Todd).

Soederberg, Susanne, *The Politics of the New Financial Architecture* (London: Zed Books, 2004).

Tawney, R.H., *The Acquisitive Society* (London: Bell & Sons, 1921).

Toftoy, R.P., 'Now playing: Corporate codes of conduct in the Global Theater, Is Nike just doing it?', *Arizona Journal of International and Comparative Law*, Vol. 15, No. 3 (1998) 905–29.

UNCTAD (United Nations Conference on Trade and Development), *Social Responsibility*, UNCTAD Series on Issues in International Investment Agreements (New York and Geneva: United Nations, 2001).

UNDP (United Nations Development Programme), *Human Development Report 1999: Globalisation with a Human Face* (New York: Oxford University Press, 1999). http://hdr.undp.org/reports/global/1999/en (accessed in June 2008).

UNECE (United Nations Economic Commission for Europe), *Governments Reach Agreement on New United Nations Treaty on Pollution Information Disclosure*, Press Release ECE/ENV/03/P01 (Geneva: UNECE, 31 January 2003).

United Nations, *Secretary-General Proposes Global Compact on Human Rights, Labour, Environment, in Address to the World Economic Forum in Davos*, UN Press Release SG/SM/6881 (New York: United Nations, 1 February 1999).

UNRISD (United Nations Research Institute for Social Development), *Corporate Social Responsibility and Business Regulation*, Programme on Technology, Business and Society, Research and Policy Brief No. 1 (Geneva: UNRISD, 2004).

——, *States of Disarray: The Social Effects of Globalization* (Geneva: UNRISD, 1995).

Utting, Peter, 'Social and environmental liabilities of transnational corporations: New directions, opportunities and constraints'. In Peter Utting and Jennifer Clapp (eds), *Corporate Accountability and Sustainable Development* (New Delhi: Oxford University Press India, 2008).

——, 'Regulating business via multi-stakeholder initiatives: A preliminary assessment'. In NGLS and UNRISD (eds), *Voluntary Approaches to Corporate Responsibility: Readings and a Resource Guide* (Geneva: NGLS and UNRISD, 2002).

——, *Business Responsibility for Sustainable Development*, Occasional Paper No. 2 (Geneva: UNRISD, 2000).

Veblen, Thorstein, *Absentee Ownership and Business Enterprise in Recent Times* (New York: Huebsch, 1923).

——, *The Vested Interests and the State of the Industrial Arts* (New York: Huebsch, 1919).

——, *The Theory of Business Enterprise* (New York: Scribner's, 1904).

Vives, A., 'The role of multilateral development institutions in fostering corporate social responsibility', *Development*, Vol. 47, No. 3 (2004) 45–52.

Wedderburn, K.W. 'Companies and employees: Common law or social dimension?' In K.W. Wedderburn, *Labour Law and Freedom* (London: Lawrence & Wishart Ltd., 1995).

——, *Company Law Reform* (London: Fabian Society, 1965).

Wood, Franklin S., 'The status of management stockholders', *Yale Law Journal*, Vol. 38 (1928) 57.

World Commission on Environment and Development, 1987. *Report of the World Commission on Environment and Development: Our Common Future*, UN Doc. No. A/42/427, June. www.un-documents.net/wced-ocf.htm (accessed in September 2007).

Zammit, A., *Development at Risk: Rethinking UN–Business Partnerships* (Geneva: South Centre and UNRISD, 2003).

4
Linking Corporate Social Responsibility and Social Policy in Zambia

Ndangwa Noyoo

Introduction

Corporate social responsibility (CSR), with its emphasis on corporate self-regulation and voluntary initiatives, is often seen as an approach that is largely independent of the state and public policy. This chapter questions this claim by showing how the trajectory and substance of CSR in particular country contexts has been conditioned by social policy and development strategies. It does so by examining the evolution of CSR through different phases of development in Zambia. Thus, social investment by business as well as the social policy of different political administrations, spanning a period of almost 50 years, will be considered.

The chapter is organized as follows: the first section deals with historical and conceptual dimensions of CSR and social policy. The analysis then turns to variations in the nature of CSR and its links with public policy through different phases of development. The analysis considers both the colonial era and several post-independence periods. These include 1964–68, that is, prior to the nationalization of industries and when Zambia was a budding democratic state; 1969–72, when the commanding heights of the economy were beginning to be controlled by the state but in the context of a pluralistic political system; 1973–90, during the one-party state; 1991–2001, when Zambia reverted to multiparty democracy and vigorously liberalized the national economy in line with the prescriptions of the World Bank and International Monetary Fund (IMF), and recent years when development strategy has again changed direction. A concluding section considers various challenges and policy implications with regard to CSR in Zambia that flow from the analysis.

Historical and conceptual dimensions of CSR

Various authors have referred to the ascendancy of a 'CSR movement' in recent decades, while others consider it a more recent phenomenon

(Crowther and Rayman-Bacchus 2004). It can, however, also be argued that CSR has been in existence for several centuries, from when corporations were first established. Contextually, CSR draws much of its meaning from the West that is also the birthplace of capitalism. Over the last three hundred years or so, the corporation has evolved from being an instrument of government chartered for a specific purpose, to being an entity granted a statutory life independent of government, with the right to carry out any (lawful) activity. During this time the close relationship between the state and corporation has not dissolved but rather evolved (Rayman-Bacchus 2004). Arguably, this relationship was initially hatched during the mercantile and slave trade eras when both parties benefited in the mutual exploitation of resources of 'the new world'. The European corporation was created by governments in the seventeenth and eighteenth centuries for a range of specific purposes: as an instrument of colonial expansion or to finance and manage public projects and works. 'At one end of the spectrum of influence, charters were granted to explore and exploit new territories (for example, Casa de San Giorgio of Genoa and the East India Company of Britain)' (Rayman-Bacchus 2004: 23).

The European corporations that eventually spread their tentacles to the developing world were intimately linked to the development of capitalism, even though the two were not always mutually inclusive. In some other parts of the world, corporations took on a different persona altogether. For instance, in Japan, firms have long been associated with the community and also regarded as a fundamental part of the society to which individual employees belonged. In contrast to an Anglo-American model of community, in Japan both individuals and companies are members of society and hence responsible to it (Tange 2001, cited in Fukukawa and Moon 2004). In this setting corporations have conventionally been regarded as comparatively 'society-friendly' because of such features as corporate governance, close coordination with government economic policy and life-long employment (Fukukawa and Moon 2004). Important in this context is the notion that Japanese companies were 'organic' or 'embedded' and responded to local needs before transcending national boundaries. In the case of Africa in general, and Zambia in particular, mining corporations were foreign and represented the interests of outsiders. Furthermore, big businesses in least developed countries (LDCs) like Zambia usually acted as agents of capitalist expansion and continue to do so to the detriment of national development. Key features of this expansion were profit maximization and repatriation, exploitative social relations and enclave structures that had relatively few linkages with the local economy.

In the main, such enterprises were not particularly bothered with the needs of host countries. They not only cultivated exploitative relations with local labour and territories but also displaced commercial activities that had thrived in pre-colonial societies. The trans-Sahara trade that covered West and North Africa between the fourth and seventeenth centuries, or commercial interactions between the East coast of Africa and Asia, and the gold trade of the Great Zimbabwe in the late 1400s, all attest to vibrant mercantile activities in Africa prior to colonial conquest. During colonial rule, however, many such activities declined, to be supplanted by those of companies from the imperial countries. Furthermore, in the seventeenth and eighteenth centuries they facilitated the subjugation of the peoples of new-found lands, and had a hegemonic hold over the trans-Atlantic slave trade and other forms of commerce.

Due to this history, one may be tempted to assert that CSR is just a euphemism that has recently surfaced to 'sugar-coat' the pillage by some firms that lasted hundreds of years. Some authors trace both business enterprises and CSR to earlier times, such as ancient Mesopotamia or Rome (see Asongu 2007). In this discussion, transnational corporations (TNCs) will serve as the main point of reference, not only due to their contemporary relevance but also because we are interested in examining the relationship between CSR and public policy. These entities can influence political processes in a particular country or enjoy control over world trade and other economic processes through their financial, investment, production and trading activities.

Clarity as regards CSR is required before engaging with theories pertinent to the area under examination. Definitions of CSR differ from context to context as well as by intellectual tradition. As a result, arriving at a universal definition is extremely difficult as CSR is a container concept that encompasses many different ecological, social and economic issues (CREM 2004). Further, defining CSR is not a value-free exercise; it is often coloured by ideological leanings. Lungu and Mulenga (2005) intimate that CSR is mainly discussed from two major points of view: the first perspective, based on economics and normally considered as the traditional view, and which traces its lineage back to Adam Smith, postulates that individuals in pursuing their own self-interest are also acting in the broad interest of society. Public interest, according to this understanding, is achieved as individuals try to maximize short-run profits. Therefore, in trying to maximize profits, goods and services supplied to society as a result of individual self-interest was a sufficient contribution to society. The second notion, which may be considered as the socioeconomic model, emphasizes society's broader expectations of business. Society counts on business to provide safe and meaningful jobs, safeguard the environment and to give back to society via charitable donations. In the socioeconomic conception business is seen as a subsystem in a highly interdependent society (Lungu and Mulenga 2005).

Another interpretation is that provided by Kotler and Lee (2005), who observe that CSR is a commitment by business to improve community well-being through discretionary business practices and contributions of corporate resources. They note that the key element in their definition is the word *discretionary*. These authors assert that they are not referring to business activities that are mandated by law or which are moral or ethical in nature and perhaps therefore expected. Rather, they are referring to a voluntary commitment that business makes in choosing and implementing these practices or making such contributions (Kotler and Lee 2005). Crowther and Rayman-Bacchus (2004: 2) point out that '[t]he broadest definition of corporate social responsibility is concerned with what is – or should be – the relationship between the global corporation, governments of countries and individual citizens.' In so far as things stand in African LDCs like Zambia, most private businesses of any significance are foreign-owned and Western in origin. In such contexts, the private sector is usually in its nascent form, even after many years of independence.

Theories relating to CSR are also varied and have widespread application. For the purposes of this examination, it is noteworthy that theory provides a framework for the analysis and interpretation of phenomena linked to CSR. Theories of CSR usually tend to fall within two broad approaches: (1) those that conceptualize the firm as a pluralistic combination of various interest holders; and (2) theories that justify addressing CSR concerns from commercial or competitive advantage perspectives. The two most established theories under these approaches are stakeholder theory and resource-based theory, respectively (Burgess and Lewer 2005). Although these two former theories have been prioritized, there are also other theories, such as, for instance, social contract theory, which is mostly associated with Hobbes and Rousseau. The latter is premised on the idea that the legal and political systems only become legitimate once members of society have rationally contracted into them. This theory has been applied to the question of business in society in a similar fashion by considering what conditions would have to be met for the members of such a society to agree to allow corporations to be formed (Crowther and Rayman-Bacchus 2004). As for Marxists, the corporation is posited as generally exploitative and antithetical to socially responsible behaviour, although class struggle and the ongoing development of the 'forces of production' can lead to improvements in working conditions, labour relations, human capital and management systems. Nevertheless, the state could and should play a part in harnessing capitalism to meet societal needs. Keynes, for example, saw an interventionist role for the state in managing the demand/supply cycle and thereby reducing, if not removing social conflict (Rayman-Bacchus 2004). Clearly, the assumptions in the Marxian and Keynesian perspectives circumscribe the scope for voluntary CSR initiatives and point to the fact that big business is only likely to play a decisive role in social 'upliftment' when prodded by the state. The discussion in this chapter subscribes to this view. Foreign firms in countries like Zambia have had a poor track record in this area. It is imperative that the state (within certain bounds of legality and the rule of law) ensure that such enterprises do not simply reap huge profits at the expense of the environment and overall societal well-being.

Interestingly, Murray (2004) is of the view that CSR has evolved into quite a stylized debate that tends to concentrate on particular facets of multinational economic behaviour, for example, the treatment of workers in factories in the developing world producing goods for multinational enterprises in the textile, clothing and footwear sectors. This focus has also brought with it renewed interest in the idea of the 'sweatshop', the extreme exploitation of vulnerable workers in terms of living wages and dangerous working conditions. She further maintains that it is important to identify the potential distorting power of this emerging discourse and to broaden the attention to labour market conditions in general, but also to recognize that private initiatives do not necessarily undermine traditional means of implementing international labour standards, provided that codes of conduct are not conceived of as the sole means through which standards are to be applied (Murray 2004). In this regard, we now turn to the crucial role of social policy in structuring and promoting business behaviour conducive to human well-being.

Social policy and CSR

Social policy refers to the range of government policies and social services that aim to improve the welfare of citizens as well as the academic study of the socially oriented endeavours of the state. In recent years, the social policy debate has expanded to include social development issues such as poverty, inequality, social justice and the impact of other policies on citizens (United Nations 2004). Also, feminist concerns and the role played by non-state actors, such as non-governmental organizations (NGOs), civil associations, unions, family support networks, international institutions as well as regional formations, have enhanced the scope of social policy (United Nations 2004). Social policy will also denote the collective interventions in the economy to influence the access to, and the incidence of, adequate and secure livelihoods and income. As such, social policy has always played redistributive, protective and transformative or developmental roles (Mkandawire 2004). There are significant differences between social policies existing in developed settings and those in LDCs. In the least developed contexts, the focus, efficacy and the manner in which financial resources buttress social policy interventions are, more often than not, minimal due to weak economies. Notwithstanding its varying applications, social policy, more importantly, also signifies state intervention that directly affects social welfare, social institutions and social relations. In the context of development, there can be no doubt that the transformative role of social policy needs to receive greater attention than it is usually accorded in the developed countries and much more than it does in the current focus on 'safety nets' (Mkandawire 2004). In the case of Zambia, social policy becomes an extremely important intellectual and practical exercise in the way that it can offer solutions towards the reduction or even eradication of various social ills in the country. In one sense social policy will avail government actors and civil society formations with the blueprints necessary to intervene into the social sector, so as to arrest human deprivation (Noyoo 2008). Lastly, social policies will revolve around the collective efforts of a nation's people to address the basic welfare needs, related to health, education, employment, occupational training, housing, income security and personal social services at the local or national levels (Osei-Hwedie and Bar-on 1999).

Social policy becomes a crucial vehicle that can operationalize CSR in a particular context because of its general orientation and tradition. It could essentially provide a framework for the articulation of CSR with a development agenda. This close connection between CSR and social policy was a feature of colonial times although, as we will see below, both were heavily segmented in favour of settler populations.

Zambia under colonial rule

The driving force behind the colonization of Zambia was the discovery of mineral wealth, especially copper. The first mineral deposits of copper were discovered in 1903 near Kabwe, which was later renamed Broken Hill by the colonialists. Henceforth, the copper industry would dominate and define the country's development prospects for years to come. Colonial rule in Zambia falls under two historical epochs, namely: Charter Rule and proper British control. From 1911 to 1924, Zambia was administered by the British South Africa Company (BSAC) of Cecil John Rhodes, who had either signed concessions with local chiefs to prospect, mine and exploit natural resources in their areas or brutally crushed those that had resisted such overtures and annexed their land. Zambia was initially overseen by the BSAC as two separate territories, known as North Eastern and North-Western Rhodesia, respectively. During this period, Zambia was merely an administrative outpost and used as a reservoir of native labour for mainly South African mines and partly those of Southern Rhodesia. The BSAC was mainly inspired to exploit the colony's natural resources while being driven by the notion of profit maximization. In this regard, the charter never bothered to undertake infrastructure development in colonial Zambia but merely extracted its wealth and was not bothered with the prevailing social conditions.

In 1924, the British Government assumed direct responsibility of the two areas that were also amalgamated into a single territory known as Northern Rhodesia. Direct British involvement in Northern Rhodesia led to some infrastructure development and the establishment of administrative systems critical for governing a country. Four years later, in 1928, commercial mining commenced in the area that came to be known as the Copperbelt. Later, copper prices on the international market would soar and mining became an extremely lucrative venture. Copper exports were not only essential to the development of the colonial economy but also to that of the colonial power, Great Britain. The mining industry also became a major employer. However, all these developments in the colony were for the benefit of settler populations and not for the indigenous communities. After the Anglo-Boer War in South Africa, apart from the purely British expatriates, individuals who were attracted by new opportunities for farming, mining, trading and hunting also came to the territory (Mwanakatwe 1994). These settlers had close links with South Africa, a country that was already practising a harsh form of racial segregation and discrimination, which would later be known as apartheid. Therefore, settler domination was not only determined by the colonial political establishment, but by also the ideology of racial supremacy that barred other population groups in the territory from participating in both political and economic processes. In the same vein, this type of political arrangement also led to the creation of a welfare system that favoured persons of European descent over other racial groups in Northern Rhodesia.

Racial classification was designated in the following manner: (1) people of mixed-race origin or Coloureds were accorded social services a notch lower than those of Europeans; (2) Asians or Indians were located below bi-racial people; and (3) last on the social ladder were the Africans who received minimal or no state attention at all. Colonial Zambia's social interaction was premised on the racist settlers' ideology, known as the Colour-bar system. In this setting, CSR had racial biases. Primarily championed by the mining conglomerates of the Rhodesian Selection Trust (RST) and the Anglo-American Corporation (AAC), these mining firms greatly influenced colonial social welfare policy by investing directly in human well-being. Lungu and Mulenga (2005: 35) report that as early as 1929 the mines had become 'responsible for the provision of housing and hygiene'. This form of patronage also extended to wages, food and various other social services. It was the duty of the mine management to provide well-arranged sanitary and orderly compounds to house the employees and some mining companies went as far as offering recreation clubs and cinema shows for the workers. Europeans had far better services both in quality and quantity than their African counterparts due to the racial discrimination that was practised in the colony. All this, however, would change at independence.

Post-colonial Zambia

When Zambia won its political independence in 1964, its first president, Kenneth Kaunda, and his United National Independence Party (UNIP) raised hopes for development. Social and economic transformation did indeed occur, due largely to the rapid growth of the copper industry, driven by favourable world prices through the 1960s and early 1970s (Fraser and Lungu 2006). These events unfolded against a background of a backward country with negative socioeconomic indicators. This was in spite of the fact that during colonial times Zambia was one of the leading producers and exporters of copper, which earned it high revenues. Unfortunately, these profits were neither reinvested into raising the quality of life of Zambians nor were they used for infrastructure development, such as the building of clinics, hospitals, schools and roads. Rather, they were transferred to Europe, the United States and South Africa.

There were high poverty levels at independence and political freedom did not initially translate into human well-being for the majority of Zambians. Nevertheless, the government began to tilt the mining industry in favour of development from the said period. Indeed, after 1964, mining would transform the Copperbelt into a dynamic urban and industrial region, and with the growth of the sector, Zambia was seen as the model for a continent moving rapidly towards political and economic independence, industrialization and an end to poverty. By 1969, Zambia was classified a middle-income country, with one of the highest gross domestic products (GDP) in Africa, three times that of Kenya, twice that of Egypt, and higher than Brazil, Malaysia, Turkey and South Korea (Fraser and Lungu 2006).

To be precise, the decade after independence (1964–74) had registered impressive records in social and economic development. As a result of overt government intervention, much improved living conditions for the citizens became a reality. However, between 1964 and 1968, the new Zambian government tried in vain to convince big business to come to the fold and be a partner in the development of the newly independent nation. What needs noting in this scenario is the fact that independence had altered the status quo whereby Africans who were merely seen as cheap labour for the colonial economy were now taking an active role in their development. At the same time, the new government was spurred on by an ideology of African Socialism or Humanism that sought, among other things, to bring pride to the once downtrodden masses via social and economic development. Power relations had also changed at independence and had immediate consequences for the settler population as well as the business sector. From responding to exclusive European needs, major companies were now being asked to spread the cake to the rest of the population. However, big business was recalcitrant and blatantly expatriated huge profits. In this climate of distrust from both the government and the foreign dominated firms, drastic measures were taken.

On 19 April 1968 at Mulungushi (the birthplace of Zambia's independence), President Kenneth Kaunda startled the world with his speech to the National Council of UNIP. It was the request in his speech to various leading companies to sell to the state controlling interests in their businesses that hit the headlines. The principal reason for the takeovers was that the government did not want the bulk of the fruits of its self-created boom to be taken by foreign and expatriate enterprises, and to be consumed or reinvested outside Zambia (de Gaay Fortman 1969). Nationalization was the route taken by the Zambian government to steer business in the direction of social responsibility, on the one hand, and overall national development, on the other. Kaunda proffers the rationale for this process in this manner: 'Instead of the expatriate enterprises accepting their profits and at the same time ploughing as much as possible into the development and redevelopment of their business, it became evident that they were obsessed with "making hay while the sun shines" and expatriated increasingly large portions of their profits' (cited in de Gaay Fortman 1969: 103). Nationalization also brought forth a new dimension, known as *Zambianization*, which aimed to empower local entrepreneurs with skills and finances. It was justified accordingly:

> The banks, the insurance companies, the building societies, the hire purchase companies and the other commercial financial institutions have not been very willing to assist the Zambian businessman. In order to stimulate the rise of Zambian entrepreneurs a number of measures have been taken such as the limitation of local borrowing possibilities for resident expatriate enterprise in the hope that the banks and financial institutions will use their resultant excess liquidity for assisting Zambian business; exclusion of resident expatriate unspecialised business from the rural and 'second class' trading areas; granting of road services licences and building minerals extracting permits to Zambian companies only; and awarding of small contracts by the Public Works Department, and preferably also the large private companies, only to Zambian businessmen. (Kaunda, cited in de Gaay Fortman 1969: 100)

It can be noted that nationalization was quite encompassing and left little room for private firms to wriggle out of their social responsibility. Why such radical measures? Many of the major enterprises on the continent had essentially emerged out of colonial capitalism and thrived on the exploitation of the indigenous people. Predictably, they were not willing to invest their energies in the new nations. Rather, they wanted the former colonial social arrangements to prevail. With many nations impatient for development, some saw nationalization as the only avenue to economic independence and prosperity.

Nationalization had far-reaching implications for Zambia's economy and its overall development outlook. Although the short-term prospects of nationalization were outstanding, long-term effects proved detrimental to the country's development. Nationalization was undertaken in a period when Zambia was a multiparty democracy with a Westminster type of constitution. This meant that the ruling party still had to take on board the concerns of other sectors in the country that were not wholeheartedly convinced by the idea of nationalization. But by December 1972, the country became a one-party state. Thereafter, the ruling party became the only recognized legal political formation allowed to operate in the country. All opposition parties were officially banned after the introduction of single-party politics. In the period after 1973, the government took bold measures to manage the economy. For instance, exchange control regulations that allowed foreign-owned companies – including the two big mining firms – to remit dividends abroad only in so far as they did not exceed 30 per cent of their equity capital or 50 per cent of their profits were put in place (de Gaay Fortman 1969). Nationalization of foreign firms also paved the way for the creation of parastatal organizations, which became major catalysts in the area of social investment (Noyoo 2000). These organizations were also channels through which government could begin to increase the scope of social welfare provision, raise employment and reorient economic activity in various ways (Turock 1989). Firms were compelled by the state to engage in CSR in fundamental ways. No longer targeted (that is, only focusing on employees of particular organizations) or ad hoc, CSR was redefined in a more comprehensive way. It became the cornerstone of social development in the country.

From 1973 onwards, the government marshalled significant resources for social investment from the nationalized mining firms and the newly created parastatals. In pursuance of the vision of an egalitarian society that was guided by Humanism, the UNIP government invested heavily in education and health infrastructure, such as the University of Zambia (UNZA), the University Teaching Hospital (UTH) and thousands of schools, colleges and district hospitals which did not exist in the colonial era. These facilities opened up socioeconomic opportunities for many previously disadvantaged Zambians (UNDP 2003). The mining conglomerate, Zambia Consolidated Copper Mines (ZCCM), which materialized as a result of the nationalization of the RST and the AAC, became a major player in CSR in the country from then on. ZCCM mirrored the state's developmental philosophy and supplied social amenities much wider in scope than those offered during the colonial period, including free education for miners' children, alongside subsidized housing and food, electricity, water and transport. ZCCM literally operated a 'cradle to grave' welfare policy, even subsidizing burial arrangements for the dead (Fraser and Lungu 2006). Furthermore:

> The mines did not only just look after their workers, they also provided services to the whole community. The company managed the environment in the mine townships, maintained roads and collected refuse as well as provided cafeterias, bars and social clubs dotted over the mine townships. They encouraged the growth of economic and social activities dependent on miners' incomes, such as shops, farms to supply food to the mine areas and other industrial activities. Youth development schemes helped youths in the compounds identify skills they could pursue and formalise as careers. Women's clubs concentrated on home-craft. Social casework agencies were charged with investigating social conditions in the townships. By the time of privatisation, ZCCM had one or two hospitals at each

of its operating division. In towns like Nchanga and Konkola there were no government hospitals and non-mine employees and their dependants relied on mine hospitals for access to medical services. (Fraser and Lungu 2006: 8)

ZCCM's CSR effectively permeated Zambian society, especially the Copperbelt region. However, other parastatal organizations also heavily subsidized services in favour of Zambia's poor. For example, the United Bus Company of Zambia (UBZ) offered cheap transport throughout the country – even to the remotest parts, where private firms were not willing to operate. Other companies like the Nitrogen Chemicals of Zambia (NCZ) produced fertilizer and sold it at concessionary rates to farmers, while the Zambia Electricity Supply Corporation (ZESCO) took over from private firms and began an electrification programme that extended to all parts of the country. The creation of the Zambia National Commercial Bank (Zanaco) in 1969 was for the purposes of economically empowering citizens. It targeted lower-income groups in regard to financial services and provided loans to emerging indigenous entrepreneurs. This was the first locally-owned bank in the country. The point that needs to be stressed at this juncture is that many of the parastatal organizations were used as launch pads for the country's development. They were engaged in crucial initiatives that the private sector was not willing to pursue or which they deemed 'unprofitable'. In this vein capital-intensive infrastructure development became the domain of these organizations. To this end, the CSR practised by these organizations was heavily influenced by the ruling party's ideology of Humanism. There was an emphasis on the provision of free or subsidized social services as a way of reducing poverty. Their scope covered: agriculture, education, health care, and sport and recreation activities. It must be stated, nevertheless, that the overarching thrust of CSR in this era was employment creation and job security. Zambians were guaranteed jobs as a way of tackling poverty via access to incomes. In the main, employment became a key development imperative and an artery of social policy. Despite the parastatal's well-intentioned notions around social consciousness, many were loss-making enterprises that relied on the mining operations. Despite moves to diversify the economy, copper production remained by far the largest export earner.

The copper mines propped up all facets of the Zambian economy, a situation that was clearly unsustainable and perilous. It became evident with the onset of the first oil crisis of 1973 that triggered a world recession and led to the plummeting of copper prices on international markets. After the second oil crisis in 1979, interest rates shot up and Zambia was thrown into a severe debt crisis. For 20 years the economy collapsed at an internationally unprecedented rate as copper prices continued to fall relative to the price of imports. Between 1974 and 1994, per capita income declined by 50 per cent, leaving Zambia the twenty-fifth poorest country in the world (Fraser and Lungu

2006). The effects of the economic collapse on ordinary people were devastating. Zambia, which had created a comprehensive welfare system, could no longer guarantee services to its citizens. Companies that offered heavily subsidized social services were operating below par and merely became drains on the economy. Again, it is noteworthy that throughout the economic crisis, ZCCM was treated as a 'cash cow', milked without corresponding investment in machinery and prospecting ventures, and the mines suffered from little investment, as had been the case before 1969. With no prospects for exploration and drilling, and a lack of spares in equipment and machinery, no new mines were opened after 1979. ZCCM production collapsed from a high of 750,000 tonnes in 1973 to 257,000 tonnes in 2000 (Fraser and Lungu 2006). Additionally, real GDP per capita fell from $1,455[1] in 1976 to $1,037 by 1987 – an average of – 3.6 per cent per year. By 2000, real GDP per capita had fallen to $892 (Situmbeko and Zulu 2004).

Liberalization and privatization

The period that saw the downturn of the economy, especially after 1975, also coincided with the rise of political misrule on the part of the ruling party UNIP. This era was exemplified by arbitrary decisions made by the government, especially in economic matters, without consulting the Zambian people. Many imprudent decisions that were made in the light of managing the economy only exacerbated its free fall. It was in this atmosphere that the World Bank and the IMF entered into Zambia's economic decision-making processes, in the 1980s, through austerity programmes. They compelled the heavily-indebted Zambian government to liberalize the economy, cut down on social spending and repeal interventionist policies. It was argued that the state had to play a minimalist role in the economy and allow market forces to flourish. The effects of economic restructuring were immediate and drastic. Food prices, especially of the staple, maize meal, sky-rocketed and the cost of living rose sharply. The direct result of structural adjustments was the food riots of 1986, which forced the government to relent and reject IMF and World Bank prescriptions. It instead opted for a 'home grown' New Economic Recovery Programme (NERP). Nonetheless, this did not last as Zambia could not borrow additional funds from these two institutions needed for critical areas of the economy.

In effect, the Zambian government did not have any other options and had to re-establish ties with the two institutions. However, it had to meet the conditions of removing food subsidies, decontrol prices and devalue the currency, if it was to receive further support. Meanwhile, the ZCCM and all the parastatals were literally limping and economically not viable. Zambia could no longer make pretensions towards a welfare state as in the past eras when copper prices were buoyant. CSR policies and initiatives collapsed as the economy stagnated and following the second food riots in 1990, disenchantment with UNIP was extremely high and political opposition against the government was gaining momentum.

With the return to multiparty politics in 1991, a new political force, the Movement for Multiparty Democracy (MMD), rose up and challenged UNIP in the first multiparty elections after 17 years of single-party rule. At this stage the economy had virtually collapsed and UNIP was extremely unpopular with the mass of the Zambian people. The MMD won a landslide victory and immediately set out to vigorously implement the IMF and World Bank's Structural Adjustment Programme (SAP). The return to multiparty politics in 1991 also facilitated the liberalization of the economy. The liberalization and deregulation of the economy was followed by the privatization of all state-owned firms. There were also resultant retrenchments of workers in line with the set conditionalities of the IMF/World Bank in regard to aid. The MMD, with President Frederick Chiluba (a former labour leader) at the helm, had a mass following and wide appeal across the social spectrum. Despite the fact that liberalization of the economy led to thousands of Zambian workers losing their jobs via retrenchment, many people still felt that the MMD was following the right course.

The privatization of firms was also motivated by the need to woo foreign direct investment (FDI) into the country. This was not always forthcoming as Zambia was not an attractive destination for serious foreign investors. In the end, Zambia had to make do with all sorts of 'investors' – some with dubious intentions as they just stripped the assets of the privatized firms and moved on – leaving shells in the process. Zambia's privatization programme during this period was not well mapped out. In the case of firms that did settle in the country and engaged in business, the working conditions of local people were extremely appalling. This was especially true in the retail sector that was dominated by South African outlets, such as Shoprite Checkers, where Zambian workers were abused and not guaranteed job security. Many of these companies also practised overt racism which they transplanted from South Africa. Zambians were not used to such behaviour, having been independent for a long time. They were also acutely aware of their rights and the critical role that they had played in the fight against colonial rule in Southern Africa, having hosted many liberation movements in their country. Thus, there were serious tensions between the white South African management and the Zambian workforce in the newly privatized companies.

Indeed, there was a considerable reversal of Zambia's fortunes as regards CSR with the onset of the privatization programme. Analysing CSR during this period is instructive not only because of the extent to which it was rolled back, but also because leading firms in the privatization process, most notably AAC, were projecting themselves on the international stage as CSR leaders while allegedly engaging in practices that undermined Zambia's development (OECD Watch 2005).

As regards social development, the swing from one extreme to another that had occurred at the time of independence was replicated under privatization. The key development imperative of full employment, as well as CSR, was seriously denuded. For example, formal manufacturing employment fell from 75,400 in 1991 to 43,320 in 1998. Paid employment in mining and manufacturing fell from 140,000 in 1991 to 83,000 in 2000. Paid employment in agriculture fell from 78,000 in 1990 to 50,000 in 2000 and employment in textile manufacturing fell from 34,000 in the early 1990s to 4,000 in 2001 (Situmbeko and Zulu 2004). Privatization also led to the casualization of labour, as foreign firms were not willing to provide secure jobs because workers' benefits would reduce their projected profits. Economic reforms increased poverty levels in the country as well as social dislocation. Privatization did not provide the envisioned prosperity to the Zambian government and CSR was virtually non-existent during this period.

Furthermore, the concessions that the government made with the new investors allowed them not to be accountable to the nation. A case in point related to the sale of ZCCM. Out of the privatization of ZCCM emerged the Konkola Copper Mines (KCM) consortium in 2000. KCM's core assets comprised Zambia Copper Investments (ZCI) (65 per cent), majority-owned (50.9 per cent) by AAC, the World Bank Group's International Finance Corporation (IFC) with 7.5 per cent, the Commonwealth Development Corporation (CDC) with 7.5 per cent, and ZCCM-IH (Zambia Consolidated Copper Mines Investments Holdings Plc – largely owned by the Zambian government) with 20 per cent (Joseph 2002).

There were hefty fiscal concessions, which the government made to the newly formed KCM. The company was exempted from paying rural electricity levy and tax on dividends, interest, royalties and management fees. On the environmental side, the company received tremendous reprieves and indemnification from all historical and future liabilities (Lungu and Mulenga 2005: 45). This is despite the fact that the people living on the Copperbelt were, and still are, confronted with a barrage of toxic chemicals and other pollutants all of which undermine their rights to health. Heavy metals, such as arsenic, lead and other industrial chemicals, have contaminated streams and the main Kafue River (Feeney 2001).

It was also despite the fact that AAC was prominent internationally in the field of CSR, having assumed a proactive role at the World Summit on Sustainable Development, held in Johannesburg in 2002, and in various global CSR initiatives. Eventually the company withdrew from Zambia in 2002. It remained embroiled, however, in a complaints procedure linked to the Organisation for Economic Co-operation and Development (OECD) Guidelines for Multinational Enterprises. In 2002, the United Kingdom (UK) and Zambian civil society organizations had brought a case against AAC, alleging unfair conduct during the privatization process. Specific accusations included: manipulation of the privatization regime, anti-competitive practices during negotiations, tabling of extraordinary tax concessions, withdrawal from social provision, environmental deregulation, and inadequate disclosure and accountability (OECD Watch 2005: 61). The entity hearing the case (the UK National Contact Point) called a halt to the proceedings in May 2008, arguing that excessive time had elapsed and that AAC had sold the companies involved (OECD Watch 2008). An NGO evaluation noted that as a result of the pressure from the complaint, however, AAC had offered a better deal for the workforce when it withdrew from the country, and provided ongoing support for the resettlement programme of KCM (OECD Watch 2005: 39).

In Zambia itself, things reached breaking point in 2006 when many communities on the Copperbelt started showing severe symptoms of exposure to these pollutants. The Environmental Council of Zambia (ECZ) rushed to the scene but KCM was only slapped on the wrist, promising to be more stringent when releasing its effluents to surrounding environs. Despite KCM's professed CSR initiatives, the truth of the matter is that the sale of ZCCM meant that many critical social services formerly provided by the company were no longer available. For instance, the anti-malaria spraying that ZCCM used to provide could not even be agreed upon by KCM and the Canadian-Swiss consortium (First Quantum and Glencore who control Mopani Copper Mines). The two disagreed on sharing the relatively minor costs of spraying (Feeney 2001). Such was the privatization programme that served to increase social problems and acted against the existing CSR in the country:

Privatisation was one of the strongest features of the IMF and World Bank conditionality from 1992 onwards. But despite attracting praise from the Bank for the 'success' of its privatisation programme, the reality is that privatisation has had a very mixed record in Zambia. Although some failing State enterprises have been transferred into private hands and are now operating more effectively; post-privatisation, many companies have collapsed, jobs have been lost and welfare programmes originally performed through a parastatal have not been continued by private companies. (Situmbeko and Zulu 2004: 2)

In 2001, Frederick Chiluba's two terms as president came to an end and the administration of Levy Mwanawasa was ushered in the following year after elections. With Mwanawasa expressing misgivings about privatization, the new government was to adopt a more cautionary approach towards liberalization. From 2002, Zambia's economic prospects changed for the better. The country's GDP grew by an estimated 5.8 per cent in 2006, as a result of increased copper production, high copper prices, an exceptionally good agricultural performance and a strong expansion in construction. Moreover, GDP is expected to remain around 6 per cent in 2007 and 2008, as a result of increasing investment in mining and high demand for housing

(OECD 2007). The country also exhibited a single-digit inflation rate of 9.3 per cent (estimate as of September 2007).

In spite of the positive outlook, the benefits have not trickled down to the rest of the population. The living conditions of the majority of Zambians are still very unsatisfactory, with about 70 per cent of the population living below the poverty line (OECD 2007). New mining firms have been reaping huge profits and paying a very low corporate tax of 25 per cent, as well as royalties of 0.6 per cent (which are one of the lowest in the world). A new fiscal regime has, however, been developed, under which the royalty would increase to 3 per cent and the corporate tax rate to 30 per cent. Mining companies were expected to comply with this new regime in 2008 (Cronjé et al. 2008).

Challenges and policy implications

While there is increasing attention to the discourse on CSR in Zambia and the emergence of some specialized institutions, such as the The Partnership Forum, promoting this agenda, CSR remain heavily rooted in conventional charity. It ranges from regular sponsorship of entertainment activities, such as football, to irregular and one-off approaches, for example, giving out presents on Christmas Day to patients at hospitals or donations to orphanages or widows (Muweme 2006: 1). A number of specific community concerns, such as HIV/AIDS and environmental contamination, are also being addressed (Kivuitu et al. 2005). A major challenge, then, appears to be the narrow focus of the CSR currently being practised in that it mostly ignores issues related to 'decent work', living wages and labour rights, as well as so-called 'macro' issues related to fiscal responsibility, environmental deregulation and declining commitments to corporate social welfare.

The key challenge remains in the articulation of CSR and public policy. In order to move away from the ad hoc and inchoate there is a need to pivot CSR on public policy and specifically comprehensive social policy. However, there has to be a distinct departure from past efforts in the manner in which social policy and CSR were enjoined. As a point of departure, CSR has to be embedded in social policy and its outcomes have to be aligned to those of social policy's intents.

Presently, there is no clear legislative framework governing CSR in Zambia. There are no tangible guidelines for firms on how to implement CSR in the country. In 2006, the government made proposals for the development of a policy for public–private partnerships (PPPs). Perhaps this is one way CSR could be addressed but, thus far, this area remains fuzzy. It has been applied relatively recently in Zambia, and there is some usage of the term within policy debates. However, there remains little consensus on the meaning and application of the term, or indeed on its usefulness, and it is not widely employed (Kivuitu et al. 2005).

From the above analysis of the different phases of Zambia's development, we have seen how CSR has been shaped by public policy. In the colonial era, mining companies were expected to substitute the role of the European welfare states, providing welfare benefits for the white settler population to the exclusion of the local population. During the post-independence period, a nationalized mining industry was urged by the state to significantly expand its CSR activities not only to African employees but beyond the enterprise to the community. Even though CSR was realigned towards the fulfilment of the needs of the broader Zambian society, its achievements could not be sustained, especially in a context of sharp economic downturn. During the subsequent period of liberalization and privatization both social policy and CSR were significantly rolled back.

This trajectory of CSR calls for a rethink in the strategy as Zambia's fortunes have again improved with the economic boom of the mid-2000s. This shift should begin with the creation of mutual partnerships between the government and the private sector. In this way, the private sector will not feel alienated but rather will have a stake in the economic prospects of the country as well. It will also genuinely complement government efforts through CSR initiatives that are better informed, coordinated and implemented. Secondly, CSR has to be linked to the government's broad development agenda and, more specifically, its social development goals, such as poverty reduction.

While placing CSR in a public policy dialogue, it is important to note that public policy has to be formulated in such a way that it strengthens the alignment between public sector priorities and CSR activities. This undertaking must be executed while ensuring that the resulting interventions are both optimal, that is, good for both business and development, and feasible – in relation to the institutional constraints of public sector agencies and the value drivers of business (Petkoski and Twose 2003). In this way, the type of CSR that emerges will be shaped by the roles that the public sector plays. In order to allow for this, the government needs to set clear public policy objectives and then encourage CSR activities by businesses that can contribute to those objectives. As a response, the government can provide a functioning legal and regulatory structure and effective delivery mechanisms for public services (Petkoski and Twose 2003).

Even though bold moves were made to link social policy to CSR after independence and during the socialist period, the social gains that were achieved could not be sustained. Therefore, an approach to CSR in the present era has to take into account the critical notion of sustainability. Social policy can only give meaning to CSR in fundamental ways when it is linked to the country's overall national development agenda and its economic policy. Therefore, social policy and economic policy must be mutually reinforcing in this regard. Within this context, social and economic policies have to reflect the relative contributions of government, households, the individual and the *private sector*. In the past, Zambia failed to align social policy to economic policy. It was unable to express and execute an adequate social policy regime, while economic development proved elusive (Mhone 2004). In this light, CSR has to be part of economic planning and therefore be in-built as opposed to its present appendage status. Clear guidelines have to be established in economic-related activities. For instance, the issuing of investment permits to foreign firms should not only be related to their ability to pay the required sum of $500,000 but must also be linked to how companies are going to address specific social concerns. This should also be applicable to Zambian companies which must be compelled to link their business cases to social courses in clear and explicit terms. This approach will also broaden the outlook of CSR which is inextricably bound with the evolution of the mining industry in Zambia.

Note

1. All references to $ are to US dollars.

References

Asongu, Januarius Jingwa, 'The history of corporate social responsibility', *Journal of Business and Public Policy*, Vol. 1, No. 2 (2007) 1–18.

Burgess, John and John Lewer, *Corporate Social Responsibility and Its Implications for Governance* (2005). www.aph.gov.au/Senate/committee/corporations_ctte/corporate_responsibility/submissions/sub75.pdf (accessed on 10 June 2007).

CREM (Consultancy and Research for Environmental Management), *Corporate Social Responsibility in India – Policy and Practices of Dutch Companies* (Amsterdam: CREM, 2004).

Cronjé, Freek, Charity Chenga and Johann van Wyk, *Corporate Social Responsibility in the Zambian Mining Industry*, Southern African Development Community (SADC) Research report, commissioned by the Bench Marks Foundation in collaboration with the Peace, Principles and Participation Initiative (PPP) and supported by the Netherlands Institute for Southern Africa (NIZA) (Marshalltown, South Africa: The Bench Marks Foundation, 2008).

Crowther, David and Lez Rayman-Bacchus, 'Introduction: Perspectives on corporate social responsibility'. In David Crowther and Lez Rayman-Bacchus (eds), *Perspectives on Corporate Social Responsibility* (Aldershot: Ashgate, 2004).

de Gaay Fortman, Bastiaan, 'Humanism and the Zambian economic order'. In Bastiaan de Gaay Fortman (ed.), *After Mulungushi* (Nairobi: East African Publishing House, 1969).

Feeney, Patricia, *The Limitations of Corporate Social Responsibility on Zambia's Copperbelt* (2001). www.minesandcommunities.org/company/kcm1.htm (accessed on 20 June 2007).

Fraser, Alastair and John Lungu, *For Whom the Windfalls? Winners & Losers in the Privatisation of Zambia's Copper Mines* (2006). www.revenuewatch.org/documents/windfalls_20070307.pdf (accessed on 10 September 2007).

Fukukawa, Kyoko and Jeremy Moon, *A Japanese Model of Corporate Social Responsibility? A Study of Website Reporting* (2004). http://goliath.ecnext.com/coms2/gi_0199-3544409/A-Japanese-model-of-corporate.html (accessed on 12 September 2007).

Joseph, L., *Zambia Agreement Reached on Future of Konkola Copper Mines* (Washington, DC: International Finance Corporation/IFC, 2002). www.ifc.org/ifcext/africa. nsf/Content/SelectedPR?OpenDocument & UNID = BD434C1704D6B91E85256C 2400712A4C (accessed on 18 December 2008).

Kivuitu, Mumo, Kavwanga Yambayamba and Tom Fox, 'How can corporate social responsibility deliver in Africa? Insights from Kenya and Zambia', *Perspectives on Corporate Responsibility for Environment and Development*, No. 3, July (2005) 1–5 (London: International Institute for Environment and Development/IIED, 2005).

Kotler, Philip and Nancy Lee, *Corporate Social Responsibility: Doing the Most Good for Your Company and Cause* (Hoboken, NJ: John Wiley and Sons, 2005).

Lungu, John and Christopher Mulenga, *Corporate Social Responsibility Practices in the Extractive Industry in Zambia* (2005). www.niza.nl/docs/200505301137193579.pdf (accessed on 12 June 2007).

Mhone, Guy, 'Historical trajectories of social policy in post-colonial Africa: The case of Zambia'. In Thandika Mkandawire (ed.), *Social Policy in a Development Context* (Basingstoke: UNRISD/Palgrave Macmillan, 2004).

Mkandawire, Thandika, 'Introduction'. In Thandika Mkandawire (ed.), *Social Policy in a Development Context* (Basingstoke: UNRISD/Palgrave Macmillan, 2004).

Murray, Jillian, *Corporate Social Responsibility: An Overview of Principles and Practices* (Geneva: ILO, Geneva, 2004).

Muweme, Muweme, *The Good Company in the Zambian Context* (2006). www.jctr.org.zm/downloads/muwemeCSR.pdf (accessed on 13 August 2007).

Mwanakatwe, John, *End of Kaunda Era* (Lusaka: Multimedia Publications, 1994).

Noyoo, Ndangwa, *Social Policy and Human Development in Zambia* (Lusaka: University of Zambia Press, 2008).

——, *Social Welfare in Zambia* (Lusaka: Multimedia Publications, 2000).

OECD (Organisation for Economic Co-operation and Development), *African Economic Outlook – Zambia* (2007). www.oecd.org/dataoecd/27/1/38563134.pdf (accessed on 22 September 2007).

OECD Watch, *OECD Watch Quarterly Case Update, Autumn 2008* (Amsterdam: Centre for Research on Multinational Corporations/SOMO, 2008). http://oecdwatch.org/publications-en/Publication_2807/view (accessed on 18 December 2008).

OECD Watch, *OECD Watch Five Years On: A Review of the OECD Guidelines and National Contact Points* (Amsterdam: Centre for Research on Multinational Corporations/SOMO, September 2005).

Osei-Hwedie, Kwaku and Aaron Bar-on, *Sub-Saharan Africa: Community-Driven Social Policies* (1999). www.idrc.ca/en/ev-85583-201-1-DO_TOPIC.html (accessed on 12 January 2007).

Petkoski, Djordjija and Nigel Twose, *Public Policy for Corporate Social Responsibility* (2003). http://info.worldbank.org/etools/docs/library/57434/publicpolicy_econference.pdf (accessed on 1 May 2008).

Rayman-Bacchus, Lez, 'Assessing trust in, and legitimacy of the corporate'. In David Crowther and Lez Rayman-Bacchus (eds), *Perspectives on Corporate Social Responsibility* (Aldershot: Ashgate, 2004).

Situmbeko, Lishala and Jack Jones Zulu, *Zambia: Condemned to Debt* (2004). www.africafocus.org/docs04/zam0406.php (accessed on 14 August 2007).

Turock, Ben, *Mixed Economy in Focus: Zambia* (London: Institute for African Alternatives, 1989).

UNDP (United Nations Development Programme), *Zambia Human Development Report* (Lusaka: UNDP, 2003).

United Nations, *Towards Integrated Social Development Policies: A Conceptual Analysis* (New York: United Nations, 2004).

5
Business, Corporate Responsibility and Poverty Reduction

Michael Blowfield

Introduction

Should we expect business to go beyond its conventional economic roles to become a more active and accountable participant in the development process? What are the consequences both for business and wider society of the private sector becoming a development agent? What does the field of 'corporate responsibility' have to offer in creating a bridge between conventional business agendas and poverty alleviation?

These are the key questions addressed in this chapter. Its starting point is not whether business has a role to play in economic growth, but whether business can be a development agent which consciously endeavours to deliver developmental outcomes. To answer this, we need first to understand the different ways that business relates to poverty – as its cause, its victim, and its solution. The nature of that relationship affects business's response in terms of what is required and what is actually done. We then identify the determinants and characteristics of when and how business is managing poverty, and go on to look at the impact of business involvement. What emerges from this mix of theoretical and empirical analyses are answers to what role business is playing in development. The final section considers the possibilities and limitations of that role in the future: the likelihood and circumstances under which business undertakes a developmental function, and – re-emphasizing a recurring theme of this book – is willing to be accountable for the outcomes.

Business as an agent of development

The subject of this chapter is how business interacts with poverty and how that is affected by corporate responsibility. I use corporate responsibility in a broad sense, meaning quite simply the responsibilities private enterprise has towards society, including the economies, ecosystems and institutions on which functional societies depend. It embraces both the defining of those responsibilities, and how they are acted upon, and hence includes corporate responsibility as an area of both social and management theory, and how these two fields interact and influence each other. As we will see, business self-interest is a central part of defining responsibility. But for those liberal economic purists who advocate what is variously called the Washington Consensus and American Business Model, the very idea that companies should be mindful of their responsibilities to society is dangerous. It is argued companies exist to create value for shareholders, subject to legal constraints (Friedman 1962). By so doing, they contribute to the public good: creating jobs, supplying goods and services, and helping to fund necessary social institutions. Yes, companies have a social responsibility, but it is not something that needs special consideration because profit maximization is a sufficient proxy for the various other contributions private enterprise can make.

Echoes of this argument can be heard in discussions about growth-driven development. If sustainable poverty alleviation depends on economic growth, then business as the primary creator of wealth has a central role to play. But should it be treated as a development agent, consciously striving to deliver and, moreover, be held to account for developmental outcomes? Or should it be considered a development tool, no more responsible for positive or negative outcomes than a hammer is for a carpenter's thumb?

When business acts as a development tool, the outcomes can be positive – creating jobs, generating wealth, meeting people's needs through the provision of goods and services. Two studies of Unilever's impact on the poor, and its economic footprint in Indonesia and South Africa, respectively, show the complex economic outcomes that can result from a multinational producing and marketing goods in developing countries (Clay 2005; Kapstein 2008). Simply by doing 'business-as-usual', the development tool may affect poverty more significantly than consciously attempting to engineer particular developmental outcomes (Newell and Frynas 2007). 'Whether it is altering the sustainability of local livelihoods or bringing cleaner production processes and improved technologies, displacing local industry or boosting it, fuelling war through investment in conflict zones or providing much needed resources to resolve such conflict, it is in the day-to-day management of the firm and through the taking of key investment decisions that development gains come to be realised or denied' (Newell and Frynas 2007: 674).

However, the question is not simply whether business has an impact on poverty, but whether or not it can, and should, be accountable for causing, preventing and alleviating poverty. For instance, the development tool might create jobs, but business as a development agent takes responsibility for the number of jobs it creates, their location and the quality. The development tool might make products available in poor countries, but the development agent makes products suited to the needs of, and accessible to, poor segments of the population. And whereas the business-as-usual approach to development emerges from managerial calculations related to costs, returns and competition, business as a development agent is also motivated by stakeholder concerns, pressures and demands.

In this chapter, we are interested in private enterprise as a development agent: something that not only affects poverty, but is the subject of conscious actions undertaken because of poverty. The agent can be a company, an industry, an inter-company alliance, a multisector partnership, or any other entity where the actions of the private sector are influenced by an awareness of poverty. Our main interest will be company actions (for example, by management or investors), but we will also explore how others, such as international development agencies, have influenced the private sector.

A brief history of business as a development agent

There is nothing new about companies being development agents. From the Dutch East India Company in Indonesia to the British South Africa Company in Zambia in the 1920s (see Noyoo, chapter 4), private companies administered vast territories, and performed governmental alongside commercial functions. The expectations of companies shift over time, and are shaped by all manner of events. In recent times, factors such as declining confidence in the state as a development agent, growth in private investment due to deregulation, the central role played by business in economic growth, and private sector delivery of developmental functions (for example, utilities, health, education) have all served to broaden the array of expectations society has of business.

What these examples and other histories (for example, Fig 2007a; Newell and Muro 2006; Robins 2007; Glover 2007) highlight is that, while definitions of responsibility shift, the idea of companies having responsibility towards society remains constant. These shifts can create the impression that corporate responsibility is a fad. But more accurately they reflect the array of internal and external, local and international, social and economic, and cultural and political factors that influence what constitutes the responsibilities of companies. One only has to consider the changing attitudes towards security of employment or corporate taxation to see how one era's expectations become controversial a generation later. While various overarching theories to define corporate responsibility have been proposed (for example, Carroll 1999; Davis 1973; Berle and Means 1932), in reality the scope of corporate responsibility is set by, or negotiated within, the predominant political economic narratives of the age. At issue is not whether change happens, but how, and for whose benefit.

Despite the evidence that the responsibilities of corporations shift over time, corporate responsibility theory has failed to produce a substantive theory of change. The analysis other disciplines bring to the relationship of businesses with society are not widely used in corporate responsibility theory (Levy and Newell 2002; Blowfield 2005). For instance, there is a

considerable body of scholarship about business and international development, concerning areas such as corporate imperialism, and influence over
newly independent post-colonial states (Newell and Frynas 2007), but it has
not significantly influenced discussion about corporate responsibility and
poverty.

There are exceptions, such as Ruggie (2003), who draws on Polanyi's theory of embedded and disembedded economies to explain general shifts in the
nature of the business–society relationship: '[Corporate responsibility] may
be seen as a voluntary effort to realign the efficiency of markets with the
shared value and purposes that societies demand, and that markets themselves require to survive and thrive' (cited in Nelson 2007: 58). But more
typically, the responsibilities of companies are presented as ahistorical. Shifts
over time are treated as normative, and there is little attempt to explain why,
for instance, the radical agendas of the 1930s have been replaced with something much less ambitious in recent times (see Ireland and Pillay, chapter 3).
If structural analysis of the business–poverty relationship is ignored, what
we are left with is explanations of corporate responsibility as management
practice wherein poverty is presented as a problem suited to technical and
instrumental solutions.

Corporate responsibility as management practice

One of the most significant changes in business over several decades concerns
the role of the manager. Khurana (2007) argues that early strands of management theory that saw managers as arbitrators between the competing claims
of different constituencies – what would now be called stakeholders – has
given way to managers having become 'hired hands' serving the interests of
investors. When business is discussed as a development agent, and ascribed
a role in combating poverty, this might be interpreted as a return to the idea
of management for the public good.

   In practice, however, managers have adopted very different responses to
corporate social responsibility (CSR). Van Tulder (chapter 6) refers to inactive, reactive, active and proactive approaches. Kramer and Kania (2006)
distinguish between 'defensive' and 'offensive' approaches. Defensive strategies are those intended to address a company's vulnerabilities and external
risks, help protect its reputation, and reduce its legal liabilities. The codes of
practice used to manage issues from human rights to sustainable forestry are
examples of defensive corporate responsibility. An important characteristic is
that they address problems of business's own making. Offensive strategies, by
contrast, address issues where business is not necessarily being blamed. They
involve companies investing their resources and competencies, sometimes
alone, sometimes in partnership with others. Funding the construction of
a local school, or promoting the use of local entrepreneurs as suppliers are
examples of offensive corporate responsibility. Defensive corporate responsibility is able to protect a company's reputation, but does not distinguish it.

Offensive corporate responsibility can distinguish that reputation, but does not protect it.

The four ways that business can affect poverty identified by Nelson (2007) – legal compliance; control of risks, liabilities, and negative impacts; charity and community investment; and creating new markets and social value – can be divided between these two categories, as can the options for engaging in poverty alleviation highlighted by Warden (2007): compliance with standards, charitable giving, committing resources, fostering entrepreneurship and advocating for development. However, there are limits to the usefulness of the offensive/defensive distinction. First, it explains why a company might want to respond (the instrumental value), but not what issues it should take responsibility for from anything other than a commercial perspective. Second, it does not adequately accommodate what we will see as a significant set of company responses where business is neither the cause of, nor the solution to, poverty, but where it is its victim.

Business practice and theories of development

The distinction between defensive and offensive types of corporate responsibility tells us something about why companies choose particular approaches, but emphasis on the business rationale alone offers little insight into what the developmental role of business could, or should, be. The potential trap here is that the scope of companies' responsibilities comes to be defined from within the framework of management theory, rather than that of development. Yet the development agent role can be constructed quite differently depending how we think about development. For example, Utting (2007) discusses the relationship between corporate responsibility and an equality/equity approach to development. If such an approach were used to inform business strategy, then the responsibilities of business would include aspects of social protection, rights, empowerment and redistribution.

Current approaches to corporate responsibility as management practice are stronger in some areas than others. For example, despite the widespread adoption of core labour rights into the responsibility discourse, meaningful interventions have proved difficult, especially on issues such as freedom of association and the rights of women. Moreover, the role of business looks different again if one emphasizes the rights-based, empowerment, redistributive or neoliberal elements of development agendas (Utting 2007). However, the distinct responses demanded by such differing ideas of development are often blurred in business-poverty discussions, something that can lead to unwarranted criticism and praise of the private sector's role (Bond 2006).

International agencies, such as the United Nations Conference on Trade and Development (UNCTAD), the United Nations Development Programme (UNDP), the World Trade Organization (WTO), the World Bank, and the Organisation for Economic Co-operation and Development (OECD), have set out various ways business can help alleviate poverty (Kolk and van Tulder 2006). For example, the International Labour Organization (ILO) highlights low wages and vulnerable employment as causes of poverty, the OECD stresses the consequences of short-termism among multinational corporations, and their abuse of political and economic muscle, while UNCTAD concentrates on the importance of backward linkages, and embedding companies into local economies. The United Nations Industrial Development Organization (UNIDO) distinguishes between the substantive dimension to corporate responsibility (that is, the particular issues that get addressed), and the process dimension (the ways business goes about addressing these issues, and identifying the boundaries of accountability) (Nelson 2007). Various international organizations emphasize the importance of this process dimension as a determinant of the effectiveness of poverty interventions, including support for the self-organization of the poor at community level or workers in factories, a cognizance of local conditions, and cross-sector coordination (Kolk and van Tulder 2006).

However, there is a mismatch between this kind of aspirational development agenda and what companies are actually doing as development agents. The array of substantive issues being addressed is incomplete, but is nonetheless more comprehensive than that of process ones which may not be included at all (Kolk and van Tulder 2006). Various questions arise from this observation. Is it the case that business has an ad hoc poverty agenda, and if so how has that come about, and what are the likely outcomes? Can business be more effectively integrated into established agendas, and what would this take? Or is it that business is already part of an alternative poverty agenda, and what are the implications of this? We will explore these questions in the coming sections.

The business–poverty framework

Irrespective of whether we consider business to be a development tool or a development agent, to have a bit-part or the starring role in tackling poverty, we need to understand that there are multiple facets to the business–poverty relationship. This is implicit in the distinction between the defensive and offensive approaches to managing corporate responsibility mentioned previously where companies adopt different strategies according to what they are trying to accomplish. However, if we look at business from the viewpoint of society, a two-dimensional model does not capture the variety of ways that business affects, or is affected by, poverty. To do this, we need to give equal consideration to three dimensions: business as a cause of poverty, its victim and a solution.

There is also a fourth dimension that is not explored, but that is worth noting, that is, that business can be indifferent to poverty, seeing it as neither a threat nor an opportunity, but simply as something that is not factored into decisions. Thus, for instance, decisions about investment are not typically based on their impact on poverty, but what will bring the best return on investment (ROI). Sometimes poverty might be appraised as an opportunity in those deliberations (for example, low labour costs), or it might be a barrier (for example, weak infrastructure), but in many instances (perhaps in the majority of investment decisions) poverty is not a consideration, and business positions itself as a bystander.

Business as a cause of poverty

In the free market system, an inefficient company has the potential to cause poverty if it fails to generate wealth, create jobs, and provide goods and services (that is, when it fails as a development tool). However, it is the way seemingly efficient companies can cause or exacerbate poverty that is of interest here. At one level, some argue that the very functioning of international markets may exacerbate poverty, although for reasons too complex to do justice to here.[1] Equally, business and government in developed economies have been accused of protecting parts of their markets from developing economy competition, and also for denying developing economies the kind of protections some feel are essential for economic development (Chang 2002).

Advocates of free markets having a singularly important role *pace* the Washington consensus, make the case that business cannot cause poverty if it acts rationally because the market is the most effective way of determining price and allocating resources. Even if one accepts this, power asymmetries that favour certain business actors mean that there are wide disparities in how the proceeds of trade are distributed, and that poor producers in particular (for example, marginal smallholder farmers) can find themselves selling their produce for even less than the cost of production (Raynolds et al. 2004). Similarly, the power some brand-owners hold as gatekeepers to lucrative consumer markets means that some manufacturers have limited bargaining power regarding price or specification, making labour one of the few areas where management can influence profitability. Hence, low wages, long hours and other abusive labour practices are the norm in places where low-skilled labour is plentiful, the opportunity cost of relocation is low, and law enforcement is lenient (Graham and Woods 2006). As one buying agent in Hong Kong said of Chinese manufacturers, 'Suppliers still have places where they can cut fat, but the easiest fat to cut is workers' wages' (Chan and Siu 2007: 8).

In the long run, developing economy labour markets may obey the scientific laws claimed of liberal economics and, if so, wages will rise with the overall upgrading of a country's economy. But in the short term, wages at less than the cost of survival and reproduction put enormous burdens not only on individual workers, but also their families and social networks. For example, in a sample of factories in China producing for Wal-Mart, the hourly wage is less than the legal minimum, and overtime hours exceed the legal maximum (Chan and Siu 2007). Only by working excessive overtime can they achieve earnings approximating a living wage. Rural to urban migrants often face particularly difficult conditions in terms of stagnating real wages and having to pay for health care and education (Pearson 2007).

Sudden injections of wealth, and unequal distribution, can have long-term consequences. For example, the promotion of cocoa production in parts of Sulawesi, Indonesia, in the 1990s together with weak enforcement of traditional land rights, allowed certain migrant ethnic groups to prosper using land alienated from the indigenous population (Blowfield 2004). Other impacts of private sector activity are also experienced differently by different sections of the population. For example, labour markets are gendered institutions that impact differently on women than men, not least because of the former's need to balance productive and reproductive responsibilities. Poverty as experienced by women is not just a matter of unequal wages, but also relates to issues such as childcare, maternity leave and care of the elderly, aspects that are often neglected in the CSR initiatives of companies that either do not understand, or are not concerned about, the connections between reproductive work or care, and both business and societal sustainability (Pearson 2007).

These are examples of the substantive dimension to the relationship of business to poverty, but we should not forget what we earlier called the process dimension, including, for example, the issue of empowerment. Poverty is often associated with disenfranchisement, marginalization, and the lack of capacity or opportunity to advocate for one's own interests. Freedom of association and collective bargaining are among the rights business has been accused of interfering with, the absence of which can perpetuate poverty. Companies can also affect the process of poverty alleviation by paying low wages, or avoiding or evading taxes, thereby denying governments essential resources that potentially could be used to invest in the poor (Jenkins 2005). And short-term contracts with suppliers may ultimately limit the opportunity to build up the capacity of poor producers and their communities (Macdonald 2007).

There are other areas where business relates to poverty, if not as the direct cause, then at least as the apparent beneficiary. The poverty that is behind child labour, forced labour and labour trafficking is something that has benefited business in some circumstances. In an indirect way, business is held responsible for these types of poverty, not just because it is seen as a beneficiary of the global economic system within which such poverty exists, but because it is associated with the changing patterns of governance that are characteristics of that system.

Bad (that is, corrupt) and weak (that is, ineffective) government is one cause of poverty, and business has variously supported, tolerated and resisted such practices. Corporate ambivalence in this regard can be seen from the positions taken by the private sector during the apartheid era in South Africa where parts of the business community both supported and undermined the government (Fig 2007b). Generalizations, however, are difficult to make.

While good public governance is generally accepted as essential to alleviating poverty, it remains to be seen if that is true of the alternative models of governance of which business is a part. Companies have played a part in the process of deregulation, and the subsequent emergence of an international regulatory system that is highly skewed towards the protection of capital and non-human corporate assets (Graham and Woods 2006). For Ruggie (2003), companies must play a role in redressing the imbalances of the global governance system, and 'the key governance question before us' is how much burden companies and, in particular, the kind of voluntary efforts associated with corporate responsibility management, should bear. Wrapped inside that question are issues of regulatory capture by the private sector, and how well self-regulation and voluntary regulation protect the interests of the poor.

The specific relationships between business and poverty are important to understand because they affect how companies behave as development agents. For example, the relocation of factories in contexts of de-regulation can have serious impacts in terms of lost employment and downward pressures on wages and working conditions in former host countries. The lifting in 2005 of the Multi-Fibre Agreement (MFA), which had helped developing countries build up export-oriented garment industries, threatened to have negative consequences for workers, communities and local and national economies, as competition from China forced factories to close in several countries. This prompted the formation of the Multi-Fibre Alliance Forum that proposed solutions for garment industries in countries, such as Bangladesh and Lesotho. Another dimension of the business–poverty nexus, namely the bias of markets against the poor, in terms of both the difficulties small producers have in accessing international markets and the unequal distribution of value along the trading chain, is addressed by the fair trade model. Elements of fair trade, which involve the payment of a premium price to small producers and the organization of producers into associations, are finding their way into large companies' trading practices, such as Starbucks' Coffee and Farmer Equity (C.A.F.E.) Practices (Macdonald 2007; Perez-Aleman 2007).

To date, when business has been accused of causing poverty, if it has not denied the charge (as has typically been the case with regard to disinvestment, relocation, and corporate tax avoidance and evasion), it has for the most part sought to protect its reputation, notably by adopting new regulatory systems, such as company, industry or multistakeholder codes of conduct that promise some form of social accountability. The most significant approach in the development context is the use of multistakeholder or non-governmental systems of regulation involving multiple actors in new roles and relationships, and new processes of standard-setting, monitoring, benchmarking and enforcement. Examples include the Fair Wear Foundation (FWF), the Ethical Trading Initiative (ETI) and the Fair Labor Association (FLA).

Business as poverty's victim

One only needs to look at the facets of poverty set out in the Millennium Development Goals (MDGs) to see how business can be a victim of poverty. The goals are indicators of human development, and failure to achieve them is indicative of the insufficiencies that can hamper business in developing economies. For example, the fact that half the world lives on less than two dollars a day, and 1.1 billion people live in 'extreme poverty' – less than a dollar a day – shows how much greater the market for goods and services could be if only people had more income. The number of children who do not finish primary school is a warning of how difficult it can be for companies to fill even relatively low-skilled positions. Women are less likely to get education, more likely to work at home, and less likely to obtain full-time salaried positions, and gender inequality and disempowerment can harm companies that need educated and independent workers and consumers.

Goals 4, 5, and 6 of the MDGs concern health (child mortality, maternal health and major diseases, such as HIV/AIDS, respectively), and high morbidity, failing health care systems, malnutrition, and disabling or terminal diseases can all harm business. Companies, such as SABMiller in South Africa, have invested in programmes to prevent AIDS and provide anti-retroviral drugs because of the attrition the disease was causing among experienced personnel. Wall (2007) shows how, in Kazakhstan, oil companies are having to compensate for the declining quality of state health care provision.

Weak public governance and the failure of government as development agents are underlying themes of the MDGs. They are equally factors in business being a victim of poverty. Though not explicit in the goals themselves, the idea that the private sector can compensate for weak government is evident in crucial agreements and policies surrounding the MDGs. For example, the 2002 Monterrey Consensus, which announced United States support for the MDGs, bound the MDG implementation process to the mainstream neoliberal strategic and policy framework (Bond 2006). To some degree, the distrust of government has been beneficial for business because important elements of the MDGs, such as the provision of safe drinking water (Goal 7: Sustaining the environment), have become in part the responsibility of the private sector. However, to the extent that weak governance is associated with poor health and education, inadequate infrastructure, corrupt institutions, poorly managed economies, and underdeveloped small and medium-sized enterprises, it can be viewed as harmful to business (Nelson 2007).

According to Saith (2006), one of the problems with the MDGs is that they are silent on certain important dimensions of global poverty. Rising inequality, for example, is something that poses particular threats for business. This situation creates all manner of uncertainties that risk-averse companies might rather not face, such as mass migration, conflict over natural resources and political unrest. Moreover, it should not be forgotten that an earlier era of economic globalization in the 1900s came to a halt because of a political backlash against globalization's distributional effects (O'Rourke and Williamson 1999).

There are innumerable examples of companies addressing issues which could affect their long-term prospects, particularly in relation to education. Mining companies in Africa, such as Anglo American, have had to engage seriously with the issue of HIV/AIDS, particularly in Africa. In addition to investing in human capital, companies respond to other weaknesses in their value chain. The Forest Stewardship Council (FSC), for example, has enabled companies to reduce reputational and supply risks arising from weak governance of forest resources (Leigh-Taylor 2005). Recently, Cadbury launched its Cocoa Partnership to address the risk of long-term shortages of cocoa should the lack of investment continue.[2] And one of the United Nations Global Compact's aims is to increase the commitment of businesses to reach the MDGs, several of which relate to business as a victim of poverty (Blowfield and Murray 2008).

Business as a solution

Increasing attention is being paid to the idea of business as a solution to poverty. This is not simply a restatement of the centrality of business to the capitalist economy as the source of employment, goods and services, and wealth. Rather, it is the belief that business can consciously invest in ways that are simultaneously commercially viable and beneficial to the poor. This relates to, and overlaps with, ideas of social entrepreneurship, a concept with many definitions, but where typically business methods are employed for social development ends but profitability is not a defining criteria (Dees 1998; Bornstein 2004; Seelos and Mair 2005). In contrast, Hammond, Hart, and Prahalad in their influential work on the 'fortune at the bottom of the pyramid' (BOP) emphasize that there are genuine commercial, market-based opportunities to be had by targeting the poor (Prahalad and Hart 2002; Prahalad 2005; Hart 2005; Hammond et al. 2007). They argue that, whereas the richest 0.8 billion people represent a largely saturated and over-served market, and despite there being significant opportunities to serve the 1.5 billion emerging middle class, the greatest unexplored opportunity is the $5 trillion market of 4 billion people who individually or as households have low incomes, but as a group account for a significant percentage of national income and expenditure (Prahalad and Hart 2002; Prahalad 2005; Hart 2005; Hammond et al. 2007).

While these figures are controversial, given the varying income thresholds that have been suggested (Hammond et al. 2007; Karnani 2007), the insight that the poor control considerable wealth is important because it suggests that what is considered the untapped purchasing power at the BOP provides an opportunity for companies to profit by selling to these unserved or underserved markets.

If that was the extent of the BOP model's proposition, it would have little direct relevance to the idea that business can be a development agent because all it would imply is that the poor represent a rational, if overlooked, business opportunity. However, bottom of the pyramid advocates say that by meeting the needs of the poor, business can increase their productivity and incomes, and be an engine of empowerment, not least by allowing them to enter into the formal economy. In other words, by selling to the poor, companies can help eradicate poverty. Prahalad (2005), in particular, emphasizes the role multinationals can play in this by allowing the poor to benefit from both the quality of their products and the efficiencies of their systems.

A large number of companies invest in building the capacity of local entrepreneurs, for example, in response to government policy, such as the Black Economic Empowerment (BEE) programme in South Africa, or as a result of business initiatives, such as Business Action for Africa, and creating markets for their produce. Organizations, such as Market for Change and the Shell Foundation, are building on this by helping link small businesses with buyers. In a different way, the consultancy Accenture is giving the private sector in developing economies access to management and technological expertise through its Accenture Development Partnerships programme.

Microfinance is perhaps the most widespread example of business providing a solution to the problems of the poor. Put simply, it is a system that enables poor people without conventional collateral to access loans at affordable rates of interest, making them less dependent on traditional moneylenders, and providing them with a form of savings, insurance and investment. In recent years, several commercial banks have offered microfinance services, including Citigroup, Deutsche Bank and ABN Amro. There are a number of examples, such as ICICI Prudential, Hindustan Lever Limited (HLL) and Grameen Phone, where the infrastructure developed for microfinance has been used to develop other services, such as retail and distribution.

A major criticism of the BOP theory is that it places too much emphasis on integrating the poor into consumer markets and treating the poor as consumers, when in fact they might be better served if they had better jobs or access to markets as producers (Karnani 2007). It is inaccurate to say that the BOP theory entirely ignores the role of the poor as producers. Indeed, organizations, such as the Shell Foundation (for example, through their collaboration with the retailer Marks & Spencer to promote flower-growing groups on the Agulhas Plain, South Africa) and others involved in Business Action for Africa, are focused on the production opportunities for the poor, and especially the promotion of entrepreneurship.

However, within the BOP theory and practice the role of the poor as consumers is very important. Many companies that identify with the BOP approach emphasize precisely this aspect. Companies, such as Coca Cola and Procter & Gamble, have invested in making their products available to the poor, and organizations, such as KickStart (capital equipment), Freeplay Foundation (sustainable energy) and Aravind (healthcare), specialize in serving poor communities. Vodafone is among the telecommunication companies that has recognized the need of migrant workers to remit money home, and has launched its mobile phone-based M-Pesa remittance system in Kenya, and is exploring a system for international remittances with Citigroup. Companies as diverse as Philips, Intel, Infosys, and Godrej have also developed new products tailored to the needs of poor communities.

To understand the theory behind this 'consumerist' dimension of BOP, one needs to consider the situation facing many poor people. Not only do they have low incomes: (a) they have significant unmet needs; (b) they are typically part of an informal or subsistence economy (the ILO estimates that 70 per cent of the workforce in developing economies is in the informal sector); (c) they are part of high cost micro-economic systems where they pay more for goods and services (for example, water is more expensive in a Nairobi slum than in central New York); (d) they are often 'prisoners' of local monopolies (for example, moneylenders); and (e) they lack access to quality products. Therefore, according to C.K. Prahalad, if companies compete to serve the poor, the upshot will be lower living costs (for example, because interest rates will fall), increased productivity (for example, because if medicines are more affordable, people will be healthier), and new employment opportunities (for example, from selling the products).

One of the issues in relation to this model as a conscious approach to tackling poverty is the degree to which, having identified the opportunity, the market alone will deliver developmental benefits. The difference between certain proponents and critics of the BOP is to a degree a moral one, with the former reluctant to make choices about what the poor should have access to, and the latter arguing that high spending by some poor people on tobacco, alcohol and gambling suggest they do not always make 'wise' purchasing decisions. This tension is evident in case studies of the BOP (see, for instance, the contributions to Rangan 2007), but if we are thinking of business as a development agent, then it is important to distinguish between companies that serve the poor, and ones that factor poverty alleviation outcomes into their decisions and strategies. This is not straightforward. For example, at first glance it may seem that HLL supply of shampoo to rural women is less beneficial than Aravind's provision of low-cost cataract surgery, yet this conclusion ignores the increase to rural women's incomes arising from new opportunities to sell shampoo and other household items. However, in the business-poverty context, the key point is that financial performance ultimately should be less important an indicator than social outcomes.

This is not to say that companies should approach poverty as a social enterprise where profits are unimportant (see Karnani 2007), although successful examples of targeting the poor, such as Aravind in India, HealthStore Foundation in Kenya and the Grameen Bank in Bangladesh, have been run on a not-for-profit basis, or involve some form of subsidy or alternative funding. However, profitability may require unconventional business models, not only in terms of understanding the market, or designing products, but equally in the collaborations that are required. There are various examples of companies collaborating with non-governmental organizations (NGOs) to identify needs, and deliver products: these include Telenor and Grameen's collaboration to create Grameen Phone, ICICI Prudential's collaboration with women's groups in India on insurance products, and Accion International's collaboration with ABN Amro on microfinance. Brugmann and Prahalad (2007) view these collaborations as part of a trend towards 'co-creation', where business and NGOs or grassroots organizations create hybrid business models suited to the very different conditions for commercial and social success when dealing with poverty. HLL (the Indian subsidiary of Unilever) decided to partner with the numerous women's self-help groups that had emerged from the boom in microfinance in Project Shakti. It brought HLL into partnership with the cooperatives that were federations of self-help groups and the NGOs that helped build cooperative capacity. At first, the project was more successful in raising awareness of HLL brands than it was in raising group members' incomes, but removing the cooperatives from the chain, and providing direct support to the women eventually raised sellers' profit margins, doubling their household incomes. The project now covers 13 states, and has given HLL access to 50,000 new villages, or one million homes.

To a degree, these collaborations are about scaling up the success of NGO innovations as could be said about the entrance of commercial banks, such as Citigroup and Deutsche Bank, into the world of microfinance. However, companies, such as Standard Chartered, are bringing new capacities to existing sectors (for example, raising capital for microfinance on international markets), while partnerships, such as that between World Diagnostics and Ugandan NGOs, allow existing networks to be used to provide new types of health services. This is not without its problems. For instance, ICICI's collaboration with women's self-help groups in India was criticized by some NGOs for undermining their wider social development goals, and there will be fundamental shifts in relationships as collaborations require NGOs to privilege task-driven partnerships with companies over ideology-driven dialogues (Brugmann and Prahalad 2007). Moreover, such partnerships are becoming a defining (and perhaps legitimating) feature of initiatives affecting the poor's access to, and control over, essential resources, such as water privatization, projects associated with the Clean Development Mechanism (CDM), and now forest management in the context of voluntary emissions trading. We discuss the implications of this kind of change later, but we should recognize that, in emphasizing partnerships with large companies, we risk further marginalizing the contribution local small and medium-sized companies make, and the local partnerships of which historically they have been a part.

Assessing the business response

The previous discussion of business acting as a development agent provides a framework of the different types of interaction (that is, based on cause, solution and victimhood). What it does not reveal is: (a) the conditions under which business will actively manage its relationship with poverty; and (b) the effectiveness of its taking on a development role. It is this I turn to now.

Features of managing poverty

The business–poverty relationship can be the focus of different spheres of business activity, such as core business operations, social investment and philanthropy, as well as policy dialogue and advocacy (Brainard 2006). As we have also seen, the actions taken may assume a variety of forms. In some instances, for example, when creating or destroying jobs, or choosing where to locate factories, business clearly impacts economic and social development,[3] but does so as a development tool, not as a development agent consciously negotiating its relationship with poverty. Under what conditions might companies act as development agents?

The examples in the previous section suggest that there are three basic conditions that dictate under what circumstances business can take on the development agent role.

Condition 1: Business is more likely to act when poverty is associated with an identifiable risk to a company or industry, including risks to reputation, to the availability of commodities, to production, and so on. This condition accounts for genuine innovations with respect to supply chain governance, and responsibility towards producing communities. It also accounts for some of the links created between companies and development organizations. Examples include the FWF, the ETI, Worldwide Responsible Apparel Production, the FLA, C.A.F.E. Practices, the FSC and Cadbury's Cocoa Partnership.

Condition 2: Business is more likely to act when poverty offers a favourable ROI. This accounts for services to underserved markets, new market opportunities for the poor and, in some cases, a re-engineering of the benefits of trade in favour of the poor. Initiatives that seek to deliver social return on investment (SROI), in addition to ROI, can position the poor as producer or consumer. Examples include fair trade, microfinance, enterprises such as Freeplay, M-Pesa or the Shakti Project, and Merrill Lynch's investment in Ulu Masen.

Condition 3: Business is more likely to act when poverty is associated with inefficiency. This accounts for initiatives to combat corruption, enhance the poor's productive capacity, increase health and safety standards, invest in education and improve living environments. Examples include the Extraction Industry Transparency Initiative, investment in AIDS prevention by firms, such SABMiller and L'Oreal, and the education programmes of companies, such as Anglo American and Cisco Systems.

Any of the initiatives undertaken by business as a development agent mentioned in this chapter can be explained by appeal to one or other of the above three conditions. Likewise, dimensions to development that lie outside the scope of these conditions are unlikely to be addressed by business overtly. For example, redistributive elements, such as corporate taxation, though part of debates about development economics, are not normally incorporated into normative debates about the responsibilities of business. Neither is there any thorough consideration of power and conflict, even though some of the areas where business affects development are historically the sites of dispute and tension (for example, relations between buyers and small contract farmers or outgrowers). The gender dimensions to poverty are frequently ignored, and this is part of a general pattern of preferencing where the individual good is preferred to the communal, financial wealth is favoured over non-financial, and issues, such as class, ethnicity, sexuality and other determinants of privilege, are discounted or isolated from their wider context. It is not that these dimensions are absent from debates about development: indeed, it is their importance to development theory that makes their absence from corporate responsibility in the development context so noticeable. These and other types of exclusion are made more apparent when we look at the impact of business initiatives.

Impact

For all the excitement surrounding the contributions business could make as a development agent, there is surprisingly little information about what has been achieved (Blowfield 2007; Hamann 2007). This is not to say that we know nothing about corporate responsibility's impact: on the contrary, we know a considerable amount about certain areas of impact, but the information we have is quite specific and tells us little about the real outcomes for the poor. There has been some interest from companies in showing the cash value added of operations, but this does not really tell much about the social or even economic return on investment, and how the data relate to the investment priorities of the poor (Ellis 2008).

There are three main sources of information commonly used in talking about impact – case studies, company corporate responsibility reports, and company ratings – as well as reports documenting the progress of companies within particular partnerships (for example, the ETI's annual report). Often the growing number of case studies, reports and ratings is itself offered as proof that corporate responsibility is having an impact. However, the information on corporate responsibility's impact is, for the most part, slanted towards instrumental benefits, and impact assessment methodologies used in development agencies (that not least demonstrate the complex nature of social impact) have not been widely used by companies.[4] While there is considerable information about how attention to corporate responsibility is changing business practice and stakeholder behaviour, and how attention to development issues relates to business performance, there have been few systematic attempts to learn how business investment in corporate responsibility management is affecting poverty. Companies, such as Anglo American, have been complimented on their efforts to develop more sophisticated social assessment tools, and use these to report their performance. However, this is a relatively recent development and does not yet explain much about impact, while experience suggests that efforts to measure impact to date have been flawed (Hamann 2007).

The ETI is one of the few examples in the public domain of a long-term commitment to assessing impact, in this case the outcomes of monitoring labour conditions in global supply chains (Barrientos and Smith 2007). It highlights not only the challenges for multistakeholder regulation in delivering benefits to poor people, but some of the difficulties any initiative faces in being an accountable development agent. Examining 18 worksites in three countries, the study identified demonstrable impacts relating to certain aspects of the ETI's labour code of conduct, notably under the provisions on health and safety, and on legal employment entitlements, such as the minimum wage, working hours and deductions for employment benefits, such as health insurance and pensions. At most workplaces, workers' physical and social well-being was enhanced through health and safety improvements (for example, information and training; fire safety; safety guards; protective equipment; improved toilets and drinking water), and reductions in working hours. Other improvements may have already occurred prior to the study: for instance, the assessment did not discover any child labour. Some improvements were limited to certain types of worker so that, for example, there was evidence of improvement in the treatment of permanent and regular workers, but contract labour was still poorly treated in most countries.

The benefits were not limited to workers. For example, workers no longer took home their work clothes or touched their children after handling chemicals. Some permanent workers said their houses were cleaner because of improved factory conditions. Reduced working hours meant more time for family life and, especially for women, domestic responsibilities.

However, there were other areas where the impact was either mixed or unclear. This is especially true when considering process rights (that is, intrinsic principles of social justice that, under ILO Conventions, are what enable workers to uphold their rights). For example, codes have not led to wage increases through Collective Bargaining Agreements, which along with Freedom of Association is considered a major process right. Without process rights, advocates argue, other changes do not follow. Codes have not led to a substantial increase in income in terms of guaranteeing a living wage, for instance. Indeed, wages do not appear to have improved as a demonstrable result of the codes. The reduction of excessive overtime can have ambivalent effects in terms of decreased take home pay but more leisure time.

In some areas where codes may have had a positive impact, the benefits are limited to certain types of worker. For example, if suppliers pay into state insurance and pension schemes, workers' vulnerability to poverty in the event of childbirth, illness or old age is reduced, but these types of employment benefit are often limited to permanent workers who constitute only a part of the workforce. Although contract and other casual workers are a large part of the workforce, the ETI code's provision on security of employment has not had much impact, and the assessment found anecdotal evidence that shortening lead times by ETI member companies led to increased usage of temporary and contract labour in order to fulfil orders.

The challenge of understanding impact

Research on fair trade also reveals problems to do with the distribution of benefits and the alienation of the intended beneficiaries (that is, small producers) from the very processes intended to raise their standards of living and to empower them.[5] In part this is because of the capture of benefits by elite groups within local communities (a common phenomenon in conventional development), but it is also because of the very process of monitoring and auditing which can create distrust and deception (Blowfield and Dolan 2008).

Various organizations, including the International Finance Corporation (IFC), the World Business Council on Sustainable Development and the Overseas Development Institute (ODI) (WBCSD 2008; Ellis 2008), are engaged in initiatives that may provide more information on impact. They are building, however, on conventional management tools, the suitability of which for the task at hand is unknown. Thus, it is not simply that we know little about the impact of corporate responsibility: the instruments used to implement certain corporate responsibility programmes – instruments adapted from conventional management's arsenal – may prevent us from knowing the actual impact, or at least limit our knowledge to a sanitized view that resonates with preconceptions about what development means.

'Entrepreneurship' is a good example of how the norms and language of business can affect our perception of development. As part of the increasing emphasis put on offensive corporate responsibility, particular attention is being paid to the significance of small and medium-sized enterprises, and the financial and developmental benefits of building the capacity of local entrepreneurs (Wilson 2006). For the most part, these are referred to as objects of corporate responsibility (something larger companies should invest in and create backward linkages with) (for example, Wilson 2006; WBCSD 2007; Nelson 2007), rather than as adopters of corporate responsibility. The importance attached to entrepreneurship (and its association with empowerment) is evidence of the way corporate responsibility, for the most part, represents a managerial vision of the role of business in development. Once an aspect of poverty is framed in ways management understands, it is more likely to be accepted (and hence legitimized) into the business–poverty agenda.

As noted earlier, a criticism of the way the role of business in relation to poverty has been conceived is that it overlooks process dimensions, such as empowerment, in favour of substantive ones, such as the minimum wage and farm-gate prices. Yet building entrepreneurial capacity is repeatedly described in terms of empowerment (WBCSD 2007; Wilson 2006; Rangan 2007), a term that is variously emphasized and deemphasized according to what aspect of the business–poverty agenda is being dealt with. If we are to better understand impact in the future, we will need to attend not only to the outcomes for the poor, but the influences exerted on ideas of development and the fact that poverty is being tackled from a managerial rationale (SustainAbility et al. 2002) or a perspective of 'technocratic rationalism of responsible competitiveness' (Rajak 2006).

Conclusion

When we examine the role of business as a development agent today, what we are witnessing is part of a constantly shifting debate about business's contribution to society that plays out differently according to place, time and culture, but is ultimately about how the norms and values of capitalism, as embodied in the modern enterprise, can be accommodated, harnessed and utilized for societal good.

The framework of business' interactions with poverty used in this chapter shows that, even if a company focuses on its financial mission, there can be good reasons to consciously manage the relationship with society. However, companies are under no formal compulsion to do this, and although there are informal pressures, there is a case to be made that companies are renegotiating their social and environmental responsibilities in ways that meet the requirements of commercial competitiveness rather than societal good. It is evidence of this kind of shift (for example, in relation to pensions, labour relations and taxation) that make some people fearful of companies acting as development agents because, ultimately, they might pick and choose what constitutes societal good and co-opt the development process. Private sector involvement can be seen as part of a process of neo-constitutionalism whereby those responsible for managing the global economy see their rights being secured in law but are increasingly isolated from popular scrutiny (see Sum, chapter 2).

There is certainly evidence that business interacts with development in particular ways and there is reason to be concerned that it constricts the meaning of development itself (Blowfield 2005). As the business–poverty framework shows, it is something that can lead companies to rethink their relationships, but does not undermine them. Moreover, elements of the business response (for example, the adaptation of conventional management tools and concepts for development purposes; the depoliticization of economic opportunity; the reduction of complex social, cultural and economic factors to technical problems) are ones that are characteristic of contemporary development itself (Ferguson 1990). Therefore, it may be harder to argue that business might co-opt development than to make the case that business as a development agent mirrors the established norms of the predominant development discourse.

Rather than examining the role of business as a development agent that is subversive either to business or development, the main focus of this chapter has been on the possibilities and limitations of the current and likely contribution of businesses. In much of the mainstream literature on business and development there is a tendency to stress the generic strengths of private enterprise to explain the significance of the role of business in development (for example, client-focus; ability to raise capital; specific skills, tools and competencies). However, the role any single company or industry can play is greatly affected by the type of relationship it has with poverty (for example, victim or cause), whether offensive or defensive strategies are pursued, and the location and context (for example, whether or not there is a functioning civil society and state regulatory capacity). Too often, in making the case for business to act as a development agent, advocates overlook the context-specific variables and complexities that can ultimately influence outcomes in a given situation, as much as flaws in execution can.

Yet even such contextual variables are of secondary importance to the three conditions that predicate any corporate engagement in development, that is, the association of poverty with risk, opportunity and inefficiency. The examples of business responses in this chapter demonstrate that at least one of these conditions needs to be met for companies to act as development agents. However, our knowledge of how the conditions influence development is far from complete. For example, when poverty is associated with risk, it has led to genuine innovations (for example, in supply chain governance; responsibility towards producing communities; linkages between business and development organizations). To date, success has been measured in terms of the instrumental benefit for companies, not the developmental benefit for communities, and while the poor may participate, they do not have the means to hold others to account for the outcomes. Similarly, while a positive association between poverty and ROI can stimulate companies to deliver a SROI, there can be a tension between developmental outcomes and commercial imperatives, evident, for example, in how the demand for certified timber has been met largely by sourcing from developed nations rather than developing ones, and concerns that the expansion of fair trade is weakening the relationships between producers, buyers and consumers. The emphasis on the financial success, and the limited information on the social impacts, of initiatives of this kind suggest that developmental consequences can be lost or overlooked once ROI attracts more attention than SROI.

The least understood of these conditions is the association between poverty and inefficiency that may account for initiatives to combat corruption and enhance the productive capacity of the poor. Some of the optimism surrounding corporate responsibility stems from surprise about what can be shown to be an inefficiency. For example, it is possible that, if as part of lean manufacturing, workers come to be treated more as assets than commodities, dislike of inefficiency will prompt more investment in the workforce. Equally, some of the pessimism about corporate responsibility relates to the lack of action around aspects of poverty that constitute an efficiency such as casualization of the workforce, and the role of women in production.

Recognizing these conditions is an important step in understanding the parameters of possibility for business as a development agent, and in particular what dimensions of poverty are likely to be included or excluded. However, we should not treat these parameters as static. It is tempting to say that certain dimensions of poverty are excluded for structural reasons because their inclusion cannot be justified under the three conditions. Kilgour (2007) argues that some issues represent differences of interest that are inherently political and conflictual, whereas formalized corporate responsibility management assumes a degree of equality among stakeholders, and equates conflict with differences of opinion that can be resolved through dialogue. The fact that more progress has been made with the substantive dimensions to development than the process ones, such as empowerment, suggests that such a conclusion could be true. However, it might be too early to pass judgement, given instances such as the recent change in emphasis from simply expecting suppliers to comply with standards, to major brands working with supplier management and workers to increase local capacity, including creating spaces in oppressive regimes where workers can organize and collaborate. This offers the promise of a more effective way of dealing with reputational issues arising from allegations of exploitation. As the possibilities of this kind of intervention are explored, and companies become more innovative in how they address the three conditions for their being a development agent, it might be worth keeping a somewhat open mind about the extent to which business is able to develop and accommodate a more nuanced view of the poor and poverty than it has shown until now.

At the same time, certain aspects of social development that complement the interests of business are being normalized, and this could explain why they appear less likely to be critiqued. These include, for instance, flexible labour markets in contrast to the emphasis on secure employment in previous eras, private ownership of natural resources and the free flow of capital. From the perspective of business as a development agent, these trends will not be opposed because they do not represent a risk, opportunity or inefficiency. While it is hard to claim that the role of business in development exacerbates such trends in a significant way, there are issues of legitimization and delegitimization that need to be addressed. Corporate responsibility plays an important role in framing our understanding of poverty and development. We have seen, for example, how modern management rationalism has been incorporated into the way poverty is understood and approached. Similarly, we have seen examples where a term, such as empowerment, has come to be associated with a business quality, such as entrepreneurship, thereby imbuing business behaviour with a new moral creditworthiness. This is problematic morally if notions of good come to be reassessed using commercial criteria (Blowfield and Dolan 2008), but also from a technical developmental perspective where a distinction has to be drawn between very different types of entrepreneurs some of whom play an essential role in growth and innovation that is conducive to poverty reduction, while others create few jobs and have little security.[6]

However, there are examples of issues that are developmentally important being accommodated even though this means challenging conventional business wisdom. For example, features of fair trade, such as supply chain trust and equity, long-term contracts and investment in producers, have found their way into the language and programmes of companies, such as Starbucks (Macdonald 2007). As Kolk and van Tulder (2006) show in the context of voluntary standards, a variety of pressures contribute to what is ultimately legitimized or ignored, and often what emerges is a 'sector conditioned morality' that reflects a minimum level of expectation from civil society, on the one hand, and a ceiling level acceptable to an industry, on the other.

The experience of corporate responsibility and business as a development agent suggests that development ends can best be served when there is genuine collaboration whereby different sectors pursue shared or complementary poverty objectives. This conclusion can be challenged on the grounds that it relies on evidence about large companies, and says nothing about the smaller firms and informal sector that are such an important feature of developing economies. It also disregards changes associated with the new influx of foreign direct investment from countries, such as China and India, and the different types of relationship that may emerge as a result, just as it ignores the role large domestic companies played in the development of countries such as the Republic of Korea, Singapore and Taiwan. However, even if consideration of these dimensions to business in developing economies revealed very different features of managing the relationship with society, a significant part of the business community would still be looking to employ collaborative models. Until now, collaboration has often been seen as synonymous with partnership, but although the contribution of partnerships can be important, collaboration can take a range of forms. For example, it could be as simple as making community development expertise available to a bank investing in forest conservation. But it could involve intersectoral collaboration to achieve the appropriate balance between voluntary regulation of supply chains and statutory regulation of factories. It could mean finding the right mix of international engagement and local activity to sustain the kind of producer-to-consumer bond envisaged by some proponents of fair trade. There are enormous challenges about how to realize these collaborations so that, for example, they are not fatally distorted by power asymmetries, or they succeed in valuing non-financial returns. They raise important questions about the future of development planning and prevalent command and control, input-output models. There are implications for the role of business, but also for conventional development agents.

Nonetheless, based on the current pattern of corporate engagement in development, there are good reasons to think a more sophisticated collaborative intersector model than exists at present would be appealing. However, a stumbling block could be companies' unwillingness to be accountable for development objectives in any rigorous way. A test of how far this can be overcome may be the recent wave of socially-oriented entrepreneurs claiming a blend of social and commercial vision. If these find viable ways to demonstrate social returns, they may influence other companies that recognize a role as development agent, but limit their accountability to internal rationalization.

To date, there is evidence that some companies are mindful of poverty, showing a degree of innovation in how they respond. But they have a narrow perspective on what to be accountable for and to whom, and the incentives to be more rigorous about this are lacking. At present, the conditions under which business engages in poverty alleviation are ones rooted in self-interest. What are presented as countervailing agents have made some progress in expanding this definition of self-interest, but government and non-government agents have had more success in getting companies to commit to development objectives than they have in holding them to account for delivering on them. By clarifying how business relates to poverty, and under what conditions it chooses to act as a development agent, we may establish a more solid base for holding companies to account, and making it in their interests to be more accountable. Without this accountability there will always be a randomness and unpredictability to business's interpretation of its responsibilities, leaving open the possibility that for all of the justification for business to be a development agent, it will remain a development maverick.

Notes

1. See, for instance, the very different perspectives of Immanuel Wallerstein, Antonio Negri, Joseph Stiglitz and David Henderson.
2. The partnership involves farming communities, NGOs, the UNDP and government agencies, as well as some more modern elements of community development, such

as microfinance, support for entrepreneurs, promoting crop diversification and biodiversity projects.
3. See, for example, the studies of Unilever-Indonesia and South African Breweries (Clay 2005; Kapstein 2008; BER 2008).
4. This complexity is evident in impact work commissioned by Unilever, but those studies focus on that company as a development tool rather than a development agent.
5. Catherine Dolan, discussions with author, July 2008.
6. Christensen et al. (2006); Karnani (2007); Patricof and Sunderland (2006).

References

Barrientos, S. and S. Smith, 'Do workers benefit from ethical trade? Assessing codes of labour practice in global production systems', *Third World Quarterly*, Vol. 28, No. 4 (2007) 713–29.

BER (Bureau for Economic Research), *The Contribution of South African Breweries Limited to the South African Economy* (Cape Town: Bureau for Economic Research, 2008).

Berle, A.A. and G.C. Means, *The Modern Corporation and Private Property* (New York and Chicago: Commerce Clearing House, Loose leaf service division of the Corporation Trust Company, 1932).

Blowfield, M.E., 'Reasons to be cheerful? What we know about CSR's impact', *Third World Quarterly*, Vol. 28, No. 4 (2007) 683–95.

———, 'Corporate social responsibility – The failing discipline and why it matters for international relations', *International Relations*, Vol. 19, No. 2 (2005) 173–91.

———, 'Implementation deficits of ethical trade systems: Lessons from the Indonesian cocoa and timber industries', *Journal of Corporate Citizenship*, No. 13 (2004) 77–90.

Blowfield, M.E. and C. Dolan, 'Stewards of virtue: The ethical dilemma of CSR in Africa', *Development and Change*, Vol. 39, No. 1 (2008) 1–23.

Blowfield, M.E. and A. Murray, *Corporate Responsibility: A Critical Introduction* (Oxford: Oxford University Press, 2008).

Bond, P., 'Global governance campaigning and MDGs: From top-down to bottom-up anti-poverty work', *Third World Quarterly*, Vol. 27, No. 2 (2006) 339–54.

Bornstein, D., *How to Change the World: Social Entrepreneurs and the Power of New Ideas* (Oxford: Oxford University Press, 2004).

Brainard, L., *Transforming the Development Landscape: The Role of the Private Sector* (Washington, DC: Brookings Institution Press, 2006).

Brugmann, J. and C.K. Prahalad, 'Cocreating business's new social compact', *Harvard Business Review*, February (2007) 80–90.

Carroll, A.B., 'Corporate social responsibility: Evolution of a definitional construct', *Business and Society*, Vol. 38, September (1999) 268–95.

Chan, A. and K. Siu, *Wal-Mart's CSR and Labor Standards in China*, International Research Network on Business, Development and Society Workshop, Copenhagen, 12–14 September 2007.

Chang, H., *Kicking Away the Ladder: Development Strategy in Historical Perspective* (London: Anthem, 2002).

Christensen, C.M., H. Baumann, R. Ruggles and T. Sadtler, 'Disruptive innovation for social change', *Harvard Business Review*, December (2006) 94–102.

Clay, Jason, *Exploring the Links between International Business and Poverty Reduction: A Case Study of Unilever in Indonesia* (Oxford: Oxfam GB, Novib [Oxfam Netherlands], and Unilever, 2005).

Davis, K., 'The case for and against business assumption of social responsibilities', *Academy of Management Review*, Vol. 16, Issue 2 (1973) 312–22.

Dees, J.G., *The Meaning of 'Social Entrepreneurship'*, comments and suggestions contributed from the Social Entrepreneurship Funders Working Group, 31 October (1998). www.fntc.info/files/documents/The%20meaning%20of%20Social%20Entreneurship.pdf (accessed on 17 March 2009).

Ellis, K., *Assessing Business Development Impact: A Management Framework for Improved Economic and Socio-Economic Performance Reporting* (London: Overseas Development Institute, 2008).

Ferguson, J., *The Anti-Politics Machine: 'Development,' Depoliticization, and Bureaucratic Power in Lesotho* (Cambridge: Cambridge University Press, 1990).

Fig, D. (ed.), *Staking Their Claims: Corporate Social and Environmental Responsibility in South Africa* (Scottsville: UKZN Press, 2007a).

——, *Corporations and Moral Purpose: South Africa's Truth and Reconciliation Commission and Business Responsibility for Apartheid*, paper prepared for the Business in Development Workshop, Copenhagen Business School (Copenhagen: Copenhagen Business School, 2007b).

Friedman, M., *Capitalism and Freedom* (Chicago, IL: University of Chicago Press, 1962).

Glover, D., 'Monsanto and smallholder farmers: A case study in CSR', *Third World Quarterly*, Vol. 28, No. 4 (2007) 851–67.

Graham, D. and N. Woods, 'Making corporate self-regulation effective in developing countries', *World Development*, Vol. 34, No. 5 (2006) 868–83.

Hamann, R., 'Is corporate citizenship making a difference?', *Journal of Corporate Citizenship*, Winter (2007) 15–29.

Hammond, A.L., W.J. Kramer, R.S. Katz, J.T. Tran and C. Walker, *The Next Four Billion: Market Size and Business Strategy at the Base of the Pyramid* (Washington, DC: International Finance Corporation/World Resources Institute, 2007).

Hart, S.L., *Capitalism at the Crossroads: The Unlimited Business Opportunities in Solving the World's Most Difficult Problems* (Upper Saddle River, NJ: Wharton School Publishing, 2005).

Jenkins, R.O., 'Globalization, corporate social responsibility and poverty', *International Affairs*, Vol. 81, No. 3 (2005) 525–40.

Kapstein, E.B., *Measuring Unilever's Economic Footprint: The Case of South Africa* (London: Unilever, 2008).

Karnani, A., 'The mirage of marketing to the bottom of the pyramid', *California Management Review*, Vol. 49, No. 4 (2007) 90.

Khurana, R., *From Higher Aims to Hired Hands: The Social Transformation of American Business Schools and the Unfulfilled Promise of Management as a Profession* (Princeton: Princeton University Press, 2007).

Kilgour, M., 'The UN Global Compact and substantive equality for women: Revealing a "well hidden" mandate', *Third World Quaterly*, Vol. 28, No. 4 (2007) 751–73.

Kolk, A. and R. van Tulder, 'Poverty alleviation as business strategy? Evaluating commitments of frontrunner multinational corporations', *World Development*, Vol. 34, No. 5 (2006) 789–801.

Kramer, M. and J. Kania, 'Changing the game: Leading corporations switch from defense to offense in solving global problems', *Stanford Social Innovation Review*, Spring (2006) 20–7.

Leigh-Taylor, P., 'In the market but not of it: Fair trade coffee and Forest Stewardship Council certification as market-based social change', *World Development*, Vol. 33, No. 1 (2005) 129–47.

Levy, D. and P. Newell, 'Business strategy and international environmental governance: Toward a neo-Gramscian synthesis', *Global Environmental Politics*, Vol. 2, No. 4 (2002) 84–101.

Macdonald, K., 'Globalising justice within coffee supply chains? Fair trade, Starbucks and the transformation of supply chain governance', *Third World Quarterly*, Vol. 28, No. 4, June (2007) 793–812.

Nelson, J., *Building Linkages for Competitive and Responsible Entrepreneurship* (Cambridge, MA: Harvard University, John F. Kennedy School of Government, and UNIDO, 2007).

Newell, P. and J.G. Frynas, 'Beyond CSR? Business, poverty and social justice: an introduction', *Third World Quarterly*, Vol. 28, No. 4 (2007) 669–81.

Newell, P. and A. Muro, 'Corporate social and environmental responsibility in Argentina: The evolution of an agenda', *Journal of Corporate Citizenship*, No. 24 (2006) 49–68.

O'Rourke, K.H. and J.G. Williamson, *Globalization and History: The Evolution of a Nineteenth-Century Atlantic Economy* (Cambridge, MA: MIT Press, 1999).

Patricof, A. and J. Sunderland, 'Venture capital for development'. In L. Brainard (ed.), *Transforming the Development Landscape: The Role of the Private Sector* (Washington, DC: Brookings Institution, 2006).

Pearson, R., 'Beyond women workers: Gendering CSR', *Third World Quarterly*, Vol. 28, No. 4 (2007) 731–49.

Perez-Aleman, Paola, *New Standards, MNC–NGO Partnerships and the Inclusion of Small Producers in Latin America: Some Lessons for State Policy*, paper presented at the Conference on Business, Social Policy and Corporate Political Influence in Developing Countries, Geneva, 12–13 November 2007 (Geneva: UNRISD, 2007).

Prahalad, C.K., *The Fortune at the Bottom of the Pyramid: Eradicating Poverty through Profits* (Upper Saddle River, NJ: Wharton School Publishing, 2005).

Prahalad, C.K. and S.L. Hart, 'The fortune at the bottom of the pyramid', *Strategy + Business*, No. 26 (2002) 2–14.

Rajak, D., 'The gift of CSR: Power and the pursuit of responsibility in the mining industry'. In W. Visser, M. McIntosh and C. Middleton (eds), *Corporate Citizenship in Africa: Lessons from the Past, Paths to the Future* (Sheffield: Greenleaf Publishing, 2006).

Rangan, V.K., 'Business solutions for the global poor: Creating social and economic value'. In V.K. Rangan, John A. Quelch, Gustavo Herrero and Brooke Barton (eds), *Conference on Global Poverty: Business Solutions and Approaches* (San Francisco, CA: Jossey-Bass (John Wiley & Sons, Inc.), 2007).

Raynolds, L.T., D. Murray and P. Leigh-Taylor, 'Fair trade: Building producer capacity via global networks', *Journal of International Development*, No. 16 (2004) 1109–21.

Robins, N., 'The imperious company', *Journal of Corporate Citizenship*, No. 25 (2007) 31–42.

Ruggie, J.G., 'Taking embedded liberalism global: The corporate connection'. In D. Held and M. Koenig-Archibugi (eds), *Taming Globalization: Frontiers of Governance* (Cambridge: Polity Press, 2003).

Saith, A., 'From universal values to Millennium Development Goals: Lost in translation', *Development and Change*, Vol. 37, No. 6 (2006) 1167–99.

Seelos, C. and J. Mair, 'Social entrepreneurship: Creating new business models to serve the poor', *Business Horizons*, Vol. 48, No. 3 (2005) 247–52.

SustainAbility, International Finance Corporation (IFC) and Ethos Institute, *Developing Value: The Business Case for Sustainability in Emerging Markets* (London: SustainAbility, 2002).

Utting, P., *CSR and Equality* (London: Third World Foundation for Social and Economic Studies, 2007).

Wall, C., 2007, *Kazakh Public Policy and Corporate Social Responsibility: An Analysis of Health Care Provision in an Era of CSR and Kazakh Nationalism*, presented at the Conference on Business, Social Policy and Corporate Political Influence in Developing Countries, Geneva, 12–13 November 2007 (Geneva: UNRISD, 2007).

Warden, Staci, *Joining the Fight against Global Poverty: A Menu for Corporate Engagement* (Washington, DC: Center for Global Development, 2007).

WBCSD (World Business Council for Sustainable Development), *Measuring Impact beyond the Bottom Line* (Geneva: WBCSD, 2008).

——, *Doing Business with the World: The New Role of Corporate Leadership in Global Development* (Geneva: WBCSD, 2007).

Wilson, C., *Make Poverty Business: Increase Profits and Reduce Risks by Engaging with the Poor* (Sheffield: Greenleaf, 2006).

6
Transnational Corporations and Poverty Reduction: Strategic and Regional Variations

Rob van Tulder

Introduction: the need for a descriptive approach

Corporate interest in the issue of poverty is as old as the industrial revolution. In the nineteenth century, the founders of major corporations not only invested in the establishment of their factories, but also created 'company villages' and 'social programmes' with a view to enhancing the social well-being of their workers. Most strategies represented a combination of enlightened self-interest, efforts to keep the (upcoming) trade unions at bay and attempts to either prevent government regulation or fill the gaps left by laissez-faire governments. In the post-war period the poverty issue became the prime responsibility of governments (welfare states) and civil society (development aid and local charity). If any, corporations had only indirect responsibility for poverty. Gradually, since the mid-1990s and with increasing pace since the beginning of the twenty-first century, the (potential) contribution and direct responsibility of corporations to alleviating global poverty – as opposed to local poverty – has received increasing attention again (Kolk et al. 2006; Wilson and Wilson 2006; Prahalad 2005). This attention is accompanied by major controversy: in particular, the role of transnational corporations (TNCs) investing in developing countries has been heralded by some as a positive force to alleviate poverty, while others have been stressing the job-displacing and income inequalities precipitating effects of the same investments.

This chapter addresses the manner in which the world's largest firms are engaging with the issue of poverty reduction at home and abroad. It considers, in particular, whether different regional 'varieties of capitalism' (VoC)[1] or 'business systems' (see, for example, Jackson and Deeg 2008), and different industries, lead to divergent approaches towards poverty. The chapter focuses on the 100 largest firms in the world – as measured by 2006 turnover (see Annex 6.1). The sample contains sufficient representative firms from five industries and three different regions to facilitate international comparison of United States (US), European and East Asian (in particular Chinese and Japanese) firms.

This chapter is largely descriptive. It identifies and documents various strategies that can be, and are, employed by corporations to reduce poverty, and in so doing provides a first assessment on the substance of these strategies, while also considering which regional variety of capitalism (and business style of leadership) seems to have developed the most proactive strategies towards poverty reduction. The prescriptive part of the chapter deals with the question of whether an active or proactive strategy towards poverty can be considered a 'sustainable corporate story' and whether examples or components of such a story already exist. A *sustainable corporate story* requires firms to come up with a convincing analysis of the issue at hand, in which primary responsibilities are sufficiently specified and the approach chosen is credibly elaborated at both the strategic and operational levels. The partnership of logistics firm TNT with the United Nations (UN) World Food Programme (WFP) presents an interesting example. Since food is in ample supply around the world, hunger can be considered primarily a problem of unequal distribution. TNT explains its involvement in the WFP as a corporate solution to a global problem. This can be considered a relatively sophisticated 'story' at the strategic level. At the more operational level, TNT has been criticized for its aggressive employee (post deliverers) negotiations intended to suppress wages. At the operational level, thus, the story is considered less sophisticated than at the strategic level.

The more sophisticated the 'story' of a corporation is, the more it receives a 'moral authority' in relation to a particular issue, which as a consequence increases its 'licence to operate' and its overall legitimacy (Schultz et al. 2000). Stories or 'narratives' not only set the agenda from the perspective of firms, but – when contained in public statements like corporate responsibility reports and/or codes of conduct – often also represent their strategic reality (Fortanier and Kolk 2007).

Consider, for instance, the following statements/stories that have been communicated by some of the 100 largest firms in the world on the issue of poverty:

- Oil company British Petroleum:
  Our primary means of making a positive impact on poverty is through aligning our own operations with local people's needs.... We can sell affordable products that enable people to improve their standard of living, including motor and heating fuels.... Energy is a major factor in lifting people out of poverty.
- Bank HSBC:
  Supporting microfinance is one of the ways in which financial institutions can support the UN Millennium Development Goal of eradicating extreme poverty.

- Consumer electronics firm Matsushita:
  At present, the world has a large number of people living in poverty and needs a level of economic growth sufficient to raise their standard of living. At the same time we must not be allowed to damage the environment ... We are thus faced with the problem of combining economic growth and environmental conservation.... Enterprises around the world are now under pressure to put in place sustainable business models that will allow the two to be combined.

What do these exemplary statements represent? Integrated strategies or incidental cases? Window-dressing and a reaction to critical stakeholders or authentic efforts to deal with the issue? A first step towards a sophisticated approach on poverty? A 'go-it-alone' strategy or an invitation to work together on solving the issue?

An examination of the poverty-related statements of major corporations reveals a considerable diversity of approaches towards poverty. At the same time, it also illustrates the difficulty of analysing these corporate approaches on a comparative basis. The lack of sophisticated descriptive business models – that include corporate responsibility as an integral part of strategy – is probably also the main reason why so many of the existing studies on corporate approaches towards poverty have been on the basis of a few case studies or prescriptive reasoning in which the moral obligation of firms is explained and/or the opportunities of the issue for firms in general are highlighted (see Prahalad 2005; Wilson and Wilson 2006; Lodge and Wilson 2006; Hart and Sharma 2004). Prescriptive approaches suffer from 'case-study bias' or the 'advisory disease' which implies that analysts have a solution before diagnosing the real issue at hand (van Tulder 2007), which also makes them sometimes even ideological and particularly difficult to use for more general purposes in which the complexities of the poverty issue are addressed fully. The prime aim of this chapter, therefore, is descriptive and aims at reaching a more thorough understanding of the question concerning where corporations around the world are in their approach towards poverty, and whether this can be considered sufficient and credible ('sustainable') as a poverty approach.

To tackle this analytical challenge, this chapter, first, discusses how the 'issue' of poverty alleviation by corporations has developed over time. This discussion is used to identify major dimensions as well as their level of maturity in the public debate. The chapter discusses propositions made since the early twenty-first century to increase the involvement of business in poverty reduction and/or sketch an 'entrepreneurial way' out of the poverty trap, such as public–private partnerships, the 'bottom-of-the pyramid (BOP)', microcredit, supply chain management, issue management and the search for new generic business models.

Secondly, this overview of most important dimensions/categories facilitates a typology of possible international business strategies towards poverty. This typology elaborates on the well-known – but poorly understood – CSR acronym: (1) in-active (corporate self responsibility), (2) re-active (corporate social responsiveness), (3) active (corporate social responsibility), (4) pro-active (corporate societal responsibility) (see van Tulder, with van der Zwart 2006). What constitutes a 'sustainable corporate story'?

Thirdly, this strategic categorization is empirically applied to the sample of the world's one hundred largest firms. The measures taken by these firms and the initiatives supported by their chief executive officers (CEOs) will be inventoried and classified. The result provides an overview of the 'breadth' and 'depth' of the approaches towards poverty reduction of these corporations and their corporate leaders. The chapter will consider whether corporate poverty strategies are partly the result of the industry or the regional variety of capitalism from which the firm originates. The concluding section will consider to what extent the present state of affairs regarding the involvement of (big) business in poverty reduction provides grounds for optimism or pessimism.

The genealogy of 'poverty' as a business issue

Since the beginning of the twenty-first century, the potential contribution of corporations to a large number of societal issues has received increasing attention, but has already been been the subject of considerable controversy. This also applies to arguably the biggest global challenge of the moment: alleviating poverty. Until recently, the issue of poverty was largely ignored in management theory and practice (Jain and Vachani 2006). There are at least three reasons for this. First, poor people operate in the informal economy and have limited buying power. Second, the definition of poverty itself is complex. Do we consider absolute or relative poverty for instance? What about the 'working poor'? Third, the issue of poverty has many 'issue owners' and it is extremely hard to identify primary responsibilities. Poverty for some is a macroeconomic issue that is related to the growth of economies in general, to others poverty can be directly associated with the alleged unemployment effects of relocation strategies of TNCs, while others again consider poverty primarily a mental state that can largely be attributed to personal traits and abilities.

Studies that tried to establish a link between poverty and TNC strategy have focused on the relationship between foreign direct investment (FDI), employment and income inequality (Fortanier 2008). It was found, for instance, that TNC affiliates pay on average higher wages than local firms and are more capital-intensive. What this means for poverty alleviation, however, is difficult to establish. Direct TNC employment creation can be considered more beneficial to skilled than unskilled workers. The quality of the employment provided by TNCs, thereby, is more often questioned. It has also been suggested that the policy competition between governments to attract FDI can lead to less stringent safety and health regulation, as well as lower wages – sometimes below subsistence level – thus creating a subclass of so-called 'working poor'. Management studies at the moment lack the firm-specific strategic frameworks, the conceptual tools, as well as the firm-specific data to address the poverty issue in all these dimensions.

This rather ambiguous state of affairs, however, has not prevented the issue from appearing prominently on the agenda of corporate decision makers. Neither did it prevent business gurus from devising formulas in which poverty is considered an opportunity rather than a threat. Consequently, the mood towards the involvement of firms, in general, and TNCs, specifically, in poverty alleviation is changing. Will this mood-change prove sustainable or is it merely a new management gimmick? What is the influence of other issues like global warming? The answer to these questions largely depends on a proper assessment of the way poverty as a challenge has become an 'issue' for corporations. Issues generally follow a lifecycle: from birth and growth, towards development, maturity and settlement. What opportunities have developed as regards the issue of poverty-as-business-challenge/responsibility?

Birth and growth: triggering incidents and growing societal discontent

The growth of an issue occurs when those who first encounter it fail to address it adequately. The discontent grows when the issue can be clearly defined, is given a popular name and the media latches onto unsuspecting protagonists. Examples include: 'Frankenstein Food' (introduced by Prince Charles), or 'Global warming' (supported by Nobel Prize Laureates or former vice president Gore). The transition to this phase is often initiated by a *triggering event,* usually organized by a visible and legitimate stakeholder. Important triggering events of the 'poverty-as-business-challenge' issue, included meetings of international organizations like the World Trade Organization (WTO), the World Bank and the G-8 Summits. 'The Millennium Development Goals (MDGs)', 'Decent work', 'outsourcing', the 'Wal-Mart effect', and the 'race to the bottom' became triggering concepts. Triggering events and concepts varied, however, for different dimensions of poverty. Worldwide attention to the issue of 'absolute' poverty was renewed in 2000, when 189 countries formulated eight MDGs and specified halving poverty – defined as those people living on less than a dollar a day – by the year 2015, as their prime goal (MDG1). Perhaps more importantly, an instrumental goal (MDG8) was formulated, in which partnerships with private corporations and a good business climate were considered vital to achieve sustainable development. Further triggers involved the 'good governance' agenda of the World Bank and the International Monetary Fund (IMF); the G-8 Gleneagles summit and the celebrity-backed 'Make Poverty History' campaign; as well as the intellectual underpinning provided by best-selling writers like Hernando de Soto (2000), Jeffrey Sachs (2005) and C.K. Prahalad (2005).

The issue of *working poor and relative poverty* also received renewed attention during the 1990s, following the fall of the Berlin Wall and as concerns mounted about the social effects of globalization and economic liberalization. The most important allegation, notably from trade unions, was that a 'race to the bottom' had relaxed labour regulation and lowered wages and taxes to attract TNCs. Furthermore, TNCs were accused of actively stimulating such a race by playing off governments against one another in a search for the weakest possible regulation. While the extent and nature of this phenomenon is the subject of much controversy, it has motivated the International Labour Office (ILO) to intensify its campaign for 'decent work'. Since the end of the 1990s, many elections in developed countries have had the outsourcing/offshoring issue as a core point of dispute. Moreover, 'fair labour' and 'fair trade' movements also targeted the issue of working poor as a result of the unfair operation of the international trading system and the (perceived) negative consequences of the inclusion of workers in the international supply chains of multinationals. More recently, the struggle for decent wages and the problems associated with 'working poor' received a boost through the so-called 'Wal-Mart effect'. As had occurred some years earlier through 'the McDonaldization of society' (Ritzer 1993), a new corporate icon triggered interest in an issue.

Development and maturity: measurement and implementation

An issue enters the development phase when important stakeholders, either individually or collectively, demand concrete changes to corporate policies and scholars develop models, approaches and strategies that can solve the issue. In the mature or settlement phase, the issue is addressed by concrete strategies, new legislation and the like, which implies that the 'expectational' gap gets bridged. If corporations do not develop credible strategies in this phase the issue remains controversial – depending on the relative strength of the stakeholders and on the extent to which 'issue fatigue' can also appear. The above triggering events precipitated a large number of initiatives, some of which already existed, in some form, long before the actual events appeared. Key initiatives include the following:

- *MDGs:* Attempts to measure the concrete contributions of corporations to achieving the MDGs.
- *Labelling:* Using labelling, notably fair trade labels, to demonstrate a company's or a group of companies' commitment to society and poverty alleviation, and provide consumers with information on the quality and contents of products.

- *Codes of conduct:* Adopted by companies, industry bodies or multistake-holder entities, codes often refer to the issue of relative poverty and the working poor, through provisions on labour conditions.
- *Bottom of the pyramid (BOP):* An approach that aims to tap the multi-trillion dollar market among the world's 4 billion living on less than US$1,500[2] and to 'eradicate poverty through profits' (Prahalad 2005). There are, in fact, two approaches: a 'narrow BOP' strategy that only focuses on the market opportunities and a 'broad BOP' strategy that takes the wider repercussions and the net effects of the strategy into consideration.[3]
- *New business models:* These aim to go beyond treating the poor as consumers and aim to reduce both poverty and risk by addressing elements that are 'missing' from the physical, economic and legal infrastructure of a developing economy and then finding alternatives (Wilson and Wilson 2006: 128) that are both economically feasible and socially desirable.
- *Microcredit:* An entrepreneurial way out of poverty, providing, in 2006, an estimated 125 million people with access to loans at rates considerably below those charged by money lenders, but also high yields for the financial institutions involved.
- *Partnerships:* Since the 2002 World Summit on Sustainable Development (WSSD) in Johannesburg, so-called 'cross-sector' partnerships have become important instruments for addressing problems of global development and reaching the Millennium Development Goals (MDGs), in which the contribution of companies is seen as crucial. Additionally, there has also been increasing interest in public–private partnerships, in which companies cooperate with governments or international organizations (Chataway and Smith 2006; Samii et al. 2002).
- *Poverty as issue and stakeholder management:* Strategic management of firms is increasingly aimed at 'issues' and related reputation management and corporate branding (van Tulder, with van der Zwart 2006; Fombrun and van Riel 2004). More and more firms are engaging in so-called 'stakeholder dialogues', which, in turn, encourage a more pro-active response from companies and their leaders.

So what are the critical societal issues according to business leaders? In the introduction to this chapter we noted already a number of statements that make clear that business leaders have discovered 'poverty' as an issue, but there are also other issues. What is the relative ranking given to various issues? Research by the Rotterdam School of Management (RSM) Erasmus University (Kaptein et al. 2007), using a representative sample of the CEOs of the 200 largest firms in Europe, shows that these firms (over the 1990s and early twenty-first century) have started to integrate CSR strategies into their mainstream or 'core' strategies. This means that the CSR staff increased, and that the CEO (33 per cent) or another board member (34 per cent) has become responsible within the company, for leading a growing number of initiatives intended to operationalize this strategy (for example, reports, whistle-blowing procedures, standardization, codes, CSR issues in marketing campaigns). Furthermore, attention to a large number of issues – including poverty – has increased substantially since the 1980s. In 2007, CEOs indicated that they perceived the following issues as having the highest impact: corruption (4.6 on a scale of 5), transparency, health and safety (4.5), labour rights, climate change (4.3). They scored the following as having somewhat less impact: income equality, fair wages, fair trade and procurement (3.9), ecological diversity (3.7), education (3.5) and poverty (3.0). However, even the general issue of poverty scored above the mean and demonstrated a significant increase from the 1990s.

Business strategies towards poverty reduction

Poverty eradication as a business challenge is still in the approximate development phase of its lifecycle. Triggering events have resulted in relatively concrete aims and goals; new concepts have been developed that structure the debate; but the issues are not yet clearly addressed, let alone resolved. New concepts are not undisputed, the operationalizations are not always clear and are not well coordinated, while the relationship between business strategies and the resolution of the issue at hand are not yet clear. There is abundant room for the public relations (PR) activities of firms in which a concept (like microcredits or the BOP) can be embraced only to ward off critical stakeholders. With regard to corporate statements on poverty: what makes these core firm strategies and beliefs, rather than marginal public relation statements?

The assessment of corporate strategies on societal themes represents the area of corporate responsibility, often abbreviated as 'CSR'. But the catch-all category of 'CSR' in fact obscures important strategic variability and contextualization. The alignment of CSR strategies and the interests of the poor depends on the circumstances and the concrete elaborations of business strategies in developing countries (see Blowfield 2005, and in chapter 5). In that context, four CSR approaches with different procedural attributes can be proposed in which the very CSR abbreviation also has four different meanings: in-active, re-active, active and pro-active (see Preston and Post 1975; van Tulder, with van der Zwart 2006). The continuum of CSR business strategies is conceptually related to the basic distinction in conventional moral theory between what is required and what is desired, or between the 'morality of duty' and the 'morality of aspiration' (Michaelson 2006). Table 6.1 summarizes the most important characteristics of these four approaches to CSR and gives some operationalizations of indicators of corporate poverty strategies.

Inactive approaches

The *inactive* approach reflects Friedman's classic notion that the only responsibility companies (can) have is to generate profits, which, in turn, generates

Table 6.1 Four CSR approaches towards poverty

In-active	Re-active	Active	Pro-active
Corporate *self* responsibility	Corporate social *responsiveness*	Corporate social *responsibility*	Corporate *societal* responsibility
Legal compliance and utilitarian motives	Moral (negative) duty compliance	Choice for responsibility and virtue	Choice for interactive responsibility
Efficiency	Limit inefficiency	Equity/ethics	Effectiveness
Indifference	compliance	integrity	Discourse ethics
Inside-in	Outside-in	Inside-out	In-outside-in/out
'Doing things right'	'Don't do things wrong'	'Doing the right things'	'Doing the right things right'
'Doing well'	'Doing well and doing good'	'Doing good'	'Doing well by doing good'
Poverty approach: • No explicit statements on poverty • We create jobs and employment (as by-product of profit maximization) • Payment of taxes • Affordable products • No code of conduct and/or low compliance likelihood • No support for labels • No separate business model for poor	*Poverty approach:* • Contribution to economic growth • Narrow BOP: mention of market changes in poor regions • Creation of local employment used defensively • Microcredits as (small) part of philanthropy • Transfer of technology and knowledge mentioned, but not specified • Vague code and low specificity as regards poverty • Support for Global Compact and modest support for Global Reporting Initiative (GRI) • Dialogue vaguely mentioned	*Poverty approach:* • Explicit statement on moral unacceptability of poverty • Definition of decent wage • Broad BOP: explicit view on how this strategy addresses poverty alleviation (net effect) • Creation of local employment opportunities at suppliers • Microcredits as part of business strategy • Transfer of technology and knowledge is specified • Explicit support for MDG1	*Poverty approach:* • Strategic statement on poverty • Explicit support for all MDGs (including Goal 8 on partnerships) • Active partnerships with non-governmental organizations (NGOs) and international organizations on poverty • Very explicit code and support of highest possible transparency (GRI) • Transfer of technology and knowledge is specified and discussed for its impact on poverty alleviation

(Continued)

Table 6.1   (Continued)

In-active	Re-active	Active	Pro-active
		• Wholehearted support for GRI • Philanthropy is aimed at poverty in general • Specific code and/or labelling on poverty and/or fair trade	• Codes and labelling activities part of a contract with third parties (high specificity and high compliance likelihood) • Dialogues as an explicit tool to raise strategic effectiveness • Search for a separate (strategic) business model for the poor
'What is required' Economic responsibility (Wealth oriented) Narrow (internal) CSR		← — — — →	'What is desired' Social responsibility (Welfare oriented) Broad (external) CSR

Source: Compiled by the author.

jobs and societal wealth. This is a fundamentally inward-looking (inside-in) business perspective, aimed at efficiency in the immediate market environment. Entrepreneurs are particularly concerned with 'doing things right'. Good business from this perspective equals operational excellence. CSR thus amounts to 'corporate *self* responsibility'. This narrow approach to CSR requires no explicit strategy towards poverty alleviation. It aims at the prime 'fiduciary duties' of managers vis-à-vis the owners of the corporation, which could imply affordable products, the growth of the corporation, paying taxes and job/employment creation, but only as the indirect by-product of a strategy aimed at profit maximization. When faced with the trade-off between job creation and efficiency enhancement (or shareholder value maximization), these firms will choose the latter. The company is relatively indifferent towards the issue of poverty. The corporation stresses economic growth (general efficiency) and its general contribution to that as a precondition for poverty alleviation, without further specification of its own contribution. The company is relatively indifferent towards including poverty-related initiatives in its (core) business practices.

Reactive approaches

The *reactive* approach shares a focus on efficiency but with particular attention to not making any mistakes ('don't do anything wrong'). This requires an outside-in orientation. CSR translates into corporate social *responsiveness*. Corporate philanthropy is the modern expression of the charity principle and a practical manifestation of social responsiveness. In this approach the motivation for CSR is primarily grounded in 'negative duties' where firms are compelled to conform to informal, stakeholder-defined norms of appropriate behaviour (Maignan and Ralston 2002). The concept of 'conditional morality' in the sense that managers only 're-act' when competitors do the same, is also consistent with this approach. This type of firm deals with the issue of poverty primarily when confronted with actions of critical stakeholders, for instance in the area of 'working poor' and in an effort to limit the negative influences of firm strategies on poverty or restore corporate legitimacy (Lodge and Wilson 2006). Primarily in reaction to concrete triggering events – and often not spontaneously – these companies legitimize their presence in developing countries or in socially deprived regions by arguing that they potentially transfer technology, contribute to economic growth and create local job opportunities, but without specifying it in concrete terms or taking up direct responsibility. The company wants to reduce its vulnerability as regards the issue of poverty. Poverty becomes, in particular, an opportunity when the growth possibilities in the existing markets are declining. The BOP is primarily the 'base' of the pyramid. Support for guidelines like the UN's Global Compact – that are neither specific nor require high compliance – is the typical approach of a re-active CSR strategy (see Kolk and van Tulder 2005). Companies consider philanthropy a sufficient channel through which concrete poverty issues (in particular, related to disaster relief and other ad hoc events) can be dealt with.

Active approaches

An *active* approach to CSR is explicitly inspired by ethical values and virtues (or 'positive duties'). Such entrepreneurs are strongly outward-oriented (inside-out) and they adopt a 'positive duty' approach. They are set on doing 'the right thing'. CSR in this approach gets its most well-known connotation – that of corporate *social* responsibility. This type of firm has a moral judgement on the issue of poverty and tries to come up with a number of activities that are strategic (core activities) and/or complementary to its own corporate activities. Such firms, for instance, can define what 'decent wages' are and can come up with substantial philanthropic activities towards poverty alleviation in markets where it is not active. The re-active firm will primarily locate its philanthropy in the vicinity of its corporate activities (thus the growing attention for so-called 'strategic philanthropy'). The active company accepts (partially) responsibility for the issue of poverty in particular where it is directly related to its own activities and responsibilities. Poverty (the BOP) is explicitly addressed as a morally unacceptable issue for which perhaps entrepreneurial solutions exist. The (indirect) job-creating effects of the company with its suppliers are also specified. In case this company embraces, for instance, microcredits, it is not only seen as a regular market opportunity or a PR instrument, but as a strategic means for reaching the real BOP for which concrete criteria should be developed to measure its effectiveness and create ethical legitimacy.

Proactive approaches

A proactive CSR approach materializes when an entrepreneur involves external stakeholders' right at the beginning of an issue's lifecycle. This proactive CSR approach is characterized by *interactive* business practices, where an 'inside-out' and an 'outside-in' orientation complement each other. In moral philosophy, this approach has also been referred to as 'discourse ethics', where actors regularly meet in order to negotiate/talk over a number of norms to which everyone could agree (Habermas 1990): 'doing the right things right' (or 'doing well by doing good'). This form of corporate *societal* responsibility (Andriof and McIntosh 2001: 15) shifts the issue of CSR from a largely instrumental and managerial approach to one aimed at managing strategic networks in which public and private parties have a role and firms actively strike partnerships with NGOs to come up with more structural solutions to poverty. The CEO of Unilever, Anthony Burgmans, in this context likes to elaborate CSR as 'corporate *sustainable* responsibility'. Firms that aim at a proactive poverty strategy are most open to the complex and interrelated causes on poverty and acknowledge that poverty can only be solved through partnerships and issue ownership of all societal stakeholders involved. This type of firm is also willing and able to see the problematic relationship between low wages and/or low prices with low economic growth, which could hamper a more structural approach to poverty. A possible legal elaboration has been provided by Lodge and Wilson (2006) who introduced the construct of a 'World Development Corporation' – a UN-sponsored entity owned and managed by a number of TNCs with NGO support.

A sustainable corporate story?

The transition from an inactive to a more proactive approach can generally be considered to mirror ever more sophisticated corporate stories in which firms not only go beyond 'philanthropy' or their general 'fiduciary duty', but increasingly engage in partnerships with other stakeholders to deal with the more structural dimensions of poverty. The move from an inactive to an active approach is part of an 'internal alignment' process in which firms face the challenge of overcoming internal barriers to change. This relates to functional areas of management, for instance, in cases where the marketing department is not aligned with the purchasing or the Human Resource Management department. Companies face increased internal coordination problems and will have considerable difficulties in developing a coherent corporate story towards their primary stakeholders: employees, suppliers, distributors, owners/financiers and competitors. The move from a re-active to a proactive approach is part of an 'external alignment' process in which companies face the challenge of overcoming external barriers to change. In this case the relationship with secondary – often single-issue – stakeholders has to be managed in a sophisticated manner. As regards the issue of poverty, this, in particular, relates to such secondary stakeholders like human rights and fair trade organizations and/or international trade unions that have no direct link with the company's employees.

The more firms consider poverty alleviation strategies as part of their core business/competencies, the more they need to develop sustainable corporate stories. A sustainable story then becomes part of a 'sustainable competitive advantage' (Porter 1990) and philanthropy becomes part of a strategic partnership with relevant stakeholders and not an isolated strategy. The latter is the case when the poverty alleviation strategy is managed by a foundation that is relatively independent of the company, instead of part of the strategic planning of the whole company. In that case the poverty alleviation strategy becomes part of the search for a new business model that might contribute to a structural poverty alleviation approach.

Illustrative of stories and statements that might apply for the status of a 'sustainable corporate story' are quotes often found in company reports and websites, as the examples below indicate:

> 'Our primary means of making a positive impact on poverty is through aligning our own operations with local people's needs. . . . We can sell affordable products that enable people to improve their standard of living, including motor and heating fuels.' (p. 50) 'Energy is a major factor in lifting people out of poverty.' (p. 58) (British Petroleum, *Making Energy More: Sustainability Report 2005*)

> '. . . broad sustainability challenges set the context for all of the lifecycle stages. These include population growth, urbanization, poverty, education, gender equality, child mortality, maternal health, infectious diseases, biodiversity and loss of ecosystem services.' (p. 6) 'Climate change is linked to social concerns including population growth, access to mobility and poverty alleviation.' (p. 22) (Ford Motor Company, *Ford Sustainability Report 2004/5*)

> 'Supporting microfinance is one of the ways in which financial institutions can support the UN Millennium Development Goal of eradicating extreme poverty.' (p. 12) (HSBC Holdings plc, *HSBC Corporate Social Responsibility Report 2005*)

> 'While we remain humbled by the scale of poverty and disease and lost human opportunity that the world faces, we feel we are making progress towards our vision of sustainable development.' (p. 3) 'A key challenge when linking business opportunities with corporate responsibility is whether we can create new business models appropriate to low-income developing markets.' (p. 12) (Procter & Gamble, *Sustainability Report 2005*)

> 'In the wider picture of our global activities, what motivates us is the ongoing quest to improve the quality of life in the communities in which

we operate. Our initiatives are in areas such as job creation, income generation, combating poverty and hunger, guaranteeing the rights of children and adolescents, the promotion of citizenship and equality in terms of race and gender, as well as preservation of the environment.' (p. 2) (Petrobras, *Social and Environmental Report 2005*)

The following observations can be made on the basis of these and other quotes found in the annual reports of the 100 largest firms in 2006 (Annex 6.1):

General emphasis

Many firms acknowledge their status as a multinational corporation, and link this to their general interest in making 'globalization good':

- Most companies link their statement on poverty to the process of 'globalization' (making 'globalization good' implies addressing the perceived negative consequences of globalization).
- Companies also tend to explicitly mention when they operate in the 'poorest regions' of a country (see, for instance, Nissan Motor Company 2006).
- Many companies stress the importance of the creation of effective markets and improve the 'risk taking capacity of the poor' (see, for instance, Aviva 2006).
- Numerous companies link their CSR strategies to programmes in support of local communities or with reference to some of the global poverty projects (such as Global Compact or the MDGs); not often are strategies explicitly related to national poverty programmes – probably because they tend to be too political and may have to be altered if governments change. Exceptions to the latter rule can be found with state-owned companies – such as Petrobras (Brazil).
- Many firms stress their commitment to paying decent wages, and thus helping poverty alleviation through their employment creation abilities.
- Only a few explicitly stress the need for 'new business models' (such as Procter & Gamble).

Specific emphasis

Specific industries tend to address, in particular, those dimensions of poverty that are directly related to their industry:

- Energy and automotive companies stress the link between energy and poverty.
- Financial services look at the provision of microfinance and access to capital in general; some like to show that they are leading in this area (we are at the forefront; like Lloyds).
- Consumer product corporations (retail and food processing), as well as utility producers, stress the poverty alleviation potential of providing

'affordable products'; they also stress that economic growth is a necessary condition for more structural poverty alleviation (or 'raising standards of living'). The poor are primarily considered a 'market' and developing countries thus become 'developing markets' (see Procter & Gamble). Compared to other issues these firms explicitly attach priority value to the issue of poverty (see, for instance, explicit statement of Electricité de France/EdF). A number of firms explicitly uses the phrase 'sustainable development', but without exactly elaborating that term.

- Retailers (like Tesco) link the poverty issue to trade liberalization and thus directly to their supply chain, which is most vital to their competitive position.

Partnership emphasis

Many firms mention that they are partnering with NGOs or international organizations on areas that are related to the issue of poverty: community development, microfinance, literacy programmes and the like. 'Public–Private partnerships' have already been classified as indicative of a proactive strategy. But the extent to which this is the case depends strongly on the nature of the partnership and the issue involved. In case of partnerships that were (temporarily) founded for disaster relief for instance – in the case of ecological disasters like tsunamis, earthquakes or hurricanes – the approach has to be qualified as 'reactive' at best. Table 6.2 shows how specific types of partnerships can be positioned in the basic scheme of CSR approaches (see also Table 6.1).

Table 6.2 An application to partnership strategies

In-active	Re-active	Active	Pro-active
No partnership			
Disaster relief	Sponsorship		
		Microfinance (narrow approach)	
		Education	
		Literacy	
		Health (HIV/AIDS)/water provision	
			Community development; Sustainable/fair trade/labour/wages/food/taxes; Financial sector development (broader than microfinance)

Source: Compiled by the author.

Regional varieties of capitalism (VoC) and poverty approaches

What patterns can actually be found in the strategies of the 100 largest Fortune Global firms (Annex 6.1)? This chapter gives a first inventory of the poverty-related strategies of these companies for the years 2005/2006. It applies the framework of Tables 6.1 and 6.2 to each of these firms. Codes of conduct, websites, and corporate sustainability reports of each of these firms were analysed. Half of the Global Fortune 100 list of 2006 comprises European firms; around one-third is American, whereas one-sixth is Asian. This composition allows us to distinguish between general strategies and sectors, as well as regional variations and the different 'varieties of capitalism' associated with them.

General patterns

Around 58 of the largest 100 corporations had undertaken some initiative on the issue of poverty reduction. At least four firms (Citigroup, No. 14 on the list, Deutsche Bank, No. 48, Electricité de France, No. 68, and Deutsche Post, No. 75) explicitly communicated a moral statement that poverty is unacceptable. Some corporations acknowledge the issue of poverty, but link it primarily to economic growth – thus supporting the mainstream approach to poverty alleviation, which does not require an active corporate involvement. Matsushita Electric Works (No. 47 on the list), for instance, argues in its 2006 CSR report that 'at present, the world has a large number of people living in poverty and needs a level of economic growth sufficient to raise their standards of living' (Matsushita Electric Works 2006: 8). Other corporations express more explicit (active) concern over the issue of poverty and link it to their own corporate responsibilities. For instance, BP (No. 4) in its 2005 Sustainability Report states that its 'primary means of making a positive impact on poverty is through aligning our own operations with local people's needs' (BP 2005: 50). Petrobras (No. 86) states in its *Social and Environmental Report* of 2005 'what motivates us is the ongoing quest to improve the quality of life in the communities in which we operate. Our initiatives are in areas such as job creation, income generation, combating poverty and hunger' (Petrobras 2005: 2).

One out of five corporations is searching for 'partnerships' with NGOs and international organizations on the issue of poverty. One out of five corporations had also developed poverty-oriented programmes in their philanthropic activities. The Shell (No. 3) Foundation, for instance, aims to support sustainable solutions to social problems arising from the links between energy, poverty and environment with a $250 million endowment. It issued a well-received report titled *Enterprise Solutions to Poverty* (Shell Foundation 2005). However, intentions and philanthropy activities do not necessarily reveal the implementation of concrete core strategies. So we considered in more detail to what extent the 100 largest firms in the world at the moment are making their commitment to alleviate poverty more concrete. One out of ten firms on average – in particular American and Japanese firms – consider the provision of 'affordable products' as an important contribution to poverty alleviation. One out of four firms on average (24 firms) identified the creation of local employment opportunities as a major issue; half of this group (12) further specified that this also included indirect employment at suppliers. Decent wages, however, were only specified by four corporations.

Another way of concretizing a commitment is to link it to international initiatives and codes. For instance, 43 of the 100 largest firms subscribed to the UN's Global Compact in the 2000–2006 period (36 of which were European). But the Global Compact only provides general and indirect reference to poverty, while it is very weak on ensuring corporate compliance with any of its Ten Principles. Some 17 corporations expressed general support for the MDGs. One-quarter of the European firms, and less than 7 per cent of the American and Asian firms, supported the MDGs. Several firms, notably European, had been very active in further operationalizing the MDGs for their business context. Firms, like Royal Dutch Shell (No. 3) and ABN Amro (No. 82), have explicitly linked their sustainable reporting to each of the eight MDGs. As regards poverty-related international codes and labelling initiatives, the most popular initiative to date has been the 'Fair Trade' label, which has been endorsed by at least four international retailers for a number of products in their product range. The Ethical Trading Initiative is supported by three corporations, of which two are American computer and office equipment producers. On average, however, by 2006 most large companies still tended to favour their own labels and poverty-related codes, while not endorsing already existing codes or standards – such as the ILO standards.

Finally, several firms promote two entrepreneurial approaches towards poverty alleviation – microcredit and the BOP. Nearly a quarter of the top 100 firms (23) from a wide variety of industries consider microcredit an option and a complement to their main business strategy. For instance, ExxonMobil has a number of partnership projects with the United States Agency for International Development (USAID) on microfinance in areas related to its oil projects (Kazakhstan and Sakhalin). The corporation presents its microfinance activities as 'one of the many ways ExxonMobil fosters education and increased opportunities for women ... as part of the company's community investment initiative' (ExxonMobil 2005: 62). An additional nine of the 17 banks of the sample present microcredit as an interesting part for their general business strategy. The Dexia Group (No. 55), for instance, asserts itself as one of the world leaders of the international financial market of microfinance, with total assets of around $89 million in 2005 (Dexia Group 2006: 3). Other international banks have followed suit, making microcredits a mainstream instrument. The actual volume of the efforts, however, remain rather limited, which serves as an illustration of the relative difficulty with which this market can be developed. Microcredit, therefore, remains a relatively marginal activity for most banks.

As regards the BOP strategy, leading firms are still rather ambiguous. Eight of the 100 largest firms mentioned the BOP as a possibility, but have primarily embraced it as an opportunity to sell products in a poor region. Only two firms (Citigroup, No. 14; Nestlé, No. 53) have been arguing in favour of a broader BOP strategy in which they are developing an explicit view on how this strategy actually addresses poverty alleviation as a result of direct and indirect effects.

Regional VoC

Table 6.3 shows some excerpts from the poverty 'scoresheet' that was drawn up on the basis of the previous indicators for the 100 largest Global Fortune corporations in 2006. Forty-three of these firms could be positioned in one of the four CSR categories, 52 firms combined two (adjacent) CSR categories, while four spread their activities over three categories. Around two-thirds of the corporations have adopted an inactive and/or a reactive strategy towards poverty. The four corporations classified as 'proactive' have in fact adopted rather modest strategies in this area, while also embracing re-active and active traits. No corporation can be classified as wholly pro-active, whereas 40 per cent of the corporations can indeed be classified as 'inactive'.

Table 6.4 summarizes the main scores for each regional variety of capitalism. Typical (pro)active strategies are primarily embraced by European corporations, whereas the typically inactive strategy is embraced by Asian corporations. American corporations are somewhere in between, however, with a strong inclination towards the adoption of inactive and reactive strategies. This involves a 'buffering attitude' towards critical NGOs that address the issue of poverty. A good example is provided by Wal-Mart (No. 2) which, in response to the allegations contained in the Wal-Mart effect, first, created a PR 'war room' in 2005 and, next, sponsored a 'working Wal-Mart families' site which stresses the importance of the jobs provided by Wal-Mart for the local community. Wal-Mart stresses in its other communication, in particular, the fact that it offers affordable products to customers – with the suggestion, although not specified, that this might substitute for the weak buying power of its employees. 'If we can go without something to save money, we do. It's the cornerstone of our culture to pass on our saving. Every penny we save is a penny in our customer's pocket'.[4] Most of the action of Wal-Mart can be interpreted as re-active, with no efforts to work on the issue of poverty in collaboration with critical societal groups.

As regards specific industries, motor vehicles, electronics firms and retailers are, on average, the least active in the area of poverty alleviation. In these sectors, the internal sector dynamics has put a 'ceiling' on individual activities towards poverty alleviation. Active and proactive attitudes towards the issue of poverty involve 'bridging'[5] strategies. These bridging strategies are more easily adopted in Europe and, in particular, by the banking and petroleum refining industry. Regulation in Europe, as well as with these specific industries, has created a 'floor' on which more active poverty alleviation strategies have been required (see Kolk et al. 2006).

Table 6.3 A Poverty Score Sheet: Exemplary strategies, 2006

Fortune 500 position	Company	Country	Sector	Approach to poverty			
				Inactive	Reactive	Active	Pro-active
1	ExxonMobil	United States	Petroleum refining	▓	▓		
2	Wal-Mart Stores	United States	General merchandizers	▓	▓		
3	Royal Dutch Shell	Netherlands	Petroleum refining		▓	▓	▓
9	Ford Motor Company	United States	Motor vehicles and parts	▓	▓	▓	
14	Citigroup	United States	Banks: Commercial and savings		▓	▓	
17	Volkswagen	Germany	Motor vehicles and parts		▓	▓	
23	Sinopec	China	Petroleum refining	▓	▓		
24	Nippon T&T	Japan	Telecommunications		▓	▓	
25	Carrefour	France	Food and drug stores		▓		
32	State Grid	China	Utilities	▓	▓		
46	Samsung Electronics	Rep. of Korea	Electronics, electrical equipment	▓	▓	▓	
47	Matsushita Electric Ind.	Japan	Electronics, electrical equipment		▓	▓	▓
53	Nestlé	Switzerland	Food consumer products		▓	▓	
59	Tesco	United Kingdom	Food and drug stores		▓	▓	
68	Electricité de France	France	Electric and gas utilities		▓	▓	
69	Nippon Life Insurance	Japan	Insurance: Life, health (mutual)	▓	▓		
81	Procter & Gamble	United States	Soaps, cosmetics		▓	▓	

Source: Compiled by the author.

Table 6.4   Poverty approaches of Fortune 100 corporations, 2006 (% of row category; overlap possible*)

	Inactive (%)	*Re-active (%)*	*Active (%)*	*Pro-active (%)*
Total (N = 100)	63	55	33	4
Europe** (N = 52)	48	67	52	8
of which United Kingdom (N = 10)	60	60	40	10
United States*** (N = 30)	77	47	13	0
Asia**** (N = 15)	93	27	7	0
Developing (N = 3)	33	66	33	0
Petroleum refining (N = 14)	50	71	36	14
Banks (N = 17)	59	47	47	6
Insurance (N = 13)	62	39	31	0
Electronics, computers, telecom (N = 15)	74	53	27	0
Motor vehicles and parts (N = 13)	69	46	23	0
Retailers, general merchandise, wholesalers (N = 12)	75	42	17	0

Notes: * Overlap occurs because companies may score on multiple indicators. For instance, a company can simultaneously be classified as 're-active' and 'active', which basically shows that it is in a state for transition, combining characteristics from two approaches and attitudes. ** Includes: Netherlands (4), Belgium (2), Germany (14), France (11), Italy (3), United Kingdom (10), Ireland (1), Norway (1), Spain (2), Switzerland (4). *** Includes: Venezuela, Brazil, Mexico. **** Includes: Japan (9), China (3), Republic of Korea (3).
Source: Compiled by the author.

A larger number of European firms have embraced partnerships and in a much more (pro)active manner than leading American firms. This is relatively independent from the actual number of partnerships. American firms embrace partnerships more often and more (re)actively than leading Asian firms. This pattern fits with the general CSR strategies of these three regional varieties of capitalism. This conclusion is also further supported by other studies. For instance, Muller and Whiteman (2008) analysed the 'geography of corporate philanthropic disaster responses' among the Fortune Global 500 firms. They observe a process of 'regionalization' in disaster relief efforts. The response of firms to a selected number of natural disasters varies systematically across regions. Asian firms show relatively low cash value of donations. American and European firms were more generous, but in the case of American donations they were more strongly linked to the advancement of the private sector in order to increase the disaster preparedness of the population and the efficiency of the actual relief effort (namely, the US Business Roundtable's Partnership for Disaster Relief). European firms seem to have been more inspired by normative considerations. These observations, however, need additional research (Muller and Whiteman 2008).

Conclusion: preconditions for a sustainable corporate story?

Does the present state of affairs regarding the involvement of (big) business in poverty reduction give ground for optimism or pessimism? Although most entrepreneurs and corporations do not yet see the alleviation of global poverty as a strategic priority (Kaptein et al. 2007), this contribution has illustrated the extent to which the issue itself has climbed up the corporate strategy ladder. The bottleneck of making it a real strategic priority – in which firms adopt active or proactive strategies – has less to do with the complexity of the issue and more with the conceptual and strategic 'poverty' that surrounds the issue. Rather narrow approaches for entrepreneurial solutions to poverty still prevail and only a few proactive approaches have been tried, which makes it yet impossible to come up with convincing 'sustainable corporate stories', in which at the operational as well as the strategic level leading firms have developed and implemented poverty alleviation strategies. This chapter has also shown that the chances that a sustainable corporate story will materialize are greatest with some of the leading European firms. They have developed the most interesting examples as regards partnerships, broader approaches to the BOP, and novel business models. But even for these firms, it proves difficult to change their strategic orientation.

TNCs are still strongly influenced by their 'countries of origin' (varieties of capitalism) as regards their CSR strategies. This is partly due to the regulatory framework in these countries, but also to sectoral dynamics. Different sectors face different problems and are at different stages when it comes to engaging with poverty reduction. So a way forward in this regard might therefore be to not approach single, individual (often high-profile) TNCs, as some NGOs and international organizations tend to do, but to create an enabling environment that facilitates dialogue and subsequent action at the sector level. In a complementary manner, the Global Reporting Initiative (GRI) and other international organizations might develop reporting guidelines and develop specific poverty alleviation indicators per sector.

A final, and perhaps the most worrying, dimension of the business interest in poverty originates in the very dynamics of issue management. Issues are always prone to strategic re-assessments by CEOs. The research covering 200 European CEOs that was referred to earlier (Kaptein et al. 2007), also asked the expected increase in urgency of the ten selected CSR issues (Table 6.5). The CEO could indicate the expected importance of the issue on a scale from 1 (not at all) to 5 (very much).

Considering that European CEOs and corporations have been leaders in the business world in trying to address the issue of poverty, we can expect that its urgency is not likely to increase in the near future. The expected attention of corporate CEOs for poverty is above average (2.5), but remains stable. This represents a breach of the trend of increasing attention for

Table 6.5   Future urgency of issues

Expected increase in issue urgency	Mean
1. Global warming	4.4
2. Transparency of business practice	3.8
3. Ecological diversity	3.7
4. Fair trade and fair procurement	3.5
5. Corruption prevention	3.5
6. Labour rights	3.4
7. Health and safety	3.4
8. Education	3.2
9. Income equality and fair wages	3.1
10. Poverty	3.0

Source: Kaptein et al. 2007.

the issue over the past decade. More importantly, a number of poverty-related issues, like income equality and fair wages, as well as education, are declining in importance. This is a worrisome development that is caused by at least two factors inherent to 'issue management'. First, the issue of 'global warming' has been receiving considerable attention in both the public debate ('the Gore effect') as well as with stakeholders and shareholders of large corporations. (As recently as late-2008, the global financial crisis had – temporarily – made global warming a secondary issue.) This 'crowds out' other issues like poverty. Secondly, evaluations of progress in attaining the MDGs in 2007 have stressed that several MDGs, notably MDG1 (halving poverty), might be reached. In issue management, the relative urgency defines the willingness of managers to address the issue. As soon as policy makers started to emphasize that MDG1 might be reached, the issue lost importance. The issue of poverty, therefore, runs the risk of falling victim not only to a substituting issue (global warming), but also to the claimed success in addressing it. This poses a problem, since the issue will certainly not be solved. It can be anticipated that relative poverty will not decrease in many regions and Africa, in particular, will not even reach MDG1.

It can be concluded that the business involvement in addressing the issue of poverty is far from settled. First, this is due to a lack of meaningful benchmarks, approaches and measurement tools, not to a lack of 'best-practice' cases. Second, however, it was also suggested that overly optimistic expectations might also dampen the efforts of the business sector in explicitly addressing poverty. Perhaps the next sustainable corporate story should be formulated by governments rather than by the firms themselves, and should include a mixture of self- and mandatory regulation, as well as partnerships and transparency-increasing measures.

Annex 6.1: Firm sample – Fortune's 100 largest global companies, 2006

Fortune 500 position	Company	Country	Sector
1	ExxonMobil	United States	Petroleum refining
2	Wal-Mart Stores	United States	General merchandisers
3	Royal Dutch Shell	Netherlands	Petroleum refining
4	BP	United Kingdom	Petroleum refining
5	General Motors	United States	Motor vehicles and parts
6	Chevron	United States	Petroleum refining
7	DaimlerChrysler	Germany	Motor vehicles and parts
8	Toyota Motor Corporation	Japan	Motor vehicles and parts
9	Ford Motor Company	United States	Motor vehicles and parts
10	ConocoPhillips	United States	Petroleum refining
11	General Electric	United States	Diversified financials
12	Total	France	Petroleum refining
13	ING Group	Netherlands	Insurance: Life, health (stock)
14	Citigroup	United States	Banks: Commercial and savings
15	AXA	France	Insurance: Life, health (stock)
16	Allianz	Germany	Insurance: P & C (stock)
17	Volkswagen	Germany	Motor vehicles and parts
18	Fortis	Belgium	Banks: Commercial and savings
19	Crédit Agricole	France	Banks: Commercial and savings
20	American Intl. Group	United States	Insurance: P & C (stock)
21	Assicurazioni Generali	Italy	Insurance: Life, health (stock)

(Continued)

Annex 6.1: Continued

Fortune 500 position	Company	Country	Sector
22	Siemens	Germany	Electronics, electrical equipment
23	Sinopec	China	Petroleum refining
24	Nippon T&T	Japan	Telecommunications
25	Carrefour	France	Food and drug stores
26	HSBC Holdings	Un. Kingdom	Banks: Commercial and savings
27	ENI	Italy	Petroleum refining
28	Aviva	United Kingdom	Insurance: Life, health (stock)
29	IBM	United States	Computers, office equipment
30	McKesson	United States	Wholesalers (health care)
31	Honda Motor Company	Japan	Motor vehicles and parts
32	State Grid	China	Utilities
33	Hewlett-Packard	United States	Computers, office equipment
34	BNP Paribas	France	Banks: Commercial and savings
35	PDVSA	Venezuela	Petroleum refining
36	UBS	Switzerland	Banks: Commercial and savings
37	Bank of America Corp.	United States	Banks: Commercial and savings
38	Hitachi	Japan	Electronics, electrical equipment
39	China Nat. Petroleum	China	Petroleum refining
40	Pemex	Mexico	Mining, crude oil production
41	Nissan Motor Company	Japan	Motor vehicles and parts
42	Berkshire Hathaway	United States	Insurance: P & C (stock)

(Continued)

Annex 6.1: Continued

Fortune 500 position	Company	Country	Sector
43	Home Depot	United States	Specialist retailers
44	Valero Energy	United States	Petroleum refining
45	J.P. Morgan Chase	United States	Banks: Commercial and savings
46	Samsung Electronics	Rep. of Korea	Electronics, electrical equipment
47	Matsushita Electric Ind.	Japan	Electronics, electrical equipment
48	Deutsche Bank	Germany	Banks: Commercial and savings
49	HBOS	United Kingdom	Banks: Commercial and savings
50	Verizon Comm.	United States	Telecommunications
51	Cardinal Health	Ireland	Wholesalers (health care)
52	Prudential	United Kingdom	Insurance: Life, health (stock)
53	Nestlé	Switzerland	Food consumer products
54	Deutsche Telekom	Germany	Telecommunications
55	Dexia Group	Belgium	Banks: Commercial and savings
56	Metro	Germany	Food and drug stores
57	Credit Suisse	Switzerland	Banks: Commercial and savings
58	Royal Bank of Scotland	United Kingdom	Banks: Commercial and savings
59	Tesco	United Kingdom	Food and drug stores
60	Peugeot	France	Motor vehicles and parts
61	US Postal Service	United States	Mail, package and freight delivery
62	Altria Group	United States	Food and tobacco
63	Zurich Financial Serv.	Switzerland	Insurance: P & C (stock)
64	E.ON	Germany	Energy

(Continued)

Annex 6.1: Continued

Fortune 500 position	Company	Country	Sector
65	Sony	Japan	Electronics, electrical equipment
66	Vodafone	United Kingdom	Telecommunications
67	Société Générale	France	Banks: Commercial and savings
68	Électricité De France	France	Electric and gas utilities
69	Nippon Life Insurance	Japan	Insurance: Life, health (mutual)
70	Statoil	Norway	Mining, crude oil production
71	France Télécom	France	Telecommunications
72	LG	Rep. of Korea	Electronics, electrical equipment
73	Kroger	United States	Food and drug stores
74	Munich Re Group	Germany	Insurance: P & C (stock)
75	Deutsche Post	Germany	Mail, package and freight delivery
76	State Farm Insurance	United States	Insurance: P & C (mutual)
77	Marathon Oil	United States	Petroleum refining
78	BMW	Germany	Motor vehicles and parts
79	Fiat	Italy	Motor vehicles and parts
80	Hyundai Motor	Rep. of Korea	Motor vehicles and parts
81	Procter & Gamble	United States	Soaps, cosmetics
82	ABN AMRO Holding	Netherlands	Banks: Commercial and savings
83	Royal Ahold	Netherlands	Food and drug stores
84	Repsol YPF	Spain	Petroleum refining
85	Legal & General Group	United Kingdom	Insurance: Life, health (stock)
86	Petrobras	Brazil	Petroleum refining

(Continued)

Annex 6.1: Continued

Fortune 500 position	Company	Country	Sector
87	Toshiba	Japan	Electronics, electrical equipment
88	Dell	United States	Computers, office equipment
89	Lloyds TSB Group	United Kingdom	Banks: Commercial and savings
90	ThyssenKrupp	Germany	Industrial and farm equipment
91	Boeing	United States	Aerospace and defence
92	AmerisourceBergen	United States	Wholesalers (health care)
93	Santander	Spain	Banks: Commercial and savings
94	BASF	Germany	Chemicals
95	Costco Wholesale	United States	Specialty retailers
96	Suez	France	Energy
97	Target	United States	General merchandizers
98	Morgan Stanley	United States	Securities
99	Robert Bosch	Germany	Motor vehicles and parts
100	Renault	France	Motor vehicles and parts

Notes

1. The classic conceptualization of varieties of capitalism (VoC) (Hall and Soskice 2001) distinguishes between coordinated market economies (CMEs), where non-market institutions play a key role in structuring intra- and inter-firm relations, and liberal market economies (LMEs), where hierarchy and competitive market pressures are more significant. The data and analysis in this chapter refer primarily to regional variations, notably the United States, Europe and East Asia.
2. All references to $ are to US dollars.
3. See, for example, the study of the poverty-related impacts of Unilever's operations in Indonesia, carried out jointly by Oxfam/Novib and Unilever (Clay 2005).
4. See http://walmartstores.com/ (accessed in March 2007).

5. The term refers to the ability of firms to overcome differences with stakeholders by discussion, dialogue or other means of communication.

References

Andriof, J. and M. McIntosh (eds), *Perspectives on Corporate Citizenship* (Sheffield: Greenleaf Publishing, 2001).

Aviva, *Corporate Social Responsibility Report 2006* (2006). www.aviva.com/csr06/index. asp (accessed on 4 February 2009).

Blowfield, M., 'Corporate social responsibility: Reinventing the meaning of development?', *International Affairs*, May, Vol. 81, Issue 3 (2005) 515–24.

BP (British Petroleum), *Making Energy More: BP Sustainability Report 2005* (2005). www.bp.com/liveassets/bp_internet/globalbp/STAGING/global_assets/downloads/S/ bp_sustainability_report_2.pdf (accessed on 4 February 2009).

Chataway, J. and J. Smith, 'The International AIDS Vaccine Initiative (IAVI): Is it getting new science and technology to the world's neglected majority?', *World Development*, Vol. 34, No. 1 (2006) 16–30.

Clay, Jason, *Exploring the Links between International Business and Poverty Reduction: A Case Study of Unilever in Indonesia* (Oxford: Oxfam GB, Novib [Oxfam Netherlands], and Unilever, 2005).

de Soto, H., *The Mystery of Capital: Why Capitalism Triumphs in the West and Fails Everywhere Else* (New York: Basic Books, 2000).

Dexia Group, *Sustainable Development Report 2005* (2006). www.dexia.com/docs/2006/ 20060510_AG/VoletC_UK/20060510_VoletC_UK.pdf (accessed on 4 February 2009).

ExxonMobil, *2005 Corporate Citizenship Report* (2005). www.exxonmobil.com/Corporate/Files/Corporate/ccr05_fullreport.pdf (accessed on 4 February 2009).

Fombrun, C. and C. van Riel, *Fame and Fortune: How Successful Companies Build Winning Reputations* (New York: Financial Times/Prentice Hall, 2004).

Ford Motor Company, *Our Route to Sustainability: Connecting with Society – Ford Sustainability Report 2004/5* (Dearborn, MI: Ford Motor Company, 2005). http://www.ford.com/doc/2004-05_sustainability_report.pdf (accessed on 4 February 2009).

Fortanier, F., Multinational Enterprises, Institutions and Sustainable Development, PhD Disseration (Amsterdam: University of Amsterdam, 2008).

Fortanier, F. and A. Kolk, 'On the economic dimensions of corporate social responsibility: Exploring Fortune Global 250 reports', *Business and Society*, Vol. 46, No. 4, 1 December (2007) 457–78.

Habermas, J., *Moral Consciousness and Communicative Action* (Cambridge, MA: MIT Press, 1990).

Hall, P. and D. Soskice (eds), *Varieties of Capitalism: The Institutional Foundations of Comparative Advantage* (Oxford: Oxford University Press, 2001).

Hart, S. and S. Sharma, 'Engaging fringe stakeholders for competitive imagination', *Academy of Management Executive*, Vol. 18, No. 1 (2004) 7–18.

HSBC Holdings plc, *HSBC Corporate Social Responsibility Report 2005* (London: HSBC Holdings plc, 2006).

Jackson, G. and R. Deeg, 'Comparing capitalisms: Understanding institutional diversity and its implications for international business', *Journal of International Business Studies*, 39 (2008) 540–61.

Jain, S. and S. Vachani (eds), *Multinational Corporations and Global Poverty Reduction* (Cheltenham: Edward Elgar, 2006).

Kaptein, M., L. Koning, R. van Tulder and L. van Vliet, *2007 Report on European CSR Survey* (Rotterdam: RSM Erasmus University, July 2007).

Kolk, A. and R. van Tulder, 'Setting new global rules?', *Transnational Corporations*, Vol. 14, No. 3 (2005) 1–17.

Kolk, A., R. van Tulder and B. Westdijk, 'Poverty alleviation as business strategy? Evaluating commitments of frontrunner multinational corporations', *World Development*, Vol. 34, No. 5 (2006) 789–801.

Lodge, G. and G. Wilson, *A Corporate Solution to Global Poverty: How Multinationals Can Help the Poor and Invigorate Their Own Legitimacy* (Princeton, NJ: Princeton University Press, 2006).

Maignan, I. and D. Ralston, 'Corporate social responsibility in Europe and the US', *Journal of International Business Studies*, Vol. 33, No. 3 (2002) 497–514.

Matsushita Electric Works, *Matsushita Electric Works CSR Report 2006* (2006). http://panasonic-denko.co.jp/e/corp/csr/backnumber/2006/pdfs/5-8.pdf (accessed on 4 February 2009).

Michaelson, C., 'Compliance and the illusion of ethical progress', *Journal of Business Ethics*, Vol. 66, Issue 2 (2006) 241–51.

Muller, A. and G. Whiteman, 'Exploring the geography of corporate philanthropic disaster response: A study of Fortune Global 500 Firms', *Journal of Business Ethics*, Vol. 84, No. 4 (2008) 589–603.

Nissan Motor Company, *Sustainability Report 2006* (2006). www.nissan-global.com/EN/COMPANY/CSR/LIBRARY/SR/2006/ (accessed on 4 February 2009).

Petrobras, *Social and Environmental Report 2005* (2005). www2.petrobras.com.br/ResponsabilidadeSocial/ingles/pdf/BS_completo.pdf (accessed on 4 February 2009).

Porter, M., *The Competitive Advantage of Nations* (New York: Free Press, 1990).

Prahalad, C.K., *The Fortune at the Bottom of the Pyramid: Eradicating Poverty through Profits* (Upper Saddle River, NJ: Wharton School Publishing, 2005).

Preston, L. and J. Post, *Private Management and Public Policy* (Englewood Cliffs, NJ: Prentice Hall, 1975).

Procter and Gamble, *Sustainability Report 2005: Linking Opportunity with Responsibility* (Cincinnati, OH: Procter and Gamble, 2005).

Ritzer, G., *The McDonaldization of Society* (Thousand Oaks, CA: Pine Forge Press, 1993).

Sachs, J., *The End of Poverty: How We Can Make It Happen in Our Lifetime* (London: Penguin Books, 2005).

Samii, R., L.N. Van Wassenhove and S. Bhattacharya, 'An innovative public–private partnership: New approach to development', *World Development*, Vol. 30, No. 6 (2002) 991–1008.

Schultz, Majken, Mary Jo Hatch and Mogens Holten Larsen (eds), *The Expressive Organization: Linking Identity, Reputation and the Corporate Brand* (Oxford: Oxford University Press, 2000).

Shell Foundation, *Enterprise Solutions to Poverty: Opportunities and Challenges for the International Development Community and Big Business. A Report by Shell Foundation*, March (2005). www.shellfoundation.org/download/pdfs/Shell_Foundation_Enterprise_Solutions_to_Poverty.pdf (accessed on 4 February 2009).

van Tulder, R., *Skill Sheets: An Integrated Approach to Research, Study and Management* (Amsterdam: Pearson Education, 2007).

van Tulder, R., with Alex van der Zwart, *International Business–Society Management: Linking Corporate Responsibility and Globalization* (London: Routledge, 2006).

Wilson, G. and P. Wilson, *Make Poverty History: Increase Profits and Reduce Risks by Engaging with the Poor* (Sheffield: Greenleaf Publishing, 2006).

7
Cross-Sector Partnership as an Approach to Inclusive Development

Ruth Findlay-Brooks, Wayne Visser and Thurstan Wright

Introduction

Cross-sector partnerships have emerged as a key development approach, with many governments and international agencies viewing them as an effective way to deal with complex and intractable development problems that have defeated single-sector interventions. Following the perceived shortcomings of the 1980s Structural Adjustment Programmes in developing countries, public–private or multi-sector partnerships are perceived as a more sustainable option, with donor agencies giving direct budget support to governments, along with the encouragement of partnership between development agencies, national governments and business. Tennyson (2003a: 3) asserts that 'only with comprehensive and widespread cross-sector collaboration can we ensure that sustainable development initiatives are imaginative, coherent and integrated enough to tackle the most intractable problems.'

However, partnerships are not a straightforward option. Some see them as merely a 'phase of policy experimentation' (Geddes 2000: 797) – a short-term response to rapid global change. There can also be issues of accountability and power imbalance, when unelected corporations and non-governmental organizations (NGOs) have influence in states where governments are weak or failing. Even where they are the best solution, there can be real obstacles in both the development and management of partnerships which are too easily ignored.

The increasing popularity of partnership as a development solution, however, makes it all the more important to take a realistic view and to test the assumptions. Unless a robust approach is adopted, then partnering risks suffering a backlash from unmet, unrealistic expectations which could result in its positive potential being lost.

Even the first step of agreeing on a definition of 'partnership' is difficult; as Rein et al. (2005) point out, the term has been used interchangeably with many others such as alliance, compact and collaboration. Perhaps the clearest definition comes from a United Nations (UN) report to the General Assembly: 'Partnerships are commonly defined as voluntary and collaborative relationships between various parties, both State and non-State, in which all participants agree to work together to achieve a common purpose or undertake a specific task and to share risks, responsibilities, resources, competencies and benefits' (United Nations 2003: 4).

Within these parameters, however, Utting and Zammit (2006: 9) highlight the complexity of the term: 'It has come to be an infinitely elastic concept, embracing a range of actors, each inspired by different motivations and objectives, and involving varying types of relationships between the partners.' The partnerships referred to in this chapter reflect this complexity (see Box 7.1).

This chapter examines the experience of partnerships that purport to promote inclusive development. It draws on research carried out under the University of Cambridge Programme for Sustainable Leadership (CPSL), which has many years' experience of partnership work, notably through its Postgraduate Certificate in Cross-sector Partnership (PCCP) course. Through exploring the experiences of partnership practitioners that have participated in the course, as well as current thinking on the topic, the chapter considers the rise of partnerships; the determinants of success and failure; issues of participation, power and accountability; and ways of enhancing the contribution of partnerships to inclusive development. A concluding section suggests that if the international development community is to rely on partnerships to bring about structural change and long-term development impacts, then this approach needs to be firmly grounded on genuinely inclusive consultation processes, operate within accountability frameworks, be properly supported and evaluated and, where appropriate, lead ultimately to policy change.

The research included three main stages. First, it examined the experience of participants in the PCCP. The programme's alumni number about 200 from 47 countries across Africa, Asia, Western and Eastern Europe, the Americas and Australasia, and all are practitioners who are leading their organizations in the development and implementation of Cross-Sector Partnerships. Following a literature review and initial scoping interviews, an online questionnaire was designed and around 100 PCCP students and alumni were invited to respond. The questionnaire was completed by representatives of 27 partnerships, based in 13 different countries across five continents, and representing a total of 311 partners. Detailed telephone interviews were then carried out with a cross-section of seven partnerships. The initial findings were then tested with a focus group of partnership practitioners from a range of countries attending the second residential workshop of the 2007 PCCP course. The chapter also draws on research carried out by Rein et al., and published by Cambridge Programme for Sustainability Leadership in 2005 as *Working Together – A Critical Analysis of Cross-Sector Partnerships in Southern Africa*.

Box 7.1   Types of partnership

The 27 partnerships explored in this study have a broad geographical spread. They include eight based in Africa, five in the United Kingdom (UK), and two in Switzerland (operating internationally). Four are based in Australia and two in South America; two operate globally, while the others represented are based in Croatia, India and the Republic of Ireland.

While the PCCP course is aimed at partnerships for sustainable development, they relate to a variety of issues. The most common aims are improved water and sanitation for the poor, and education, followed by development and poverty alleviation. Three partnerships are targeting biodiversity and conservation awareness as a component of sustainable development. Housing for the poor is the aim for two partnerships, while one focuses on refugee children and one on social inclusion.

Of the 311 partners involved in the 27 partnerships, 102 are community groups. Civil society (67) and the private sector (66) come next, followed by 61 government partners and 15 intergovernmental organizations.

To illustrate the types of partnership in the study, one example is the Sustainable Communities Initiative (SCI), developed by the Australian national research agency. This is a three-year action learning programme that brings together organizations from across public, private and civil society sectors to work in partnership with communities to develop and deliver solutions to local sustainability issues. There are approximately 12 projects in this portfolio. Individually, SCI projects deliver solutions to local sustainability issues, and collectively they inform community-scale sustainable development policy, programmes and practice across Australia.

A second example is a partnership designed to promote social inclusion in Ireland; this initiative includes the state sector, the community and voluntary sector, employers and trades unions, and has been operating for over 30 years. Others in the study include a partnership between a UN department, a large extractive industry in Russia, and five municipal government departments – aiming to promote socioeconomic development, and a UK-based partnership operating in Asia and Africa to improve water and sanitation for the poor. This partnership includes two corporates, two governments, four NGOs and one community group. There is no such thing as a 'typical' respondent, and the diversity of the group illustrates the wider diversity and complexity of multisector partnerships involved in development.

The rise of partnerships

Given this diversity, what differentiates 'partnership' from other forms of cooperation and association? Caplan (2006: 11) points out that 'The term partnership elicits much confusion. It is used to describe widely different constructs from loose networks and alliances to more institutionalised joint ventures'. Looking for common features, Caplan suggests that partnership indicates shared power and different kinds of resources beyond finance. He suggests that partnerships can be defined as involving 'two or more organizations that enter into a collaborative arrangement based on (1) synergistic goals and opportunities that address particular issues or deliver specified tasks that single organizations cannot accomplish on their own as effectively, and (2) whose individual organizations cannot purchase the appropriate resources or competencies purely through a market transaction.'

In considering why multisector partnerships have emerged as an important institutional arrangement in contemporary development thinking, policy and practice, two key perspectives stand out. The first, emphasized in Kaul and Conceição (2006) is the changing role of the state in a global context. Whereas previously, governments largely had autonomy in internal decision making and finance, the increasing power and financial influence of the private sector, on the one hand, and the international pressures of globalization, on the other, have shifted their role. Increasingly they are becoming intermediaries, adjusting their policies to accommodate the demands from internal and external influencers. For example, NGOs are having an increasing influence on developing country governments. The response from some states has been to shift from a 'brokering' role to that of a participant in public–private partnerships (PPPs) that harness these demands, along with the resources and capacity of the corporate and civil society sectors making them.

Utting and Zammit echo this view, suggesting that the drive to partnerships arose partly as a response to pressure from civil society organizations (CSOs) concerned with the 'perverse effects of corporate globalization' (2006: 7). As the influence of corporations grows and spreads, recruiting them as allies in the battle against poverty, rather than seeing them as the 'enemy', offers a much more positive approach and one which brings new potential for tackling 'insoluble' development problems.

Another perspective on the drivers of multisector partnerships, that of complementarity, is emphasized by Tennyson (2003a: 3):

> Working separately, different sectors have developed activities in isolation – sometimes competing with each other and/or duplicating effort and wasting valuable resources. Working separately has all too often led to the development of a 'blame culture' in which chaos or neglect is always regarded as someone else's fault.
>
> So partnership provides a new opportunity for doing development better – by recognising the qualities and competencies of each sector and finding new ways of harnessing these for the common good.

A common feature of these two perspectives is the context of increasing complexity – both of political frameworks and of development challenges – and therefore the need for more complex and sophisticated approaches to tackling development.

This is not, however, necessarily matched by sophistication in understanding the implications of partnership solutions. One of our interview respondents commented: 'There's a lot of support for the idea of partnership and for people working together, but no understanding of what it really means'. Her observation at a local level seems to reflect a global level drive to partnership – sometimes with a similar lack of understanding of the full implications.

The high expectations of a partnership approach are illustrated by the optimism that surrounded the setting up of UN–business partnerships to work towards the Millennium Development Goals (MDGs): 'These multi-stakeholder and cross-sector approaches to problem-solving offer one of our greatest hopes for meeting, together, the challenges of the twenty first century' (Nelson 2002: 36–7). Matthews counters this with a more cautious approach: 'Multi-sector partnerships have the potential to contribute significantly to efforts to accelerate progress towards the Millennium Development Goals, but they are not a panacea and it would be foolish to underestimate the difficulties involved in building relations across sectors and between non-traditional partners' (2005: 6).

The potential offered by different sectors working together to achieve development goals is viewed positively by many: 'partnerships can be as diverse as the creativity of governments, NGOs and business allows. This gives them an experimental quality that may lead to breakthrough approaches to development problems' (Hale and Mauzerall 2004: 223).

The concept of different sectors pooling their complementary skills and resources to deal with complex, intractable problems was the most commonly cited motivation for the respondents in our study. One interviewee in a multisector partnership working on community development in Australia commented that the government partners had been 'on top of the simple stuff, but not the complex interface "wicked" problems where social, economic and environmental issues meet'. As another respondent succinctly put it: 'By and large the problems we're dealing with are ones where other people have tried and failed'.

This is an important point to bear in mind when looking at partnerships; if by definition they are likely to be tackling intractable problems that have defeated other approaches, then expectations should not be unrealistic. A cooperative approach may be more effective than a single-sector one, but it still needs time to bring about change.

Whatever the nature of the overall partnership aims, the individual sectors may have different motives for collaborating. Frequently cited reasons among the respondents in our study included enhanced reputation and funding, while for one partner it was gaining access to politicians. A 'licence to operate' is another frequent motivator for partnering.

For corporations, particularly in the extractive industries, partnering with intergovernmental organizations, civil society and/or community groups can give much-needed legitimacy. The resources and funding they provide in return are sufficient motive for prospective partners. On the other hand, for the United Nations or for NGOs wishing to operate in areas where they have little sway with governments, the economic power of large corporations can be a useful influence – an example given was helping refugees in a country that had not signed up to an international treaty.

But the same motives which bring partners together can also get in the way of the partnership's expressed aims. As a respondent explained: 'One partner wants money, the other wants legitimacy by association. The mere act of coming together satisfies these underlying needs of the separate partners, which may be termed success, even if the written objectives are not achieved.'

Inevitably, many partners from all three sectors will have 'covert' motives for partnering which are different to the project outcomes, whether this is the pursuit of funding, credibility, or a licence to operate. If the disconnect between the motives of the partners and the desired outcomes of the part-nership itself leads to partners feeling they have succeeded because they have gained what they were looking for and they are seen to be doing something, this can be at the expense of making real steps in development goals. In this case, partnership could be viewed as an expensive distraction which appears to involve action in response to development challenges, while, in reality, soaking up large amounts of time and money.

The second problem with covert (and potentially conflicting) motives for partnering is the risk of misunderstanding between partners. Rein et al. (2005) stress the importance of real honesty and clarity about the goals of the part-ners and of the partnership, particularly where partners are very different to each other.

Perhaps for these reasons, many of our respondents gave single-issue motives – for any of the three sectors – as a reason *not* to partner. For example:

- where money is the main driver, or profit the only goal;
- where a company is simply trying to improve a poor image through part-nering with a 'credible' organization,[1] or just wants to 'sell more soap' with no interest in long-term solutions;
- where governments are trying to offset social injustice by placating civil society, are too weak to manage private sector inputs, or cannot accept equality and shared decision-making.

This is reinforced by Hale and Mauzerall's even more critical view of motives for partnering: 'corporations, governments, and IGOs [intergovern-mental organizations] may use partnerships as a showcase for sustainable development to divert attention from their other environmentally and socially unfriendly activities' (2004: 223). Utting and Zammit put this in a wider context, seeing the partnership movement as constrained and dominated by a 'global economic system that is not only increasingly interdependent and interconnected but also moulded and controlled by global corporations and corporate elites' (2006: 6).

In view of this, it is understandable that many respondents to the questionnaire felt partnership is only an appropriate approach where goals or motives are compatible, sectors are linked or at least understand each other, and partners agree. Partners need to be committed to finding common ground for a partnership to work.

Finally, there was a concern among respondents that partnership should be avoided where it puts the intended beneficiaries at risk, either through power imbalance 'where control is hierarchical and/or local people are not consulted in changes that will affect their lives', or where people may be harmed – through delay caused by consultation in emergency situations, or through participation within a context of conflict.

Determinants of success and failure

Having come together to form a partnership, what are the factors that can assist or hamper success? The study showed that there are numerous success factors, with little difference in their relative weight, posing a significant challenge to partnerships and practitioners, which need to be taken into consideration.

However, the factor that rated slightly higher than the others in the study, and several of the interview respondents also stressed its importance, was the mutual commitment of partners. An interviewee from a community development partnership explained that: 'The commitment of the partners has been very important ... the organizations were in it together to address the problem and all had a common goal.'

This was echoed by a Swiss-based intergovernmental organization representative: 'The corporate partners were keen to work with an operational humanitarian organization. On the other hand, our senior management was willing to experience a new type of partnership, different from the NGO/government partnership.'

According to the survey respondents, it is also important for partnerships to find the right balance between mutual commitment and compatibility, and the complementarity of expertise that the different sectors can bring.

On a more practical level, adequate resources are seen as a major success factor, tying into the problems with funding, discussed below. Good planning is considered important, and a clear partnership agreement – although it seems to be the process of preparing and agreeing this document that has the most impact in clarifying partners' expectations and commitment. Once the partnership is underway many agreements and Memorandums of Understanding (MOUs) are no longer seen as important. One respondent from an Australian education partnership reflected a common view: 'A firm agreement was put in place at the start of the partnership, although the partnership functioned without this playing a significant part.'

Another important factor for partnership success is an enabling environment, where national or local government is supportive through policy, funding, or both. A respondent from an Irish social development partnership commented: 'There was a commitment at national level to social partnership and we've had significant funding as part of that initiative. Thus we have benefited from an enabling environment both financially and legislatively.'

Rein et al. also stress the importance of environment and context, from their study of partnerships in Africa:

> The issue of context is central to our findings. One of the undoubted dangers of the fashionable status that partnership currently enjoys is the assumption that there is a model of partnership which can be applied to each and every situation. Our research suggests that partnerships need to be built very carefully both on established good practice and on the constraints of local conditions. (2005: 125)

Interestingly, however, engagement of beneficiaries and/or stakeholders only ranked joint fifth in the questionnaire results out of eight success factors, which appears to tie in with the lack of consultation with beneficiaries noted below – the relationship between partners is viewed as much more important than the relationship with the target group. This raises interesting questions in relation to inclusive development.

Inevitably, in practice, partnership is not a straightforward option. One respondent commented: 'For a partnership to work, people with a vision are needed at the outset, people to communicate the objectives and really make the partnership happen.'

By far the largest set of challenges to effective partnership identified by the study respondents relate to the relationship between the partners themselves. The questionnaire responses show that the greatest of these is a difference of expectation and/or commitment between partners, followed by a power imbalance and communication problems. Matthews confirms these points: 'problems can result from the asymmetries of power and resources between partners, from their divergent decision making processes and even from the latent hostility that sometimes exists between partners as a result of past antagonisms' (2005: 6).

The other two key barriers mentioned by the questionnaire respondents are lack of resources, and lack of an enabling environment – the flipside of the success factors discussed above.

The importance of practical factors in implementing partnerships was illustrated by one respondent: 'Barriers to partnerships are often resource-driven, because these resources are needed to move from the *vision* of a partnership to achieving outputs.' This bridge between vision and implementation can be hampered, as Rein et al. (2005) illustrate, by the difficulties of matching up the different sectoral approaches to timing of funding, decision making and so on.

As one interviewee from an Australian community development partnership explained:

> Things were lining up at a conceptual level – so the ideas were all fine and everyone's on board, but the logistics and practicalities, particularly with more than one funder and a co-investment approach, this was the challenge ... We're at this part of the budget cycle, this part of the political cycle ... getting everything lined up is a huge challenge.

Inevitably, however, the most important factor in most cases is funding. The issue of funding for partnerships involved in development is not just about the amounts available, or the problems of different accounting systems, but also the reliance on short-term funding when tackling long-term problems. The tendency for funders to look for short-term successes with easily quantifiable outcomes is unlikely to be compatible with sustainable, inclusive development within challenging contexts.

Two partnerships which rely mainly on government funding highlight the challenges: 'A Government department gave us a small amount of money – we could only get funding for the first year, and the private sector guys put in three years' funding but it was only a small amount per partner per year.'

A second interviewee agreed: 'Longer-term funding certainly enables you to be more creative and to think more broadly. Short-term funding can be a huge problem. It's hard to retain expertise where there's no security of tenure.'

According to our study, the complexity inherent in the partnerships represents considerable risk as well as great opportunity for innovative approaches. Inevitably, partners will find working with organizations from different sectors challenging, and in setting up a partnership it is essential for them to recognize and allow for the differences. However, there is a responsibility for the public sector, if they see partnership as a meaningful approach to development, to recognize the particular challenges that it can present as a partner, and to seek ways of mitigating these. For this reason, we explored the challenges of partnering with government and with inter-governmental organizations in more detail.

Virtually all of the partnerships involving government departments highlighted the challenges of working with the public sector. In spite of these obstacles, there was agreement that, as one respondent stressed: 'Governments should not be left out of the equation ... It is important to work with governments in developing countries to improve public policy and acceptability.'

There was some perception that operating within a 'weak' state is inadvisable, and this is discussed further in the section on accountability. However the general reaction showed that all governments – whether 'weak' or not – present a particular challenge to working in partnership. Along with the difficulties of short-term funding cycles discussed above, the other two key difficulties are the segmented nature of government, and the rapid turnover of staff.

On the first of these, one respondent explained: 'The challenge was how to bring together a lot of government departments. It's difficult for government departments which are arranged on themes; they're fine for the simple things, but when you're sitting in a place where it hasn't rained for three years then you really don't care who helps or what they're called.'

The difficulties of reconciling rapid staff turnover, characteristic of governments in both developing and developed countries, with long-term partnership commitment, were illustrated by several respondents. One from an IGO–corporate–government partnership in Africa said: 'I know there are a lot of problems with government bureaucracy, but it's doubtful whether that's because it's a "weak state" – more because of bureaucratic structure, as with many governments! Four months ago we had a meeting with our government partner; days later the government partners all changed.' This is by no means a specifically African problem – very similar challenges were described by respondents working in many geographical areas.

While partnering with government in development initiatives is seen by partners as important, and often essential, the frustrations of rapid staff turnover and short-term funding cycles undermine the enabling environment that is so critical to success. The principles of neoliberalism, initiated in the West and often imposed upon developing countries over the last 20 years, have seen the rolling back of the state and relative reduction in state expenditure. This weakening in the capacity of the public sector undermines its ability either to be a fully effective partner in large-scale development projects, or to create an environment in which development projects can be successful and sustainable, rather than short-term 'fixes'. The repercussions of this are discussed later in this chapter.

The challenges of partnering with intergovernmental organizations need to be viewed in perspective, as there are many successful UN–private partnerships, two of which were described by our respondents. In these instances, corporate funding, drive and expertise had been successfully aligned with UN development goals. However, there are also unique obstacles to partnering with intergovernmental organizations, highlighted by two projects where the United Nations partnered with large corporations, one a humanitarian partnership, the other focusing on development. From the intergovernmental organization perspective:

> Organizational cultural differences were a major challenge. They [the corporate partners] could easily make the decisions and go ahead with the implementation. We [UN department] had to focus on the process by consulting different technical divisions, different regional offices and desks, different budgetary units.

From the corporate perspective:

> There has been some discussion about how to account for the money intended for the local area. There were differences in the accounting systems between the two organizations which have caused problems. The United Nations just sends a summary of expenditure, which is not adequate for us to report back to the government.

These issues are further explored by Stott (2007) in her study of a UN–corporate partnership. Stott outlines some of the obstacles that, despite goodwill on both sides, ultimately led to its failure:

- A difference in culture – creative versus bureaucratic. While the company was fast-moving and creative, the UN 'decision-making was slow and there was hesitancy about making quick choices and assessment without careful consultation and sign-off' (Stott 2007: 6);
- A difference in goals, and misunderstanding between the two organizations;
- The view of the corporate partner as primarily a source of cash, when they wanted wider involvement;
- Difficulties over aligning funding cycles and decision-making processes;
- Within the UN department 'personnel were generally divided between those who welcomed the engagement with [the corporate] as a "cash cow" and little more, and those who saw the relationship as a dangerous precedent with business playing too great a role in the development of UN programmes at the expense of the credibility of the institution' (Stott 2007: 7).

Participation, power and accountability

Having explored the relationship between the various partners, we went on to look at the partnership's relationship to the beneficiaries or target group. As discussed above, questionnaire respondents rated engagement with beneficiaries/stakeholders only joint fifth out of eight success factors. However, it is reasonable to assume that an inclusive approach to development will be based on a meaningful consultation with the intended beneficiaries. As well as helping to ensure the appropriateness of the intervention, this also gives stakeholders more sense of ownership of the partnership activities. The first stage of this would be during the partnership scoping stage, and might be expected to include a needs analysis involving the target group. It is interesting to note therefore that, although 22 out of the 25 partnerships who responded to this question had carried out a consultation exercise, at least 11 of these had not included the intended beneficiaries. Some of the partnerships viewed their civil society partners as having strong enough links with the beneficiaries to represent them, while others considered that as they were delivering part of a global or international programme for which a need had been identified, consultation with local groups or a full scoping exercise was unnecessary. Eight of the 11 partnerships mentioned had taken subsequent steps to ensure inclusivity *after* the launch of the partnership, including stakeholder meetings, focus groups and 'capacity-building' for beneficiaries.

A more detailed discussion with the interview respondents gave some interesting – and contrasting – perspectives:

- A large scoping exercise was put in place at the start of the project. This had an element of financial risk for the funding agency because if a project is not deemed viable as a result of the scoping then the money spent has been wasted. However ... the scoping exercise gave the partnership legitimacy and a major foundation.
- The beneficiaries are represented on a national level, but it is difficult to get representation from communities because they are, by definition, very diverse and very localized.
- Discussions between the partners took place for three or four months and an MOU was signed. After the main structure was put in place the local communities were consulted. The programme is very flexible though and changes occurred throughout as a result of community and expert consultation.

Some partnerships, however, do go to great lengths to try to be inclusive in their scoping, while recognizing the barriers. As a respondent explained:

We do our best but those who are most excluded and need it most are least likely to participate. You would try and use the structures that are already there in the community. You can go to where they go rather than expecting them to come to you. We go to the local community centre, schools and crèches. We have also had some research done door to door.

Difficulty of access is not the only challenge to consultation and, in an attempt to be inclusive, it is clearly important to avoid naivety: 'Consultation can be high-risk both for the researcher and for the respondent. Where there are high levels of criminality and intimidation you need to be careful about not putting people in danger.'

In emergency situations, too, carrying out a consultation with the target groups can put them at risk – this time through delays and unnecessary bureaucracy. However, this is not an easy circle to square, as one of our respondents described instances when, in trying to react quickly, humanitarian missions rush in with clothes and food which turn out to be unacceptable or inappropriate to the recipients.

Related to the question of inclusivity in scoping consultations is the problem of determining which groups to work with and what activities to focus on once the partnership is underway. Hale and Mauzerall (2004: 232) point out that 'a barrier to grassroots involvement is a lack of economic resources and human capacity. Those communities and organisations that would most benefit from partnership are, more often that not, precisely those without the ability to participate.'

This dilemma was clearly echoed by many of the partnerships in our study, who recognized that those most in need of support are the least able to ask for it. To take one example from an Australian community development partnership:

> It became clear there was diversity around the capacity of communities: the communities that are proactive and who are innovators; then communities that are reactive, who think they're okay until something comes along like the drought; then the third group are the inactive, and they need the leg-up more than anyone else. There are a small group which will always be ahead of the curve and we want to help communities like that because there we can innovate, but we also have an obligation to work with the ones that need us most.

Another partnership had gone to considerable lengths to ensure balanced representation:

> We have 10 representatives. The most deprived areas are all represented. The umbrella groups for each area decide who should be the representatives, but we have a rule that they *must* actually be resident in the areas. There is also a seat for special interest groups, such as travellers, youth, those with disabilities, and so on. The nominating bodies for these again would be umbrella groups, for example, the local branch of the national disability group would appoint that person.

In other areas the approach – although still attempting to be inclusive – is very different: 'There is a committee comprised of community representatives who were selected by the two main partners. They meet a couple of times a year – it's not a very large group, however, so it's difficult for them to challenge project decisions.'

In our initial analysis of the questionnaire and interview data, there appeared to be a clear contrast between the partnerships working in 'developed' and 'developing' countries. Although the sample is too small to reach broad conclusions, the pattern indicated that partnerships working in developed countries are more likely to go to considerable lengths to ensure that processes are inclusive and that all stakeholders are fully represented both in planning and implementing the partnership activities. In developing countries, however, the tendency appeared to be for outside agencies to decide what the problems are, and then to move in and attempt to 'solve' them. The difference of approach is between working *with* local people on mutually identified issues, and approaching them with predetermined answers to problems they have not necessarily been consulted about. Government and IGO partnerships, as well as philanthropic initiatives, seem particularly to favour the latter approach. One respondent commented: 'You can't just rock up and say to someone, *you have a problem – we're here to help'*, but in many cases that's exactly what seems to happen.

However, the focus group which reviewed the initial findings, made up of PCCP participants, took the view that it is the capacity of the target community rather than its geography which determines how involved it is in the process. Examples were given of partnerships working in Canada and Australia where the involvement of indigenous communities was quite different – and much less inclusive – than that of non-indigenous groups. This led to the question of capacity building, and the focus group felt strongly that to talk about the need to build capacity within some communities to work better with development partnerships is a very patronizing approach. In their view, it is often the partnerships and the outside agencies who need to build their capacity to understand the groups they are working with, and to learn to listen to them rather than making assumptions.

One of the difficulties in achieving genuine communication between different groups comes from their conflicting worldviews and ways of talking about things. One of our focus group members gave the example of agreeing on locations, when the indigenous community relates to the landscape in terms of sacred sites and ancestral connections, while an extractive company trying to negotiate with them sees it in terms of map references and geological features.

Idemudia (2007: 20) confirms this view:

> The problem with this tendency by oil TNCs [transnational corporations] to frame the situation in scientific terms is that it clashes with the worldviews held by local communities, which are often based on beliefs and perceptions ... This clash in worldview and expectations ... invariably fosters the violation of the psychological contract that exists between

local communities and oil TNCs from the perspective of the communities. Oil TNCs are, therefore, often not given the benefit of doubt in the event of crisis or accidents, while corporate-community relations remain largely conflictual and community development partnerships have limited impact on community development.

The results of our study do appear, as discussed above, to indicate a tendency for partners to view their relationship with their partners as much more important than the relationship with beneficiaries. It is difficult to see how partnerships can contribute to inclusive development unless they genuinely engage with their target groups rather than seeing them as passive recipients. However, it is essential to avoid simplistic assumptions. Genuine mutual understanding and the development of common aims may be essential, but it is not an easy, quick solution. It may be that the capacity building needed is to find a common language to engage in dialogue, not just consultation, between partnerships and stakeholders/community groups, in order to understand how each other works and find collective ways to identify problems and solutions.

One of the key difficulties in genuine stakeholder participation, as well as in partnership more generally, is the issue of power. There can be inequities within and around partnerships, between partners and with and between beneficiaries. Partnerships operate within existing power structures, and can unsettle, cut across or reinforce them. Rein et al. point out the importance, but also the potential implications, of stakeholder participation. Through engaging or excluding particular groups, while seeking to be participatory, partnerships can reinforce or unsettle pre-existing power relationships within and between communities. They suggest that further analysis is needed of 'terms such as community engagement and stakeholder engagement' (2005: 10). On what basis are stakeholders engaged? Does the appearance of collaboration mask asymmetries of power?

One reaction to the difficulty of dealing with unequal power can be the temptation to partner only with similar organizations. Hale and Mauzerall point out that in the partnerships arising from the World Summit on Sustainable Development (WSSD), 'only a handful of the largest and richest [governments] have taken an active lead in promoting partnerships. Additionally, most of the NGO partners are large, Northern organisations. Small businesses are completely absent from leading roles' (2004: 231).

Another interviewee addressed the issue of working with community groups:

> Power imbalance always needs to be kept an eye on. To begin with I believed that of course we are equal, but now I've come to realize that we're not equal at all, but that we have respect for the experience of everyone whoever they are. A community organization sitting at table with the

person who funds it can't be there on an equal basis, but if they can respect my contribution as the person who has the local knowledge, then they can respect me. So talking about parity of esteem is a better term than talking about equality, otherwise one can kid oneself.

Like power, accountability is an important factor to which some partnerships appear oblivious. It is a particular concern in areas where partnerships may have a lot of power, influence and/or money relative to the state or to local organizations, and where development is being carried out by organizations who have not been elected and whose mandate may be questionable. This is an issue for corporates, for NGOs and for intergovernmental organizations, such as the United Nations. If CSP is to be a viable, inclusive development mechanism, then accountability frameworks need to be accessible, robust, and come to be seen as the norm rather than an optional extra. Yet as Zadek and Radovich point out, 'there are signs that accountability issues have been ignored as the floodgates to private sector collaboration have opened' (2006: 45).

While Zadek and Radovich (2006: 1) suggest that there is a growing recognition of the need for systematic governance and accountability in partnerships, this was not evident from the majority of the responses received in our survey. One partnership had gone to great lengths to adapt and implement Zadek's framework for partnership accountability and governance (AccountAbility 2006). However, for the majority of partnerships consulted, an MOU and/or financial reporting was the extent of the accountability framework they were using. There is also a gap between accountability on paper and in reality, as one respondent pointed out: 'There is an MOU partnership agreement – it covers the expectations and evaluation process. It covers a lot of things. But there is a disconnect between the formal structure on paper and the reality on the ground.'

It is not just corporate partners that can be oblivious to the need for accountability: 'The UN is not good at accountability – this frustrates corporate partners. There are too many actors involved to make accountability easy ... Large NGOs such as Oxfam or Care International are much more accountable and have better accountability structures.'

Partnerships operating within poor political governance contexts highlight the ambiguities of accountability, as one respondent pointed out: 'Partnerships can be a good idea where the state is weak or lacking the necessary capacity. There may be an issue with accountability here with an unelected body (that is, the partnership) delivering development outcomes. However, in such a situation, there would already be problems with accountability if the state was weak or not accountable to the electorate – so a partnership would improve the situation on the ground.'

For those who try to balance accountability with inclusivity, there can be opportunities and challenges: 'In the drive to regulate and to increase accountability, you can lose the community involvement. For instance the rules against participation of individuals in decisions which may benefit themselves take away empowerment.'

Issues of governance and accountability are explored further in Rein et al. (2005: 9–10), who point out that the structures partnerships adopt are crucial to their accountability. The importance of this is stressed by Zadek (2004: 12): 'Are they destined to become stable, permanent governance fixtures? And if so, on what basis and on whose terms? And how do they relate to each other? Some seek to reinvigorate and reinvent our Bretton Woods institutions in pursuit of effective global governance. But are we in practice seeking a new civil governance emerging in partnership form?' If this is the case, then proper governance and accountability structures are essential.

Enhancing the contribution of PPPs to inclusive development

Reports of success from the partnerships in our study were mixed, with the majority of questionnaire respondents feeling that their partnership was 'fairly successful', seven regarding it as 'very successful' and two as 'not very successful'. Two IGO partnerships had got very bogged down in process and had not so far managed to achieve their intended outcomes.

Measures of success varied, however, with respondents differentiating between the immediate goals of successful partnering, and the longer terms outcome goals. As one questionnaire respondent commented: 'This depends on how success is defined. Would it be based on the objectives indicated on the partnership agreement or include or be limited to the underlying expectations which most partnerships have?'

The complexity of gauging partnership outcomes is highlighted by Rein et al., who suggest that 'the value of partnerships ... lies not just in their ability to deliver tangible improvements in social services or economic goods: it can also reside in the vantage point a partnership can give to relatively weak or disadvantaged sections of the community, to enable them to express their needs, draw attention to pressing problems and build dialogue with other groups and institutions' (2005: 125).

This 'by-product' of capacity building is seen by many as a very important and positive partnership outcome. Some partnerships recognize that this is a two-way process: 'There is capacity building both within the partnership and within the communities; we're learning a lot and helping the partner organizations to know how to work together and to work with the communities.'

The process of working in partnership can in itself bring about change: 'You are bringing together partners for new initiatives who couldn't have started it themselves. Through participating in the partnership they then built up capacity and became independent. But it takes time for a partnership to get to that stage so that the individual partners are confident.'

Success in achieving partnership aims is often also dependent on the macro-level context, as the following comments suggest: 'We are working in a system that has got firmly entrenched over a period of 60 years. It will take time to get this system to move'; and 'As ever, the project turns out to be more complex than foreseen; volatile national level issues determine overall success.' When looking at partnership as a mechanism for genuine inclusive development, the distinction between achieving success at an individual or group level, and making changes at a structural level is a recurring theme. One respondent explained: 'It has been successful in making people aware of the debate but not necessarily in changing policy.' Similarly: 'Lots of people have been helped and progressed to coming into training programmes, labour programmes, education, jobs, and so on. Yet the structure still remains. I think what it would have to do to make a structural difference is to feed into the decision-making processes. To make sure that inclusion is on the agenda for those who make decisions.' This tension between change at an individual and at a structural level is an important one, and is further discussed below.

The difficulties of gauging the impact of partnerships are widely acknowledged. Their long-term nature and engagement with complex issues involving a wide group of stakeholders makes it difficult to find meaningful measures of success. Tennyson (2003b: 15) points out that evaluation needs to look at changes that have taken place for beneficiaries and stakeholders as well as for partners.

Utting and Zammit suggest that for UN partnerships, 'impact assessment is rare and is not conducted consistently' (2006: 20). However, they also acknowledge that making such impact assessment meaningful, rather than a pragmatic distraction from the wider implications of the partnership, would be extremely complex and challenging (Utting and Zammit 2006: 24). A consideration of more contested factors such as accountability and equity, as well as partnership 'value added', rather than just of factors such as relevance and effectiveness, is essential.

The mainstreaming and growth of successful partnership activities can take a number of forms, for example continuation, scaling-up, replication, or incorporation into government policies.

Utting and Zammit point out that one should not automatically assume the growth of partnership activities is a good thing: 'The case for scaling-up, and how this should be done, rests on whether it can be plausibly demonstrated that such scaling-up would, of and by itself, have a decisive impact on the problems or issues at stake. The absence of greater information derived from evaluations of existing UN-business partnerships suggests that advocating scaling-up may be premature' (2006: 19).

However, the risks of undertaking partnership activities without an assurance of long-term and sustainable resourcing are also noted: 'The partnerships themselves risk disguising the severity of the underlying problem by offering or attempting partial or piecemeal solutions that do not take enough factors into consideration. In practice, they are likely to encounter significant problems of sustainability if resources are not guaranteed in the long-term' (Rein et al. 2005: 126). Limitations on funding can restrict replication of even the most successful projects, as one of our respondents from an educational partnership in Australia explained: 'The [award-winning] partnership is already widespread within this state, but will not continue out of the state as funding comes from a regional government department.'

The majority of respondents to the questionnaire (20 out of 22) felt that their partnership would grow through replication to other areas, while only one feared that the partnership would not continue at all. Three commented that the future of the activities had been assured through their institutionalization within government policy, and this appears to be an important factor in 'mainstreaming' outcomes.

However, approaches to the long-term impact of partnerships do not have to be simplistic. Rein et al point out that: 'Replication need not necessarily imply the "copying" of activities, but rather the copying of successful process and understanding: in other words, it is the learning that is transferred from one situation to another' (2005: 125).

The importance of finding models to share learning, and if possible to inform policy, was recognized by partnerships in our study:

> In the places we worked we delivered effective outcomes, but there was no model to take the learning to share with other regions, or to do meta-analysis to inform policy at a higher level. Now we've developed an evaluation and learning model. So partnership and action learning is generic across everything with the aim of mutual benefit for everyone and the extraction of meta-level learning that can be useful for policy makers.

Similarly: 'We have always been conscious of the need to pass on the learning. We do this through evaluation and spreading the learning. There are 38 funded partnerships across the country. We are looking now at new geographical areas which were not formerly priority areas. We're looking at the type of community infrastructures that have been successfully developed in the most disadvantaged areas and rolling them out.'

In the light of this discussion and the findings of the study, can partnerships bring about inclusive development and act as genuine agents of change?

There is no doubt that many partnerships are doing good and effective work within the development field. However, the question of whether they are dealing with the symptoms or addressing the disease is an important one. The discussion above, based on the experience of the partnerships in our study, of whether development can occur at a structural level or only in helping groups of individuals (important though this is), indicates the challenges of effecting systemic change.

Idemudia (2007: 23) underlines the difficulty of effecting genuine change within complex contexts:

> The implication is that there is a need for an enabling environment for partnership in developing countries, which requires addressing the structural determinants of maldevelopment (Utting 2000) and building local individual and institutional capacity. Efforts presently geared towards institutional capacity building in existing partnership schemes will continue to yield limited dividends as long as the more fundamental issues are ignored.

But at a wider level it should perhaps be recognized that many of the institutions involved in partnerships for development are the very institutions around which the structure is built – so it would be extremely difficult for them, however good their intentions, to do anything other than reinforce it. This challenge affects not just partnerships themselves, but also the ability to look objectively at their role as agents of inclusive development. The hegemonic discourse of neoliberalism and capitalism – the framework in which partnerships inevitably operate – makes it very difficult to stand back and assess the wider ways in which they interact with complex power structures. In other words, if they are judged at all, they will inevitably be judged on their own terms. If partnerships arise out of – and can only be critiqued from within – the current paradigm, then review and revision may be possible, but not revolution.

Utting and Zammit wisely advocate moving 'beyond pragmatism' in looking at partnerships, to analysis: 'There is a tendency in the mainstream literature and best practice learning circles to suggest that reforms derive essentially from "learning by doing". In other words, pragmatism, rather than politics, is the keyword' (2006: 9).

Certainly we need to move beyond naïve models of 'best practice' which take too much as read, and towards an approach which questions the terms of reference. And yet this is still a very new field, where we are (or should be) also learning through experience. Simply theorizing partnerships becomes a hall of mirrors, where all the references lead back to each other in a never-ending circle, with only occasional injections of primary data, and where the analysis is almost always done by those in positions of power.

The conclusion has to be that, in an imperfect world, partnerships can only ever be an imperfect solution. But are they (one of) the best imperfect solutions we have? And if so, what straightforward ways are there that would at least help them to be as good as they could be? Perhaps an analytical pragmatism is needed, where we act because action needs to be taken, but in a reflective, analytical way which understands the context and which extracts the meta-learning from the process of partnership. We need to listen to the unheard voices that form part of this hybrid approach to development, so that the learning can be shared, and grown and built upon – added to by each partnership, but continually tested, and always in context.

Conclusion

It is clear from this study that partnerships work best where partners are committed to finding common ground, can balance compatibility with complementarity, and are adequately resourced. An enabling environment, through finance and policy, is also an important success factor.

Covert, over-simplistic, or conflicting motives can undermine partnerships. Partnership should be avoided where it puts the beneficiaries at risk, either through power imbalance or where people may be harmed – through delay caused by consultation in emergency situations, or through participation within a context of conflict.

Partnering across sectors brings inevitable challenges. Problems result from asymmetries of power and resources between partners. Differences in aims, accountability, and practical aspects such as reporting structures, are also a common source of problems.

A particular – and common – problem is the tension between short-term funding and reporting cycles by donors, particularly governments, and the long-term, complex nature of development work. This makes forward planning and recruitment very difficult, and undermines sustainable solutions. This reflects the difficulties of states, weakened in terms of power and expenditure by 20 years of neoliberal reforms, playing a full part either in creating an enabling environment for partnership, or in being fully effective partners themselves.

The results of the study show a tendency to view relationships with partners as more important than those with beneficiaries, and target groups are often seen as passive recipients. There is no easy, quick solution to building mutual understanding and developing common aims, but genuine dialogue between partnerships and stakeholders/community groups appears to be an essential step to understanding how each other works and finding collective ways to identify problems and solutions.

The issue of power is one of the key difficulties in genuine stakeholder participation, as well as in partnership more generally. Partnerships operate within existing power structures, and can unsettle, cut across or reinforce them, yet these issues often go unrecognized.

If cross-sector partnership is to be a viable, inclusive development mechanism, then proper accountability and governance frameworks are essential, and again this area often goes unrecognized and unaddressed.

The 'success' of partnerships is difficult to gauge. Change can occur through outcomes, but also through the partnering process itself, and both are difficult to measure. Impact assessment, in particular, is difficult in challenging, complex environments, and is rarely carried out.

Another challenge in assessing the impact of partnerships is in differentiating between short-term success and long-term structural change. Initiatives are understandably often better at addressing the symptoms of a problem than its long-term causes, and thus can be seen as doing short-term good, without necessarily making any structural changes that will prevent the problems re-occurring.

Seeing partnerships simply as a short-term solution to a specific problem can be counter-productive. Models to share learning are important, but for effective partnership activities to continue beyond the short-term, they need to feed into decision making and wider policy.

Note

1. For example, the Global Compact, the UN's flagship partnering initiative, is seen by some as a mechanism for 'bluewashing' corporations that could project a socially responsible image through their association with the United Nations (TRAC 2000).

References

AccountAbility, *Partnership Governance and Accountability. Reinventing Development Path: The PGA Framework* (London: AccountAbility, 2006).

Caplan, K., 'Creating space for innovation: Understanding enablers for multi-sector partnerships', *Partnership Matters: Current Issues in Cross-Sector Collaboration*, Issue 4 (2006) 11–14.

Geddes, Michael, 'Tackling social exclusion in the European Union? The limits of the new orthodoxy of local partnership', *International Journal of Urban and Regional Research*, Vol. 24, No. 4 (2000) 782–800.

Hale, Thomas and Denise Mauzerall, 'Thinking globally and acting locally: Can the Johannesburg partnerships coordinate action on sustainable development?', *Journal of Environment & Development*, Vol. 13, No. 3 (2004) 220–39.

Idemudia, Uwafiokun, *Corporate Partnerships and Community Development in the Nigerian Oil Industry: Strengths and Limitations*, Programme on Markets, Business and Regulation, Paper No. 2 (Geneva: UNRISD/Copenhagen Business School, 2007).

Kaul, Inge and Pedro Conceição, *The New Public Finance: Responding to Global Challenges* (Oxford: Oxford University Press, 2006).

Matthews, Petter, 'Briefing: Multi-sector partnerships for poverty reduction', *Proceedings of the Institution of Civil Engineers, Engineering Sustainability*, Vol. 158, No. ES1 (2005) 5–7.

Nelson, Jane, *Building Partnerships: Cooperation between the United Nations System and the Private Sector* (New York: United Nations Publications, 2002).

Rein, Melanie, Leda Stott, Kavwanga Yambayamba, Stan Hardman and Stuart Reid, *Working Together: A Critical Analysis of Cross-Sector Partnerships in Southern Africa* (Cambridge: Cambridge University Programme for Industry, 2005).

Stott, Leda, *Conflicting Cultures: Lessons from a UN–Business Partnership* (London: International Business Leaders Forum, 2007).

Tennyson, Ros, *The Partnering Toolbook* (London/Geneva: The Prince of Wales International Business Leaders Forum and Global Alliance for Improved Nutrition, 2003a).

———, *Institutionalising Partnerships: Lessons from the Front Line. Infocus 8* (London: The Prince of Wales International Business Leaders Forum, 2003b).

TRAC (Transnational Resource and Action Center), *Tangled up in Blue: Corporate Partnerships at the United Nations* (2000). www.corpwatch.org/article.php?id=996 (accessed in July 2006).

United Nations, *Enhanced Cooperation between the United Nations and All Relevant Partners, in Particular the Private Sector*, Report of the Secretary-General, UN Doc. No. A/58/227 (New York: United Nations General Assembly, 18 August 2003).

Utting, Peter, *Business Responsibility for Sustainable Development*, Occasional Paper No. 2 (Geneva: UNRISD, 2000).

Utting, Peter and Ann Zammit, *Beyond Pragmatism: Appraising UN–Business Partnerships*, Programme on Markets, Business and Regulation, Paper No. 1 (Geneva: UNRISD, 2006).

Zadek, Simon, 'Civil governance and partnerships: Inventing tomorrow's history', *Partnership Matters: Current Issues in Cross-Sector Collaboration*, Issue 2 (2004) 11–18.

Zadek, Simon and Sasha Radovich, *Governing Collaborative Governance. Enhancing Development Outcomes by Improving Partnership Governance and Accountability*, Accountability and the Corporate Social Responsibility Initiative, Working Paper No. 23 (Cambridge, MA: John F. Kennedy School of Government, Harvard University, 2006).

8
Growing Sustainable Business in Eastern Africa: The Potential and Limits of Partnerships for Development

Catia Gregoratti

Introduction

It has been widely acknowledged that since the 1990s the 'public–private partnerships' (PPP) paradigm has become a cardinal component of processes of global governance (United Nations 2006). More recently, it has gradually rolled out in the developing world as a result of the multilateral consensus generated at the World Summit on Sustainable Development (WSSD) (Calder 2002; Calder and Culverwell 2005). The novelty of the PPP mode of governance, or new approach to public policy, is that it seeks to complement governmental commitments to sustainable development and the Millennium Development Goals (MDGs) with non-traditional forms of multistakeholder (voluntary) cooperation involving governments, multilateral organizations and non-state actors, such as non-governmental organizations (NGOs) and the private sector. The definition of the term, however, remains loose and context-bound because the actual practice and procedures underpinning the PPP paradigm display different degrees of stakeholder engagement, varying levels of institutionalization and the pursuance of outcomes as diverse as advocacy, norm-setting, policy making, finance or market creation (Reinicke and Deng 2000; Bull et al. 2004).

Independently of their differences and specific traits, proponents of these new coalitions have praised them for their capacity to deliver expediently a non-exclusive range of public goods and for their ability to draw non-state actors into formal and informal decision-making structures. In other words, based on liberal models of cooperation, these assumptions maintain that PPPs can effectively bridge an implementation gap resulting from a lack of financial resources, knowledge and political will, as well as reducing the democratic deficit in global governance by incorporating non-state actors and underrepresented groups.[1] Beyond narrowing these two gaps, the partnership rationale goes further by postulating that, beyond achieving what no actor can accomplish on its own, all the actors involved in such formal or informal arrangements stand to gain material and non-material benefits, thereby creating 'win–win' scenarios (Nelson 2002: 38–40).

As Martens suggests, the fundamental problem with these suppositions is that the advantages of global partnerships or multistakeholder approaches 'are for the most part not based on empirical research and the widely-held notion that there is no alternative is often no more than a profession of faith' (Martens 2007: 34). Based on this observation, this chapter seeks to make a conceptual and empirical contribution to the debates on decentralized United Nations (UN)-brokered PPPs by appraising the participatory credential and developmental outcomes of the flagship partnership initiative of the United Nations Development Programme (UNDP), known as the Growing Sustainable Business (GSB) Initiative (Witte and Reinicke 2005: 70–1).

Created in 2002, anchored in the United Nations Global Compact and managed by UNDP's Business Partnership Division, the GSB seeks to facilitate 'business-led enterprise solutions to poverty in advancement of the MDGs' with the specific intent of increasing access by the poor to goods and services, employment and livelihood opportunities. The organizational features of the GSB conform to a traditional multistakeholder arrangement coordinated by a country broker and relying on the participation of governments, local and international businesses, and civil society for policy deliberation and project implementation. Between 2002 and 2006, the GSB had expanded its partnership portfolio to 12 developing countries across the continents of Africa, Europe and Asia. By the end of 2007, when the empirical research referred to in this chapter was concluded, in Eastern Africa alone a total of 22 projects were at different stages of development, ranging from conceptualization to full-scale operationalization. None of these have been systematically evaluated. This assessment seeks to add to the emerging but still limited body of literature on the GSB (Bekefi 2006) and empirical analyses on sustainable partnership projects in least developed countries (LDCs) (McFalls 2007). It also addresses the limited scope of research on PPPs in Eastern Africa by broadening the geographical focus of enquiry, which, in the African context, has mainly tended to concentrate on South Africa or Nigeria.

The first of the three main sections below introduces and appraises the thinking, key propositions and debates surrounding the emergence and rise of UN-brokered PPPs and sketches a critical framework to understand the political economy of partnerships for development. The second contextualizes the GSB and explores its inception, functions and current development. Drawing on extensive fieldwork in Kenya and Tanzania,[2] the chapter then evaluates the role of the GSB deliberation mechanisms and projects in Eastern Africa, and assesses its degree of inclusiveness and other development outcomes. In other words, the chapter interrogates the extent to which the GSB fosters local participation and ownership and whether its inclusive business models make a meaningful contribution to poverty alleviation, building local capacities and complementing, rather than replacing, local development efforts (Frynas 2005).

The chapter argues that the mode of governance emerging from the GSB structures is elitist and top-down in character. Second, from the perspective of equitable and sustainable development it maintains that the GSB's partnership projects have produced questionable and limited results. These parallel arguments call for a fundamental rethink of the way in which partnerships for development are conceptualized and implemented. By way of conclusion, it is suggested that the real potential of these interventions could be unleashed by fostering greater bottom-up participation and by aligning the objectives of the partnerships with national development strategies and priorities. Allowing and facilitating alliances of businesses and NGOs to steer development in order to serve private interests might not only exacerbate inequalities but might also undermine the legitimacy and credibility of the UNDP.

Public–private partnerships and the United Nations

The ever-increasing rise and closer relationships being forged among the private sector, NGOs and the United Nations merit some conceptual clarifications. The emergence of these new forms of governance is historically contingent and cannot be delinked from the structural changes associated with economic globalization and the ideological shifts that have emerged in response to a widespread crisis of legitimacy facing the multilateral system in the mid-1990s. While relationships between the United Nations and NGOs can be traced back to the San Francisco Conference and have been historically characterized by dynamic and more or less institutionalized encounters, the United Nations' relationships with the private sector have been markedly different. Notwithstanding the existence of UN agencies that worked with specific private sector actors throughout the Cold War period, calls for a New International Economic Order (NIEO) and the attempts to establish a binding code of conduct for transnational corporations (TNCs) contributed to fostering the perception that the United Nations manifested hostility towards the private sector. The United Nations was partially absolved from this legacy following the dismantling of the United Nations Centre on Transnational Corporations (UNCTC), prior to the 1992 Rio Earth Summit (Clapp 2005: 25). The importance of the 1992 World Summit should not be underestimated as it epitomized the first step towards rapprochement as the newly formed Business Council for Sustainable Development (BCSD) and the International Chamber of Commerce (ICC) were formally invited by the Conference Secretary Maurice Strong to contribute to Agenda 21 (Bruno and Karliner 2002: 27–32).

However, it was only with the appointment of Secretary-General Kofi Annan in 1997 that the United Nations was effectively transformed from an intergovernmental organization to a nodal point and leading proponent of complex networks of governance that included organized business interests and TNCs as key participants. This turn has been explained at several levels and with different emphases. Some commentators pointed to the UN's financial crisis and the urgent need to find 'creative' solutions to finance its operations and fulfil its socioeconomic mandate (Bull et al. 2004: 484–5), while others have praised the bold leadership and background of Kofi Annan in persuading businesses and civil society to work together with the United Nations (Tesner and Kell 2000). A more theoretically grounded approach to understanding the emergence of partnerships in the multilateral system locates their inception in relation to the evolving governance dimension of the 'new politics of contested globalisation' (Higgott 2001) where the international policy community has sought to formulate responses to suppress the hostility against liberalization, deregulation (or competitive re-regulation) and corporate globalization. From a neo-Gramscian perspective, PPPs and the associated discourse of corporate social responsibility (CSR) constitute some of the most evident institutional responses that international organizations, and the United Nations in particular, have adopted to defuse countervailing and potentially destabilizing social forces.

The intellectual foundations that facilitated the United Nations' endorsement of partnerships were provided by John G. Ruggie, architect of the Global Compact, Assistant Secretary-General and Chief Adviser for Strategic Planning to Kofi Annan between 1997 and 2001. Ruggie noted that, in the light of the progressive disarticulation between states and markets and the failure of international institutions to redress the social and environmental imbalances ensuing from the process of economic globalization, the idea of 'embedded liberalism' could be transposed at the global level. What he advanced, and for which he provided an intellectual justification, was the creation of a new compromise to re-embed markets in social values. This attempt to socialize markets would rely primarily on the dynamic interplay(s) between civil society, the private and the public sector around the idea of CSR (Ruggie 2003). Devoid of considerations over power relationships and distributional outcomes, this constructivist reading was imbued with a functional logic as it essentially postulated increased effectiveness in the management of 'public bads' and greater pluralism in global governance. The appeal of this pragmatic proposition was further reinforced by the advantages that it was said to offer to the United Nations; the UN Vision Project,[3] for example, argued that by working more closely with non-state actors, facilitating the emergence and management of public–private networks, the United Nations would be able to increase its own effectiveness and credibility (Reinicke and Deng 2000: 78).

The resonance of the partnership rationale within the United Nations was first manifested in 1998 with the creation of the United Nations Fund for International Partnerships (UNFIP) and the now-defunct UNDP's Global Sustainable Development Facility, which were shortly followed by the establishment of the Global Compact. The 2002 WSSD completed the institutionalization of these new mechanisms of governance by endorsing so-called 'Type II Partnerships' or 'Partnerships for Sustainable Development', namely voluntary, multistakeholder initiatives (MSIs) aimed at implementing sustainable development. As the United Nations was rapidly embedding partnerships with the support of Member States, concerns were being raised not on multistakeholder partnerships per se but about the increasing involvement of the private sector, particularly TNCs, in the multilateral system. Critical NGOs formed the 'Alliance for a Corporate Free UN' warning against the dangers of equating the interests of the private sector with the mandate of the United Nations and calling for greater corporate accountability; similar concerns were echoed by the opinions of some UN officials, while academics began to articulate hypotheses on the possibilities of institutional capture and policy distortion (Utting 2001: 67; Utting 2005: 384).

Early signs of resistance did not stop the partnership agenda from taking off. In a recent assessment conducted by the Global Public Policy Institute (GPPi), Witte and Reinicke (2005) argued that despite financial and human resources constraints the partnerships approach is becoming fully embedded in the UN's modus operandi. Evidence for this is provided by the growth of partnership portfolios among leading and less prominent agencies, the appointment of partnership brokers or 'focal points', the efforts to decentralize their management to country offices, the development of tailored guidelines for engagement with business and civil society, and the mushrooming of websites and publications geared towards enhancing the profile of particular MSIs and attracting new partners. While no comprehensive database of UN partnerships exists, by the mid-2000s some estimates suggested there were more than 400 in place (Utting and Zammit 2006: 18), ranging from health interventions to the provision of public services, the majority (if not all) of which claim to have a development mandate.

Assessing UN-brokered PPPs for poverty reduction

Despite the proliferation of partnerships there is no consensus as to how to evaluate them. Much of the existing evidence of their participatory credentials and effectiveness comes in the form of anecdotes produced by lead companies, UN agencies' promotional material, the international and local press, and ex ante assessments by consultancy firms which are often paid for by the companies involved and not available to the public. It also results from studies subcontracted to academic research centres, such as the Mossavar-Rahmani Centre for Business and Government at Harvard. The collective knowledge base articulated by these sources is often associated with a discourse that emphasizes the instrumental benefits accruing to firms engaged in a partnership (Blowfield 2007), while the impact of these collaborative endeavours upon the environment, intended beneficiaries or society more generally, is communicated in terms of bold claims about the desired developmental results the partners expect to achieve. In 2005 the United Nations General Assembly recognized this shortcoming and requested the UN Secretary-General, in consultation with Member States, to promote impact assessment mechanisms 'in order to enable effective management, ensure accountability and facilitate effective learning from both successes and failures' (United Nations 2006). In response to this call, in 2007, the Global Compact in collaboration with the United Nations Institute for Training and Research (UNITAR), UNFIP, the UNDP and the Boston Consulting Group produced a Partnerships Assessment Tool (PAT). The first businesses that tested the PAT unsurprisingly welcomed the introduction of this instrument, which, beyond standardizing the management of partnerships and grading their expected contributions to development, also reinforced the assumptions of the partnership rationale.

On what basis and with what theoretical lenses should UN-brokered partnerships in developing countries be evaluated? An analytical facet that has often been omitted in mainstream assessments comprises the structural conditions that have enabled the emergence of these new forms of cooperation and which might also serve as benchmarks to test the limits of these interventions. Partnerships have emerged to solve the market failures, externalities and inequalities generated by a consensus favouring deregulation and liberalization over and above interventionism. However, rather than moving beyond neoliberal economic policies, they also shield them. Utting and Zammit (2006), for example, argue that PPPs are a component of the global processes of restructuring that takes place via privatization, foreign direct investment (FDI), commodification, expanding global value chains and the cultural penetration of brands. Restructuring has also been accompanied by a progressive weakening of the developmental capacities of states (Newell and Frynas 2007), while businesses are enjoying an unprecedented degree of structural and discursive power. These multiple and intertwined dimensions are crucial in determining whether, rather than socializing markets, multistakeholder partnerships extend the hegemony of United States (US) or Northern business interests over the South contributing to increased socioeconomic inequalities (McFalls 2007).

At the level of operationalization, particularly in developing countries, the question of who defines, drives and implements a partnership is still of marginal importance in self-evaluations and internal assessments. Omitting this facet is to reinforce the apolitical notion that partnerships are 'neutral', infinitely inclusive and that all the 'stakeholders' involved have an equal say. An emerging body of critical scholarship on CSR and PPPs has observed that in multistakeholder forums and meetings those normally without a voice in society are also the ones excluded from the discussions (Newell 2005: 543); furthermore, even when these groups have a voice 'power relationships between stakeholders continue to shape the issues raised, the alliances that are formed and the issues that are identified' (Prieto-Carrón et al. 2006: 984). The issue of selective exclusion and inclusion are central to casting light into the power structures that partnerships legitimize and the political inequalities they might reinforce at the local level.

A third question that needs to be reopened, one that is intimately related to the points previously discussed, relates to impact(s), in other words, how do partnerships affect poverty through specific interventions? The UNDP has embraced the notion that partnerships can act as a powerful poverty reduction force by creating new markets and deepening existing ones (UNDP 2007). Poverty can be eradicated by developing products for those living at the 'bottom of the pyramid' (Prahalad 2004; United Nations Commission on the Private Sector and Development 2004) while striving to minimize any negative impacts and scaling up the positive ones. The emphasis on the virtues of a market-based development model reflects the assumption that businesses, large and small, can reduce poverty through their 'core competencies', benefiting both economically and in terms of reputation. In a typical multistakeholder partnership, these benefits are also expected to be shared by other partners, such as consultancies, service delivery NGOs and UN agencies that can rely on funds disbursed by donors for new partnerships and the development of market linkages.

Nonetheless, several ambiguities remain. What exactly is understood by poverty reduction or development? Who benefits from these initiatives? And what are the limits and contradictions of initiatives that aim to export and deepen capitalist relations of production in the developing world? As Newell and Frynas remind us, 'there are multiple forms of deprivation and social exclusion at work, often based on gender, race, ethnicity and class inequalities. Contributions to poverty alleviation which rest solely on the potential of business [and NGOs] to promote growth or provide jobs are therefore limited in addressing underlying causes of poverty which exclude people from labour markets in the first place' (Newell and Frynas 2007: 673). Beyond this central point, even if the only contribution of PPPs might be that of generating employment there are no requisites in place, besides the goodwill of lead business partners, for 'development partnerships' to address equity issues, such as contracts, wages, labour conditions and skill transfers, or to mitigate potentially adverse environmental impacts.

The growing sustainable business initiative

The points and questions raised in the previous discussion will serve as a basis to present an assessment of UNDP's GSB Initiative in Eastern Africa. Although the initiative is still in its infancy, experimenting with the brokerage of partnerships and seeing some immediate impacts, its institutional design, portfolio of projects and overarching objectives provide a fertile ground to comprehend the limits and potentials of reconciling market imperatives with equitable development.

A private sector idea

It was on the occasion of the Global Compact's second Policy Dialogue on Business and Sustainable Development that the concept of decentralized partnerships with a development dimension took a concrete form. The Policy Dialogue's Group on how companies contribute to sustainable development put forward the idea of contacting a group of companies that would be willing to explore sustainable business opportunities in LDCs and to work with stakeholders from those countries to develop an understanding of local needs (United Nations Global Compact 2002a). The idea of accelerating business expansion in LDCs and contributing to the eradication of poverty through profits was agreed upon by the Policy Dialogue participants and an initiative called 'Sustainable Investment and Access to Basic Services in LDCs' was constituted. Headed by Sir Mark Moody Stuart, former Chairman of the Royal Dutch/Shell and Business Action for Sustainable Development (BASD), the group was reconvened in a follow-up dialogue in Paris where the possibility was examined of a voluntary commitment by the Global Compact's signatories to grow some of their business activities in LDCs in line with the principles of sustainability. The idea was then envisaged to become a multistakeholder partnership with the twin aims of contributing to economic growth and socioeconomic development (United Nations Global Compact 2002b).

In the run up to the WSSD, Sir Mark Moody Stuart was invited by the Global Compact's Executive Director, Georg Kell, to identify a number of TNCs that would be interested in expanding their investment portfolio in sub-Saharan Africa and be part of a 'solution in support of sustainable development'.[4] The influential position of the BASD's Chair guaranteed that a number of companies responded positively to the proposed initiative, and the Global Compact in cooperation with the United Nations Conference on Trade and Development (UNCTAD), the United Nations Environment Programme (UNEP) and the UNDP seized the opportunity to present an embryonic overview of the initiative in Johannesburg. At a high-level roundtable chaired by UN Secretary General Kofi Annan and attended by heads of state, business leaders and prominent international NGOs (INGOs), the GSB was launched and was proclaimed by the UN Secretary-General as the 'most promising pathway in overcoming the poverty trap ... giv[ing] hope and opportunity to the world's poorest' (United Nations Global Compact 2002c). Shortly after the Summit, the UNDP, one of the Compact's core agencies, was delegated with the task of running the initiative, developing it further and decentralizing it to country offices. The choice of devolving the partnership initiative to the UNDP's Division for Business Partnerships was described by a UN official as 'natural', since the Office of the Secretary-General seeks to promote universal values, whereas the UNDP is the operational arm of the United Nations at country level.[5]

Objectives, structure and progress

The official launch of the initiative enabled a clearer delineation of the main aims and objectives underpinning the idea of forging partnerships for poverty through business models. In the first official document co-produced by the Compact and the UNDP, the overall contribution of the GSB was identified as being a means to alleviate poverty and promote sustainable development by 'facilitating sustainable business and investment by the private sector through a process of multi-stakeholder engagement with governments, civil society, the UN family and other development organisations' (United Nations Global Compact and UNDP 2004). Here, 'sustainable investment' is understood as a standard business activity, such as FDI, production or sales, which is based on accepted measures of social, environmental and economic responsibility as defined by the Global Compact's ten principles, but it is also a type of investment that involves and is supported by a number of state and non-state actors (Sandbrook 2002).

More specifically, the initiative wants to advance three interrelated goals. First, it seeks to facilitate increased investment activities by assisting corporate partners along with communities and relevant stakeholders through an investment cycle which encompasses opportunity identification, business model development, financing and implementation (Day et al. 2005a). Second, it wants to prove that 'sustainable business' projects can mitigate widespread poverty through the creation of new enterprises or supply chains, thus allowing the poor to access needed goods and services or employment opportunities (Day et al. 2005b). Third, the GSB aspires to support projects which are relevant to local contexts and are aligned with national priorities to achieve the MDGs, thereby making something happen for the needs of a nation and the poorest in it.

Operationally, the GSB is coordinated at both global and country levels. Globally, a small team of UNDP advisors are to encourage international companies to take action, support country-level activities and share country experiences. At the country level, where the partnerships unfold, a GSB Delivery Mechanism is established in selected LDCs 'where stakeholders agree that there is a need for such programme and where the UNDP Country Office is committed to supporting it' (Day et al. 2005a). The GSB Delivery Mechanism consists of a full-time GSB broker, who acts as an intermediary for the various stakeholders and oversees the research arm, whose role is to assist stakeholders in the creation of socioeconomic background studies, feasibility studies and the identification of sources of funding. The decision-making mechanism through which the GSB's targets are set, projects approved, and consensus on the meaning of sustainable business reached, is the GSB Coordinating Group – an umbrella group made of government representatives, businesses, NGOs, international organizations and relevant bilateral and multilateral donors (United Nations Global Compact and UNDP 2002).

In the GSB's early stages, signatories, such as Ericsson, Unilever, ABB, Tetra Pak, Shell and Total, formed the core group TNCs that undertook GSB pilot projects in Tanzania, Madagascar and Ethiopia in response to the Global Compact's invitation to offer contributions to boosting economic growth in LDCs (ABB 2005; Tetra Pak 2004). At the time, critical commentators were already pointing out that the initial 'Northern enthusiasm' for the initiative should not be overstated, since for many companies 'sustainable business' might simply equate to 'business as usual' with little but lip service to the Global Compact principles (Zammit 2003: 75) and the MDGs. Despite such criticisms, as the pilot phases drew to an end and success was proclaimed by international press coverage (Murray 2005), the GSB started to expand beyond the African continent to Eastern Europe, Central America and more recently in South-Eastern Asia (see Table 8.1). The process of expansion also corresponded to the development of a more wide-ranging approach to sustainable business partnerships; as only a comparatively small number of major TNCs had expressed interest in the initiative, the GSB's existence and continuation became more dependent on forging local PPPs with small and medium-sized enterprises (SMEs) and local stakeholders, such as local trusts and CSR foundations.

The GSB in Eastern Africa: an assessment

Since the initiative's inception, 12 UNDP Country Offices have set up a national GSB Delivery Mechanism and the only official estimate dating to 2005 indicates that the GSB has effectively brokered more than 30 partnerships with investment funds ranging from $20,000[6] to $2 million (Day et al. 2005b). Despite its steady geographical diffusion and growing project portfolio, no systematic research has yet been undertaken to unravel how the GSB Delivery Mechanisms actually operate. The fieldwork conducted in Kenya and Tanzania suggests that, within the UNDP's GSB initiative, the interaction of likeminded UN brokers and business elites has contributed to the development of unaccountable types of economic partnerships that prioritize financial soundness and profitability over and above considerations for sustainable and equitable development.

The GSB delivery mechanism: who decides what?

The main actor driving the GSB partnerships forward at country level is the GSB broker. According to UN documentation, the competencies required by the broker are an ability to convene collaborative coalitions of partners, to show significant experience in private sector work, and to have the capacity to understand and provide critical analysis of business models – including quantitative skills for the evaluation of investment projects, such as standard investment analysis and financial modelling (UNDP 2007). Nowhere does

Table 8.1 GSB delivery mechanisms worldwide, 2002–07

Launch	Country	Status	Region
2002	Ethiopia	Abandoned	Eastern Africa
2003	Madagascar	Active*	Eastern Africa
	Tanzania	Active	Eastern Africa
2005	Kenya	Active	Eastern Africa
	Zambia	Active	Eastern Africa
2006	Angola	Proposed**/Abandoned	Middle Africa
	Bosnia and Herzegovina	Broker appointed	Southern Europe
	El Salvador	Broker appointed/Abandoned	Central America
	Malawi	Active	Eastern Africa
	Macedonia	Broker appointed	Southern Europe
	Moldova	Active	Southern Europe
	Mozambique	Active	Eastern Africa
	Serbia	Active	Southern Europe
	Turkey	Active	Western Asia
2007	Cambodia	Broker appointed	South-Eastern Asia
	Indonesia	Not known***	South-Eastern Asia

Notes: The terminology for the geographical regions is according to the UN Statistics Division (http://unstats.un.org/unsd/methods/m49/m49regin.htm). * Active refers to the existence of a broker and a portfolio of projects. ** Proposal as part of the GSB expansion plan in 2006. *** Listed in the UNDP web site but without further information.
Source: The data were obtained from information posted on and at times removed from the UNDP GSB website (www.undp.org/partners/business/gsb/) between 2006 and early 2008.

the job specification require the broker to have a background in CSR, development or 'pro-poor' partnership initiatives. These omissions are important elements in understanding what kind of candidates are being sought to drive partnership processes.

In both Kenya and Tanzania the brokers appointed had extensive work experience in the private sector (that is, in business consultancy and finance) and a keen interest in development projects and processes. However, when asked what constituted 'sustainable business', they both displayed a predominantly economic understanding of partnerships and development. One broker, for example, stated that 'our priority is to develop new markets, creating employment and raising income ... development will trickle down',[7] while another broker confirmed that sustainable partnerships are to have an impact on poverty reduction by generating income.[8] Such economistic views of development seem to overshadow more pressing distributional and social questions. Despite the GSB brokers' good intentions over bridging the distributional gap through new investments, more qualitative considerations over the nature of 'sustainable investment' were not recognized. For example, it has been noted that however sustainable a business venture intends to be, a company which decides to undertake some form of profitable investment will tend to concentrate its training activities on the upper echelons of the labour force, thus bypassing the poor (Jenkins 2005: 553). Similarly, considerations regarding the location of partnerships in favour of poorer regions, environmental sustainability and gender inequalities were not being significantly explored, thereby entrenching a narrow and quantifiable understanding of development within the GSB, namely one which is predominantly defined and measured in terms of number of jobs created and potential increase in personal incomes.

The brokers are also assigned the responsibility of enabling the formation of the decision-making mechanisms at country level – the GSB Coordinating Group. The identification of the right or appropriate stakeholders did not seem to conform to the aspiration of 'closing the democratic deficit in global governance'; rather, it mirrored concerns such as individuals' status, institutional affiliation and willingness to participate in the GSB processes. In Kenya and Tanzania, the coordinating group members had a history of institutional affiliation with the United Nations or were invited to become members by virtue of the scale of their involvement in private sector and development activities. Official documentation suggests that these groups are quite heterogeneous and represent a blend of public and private interests. However, on closer inspection, in both Kenya and Tanzania the 'active' members who participate in the processes of deliberation are largely private sector representatives, and a handful of local NGOs with a long-standing interest in facilitating market expansion and deepening, such as the African Management Services Company (AMSCO) and the Kenya Gatsby Trust (KGT). The participation of donors, like the Swedish International Development Cooperation Agency (Sida) and the Norwegian Agency for Development Cooperation (Norad) in the case of Tanzania, international development institutions and NGOs can be best described as sporadic whereas labour representatives had been simply forgotten. Furthermore, despite recognizing the importance of including government officials within the coordinating mechanisms, the participation of public officials has been limited and inconsistent, particularly in Kenya.

Whereas the Kenyan coordinating group has consolidated itself into a tightly knit group of eight 'likeminded' individuals from local private sector organizations, the Tanzanian group has been mainly driven forward by foreign signatories of the Global Compact. When questioned about the 'representativity' of their respective groups, the emerging consensus was that the supposed beneficiaries of the partnerships did not have to be included in deliberations. One member of the coordinating group commented that 'when you bring the farmers in they tend to bring their own interests and they are not very objective. We, on the other hand have no direct or vested interest, we think about the whole community and not about individuals ... I would feel as if I let the farmers down if I did not attend a meeting'.[9]

Another member from the private sector added that 'the coordinating group is broad enough and if a labour union was to be invited to join they would not represent the non-unionised farmers'.[10] By the same token, the GSB brokers have never questioned the legitimacy of the groups, preferring instead to focus their attention on targets rather than political processes. Contrasting these views are those of a defiant UN bureaucrat, and former GSB broker, who advocated communities' participation and communities' ownership of partnership projects as a means to guarantee a more equitable distribution of the spoils of partnerships.[11] Similarly, a former GSB coordinating group member admitted that poorer communities affected by the partnerships catalyzed by the initiative were far removed from the 'CSR whirl', and that none of the coordinating group members could claim to speak for the interests of the Tanzanian people, as the initiative had originated in the West and had remained insensitive to the country's developmental needs and existing national and local development efforts.[12]

The particular configuration of developmental ideas and actors – the brokers and the coordinating group members – can be considered as a determinant factor in understanding how targets are set and sustainable partnerships projects are evaluated during official GSB meetings. The main trend is for all the projects proposed to be unanimously endorsed, with the provision that the lead company supplies the coordinating group with an ex ante project proposal containing a detailed business plan, a reflection on how the company believes the project is going to contribute to development with an emphasis on job creation and income generation, and a very brief assessment of the project's environmental impact and contribution to the broader partnership agenda. Unlike the assessment studies of larger projects driven by TNCs which were funded by the UNDP or attracted donors' funds, local SMEs often lacked the financial and human resources to assemble the proposal, and this was said to have caused considerable delays in getting the projects off the ground and, at times, even halting the process. However, the procedures for proposal writing were simplified with the introduction of a shorter template for SMEs.

In Tanzania, the changeover of brokers and the business-dominated composition of the coordinating group have contributed to allowing the deliberation mechanism to become not a forum to strengthen the accountability of the proposed partnerships and seriously engage with private sector and macro- and micro-development issues, but rather an opportunity for lead businesses to increasingly present new project proposals or feasibility studies which would then be automatically included in the GSB project portfolio. In a total of eight official meetings, only once were questions of gender, worker selection and ecological impact raised, in this case, in relation to Unilever's Novella partnership project to set up an Allanblackia (AB) supply chain in the Usambara region. Unilever responded to the criticisms by incorporating the comments made in a socioenvironmental study commissioned by

Norconsult. The study had addressed gender and equity dimensions, and enjoyed UNDP endorsement (Attipoe et al. 2006). It failed, however, to address how the real incremental revenue raised from a secondary farming activity paid at TSh150/Kg ($0.12) was supposed to be understood as something beyond the commercial activities of the company or one that would lift and 'empower' seasonal, predominantly female, workers out of poverty.

The deliberation processes in Kenya do not appear to diverge extensively from what occurs in Tanzania. Despite an interviewee's claim that 'we don't put a seal of approval on anything that comes by',[13] the evidence shows that almost every proposed partnership had been endorsed, with failing partnerships being praised or continued, and with failed partnerships being filed in the GSB portfolio simply as 'past projects'. As in the case of Tanzania, only once did the coordinating group raise objections to a particularly controversial plan put forward by a safari company (Gamewatchers Safari). The proposed partnership envisaged the creation of two boreholes in the Ol Kinyei Conservancy to enable the local Masai community to access water without endangering the value proposition of the company's existing eco-camp, which is built along a natural watercourse. The coordinating group objected to the project on the grounds that the community was being pushed away from their grazing land and local resources, and requested to visit the camp with the GSB broker. The visit to the camp was deemed successful, even though it lasted only three hours and the only 'local people' interviewed were the camp managers, camp employers and the community liaison officer. Of particular importance is the fact that the visit failed to assess how revenue accrued from the eco-camp would be of any benefit to the displaced cattle owners or how it would be channelled into local community projects. Nonetheless, the project was deemed financially sound and sustainable and a sum of $600 was set aside in support of a hydrological study in Ol Kinyei.

'Developmental' partnerships: *cui bono*?

If the composition and processes of the GSB Delivery Mechanisms seem to epitomize little more than another example of technocratic governance, the partnerships themselves consolidate an understanding that the ideational and material capacities of the most powerful stakeholders, particularly the private sector, shape the direction and outcomes of sustainable investment and development with little or no consideration for the limited or adverse impacts they might produce. In other words, the GSB processes and its mode of governance allow private partners to define what their developmental responsibilities are which, in practice, would appear to amount to little more than 'business as usual'. What is really UNusual, to borrow an expression popularized by Witte and Reinicke (2005), is that the UNDP appears to be facilitating the privatization of development without any significant rethink of the potential contradiction ensuing from the agency of businesses in LDCs.

The GSB official project portfolio consists of over 30 projects worldwide. However, in the context of Eastern Africa, not all the partnerships officially listed are actually being executed. In Kenya, for example, out of six officially listed partnerships only two were being operationalized as of 2006 and two additional partnership concepts were added to the portfolio in 2007. In Tanzania, only four out of 11 have moved from conceptualization to implementation. According to the Kenyan broker, 'partnerships dumped on us from New York'[14] from the Global Compact and GSB Global were proving difficult to handle, particularly those with private partners who did not have an office in Eastern Africa; additionally, fading corporate commitment and diverging interests among the partners resulted in the official abandonment of three projects.

One of the filed partnerships envisaged the linkage between the US-based information technology (IT) company Voxiva and the Kenyan NGO Pride Africa to build upon an existing transaction platform called DrumNet that gives farmers financial, market and information access. In this project Voxiva was expected to develop a tailored information system for commodities exchange, which would have enabled real-time data collection using low-cost mobile phones linked to a central database. The rationale underpinning the proposed partnership was that using low-cost technologies would allow more farmers to make better decisions, increase productivity and reduce poverty. According to Pride Africa, Voxiva was reluctant to relinquish control of a very expensive software and any changes to it would have resulted in additional costs that could not be financed, further hampering 'poor communication and responses not coming through'.[15] With funding from the Canadian International Development Research Centre (IDRC), DrumNet was able to develop an open source software to which Voxiva objected. DrumNet's project continued with an in-house research and development (R&D) team and with 'affordable' Kenyan partners, such as Nairobi's Institute for Development Studies, but the GSB Kenya no longer has a stake in it.

In Kenya, what 'seemed to have worked', namely the concepts that progressed from design to implementation, were the partnerships forged with local SMEs and between SMEs and NGOs. By contrast, in Tanzania, five foreign Global Compact's signatories with affiliates in the country or in Eastern Africa – ABB, Unilever, Tetra Pak, Ericsson and Holcim – were contributing to running the projects on the ground.

Although the brokers indicated that it is too premature to make an assessment of the developmental impact of the projects, the feasibility studies are a means of understanding what type of sustainable development is being fostered by the partnerships. One indication of the leverage conferred on the private sector is that the companies themselves are to draft these studies or choose who is to conduct the research. If the company itself produces such a study and seeks UN/UNDP endorsement or co-funding, it would hardly be surprising that the development impact predicted in the studies would be described as positive. For example, Global Entrepreneurs – an international trading and business development company with supply and sales offices in Uganda, Kenya, Colombia and India – partnered with UNDP Kenya to revive a macadamia nut supply chain with the view to exporting the produce to United Kingdom (UK) supermarkets. The ex ante project proposal, written by Global Entrepreneurs, states that 'the project will have a direct benefit to the farmers . . . they will enjoy higher income and after receiving education they will be able to make informed choices about their own situations'.[16] However, the study does not indicate how this prediction was reached or how (and if) the local revival of a supply chain linked to a global competitive market dominated by Australian, American and Brazilian producers would push risks and costs downwards. Interviews with the macadamia nut farmers also confirmed that one and a half years after the project was launched they had not seen any increment in their income and, in contrast to the views of management, even those living in close proximity to the processing factory claimed not to have received any training or extra support, such as the provision of fertilizers.

If, on the other hand, the company delegates the responsibility of the study to a consultancy group and contributes to paying the costs of the study, the company's interests in exploring the feasibility of a commercial activity are still likely to define what constitutes development. Ericsson's feasibility study, based on the idea of the 'bottom of the pyramid', was conducted by the consultancy Scanagri. Methodologically, the study did not offer a choice in purchasing preferences at a fixed income and, unsurprisingly, it revealed that Tanzanian farmers are 'clearly' interested in owning mobile phones. Furthermore, to add prestige to the investment plan, the study links its expected developmental outcomes, such as increased business opportunities and reduced time and cost in communications, to the fulfilment of the MDG 8,[17] without specifying whether this would stimulate local development, employment opportunities beyond the company's headquarters in Dar es Salaam or whether the project is in any way sustainable. Ericsson's project expects farmers to absorb all the up-front and indirect costs associated with mobile phones and it is projected to be implemented in areas already serviced by electricity. What the study appears to suggest is that 'development' would equate to the company's ordinary commercial activities and that any aspect of the developmental process that cannot be justified commercially falls outside the company's concerns.

Another indication of the potentially limited development impact of the projects is that the lead private partners are to decide where the projects are to unfold and who the beneficiaries are supposed to be. The company's commercial interests will inevitably dictate where the investment ought to be channelled. For example, in both Kenya and Tanzania the majority of operating partnerships were unfolding in geographical locations which were already relatively affluent by local standards and where there was little or no need for investment in infrastructure. Tetra Pak decided to pilot an integrated supply chain for ultra-high temperature (UHT) milk in Dar es Salaam, whereas Global Entrepreneurs chose to locate its activities in the well-serviced capital of the Embu district. If the investment projects are concentrated in the wealthiest regions, the real impact of the GSB partnerships on poverty alleviation is left open to question.

An additional concern relates to the direct benefits accruing to workers targeted by the partnerships. The academic literature claims that there is greater potential for such investment to benefit the 'poor' by creating linkages with local firms, especially where suppliers are microenterprises or smallholders (Jenkins 2005: 252). However, GSB partnerships have displayed a propensity to pay local suppliers so little that the net economic short- to medium-term impact to smallholders can be considered negligible, as exemplified by the projects of Global Entrepreneurs, Kevian and Unilever. Furthermore, partnerships that have sought to deepen an existing market or revive the fortunes of existing industries have inevitably targeted the upper echelons of the labour force or, as in the case of the Tanzanian sugar producer Kilombero, they have provided health and education services primarily to the benefit of the company's employees, who had a tradition of militancy, thus bypassing the least well off in the Morogoro region.

Finally, any potential benefits accruing to local communities and workers that the partnerships are intended to provide might be limited by the fact that long-term sustainability is driven by commercial motives. Under the GSB partnership terms, companies, with or without other partners, commit themselves to initiating sustainable and long-term investment projects; however, if the investment does not yield the expected results, the company can pull out of the partnership and relinquish its responsibilities vis-à-vis the communities and workers it was expected to lift out of poverty. In Kenya, for example, the Nairobi-based fruit juice producer Kevian entered in partnership with the Deutsche Gesellschaft für Technische Zusammenarbeit/GTZ (German Technical Cooperation) and KGT to develop a local supply chain for mangoes. GTZ and KGT provided training and much-needed extension services to the mango farmers in the Malindi region; yet when it became apparent that Kevian would have to pay for the transport cost of the fruit, the company considered pulling out of the partnership to look for more cost-efficient suppliers, temporarily leaving the farmers with no buyers. This particular example illustrates that development might be stretched only to the point where it remains profitable. Kevian nonetheless remained committed to the suppliers, since it made a substantial investment in a fruit-processing factory in Thika. Alongside the creation of a new factory, GTZ and KGT have continued to offer training in production techniques and quality standards and organize farmers in the coastal region. Ultimately, the potential of this partnership might rest in the ability of organized small-scale producers to use 'voice' in order to negotiate better prices and contractual terms with their local buyers.

Conclusion

The above analysis of the 'partnerships for development' fostered by the GSB suggests that a political reading of PPPs ought to identify the power relationships at work in their governance and operationalization. The evaluation of the GSB Delivery Mechanism revealed that private interest and a truncated, predominantly economic, understanding of development, shape the GSB's deliberation processes, and that these have encouraged the emergence of yet another form of technocratic governance that remains largely silent about the equity aspects of development. The examination of projects carried out in Kenya and Tanzania showed that the private sector's efforts to be portrayed as an integral actor in development activities is little more than a 'business as usual' approach. The empirical research demonstrated that the leverage conferred to companies by the GSB arrangements allows a company to determine what constitutes development and who the beneficiaries of these interventions should be. In practice, if sustainable development works primarily to further the commercial interests or reputation of a company, then it is evident that the GSB and its partners are not fully geared up to meet the challenges of equitable and sustainable development. Furthermore, given the absence of any mechanism that delineates the responsibilities of companies vis-à-vis the intended beneficiaries of the investment, a project that does not turn out to be viable may even have negative impacts on poverty reduction and development.

The chapter's intention has not, of course, been solely that of critiquing the UN's approach to partnership and highlighting its limitations, but to draw attention to the political nature of these new forms of engagement in order for the United Nations to directly address these critical issues. It would be naïve to think that the United Nations will abandon the route of pragmatism (Utting and Zammit 2006) in favour of a more idealistic type of bottom-up democracy or new form of multilateralism that strives for certain normative goals, such as social equity and greater diffusion of power among people, social classes and gender (Cox 1997). As this appraisal suggests, however, it is clear that the partnership paradigm must become more accountable and development-centred. Furthering the commercial interests of the business sector or, as Fox (2004) suggests, 'tinkering at the edges' is not enough.

At the outset of this chapter it was suggested that the GSB and the UNDP ought to rethink the implications and operationalization of partnerships for development. These supply-driven interventions are prone to replicate several concerns that have been identified by the more critical literature (Utting 2001; Martens 2007), such as strengthening the political power of business, the replacement of the role of governments as a provider of public goods and the corollary creation of an elitist mode of governance. These new social pacts could be perceived as more legitimate and even prove to be more effective if the expected beneficiaries were given more voice and if 'sustainable business' initiatives were selected to reinforce state-led development policies to amplify the impact of existing programmes (Newell and Frynas 2007). What does this mean for the GSB? First of all, it means reassessing the value of supply-driven intervention and abandoning the 'anything goes' approach that has characterized the initiative to date, while aligning more closely the commercial interests of the private sector to the existing national development plans and poverty eradication initiatives, such as the Mukukuta in Tanzania and Kenya's Economic Strategy for Wealth and Employment Creation. Second, opening up the GSB's decision-making mechanism to the beneficiaries of the projects or other non-strategic and less complacent stakeholders could actually improve the prospects of addressing more systematically the positive and negative qualitative impact(s) of the partnerships' projects. Ultimately, public reporting and monitoring should become an integral component of partnership building and implementation. The early efforts to post online the minutes of meetings and create public briefings were encouraging steps, but these suddenly stopped, while the issues of monitoring and assessment have yet to receive attention.

These suggestions have been advanced to offer scope for the GSB to be more effective in allowing sustainable business to work for some beneficiaries, in some places and tackling some developmental concerns. It must also be acknowledged that there will always be inherent limits and contradictions in what sustainable business and MSIs can bring to the process of development. Businesses in conjunction with international organizations, NGOs and trade unions can be invited to reflect on doing less harm and more good, whether by means of investment or philanthropic efforts, or even by championing anti-poverty campaigns through UN-led coalitions such as the newly formed 'Business Call to Action'. However, these actions also need to be judged in relation to the power of business interests, their political and lobbying activities, and the capacity (or lack of) of governments to define the role of business in society through regulatory frameworks and taxation.

Notes

1. Reinicke (1999); Reinicke and Deng (2000); Ruggie (2000); Waddel (2003); McIntosh et al. (2004).
2. The appraisal of the GSB's activities is primarily based on semi-structured interviews with UN civil servants, chief executive officers (CEOs), corporate social responsibility (CSR) practitioners, NGOs, academics and community groups. Desk-based research and primary research consisting of 43 face-to-face interviews, telephone interviews and focus groups were undertaken in London, Vienna, Geneva, New York, Kenya and Tanzania between 2005 and 2007.
3. Conceived in the late 1990s and run by the Global Public Policy Institute (GPPi) with funding from the UN Foundation, the UN Vision Project provided strategic guidance to the United Nations in formulating and implementing PPPs.

The resonance of the recommendations produced by the project was highlighted in the Secretary-General's Millennium Report *We the Peoples* (United Nations 2000).
4. Interview, Anglo American, London, 6 June 2005.
5. Interview, United Nations, New York, 9 December 2005.
6. All references to $ are to US dollars.
7. Interview, UNDP Kenya, Nairobi, 6 July 2006.
8. Interview, UNDP Tanzania, Dar es Salaam, 9 August 2006.
9. Interview, Kenya Gatsby Trust (KGT), Nairobi, 14 July 2006.
10. Interview, Export Promotion Council, Nairobi, 20 July 2006.
11. Interview, UNDP Tanzania, Dar es Salaam, 16 August 2006.
12. Interview, Independent Consultant, Economic and Social Research Foundation Tanzania, 11 August 2006.
13. Interview, KGT, Nairobi, 14 July 2006.
14. Interview, UNDP Kenya, Nairobi, 6 July 2006.
15. Interview, Pride Africa, Nairobi, 7 July 2006.
16. Interview, Global Entrepreneurs, Nairobi, 13 July 2006.
17. MDG 8 aspires to make available, in cooperation with the private sector, the benefits of new technologies.

References

ABB (Asea Brown Boveri, Ltd.), *Access to Electricity – White Paper on ABB's Initiative for Access to Electricity* (Zurich: ABB, 2005).

Attipoe, Lawrence, Annett Van Andel and Samuel Kofi Nyame, 'The Novella Project – Developing a sustainable supply chain for Allanblackia oil'. In R. Ruben, M. Slingerland and H. Hijhoff (eds), *Agro-Food Chains and Networks for Development* (The Netherlands: Springer, 2006).

Bekefi, Tamara, *Tanzania: Lessons in Building Linkages for Competitive and Responsible Entrepreneurship* (Cambridge, MA: UNIDO and John F. Kennedy School of Government, Harvard University, 2006).

Blowfield, Michael, 'Reasons to be cheerful? What we know about CSR's impact', *Third World Quarterly*, Vol. 28, No. 4 (2007) 683–95.

Bruno, Kenny and Joshua Karliner, *Earthsummit.biz – The Corporate Takeover of Sustainable Development* (Oakland, CA: Food First Books, 2002).

Bull, Benedicte, Bøäs Morten and Desmond McNeil, 'Private sector influence in the multilateral system: A changing structure of world governance?', *Global Governance*, Vol. 10 (2004) 481–98.

Calder, Fanny, *The Potential for Using the Multistakeholder Network Model to Develop and Deliver Partnerships for Implementation (Type Two Outcomes) for the World Summit on Sustainable Development*, Discussion Paper (London: Royal Institute of International Affairs, Chatham House, February 2002). www.chathamhouse.org.uk/publications/papers/view/-/id/17/ (accessed in September 2007).

Calder, Fanny and Malaika Culverwell, *Following up the World Summit on Sustainable Development Commitments on Corporate Social Responsibility* (London: Royal Institute of International Affairs, Chatham House, 2005). www.chathamhouse.org.uk/files/3878_csrwssdf.pdf (accessed in September 2007).

Clapp, Jennifer, 'Global environmental governance for corporate responsibility and accountability', *Global Environmental Politics*, Vol. 5, No. 3 (2005) 24–34.

Cox, Robert W., 'Reconsiderations'. In Robert W. Cox (ed.), *New Realism Perspectives on Multilateralism and World Order* (London: Macmillan, 1997). http://www.enewsbuilder.net/globalcompact/e_article000427880.cfm?x= b11,0,w (accessed on 9 July 2009).

Day, William, Sanjay Gandhi and Jonas Giersing, 'UNDP's growing sustainable business initiative: From policies to action', *Alliance*, Vol. 10, No. 3 (2005a) 50–2.

——,'Partnering for poverty reduction: The growing sustainable business initiative', *Global Compact Quarterly*, Vol. 1, No. 3 (2005b). http://www.enewsbuilder.net/globalcompact/e_article000427880_cfm?x=bll,o,w (accessed on 9 July 2009).

Fox, Tom, 'Corporate social responsibility and development: In quest of an agenda', *Development*, Vol. 47, No. 3 (2004) 29–36.

Frynas, George Jedrzej, 'The false developmental promise of corporate social responsibility: Evidence from multinational oil companies', *International Affairs*, Vol. 81, No. 3 (2005) 581–98.

Higgott, Richard, 'Contested globalisation: The changing context and the normative challenges', *Review of International Studies*, Vol. 26 (2001) 131–53.

Jenkins, Rhys, 'Globalisation, corporate responsibility and poverty', *International Affairs*, Vol. 81, No. 3 (2005) 525–40.

Martens, Jens, *Multistakeholder Partnerships – Future Models of Multilateralism?* Dialogue on Globalization, Occasional Paper No. 29, January (Berlin: Friedrich-Ebert-Stiftung, 2007).

McFalls, Ricarda, 'Testing the Limits of "Inclusive Capitalism" – A Case Study of the South Africa HP i-Community', *Journal of Corporate Citizenship*, Vol. 28, Winter (2007) 85–98.

McIntosh, Malcom, Sandra Waddok and Georg Kell (eds), *Learning to Talk, Corporate Citizenship and the Development of the UN Global Compact* (Sheffield: Greenleaf Publishing, 2004).

Murray, Sarah, 'Partnerships that profit the poor', *Financial Times*, 31 March (2005) 13.

Nelson, Jane, *Building Partnerships – Cooperation between the United Nations System and the Private Sector* (New York: United Nations Department of Public Affairs, 2002).

Newell, Peter, 'Citizenship, accountability and community: The limits of the CSR agenda', *International Affairs*, Vol. 81, No. 3 (2005) 541–57.

Newell, Peter and George Frynas, 'Beyond CSR? Business, poverty and social justice: An introduction', *Third World Quarterly*, Vol. 28, No. 4 (2007) 669–81.

Prahalad, Coimbatore K., *The Fortune at the Bottom of the Pyramid – Eradicating Poverty through Profits* (Upper Saddle River, NJ: Wharton School Publishing, 2004).

Prieto-Carrón Marina, Peter Lund-Thomsen, Anita Chan, Anna Muro and Bushanan Chandra, 'Critical perspectives on CSR and development: What we know, we don't know and what we need to know', *International Affairs*, Vol. 82, No. 5 (2006) 977–87.

Reinicke, Wolfgang H., 'The other world wide web: Global public policy networks', *Foreign Policy*, No. 117 (1999) 44–57.

Reinicke, Wolfgang H. and Francis M. Deng, *Critical Choices: The United Nations, Networks and the Future of Global Governance* (Toronto: International Development Research Council, 2000).

Ruggie, John G., 'Taking embedded liberalism global: The corporate connection'. In David Held and Mathias Koenig-Archibugi (eds), *Taming Globalization – Frontiers of Governance* (Cambridge: Polity Press, 2003).

——, 'Globalisation, the Global Compact and corporate social responsibility', *Transnational Associations*, Vol. 52, No. 6 (2000) 291–4.

Sandbrook, Richard, *Growing Sustainable Business for Poverty Reduction in Tan-zania* (2002). www.tz.undp.org/publications/GSB_introduction.ppt (accessed in September 2007).

Tesner, Sandrine and Georg Kell, *The United Nations and Business – A Partnership Recovered* (New York: St. Martin's Press, 2000).

Tetra Pak, *Tetra Pak Becomes a Participating Company in the UN Global Compact* (2004). www.tetrapak.com/index.asp?navid=117&show=13 (accessed in September 2007).

United Nations, *Towards Global Partnerships*. UN Doc. No. A/RES/60/215, United Nations General Assembly, New York, 29 March 2006. http://daccessdds.un.org/doc/UNDOC/GEN/N05/500/50/PDF/N0550050. pdf?OpenElement (accessed in September 2007).

——, *We the Peoples – The Role of the United Nations in the 21st Century* (New York: United Nations Department of Public Information, 2000).

United Nations Commission on the Private Sector and Development, *Unpleasing Entrepreneurship – Making Business Work for the Poor* (New York: UNDP, 2004).

UNDP (United Nations Development Programme), *Growing Sustainable Business Broker*, Vacancy 2007, Malawi (2007). http://jobs.undp.org/cj_view_job.cfm?job_id=543 (accessed in January 2007).

United Nations Global Compact, *Global Compact Policy Dialogue 2002: Business and Sustainable Development – Outcomes of the 1st Meeting* (2002a). www.unglobalcompact. org/Issues/sustainable_development/meetings_and_workshops/GCPD_Meeting_UN_Headquarters_New_York.html (accessed in September 2007).

——, *Global Policy Dialogue 2002: Business and Sustainable Development – Outcomes of the 2nd Meeting* (2002b). www.unglobalcompact. org/Issues/sustainable_development/meetings_and_workshops/GCPD_Meeting_Paris.html (accessed in September 2007).

——, *Global Compact Launches Development Initiative at Summit* (2002c). www.unglobalcompact. org/Issues/sustainable_development/meetings_and_ workshops/Global_Compact_Launches_Development.html (accessed in September 2007).

United Nations Global Compact and UNDP, *Growing Sustainable Business for Poverty Reduction* (2004). www.unglobalcompact.org/docs/issues_doc/7.3/GSB_overview.pdf (accessed in September 2007).

——, *Growing Sustainable Business for Poverty Reduction in Tanzania – ToR for the GSB Coordinating Group* (2002). www.tz.undp.org/publications/GSB_draftTOR.pdf (accessed in September 2007).

Utting, Peter, 'Corporate responsibility and the movement of business', *Development in Practice*, Vol. 15, No. 3/4 (2005) 375–88.

——, 'UN–business partnerships: Whose agenda counts?', *Transnational Associations*, No. 3 (2001) 118–29.

Utting, Peter and Ann Zammit, *Beyond Pragmatism, Appraising UN-Business Partnerships*. Programme on Markets, Business and Regulation, Paper No. 1. (Geneva: UNRISD, 2006).

Waddel, Steve, 'Global Action Networks: A global invention helping business make globalisation work for all', *Journal of Corporate Citizenship*, Vol. 12 (2003) 27–42.

Witte, Jan Martin and Wolfgang Reinicke, *Businesss Unusual – Facilitating United Nations Reform through Partnerships* (New York: United Nations Global Compact Office, 2005).

Zammit, Ann, *Development at Risk – Rethinking UN–Business Partnerships* (Geneva: South Centre and UNRISD, 2003).

9
Private Food Governance: Implications for Social Sustainability and Democratic Legitimacy

Doris Fuchs and Agni Kalfagianni

Introduction

The global food system and its governance have important implications for the question of sustainability. Engaging over half of the world's population, agricultural production provides a livelihood for a major proportion of people on the planet, and food is a commodity that touches us all as consumers. Food production and trade, moreover, have important implications for socioeconomic outcomes and, depending on their organization and distribution, can work to either enhance or detract from economic opportunities and environmental and social living conditions.

This chapter seeks to better understand how business actors, and specifically transnational corporations (TNCs), impact social aspects of sustainable development in developing countries through the creation of private institutions in food governance. Given the proliferation of private governance institutions in the area of agriculture and food, their impact on sustainability, especially its social dimension, becomes crucial. We pursue our objectives applying a power-theoretic approach, where we assume that actors draw power from material and structural as well as ideational and normative sources (Fuchs 2005a[1]). From this perspective, actors exercise power when they influence other actors' decisions (instrumental power). Actors also exercise power by influencing other actors' policy options. This kind of power is called structural power and can exist as both agenda-setting and rule-setting power. And, finally, actors exercise power by influencing other actors' perceptions concerning their own interests and thereby their preferences. This form of power can be referred to as discursive power.

In addition, the chapter discusses the democratic implications of private governance institutions and highlights the challenges private and public actors face in the global governance of food in that respect. In discussing the democratic implications, the chapter focuses both on input-oriented arguments for procedural democracy and output-oriented arguments, that is, the question of whether private institutions contribute to, or hinder, the creation of the conditions necessary to protect the poor and reduce the chasm between the rich and the poor in the long term. Moreover, the chapter also discusses the concept of deliberative democracy as an alternative source of legitimation for food governance beyond the state.

The chapter is organized as follows. The next section provides background information concerning the characteristics of global food governance, highlighting the increasing role of food retailers. We then provide some examples of private retail institutions, in particular retail standards, and go on to discuss their implications for the social dimension of sustainability and democratic legitimacy. A concluding section summarizes our findings and delineates their implications for research and policy.

Characteristics of global food governance

Today's global food governance is characterized by the increasing role of private governance institutions, such as private standards for food safety and quality, corporate social responsibility (CSR) initiatives, and public–private partnerships (PPPs). The rise of private food governance institutions can be understood within a broader set of changes in the global food and agricultural system that have taken place in the past two decades, centred around the Uruguay Round (UR) (1986–1994) of the General Agreement on Tariffs and Trade (GATT). Prior to the UR, agriculture was exempt from GATT and states had their own national strategies regarding food (for example, the green revolution). The UR focused on a reduction of barriers to trade in agricultural commodities *worldwide*, a development which culminated in the creation of the World Trade Organization (WTO) Agreement on Agriculture (AoA) (1995). As the liberal trade regime in agriculture brought dramatic changes to the food system, the pressures for competition in a global market intensified. As a consequence, there was a concentration of production and an integration of supply chains (Josling 2002). These transformations led to the strengthening of the food industry (Tansey and Worsley 1995) and the creation of big multinationals. As the agricultural sector increasingly transformed itself into a food sector, food companies, including retailers, became the main players in the global political arena.

Even though concentration in the retail sector is still less than in other parts of the food chain, such as manufacturing, it is nevertheless significant, to the point that it has been characterized as an oligopoly (Burch and Lawrence 2005; Konefal et al. 2005). In Australia, for instance, over 75 per cent of food retail distribution is controlled by three firms (FAO 2003). In Europe and the United States (US), retail concentration is high as well and has increased notably over the past decade. In the United States, for example, the five largest supermarket chains have more than doubled their market share between 1992 and 2000 (Konefal et al. 2005). Concentration, however, is also high in developing countries. Reardon et al. (2004) report that in Latin America the top five chains per country control 65 per cent of the supermarket sector. Most of the acquisitions of smaller chains and independents are taking place via foreign direct investment (FDI), with few being made by larger domestic chains (Reardon et al. 2004).[2] As illustrated in the following paragraphs, retailers are able to exercise significant structural and market power as a result of these developments. Moreover, if one takes into account that concentration in the retail sector is likely to continue to rise rapidly (Lang 2003), the implications for future trends in retail power are immense.

At the same time, a new form of retail company has developed, characterized by the control of the product chain from farm to shelf. The underlying, highly complex, logistical tasks are made possible, among other things, by new technologies of supply chain management, with shipments traced by the Global Positioning System (GPS) and deliveries handled in short time windows defined by the minute (Burch and Lawrence 2005). Moreover, competition among retail companies is currently based not only on price but also on quality (Konefal et al. 2005). Indeed, food scandals and increased health awareness, combined with shrinking time budgets of consumers in the North, have led to the emergence of new markets. Retail market data indicate that the sector has enjoyed sharp increases in revenues in the luxury, organic and health food segments as a result (Datamonitor 2006). Although these markets are still referred to as 'niche', they are the markets where most of the money will likely be earned in the near future. At the same time, however, discount retailers also enjoy a boom in developed markets on the basis of cheap bulk foods. Experts expect this soon to be true for the developing markets of the Asia-Pacific region as well, where several US supermarket chains are pursuing aggressive expansion strategies (Datamonitor 2006). Thus, large retail chains have responded in a dual fashion to the changing competitive landscape, with some opting for provision of expensive, high-quality foods and some others for cheaper, low-quality bulk foods.

What is the significance of these developments, particularly for developing countries? With the liberalization of agriculture, production has become far more export-oriented. As a result, self-sufficiency of food has been challenged, in particular in the global South where exposure to market pressures changed the character and intensity of agricultural production, increasing the vulnerability of smallholder and subsistence farmers. The pressures exercised by international organizations, specifically the World Bank, the International Monetary Fund (IMF) and the WTO to withdraw state support to farmers, compounded the issue. Numerous developing countries now have to rely on food imports to feed their populations. By the mid-1990s, half of the foreign exchange of the 88 countries that the Food and Agriculture Organization of the United Nations (FAO) classifies as low-income food deficit countries went to food imports (McMichael 2004). Of the 10 poorest countries in the world (Sierra Leone, Tanzania, Malawi, the Democratic Republic of Congo, Burundi, Zambia, Yemen, Ethiopia, Mali and Madagascar), six were found to be less prosperous than they were 20 years ago (Lines et al. 2004). These countries' economies depend heavily on exporting primary commodities (food and raw materials) to pay for food imports (Lines et al. 2004). The increase in agricultural trade, therefore, also increased food dependency.

At the same time, retailers are now able to exercise significant market power on the lower parts of the chain, and in particular on farmers, exerting downward pressure on prices.[3] Importantly, the large grocery chains prefer selling and distributing the premium national and international brands, making it extremely difficult for small or local farmers with lesser-known brands to get their products into the grocery chains. In addition, many retailers are establishing contracts with their suppliers that allow retailers to determine the quality attributes of the suppliers' products (Reardon et al. 2004: 18). This gain in market power and prominence in distribution networks implies not only the need for larger volumes and/or continuous delivery in individual transactions, but also more power to impose private standards (FAO 2003). In other words, retailers are able to exercise structural power in world and domestic markets. Private standards are a source and manifestation of structural power in the sense that retailers have the ability to determine the choice set both of countries and farmers regarding what they can produce and how.

Moreover, private standards are a manifestation of retailers' instrumental power as well. The food industry is lobbying hard to head off state regulation in addition to trying to influence the content of public standards (Agribusiness Examiner 2005; Healthmatters 2004).[4] Regarding health-related issues, for example, United Kingdom (UK) retailers have lobbied the Food and Drink Federation to drop statutory labelling of food as detrimental to health, and use the low salt/sugar/fat choices presented by retailers instead (Healthmatters 2004). In the United States, big food corporations have lobbied the Food and Drug Administration regarding the content of carbohydrates in food, aiming to generate their own 'low-carb' food labelling (Edwards and Reyes 2004). Instrumental power, then, can be used by retailers not only to influence the content of public standards, but more importantly to replace public with private standards. In that context, commentators also report on the success of the US retail lobby in keeping national minimum wages from rising (DSNRetailing Today, 25 February 2002).

Retailers are able to exercise significant discursive power as well. Food retailers do this, for instance, by presenting themselves as guardians of consumer interests with respect to both prices and quality. They emphasize their efficiency as market actors in production and distribution, but, more importantly, also in the design and monitoring of standards (Konefal et al. 2005). Their core argument is that public actors act too slowly and do not have the necessary expertise to set the most efficient standards, an argument frequently made in many other business sectors.

The exercise of discursive power takes place via advertising and public relations (PR) campaigns. Private standards form an important part of such PR strategies as well. While the standard guidelines are not communicated directly to consumers and are not included in product labelling, important communication takes place via retailers' branding efforts to create a loyal and stable customer base (Burch and Lawrence 2005; Codron et al. 2006).[5] The incorporation of private standards into retail brand items is meant to signal quality assurance as well as establish and maintain the legitimacy of retailers as major actors in food governance. It is noteworthy in this context that private standards are not only a manifestation of retailers' structural and discursive power, but also a means to extend it. Finally, and most fundamentally, retail companies' media presence is crucial to their discursive power, both as a medium to constantly communicate with consumers and to adequately present and frame themselves (see also Fuchs et al. forthcoming).

To summarize, the liberalization of agriculture and food brought significant changes to the global food system, leading to the rise of big retailers as prominent actors in agriculture and food industry governance. As a result, retailers are now able to exercise significant structural and discursive power, through private institutions, or more specifically, private standards. Moreover, lobbying efforts enable retailers to head off public standards or public influence on the content of private standards. The following section presents examples of private standards and discusses their implications for social aspects of sustainability.

Private standards and their consequences

The consequences of private food governance that relate to social sustainability have not been addressed comprehensively in the literature. More attention is paid to environmental considerations of production and distribution systems or issues, such as food safety. It should be noted that social considerations are not only equally important, but may also be more pressing at the moment. Most of the world's poor live in rural areas. It is estimated that in 2001 among the poorest 1.2 billion people in the world – who survive on less than a dollar a day – three out of four lived in rural areas (IFAD 2001). As a result, the question how these people and their livelihoods are affected by private standards set by big retailers is particularly important and has extremely relevant implications for any discussion on the sustainability of the global food system. In this section we aim to provide some answers to this question. Before doing that, however, we present an illustration of private food retail standards.

Examples of private retail standards

Private standards are a form of governance that has proliferated in recent years, especially in the retail sector. They are defined as a rule of measurement established by regulation or authority (Jones and Hill 1994). Private standards tend to be voluntary in nature and rely on various sorts of certification mechanisms to identify actors complying with the principles defined in the standard. They cover a variety of issues at all levels of the food chain ranging from food safety and quality, to environmental management and workers' rights. Most of the retail standards are developed collectively (either at the national or international level) in order to strengthen their structural power and induce supplier participation. As discussed below, by adopting the same standards retailers can constrain market choices and thereby basically force suppliers to accept them (Busch 2000). The British Retail Consortium (BRC), the Global Food Safety Initiative (GFSI), FOODTRACE, the Global Partnership for Good Agricultural Practice (Global-Gap), the International Food Standard (IFS) and the Ethical Trading Initiative (ETI) are examples of such standards. Compliance by the participating agricultural and food companies is certified through independent auditors.[6]

The BRC Technical Standard was created by the BRC in 1998 in order to evaluate manufacturers of retailers' own brand products. It consists of more than 250 requirements, including comprehensive norms for food safety and quality schemes, products and process management, as well as the personal hygiene of personnel. For most UK and Scandinavian retailers, BRC certification is required in order to consider business with these suppliers (CERES 2008). Following the Packaging Standard in the previous year, the Consumer Products Standard was introduced in August 2003 by the BRC. Each of these standards is revised and updated at least every three years.

The GFSI was launched in 2000 by a group of international retailers and global manufacturers. With 52 members and 65 per cent of worldwide food retail revenue, it aims for consumer protection and the strengthening of consumer confidence. Furthermore, the initiative sets requirements for food safety and aims to improve efficiency throughout the food chain.

The Global-Gap (known as Eurep-Gap until 2007) was developed in 1997 by a group of retailers belonging to the Euro-Retailers Produce Working Group (Eurep). While initially only applying to fruits and vegetables, it now covers meat products and fish from aquaculture as well. Completion and verification of a checklist consisting of 254 questions are required in order to acquire Global-Gap certification. This checklist is divided into 41 'major musts', 122 'minor musts', as well as 91 recommendations ('shoulds'). Traceability and food safety are covered by 'major must' practices, while 'minor musts' and 'shoulds' include environmental and animal welfare issues.

FOODTRACE was initiated by the European retail association, Eurocommerce, with the aim of promoting concerted action in Europe for the development of a traceability scheme for the whole chain. The goal is to create a practical framework for all actors involved in the chain, including the international level, thereby allowing for traceability throughout all stages of the chain. In order to ensure its application in developing countries, the proposed scheme is supposed to be technology independent but technologically supported.

The IFS is a standard developed for retailers and wholesalers to ensure the safety of own-brand products. It was initiated in 2002 by German food retailers from the Hauptverband des Deutschen Einzelhandels (HDE/Central Association of German Retail Trade). In 2003, French food retailers (and wholesalers) from the Fédération des Entreprises du Commerce et de la Distribution FCD/Federation of Commerce and Distribution Companies) joined the IFS Working Group and have contributed to the development of subsequent versions of IFS (version 4).

The ETI was formed in 1998. Its aim is to develop an agreed baseline code of conduct covering employment conditions among companies, unions and non-governmental organizations (NGOs), and examine how systems of monitoring and verification can be established. As a UK initiative, its ultimate goal is to ensure that the working conditions of workers producing for the UK market at least meet international labour standards. Scholars note that the ETI should be distinguished from fair trade or alternative trade in that it is not restricted to small producers and does not carry a specific seal of approval, although companies can advertise their association with the ETI if they so desire (Smith and Barrientos 2005). Rather, it is based on a company applying a code to its suppliers in the same way as it applies other conditions of supply covering production and product specification (Smith and Barrientos 2005).

In so far as these private governance institutions emphasize certain issues over others (food safety, for instance) have been created by a certain group of actors, and function in similar ways when it comes to monitoring, transparency and accountability, they are characteristic of developments occurring more generally in global food governance and in the role of retailers in particular. Through an examination of social dimensions of sustainability and democratic legitimacy, these characteristics are considered in more detail in the sections that follow.

Societal consequences of private retail standards

Social aspects of sustainability of food governance cover a wide array of complex issues including workers' rights, migration, gender issues, rural livelihoods and food security. In that context, private governance institutions claim to substitute for weak states, especially in developing countries that lack the capacity (and perhaps willingness) to provide and enforce social safety nets. The most important private governance institutions aiming to improve the social conditions of the food system include codes of conduct and other CSR instruments. The central feature of these standards and institutions is that they set out principles and criteria against which company performance is measured and reported upon (Blowfield 2005). Codes of conduct, for example, can be understood as written guidelines on the basis of which companies deal with their workforce, suppliers, state authorities and external stakeholders in their host country (Greven 2004: 142). Other aspects of CSR include the corporate reporting of business activities that relate to social, human rights and environmental issues. The idea is that such reporting will foster transparency and ultimately improve firms' performance on these fronts.

Social and labour standards

Social provisions, such as worker welfare, gender non-discrimination and rules against sexual harassment, are included in some mainstream standards and companies' codes of conduct (for example, Chiquita Code of Conduct), albeit playing a secondary role compared to the current understanding of food quality. Scholars report that in several cases the presence of these standards can improve labour conditions, raise wages and increase workers' security (Schaller 2007; Pearson 2007). Social standards suffer from a number of limitations, however, both in terms of their scope and implementation that severely constrain the range of benefits they generate.

More specifically, social standards tend to apply primarily to the regular employment workforce, who may benefit from the newly introduced standards and management practices promoted by retailers. However, most workers in the supply chain who are employed on a more informal basis, such as migrant and contract workers, have far fewer benefits.[7] Indeed, much of the labour force in developing countries is 'flexible', working only seasonally or 'informally', and comprising mostly of female workers who may even do unpaid jobs (Barrientos et al. 2001; Dolan 2005). The limited scope of private social standards, then, increases the gap between protected and unprotected workers (Barrientos et al. 2001), reinforcing economic and social cleavages that already exist.

The situation of women working in agriculture seems particularly problematic. Concentrated at the lower and less skilled end of the occupational hierarchy, they are particularly vulnerable to both structural and individual discrimination and abuse in terms of working conditions, levels of pay, insecurity of employment and harsh or undignified employment (Pearson 2007). Research conducted by the International Union of Food, Agricultural, Hotel, Restaurant, Catering, Tobacco and Allied Workers' Associations (IUF) on working conditions in the cut flower industry in Africa, including farms involved in several ethical codes, for example, shows that even though the sector has brought much-needed employment for women workers, these same workers have paid a heavy price in terms of ongoing problems related to the use of pesticides, repetitive strain injury and sexual harassment (Utting 2007). These concerns become particularly acute if we consider the 'feminization' of agriculture that is observed in many countries (Deere 2005).

In that context, scholars observe that gender issues are insufficiently covered by mainstream standards. More specifically, these standards fail to recognize the different priorities for female workers stemming from the gendered nature of women's obligations to meet domestic and household commitments as well as their employment-related responsibilities (Pearson 2007).[8] To some extent this reflects the fact that codes are designed to ensure equal treatment of men and women and not the issues that affect women because of their reproductive and societal role (Prieto-Carrón 2006). Such limitations, however, pose significant constraints for women as responsibility for family welfare and social provisions supporting reproductive work are crucial for them.

In addition to the limitations in scope mentioned above, implementation of social and labour standards is also difficult in practice. Research shows, for example, that Nicaraguan women agricultural workers on farms that supply Chiquita had to put pressure on male managers to acknowledge the Chiquita code that would protect them against various problems including sexual harassment (Prieto-Carrón 2006). These managers would not accept that women were working for Chiquita, a faceless company; instead they insisted that they were working for them. Such culturally determined attitudes are very difficult to change in practice and the mere existence of standards will not automatically lead to their abolition. Constant supervision and monitoring of standards, as well as facilitation of learning processes by all the actors involved (including the retailers), are fundamental requirements for the successful endorsement and implementation of standards targeting socially and culturally sensitive issues.

Food safety and quality standards

Central to the vast majority of standards presented in this chapter is the issue of food safety. Private standards for safety and quality have broader societal consequences that affect rural livelihoods, especially in developing countries. For example, the proliferation of private certification schemes is seen by many to be pushing small farmers out of the market in favour of large agribusiness and food processors (FAO 2006a; Hatanaka et al. 2005). These are impacts more generally related to liberalization, of course, but they are reinforced by the obligations demanded by the standards. More specifically, small farmers and enterprises currently are being forced out of business by the high costs of implementing new private standards for food safety and quality, especially documentation and certification costs. During the last 10 to 15 years the closing down of farm businesses and accelerated industry concentration has been a common trend, especially in developing countries. For example, thousands of small dairy operations have gone out of business in the past five years in the extended area of Latin America's Common Market of the South (Mercado Común del Sur/MERCOSUR), because they were unable to meet new quality and safety standards for milk and milk products that implied large investments in equipment, buildings, coordination and management (Reardon et al. 2001). Similar observations have been made for poultry operations in Central America (Alvarado and Charmel 2000). Likewise, experts predict that the livelihoods of hundreds of thousands of peasants in Africa will be seriously threatened by the implementation of the Global-Gap standard (ActionAid International 2005). Researchers report that in Kenya and other major horticultural exporting countries in sub-Saharan Africa, the market share of smallholders, which used to be the backbone of production, has declined significantly (Brown and Sander 2007). Instead, a few large exporters currently dominate the market sourcing predominately from large-scale production units. More specifically, while in 1992 nearly 75 per cent of fresh fruit and vegetables grown for export in Kenya were produced by smallholders, by 1998 the four largest exporters in Kenya sourced only 18 per cent of produce from smallholders. In the same year, the five largest exporters in Zimbabwe sourced less than 6 per cent of produce from smallholders (Brown and Sander 2007).

These developments contribute to mass rural exodus, which is already a strong trend in countries with long-term features of economic maldevelopment. In the past 50 years, some 800 million people have moved from the countryside to the cities. Although rural dwellers currently represent 60 per cent of the population of developing countries, that share is expected to drop to 44 per cent by 2030, with profound social, economic and environmental repercussions (FAO 2006b). Migration to nearby medium-sized and large cities does not necessarily signal a country's economic development and improvements in living standards. Rather, the fastest-growing parts of large cities are often their slums.[9] The already vulnerable members of the population become even more vulnerable when they migrate to an urban environment (see also Mingione and Pugliese 1994).[10]

In consequence, these trends add to the highly uneven and unequal development in the producing countries and regions (van der Grijp et al. 2005). At the same time, capital concentration in the retail sector and the global expansion of the operations of large retail chains are threatening the livelihoods of smaller local retailers as well. With the increasing spread of the large retail chains to Eastern Europe and Asia, for instance, thousands of smaller, locally owned retail stores have been forced to close. In Latin America the increase in the importance of supermarkets in the national retail sector taking place over the past decade is equivalent to the changes experienced by the United States over a period of six decades (FAO 2003). More specifically, the share of supermarkets in the national retail sectors of three-quarters of the Latin American economy increased from about 15–20 per cent in 1990 to 60 per cent in 2000. For the poorest one-quarter of the Latin American and the Caribbean (LAC) countries, it increased from 5 per cent to about 30 per cent over the same decade and is still rising (FAO 2003). In Southeast Asia and East Asia (excluding China), these numbers represent 15–20 per cent and 30 per cent, respectively (Reardon et al. 2004). In China, the supermarket share of national retail sales of processed food is around 20 per cent, similar to the supermarket share of overall food retail sales for Brazil and Argentina in the early 1990s. The difference is, however, that the rate of growth in the number of stores is three times faster in China than it was in Brazil and Argentina in the 1990s (Reardon et al. 2004). Hence, food retail concentration is expected to occur much faster in China than in Latin America, with dramatic consequences for local retail owners.

Optimistic views on the implications of food safety and quality standards for social sustainability also exist. However, these must be treated with caution. Some observers argue, for instance, that the formal certification process benefits farmers, as it opens up new opportunities in global export markets. For instance, firms that implement standards can increase efficiency and therefore profit rates through better intrafirm and interfirm coordination and management (Mazzocco 1996). Moreover, standards are a means for reaching more consumers by communicating and reassuring them regarding safety and quality (Reardon and Farina 2002). However, such opportunities are likely to exist only for a small subset of the original set of suppliers, and thus the benefits are minimal in relation to the total population (Reardon and Farina 2002).

Likewise, more optimistic evaluations point out that new stringent food standards could provide an incentive to modernize production. They report that, given the capacity to modernize, food standards could be a basis for competitive repositioning and enhanced export performance of developing countries (Jaffee and Henson 2004). At the moment, however, it is primarily the large retail chains and agribusinesses which have the necessary financial capacities for such measures, and it is questionable whether this will change in the near or mid-term future.

A relevant question in that respect is whether consumers in the South benefit from retail standards. Some observers note that higher standards for export markets can lead to spillover effects for domestic food safety in developing countries (Jaffee and Henson 2004). Van der Grijp et al. (2005) report, however, that the new retail standards lead to an increasing gap in quality between export and domestic food products. To some extent, however, the market in developing countries is likely to also develop a segment responding to higher demands for quality and safety, as a financially better-off consumer class emerges. Indeed, research shows that urban consumers in China are increasingly concerned about food safety requirements and are willing to pay a modest premium for certified products (Wang et al. 2008). Likewise, Berdegue et al. (2005) report that safety concerns are likely to play an increasing role in buying decisions in Latin America in the future, even though consumer awareness is still not as widespread at the moment.

When considering, then, the social consequences of private food governance, the conflict of values between producers and consumers, protected and unprotected workers, and the rural and the urban becomes obvious. Food safety and quality is a legitimate demand. The current model of providing these desirable characteristics of food products and processes, however, has negative impacts on farming populations worldwide, denying them access to nutritious food, which is a basic human right. Moreover, gender issues and the priorities of the female workforce are insufficiently addressed in social and labour standards, while implementation also proves difficult in practice. Clearly both public and private actors face significant challenges in the governance of the global food system if social considerations are to be taken into account. Next to these challenges, however, private food governance faces another fundamental concern, that of the democratic implications of private governance institutions.

Implications for democratic legitimacy

In this section we raise some ideas about the democratic implications of private retail standards (for a more extensive discussion, see Fuchs and Kalfagianni, forthcoming). We concentrate on three concepts of democratic legitimacy beyond the state frequently discussed in the literature, namely input legitimacy, output legitimacy and deliberative democracy. According to input-oriented arguments, legitimacy derives from democratic procedures and formal arrangements. These procedures and arrangements (that is, individual rights, participation in law formation, elections, and so on) are in place to ensure the autonomy of the individual and the collectivity, which are fundamental for the self-governance of a democratic society. Autonomy means that individuals feel free under law, even though they are constrained by it, because it is they who have created the law in the first place. As such, autonomy presupposes equality, as it is difficult to imagine freedom under law if it is not equally possible for all to participate in the positing of the law (Castoriadis 1997). According to output-oriented arguments, on the other hand, legitimacy derives from the effectiveness of the specific governance institution in designing policies that promote the public good. In that latter type of legitimacy, two notions are entailed: one, that the public good rather than private interest (from private or public actors) is served and, the other, that the public good is served effectively (Scharpf 2003). Finally, deliberative democracy bases its understanding of democratic legitimacy on the discursive quality of the procedures leading to the design and implementation of the governance institution. In the following, we will explore the democratic legitimacy of private food governance from each of these perspectives.

Input legitimacy

The increasing privatization of food governance clearly raises concerns from the perspective of input legitimacy. Most of the standards presented in this chapter limit access in the design process to retailers only. In some cases (for example, IFS) manufacturers are also included, albeit in an advisory role. Lack of access, which affects especially civil society and Southern actors, constitutes a serious obstacle to the provision of equal opportunities for different societal actors to influence the norms and rules that govern the food system. Lack of participation in the development of the institutions by those individuals and groups affected is fundamentally at odds with principles of autonomy and equality. But there are also exceptions. Global-Gap, for example, includes suppliers/producers in the development of standards, while the ETI invites a wider range of stakeholders, including civil society organizations (CSOs). Even in multistakeholder initiatives (MSIs), however, resource constraints remain a fundamental obstacle to participation. In the very rare cases (for example, ETI) where some financial assistance is provided to weak organizations, participation from developing countries is still limited and North–South imbalances remain (Schaller 2007).

From an input legitimacy perspective, the democratic legitimacy of private governance mechanisms is also weakened by a lack of transparency. If private actors develop their own rules, then, at least, these rules should be open to public scrutiny. Furthermore, the value of transparency is limited if scrutiny refers only to technical aspects of food production and social aspects are ignored. Even in cases where access exists, lack of transparency can render it meaningless by obscuring the real options for which actors can 'vote'. Do the standards presented in this chapter provide transparency? To some extent the answer to this question is positive. Information about standards is provided on the web and certain documents are available to all. However, most of the documents related to the development and monitoring of standards are only available to members. In addition, information for the general public is only provided after decisions have been made, constraining meaningful intervention on the part of civil society. What is more, most of the information covers issues of food safety, while broader sustainability concerns receive limited attention. Finally, access to information from developing countries due to technological constraints is also problematic (Schaller 2007).

Related to questions of participation and transparency, accountability is also a crucial issue when it comes to democratic input legitimacy. Although public actors may perform poorly as creators of governance institutions, they are at least accountable to more interests and criteria than private actors. Indeed, mechanisms to ensure accountability in private governance institutions are not predefined. Multinational business actors are, at best, only accountable to a fraction of the people affected by their activities (Utting and Clapp 2008). Most of the standards presented here provide at least internal accountability as members need to report on their activities on a regular basis. Regarding external accountability, civil society participates only in the auditing of standards that cover social aspects, as in the case of the ETI. At the moment, however, such standards are limited in the food chain.[11]

Creating and institutionalizing measures to provide input legitimacy for private governance institutions clearly is not an easy task. Ensuring equality in participation would require first a definition of who should have the right to participate. But what definition of 'equality' is most appropriate in the case of private food governance? Should it be based on a principle of universality, including all those even remotely affected by the standards, or should it be of a more restrictive nature, including only those directly affected? Secondly, such measures would require support for those facing resource or collective action constraints in participation. In the end, it is extremely difficult to define the objects of governance of private institutions. In terms of accountability, concerns also arise regarding to whom accountability should be attributed and how it can be enforced, given the context of huge information asymmetries and collective action problems. In this context, a major challenge for ensuring the accountability of private governance institutions is that many countries lack the institutions that foster 'individual and collective agency' (Marquez 2005). In China, for example, where many of the Western retailers have opened new stores, collective action involving independent trade unions is forbidden. In general, collective action through labour unions has declined considerably across the world. This is particularly apparent in Latin America, where levels of unionization have decreased by almost 50 per cent in Argentina, Colombia, Peru and Venezuela since 1980 (Sabatini and Farnsworth 2006).

Output legitimacy

Private actors usually emphasize their output legitimacy, that is, the efficient and effective provision of the public good, in contrast to the performance of public actors that are deemed to act very slowly. But how efficient and effective are retailers as providers of the public good?

Finding an answer to this question is difficult as one first needs to define 'effectiveness' and 'the public good' in the context of global food governance in order to be able to judge the performance of private governance institutions in terms of output. There is, however, no objective measure of the 'effectiveness' of a private governance institution in providing the public good. Rather we can only define the public good and measure the effectiveness of its provision with respect to the definition and interests of certain publics. More specifically, different stakeholders will define different aspects of the global food system as 'the public good'. Retailers, for instance, tend to define the effectiveness of their standards in terms of traceability and the provision of food safety in the narrow sense. If we include consumers (in the North) in the relevant public, the effectiveness of the provision of public goods will also have to be measured with respect to the promotion of some environmental norms. If, on the other hand, the public includes all those affected, then the public good is promoted effectively when safety and environmental and social norms are fostered simultaneously, that is, when the livelihoods of farmers in the South are included as well. In that respect, even though it is a common understanding in the literature that effectiveness improves in MSIs, such as the ETI, in terms of the range of issues covered and robustness of regulation (Blowfield 2005), one should be aware that, given the adoption of different criteria, effectiveness can also be attributed to initiatives involving fewer stakeholders, such as the GFSI and the IFS.

In sum, the question of how inclusive the 'public' is has to be considered, which in turn leads to questions of participation, transparency and account-ability. It is difficult to imagine that the norms and objectives relevant to a broader public will be fostered in any meaningful way without the participation of the relevant actors. Yet how are these norms and objectives going to be voiced? Who is going to ensure their effective inclusion? Elements of private governance institutions allegedly addressing questions of environmental or social responsibility frequently turn out to be window dressing rather than serious efforts at improving performance.[12] Hence, output legitimacy presupposes satisfying criteria of input legitimacy, after all.

Deliberative democracy

Deliberative democracy, as well as other conceptualizations of democracy beyond the state (for example, cosmopolitan democracy), has been developed to respond to the challenges globalization poses to traditional, territorial concepts of democracy. As the term itself suggests, in a delibera-tive democracy, legitimacy derives from discursive procedures. Influenced by Habermasian ideas, the rationale is that individuals (and indeed any actor) increasingly accept the force of arguments. Hence, the main concern of delib-erative democracy is how to optimize the discourse about which goals are to be achieved by utilizing and fostering the deliberative competence of those involved in it (Wolf 2002).

The context of deliberation takes on profound significance. According to theories of deliberative democracy, two fundamental conditions need to be fulfilled for the fostering of legitimacy: inclusiveness and unconstrained dialogue.[13] In terms of inclusiveness, the principle of 'stakeholding' is cen-tral to the deliberative argument: all those affected by, or with a stake in, the decision have a right to a voice in the governance of those matters (McGrew 2003). Membership in the relevant deliberative community is there-fore contingent upon the specific configuration of stakeholders involved in any issue, that is, those whose interests or material conditions are directly or indirectly implicated in the exercise of (public) power (McGrew 2003). That confines the relevant *demos* to those affected by the decisions. To do otherwise, that is to broaden the relevant public and give equal say to those who will not bear any consequences, is to treat the former unequally (Barry 1996). Regarding unconstrained dialogue, this requires the promotion of deliberate as opposed to strategic arguments (Smith 2003). A collective is deliberately rational 'to the extent that its interactions are egalitarian, unco-erced, competent and free from delusion, deception, power and strategy' (Dryzek 1990: 202). Such a horizontal and argumentative political style, then, has the potential to generate collective identity and mutual trust (Wolf 2002), which are considered fundamental prerequisites for deliberation itself and, consequently, the functioning of democracy beyond the territorial borders of the state.

A number of concerns associated with the deliberative democracy thesis need to be mentioned, however. Regarding the principle of inclusiveness, proponents of deliberative democracy appear to have a very clear proposal: participants in the deliberations should be those that are most affected by the decisions.[14] That automatically excludes those not affected by the decisions (and, by implication, restricts accountability and transparency of the decision-making process to a narrowly defined public as well). In terms of private food governance institutions, for instance, questions need to be answered regarding who would be excluded from the decisions and who would be the least affected. After all, numerous actors in the food chain from the farmer to the consumer are affected by private food standards. Moreover, concerns about who is going to make such decisions need to be addressed. Will governments take the responsibility to designate participants in the deliberations or will the responsibility lie with private actors themselves? But even if one happens to agree on this point, the question then becomes how to organize an inclusive, transparent and egalitarian deliberation; in other words, how to satisfy the principle of unconstrained dialogue.

From a deliberative democracy perspective, MSIs are more legitimate because they bring together different actors with opposing interests trying to reach an agreement on crucial societal issues. It is extremely difficult, however, to imagine unconstrained and uncoerced dialogue taking place among the various interest groups associated with food governance. This would presuppose a level of equality in resources, organizing capacities and reach that can hardly be said to exist between a TNC and a small NGO, a TNC and a small farmer or an independent store, a small and a large NGO, and so on. In the same way, the structural power of these different actors, that is, their ability to restrict the others' choice sets, is vastly different, as is the discursive power and associated capacity to influence other actors' ideas and perceptions. Indeed, an examination of the ETI initiative shows that even though numerous communicative forums exist and there is mutual trust among members, there is always the danger of company domination (Schaller 2007). Moreover, significant difficulties exist in integrating public and Southern stakeholders in the deliberations (Schaller 2007).

In sum, neither input nor output legitimacy, nor the concept of deliberative democracy, offer convincing solutions to the democratic deficit of private food governance institutions. Questions about participation, transparency and accountability and concerns regarding the unequal distribution of power among the relevant actors keep surfacing. The appearance of some MSIs in food governance, involving a larger diversity of actors, is a positive step towards the democratization of private food governance. However, even in these cases participation is constrained because of the unequal distribution of financial resources and structural inequalities among the actors. The result of our discussion of the issue of democratic legitimacy, then, is not an optimistic one. Rather than being able to explain on what sources of legitimacy private food governance can draw, we have to caution against too easily attributing democratic legitimacy here. Private food governance is certainly desirable in a number of ways, such as the improvements in food safety and quality. Yet its potentially negative consequences are sufficiently severe to remind us of the importance of participation, transparency and accountability in its creation as well as the need for checks and balances for the power exercised by the different actors involved, especially the large retail corporations.

Conclusions

In this chapter, we have raised concerns about the implications of the increasing political and economic power of retail corporations in food governance for social sustainability and democratic legitimacy. We have argued that large retailers have acquired rule-setting (structural) power as a result of their material position within the global economy and their control of networks and resources. As a consequence, privately set retail standards take on an obligatory quality. Their lobbying activities, especially those focusing on the content of food standards, have also contributed towards that end. In this context, retailers have benefited from their acquisition of political legitimacy and, therefore, discursive power, which results from their alleged expertise and efficiency in relation to public actors. And they have used their rule-setting activities to enhance and maintain this power.

Regarding the social implications of sustainability, we found that they have received insufficient attention. Within the context of CSR, standards providing for good working conditions have been developed. But these standards suffer from considerable limitations in scope, often failing, for example, to pay sufficient attention to gender issues. Moreover, the implementation of private standards in the areas of food safety and quality has driven many small farmers out of business. Likewise, retail concentration, having facilitated the development of private standards, has also led many small retailers out of the market. Such developments have serious implications for economic and social well-being, especially of vulnerable groups in developing countries.

Concerns also exist regarding the democratic implications of the increasing privatization of food governance. Inequality in access to the development of private standards, as well as a lack of transparency and accountability in most cases, signify a serious lack of input legitimacy in private governance institutions. Yet it is extremely difficult to identify strategies for improvement, as answers to questions regarding the inclusion of relevant publics of private institutions are neither easy nor straightforward. Similar obstacles exist with efforts to improve the output legitimacy of private schemes. In that case, too, questions arise concerning the inclusiveness of the 'public' that should evaluate the output; how to ensure its participation in both the definition of the 'public good' and the evaluation of 'effectiveness'; and related issues of transparency and accountability.

The chapter has also considered deliberative democracy as a model of democratization of private governance institutions. Deliberative democracy posits that input legitimacy determines output legitimacy and argues in favour of inclusiveness and unconstrained dialogue among the relevant actors. We pointed out major difficulties, however, associated with the identification of the relevant actors in the deliberations. Moreover, we seriously questioned the potential for unconstrained dialogue among 'equal' participants, given the existence of the major differences in structural and discursive power existing among the actors in the global food system.

It becomes obvious from this discussion that private and public actors face serious challenges in the global governance of food. Fundamental questions regarding the sustainability of the global food system remain. Without institutional transformations, the expansion of private governance institutions delineated in this chapter has highly ambivalent effects on sustainability and fails to satisfy basic criteria of democratic legitimacy. In consequence, public actors can no longer ignore their responsibility in global food governance and need to create appropriate public regulatory frameworks for private food governance institutions.

Notes

1. See also Fuchs (2005b, 2006).
2. Reardon et al. (2004: 9) also report that in the first eight months of 2002, for example, five global retailers (Tesco, Carrefour, Ahold, Makro and Food Lion) spent $120 million in Thailand, while Wal-Mart spent $660 million in Mexico for building new stores.
3. The ability to exercise this pressure today reaches all the way to farmers in industrialized as well as developing countries. In Norway, for instance, where four grocery chains (Norgesgruppen, Ica Norge, Coop Norgeand Reitan Narvesen) control almost 100 per cent of the groceries sold, studies have documented a dramatic drop in farmers' selling power (OECD 2006).
4. Data from the United States indicate that the food processing and sales sector spent $12,467,556 on lobbying during election cycle 2006. Most of this money was donated to the Republicans (www.opensecrets.com).
5. Experts report that there is a growing significance of 'own brand' products promoted by supermarkets, which gradually replace manufacturers' brands (Burch and Lawrence 2005).
6. Some supermarket organizations, however, generate their own quality assurance and safety schemes including unannounced inspections at farms, gardens and plants (for example, Albert Heijn in the Netherlands, Tesco and Sainsbury in the United Kingdom, or Carrefour in Brazil with its Seal of Meat Quality and Safety).
7. Clay (2005); Barrientos and Smith (2006); Pearson (2007).

8. An exception in that respect is the Nicaraguan Code of Conduct which has been developed by women workers themselves (Pearson 2007).
9. Regarding the case of Argentina, see Washington Post Foreign Service (2007).
10. One may argue that the displacement of the rural population due to trends related to agricultural concentration merely reflects processes of economic development that the industrialized countries once experienced and which allowed the provision of the necessary labour for industrial development. However, the displaced rural population in developing countries is frequently not finding industrial jobs in the cities.
11. Accountability to the people in a democracy differs from accountability to the people ruled by a non-democratic, potentially corrupt government, of course. Thus, one may be inclined to argue that in the case of a lack of democratically elected and accountable public actors, private governance institutions will be able to provide a more legitimate form of governance. As long as these private governance institutions are not held to some standard of accountability, however, such an assumption does not stand on firm ground.
12. For example, Gibson (1999); Haufler (2001); King and Lenox (2000); von Mirbach (1999).
13. Dryzek (1990); Smith (2003); Young (2000).
14. It is interesting to note here that Aristotle (1992) suggested exactly the opposite of the deliberate argument, that is, that those most affected by a decision should be the least involved in the decision-making processes. The logic behind this counter-intuitive argument is that society should be able to impose constraints on the self-interest of actors.

References

ActionAid International, *Power Hungry: Six Reasons to Regulate Global Food Corporations* (London: ActionAid International, 2005).

Agribusiness Examiner, 'Global food giants lobbying for reduced food tariffs and farm subsidies', *Agribusiness Examiner*, Vol. 410, 20 June (2005).

Alvarado, Irene and Kiupssy Charmel, *Crecimiento de los canales de distribucion de productos agricolas y sus efectos en el sector rural de America Central*, paper presented at the International Workshop on the Concentration in the Processing and Retails Segments of the Agrifood System in Latin America: Effects on the Rural Poor, Santiago, Chile (2000).

Aristotle, *The Politics* (London: Penguin Books, 1992).

Barrientos, Stephanie, Catherine Dolan and Anne Tallontire, *The Gender Dilemma in Ethical Trade*, NRI Working Paper No. 2624 (Chatham: Natural Resources Institute, 2001).

Barrientos, Stephanie and Sally Smith, *The ETI Code of Labour Practice: Do Workers Really Benefit?*, report on the ETI Impact Assessment (Brighton: Institute of Development Studies, University of Sussex, 2006).

Barry, John, 'Sustainability, political judgment and citizenship: Connecting green politics and democracy'. In Brian Doherty and Marius de Geus (eds), *Democracy and Green Political Thought: Sustainability, Rights and Citizenship* (New York: Routledge, 1996).

Berdegue, Julio A., Fernando Balsevich, Luis Flores and Thomas Reardon, 'Central American supermarkets' private standards of quality and safety in procurement of fresh fruit and vegetables', *Food Policy*, Vol. 30 (2005) 254–69.

Blowfield, Michael, 'Corporate social responsibility: The failing discipline and why it matters for international relations', *International Relations*, Vol. 19 (2005) 173–91.

Brown, Oli and Christina Sander, *Supermarket Buying Power: Global Supply Chains and Smallholder Farmers*, March (Winnipeg: International Institute for Sustainable Development (IISD) and Trade Knowledge Network, 2007).

Burch, David and Geoffrey Lawrence, 'Supermarket own brands, supply chains and the transformation of the agri-food system', *International Journal of Sociology of Agriculture and Food*, Vol. 13, No. 1 (2005) 1–17.

Busch, Lawrence, 'The moral economy of grades and standards', *Journal of Rural Studies*, Vol. 16 (2000) 273–83.

Castoriadis, Cornelius, 'Democracy as procedure and democracy as regime', *Constellations*, Vol. 4, No. 1 (1997) 1–18.

CERES (Certification of Environmental Standards GmbH) website, Our Services, *BRC* (2008). www.ceres-cert.com/en_brc.html (accessed on 24 November 2008).

Clay, Jason, *Exploring the Links between International Business and Poverty Reduction: A Case Study of Unilever in Indonesia* (Oxford: Oxfam GB, Novib [Oxfam Netherlands], and Unilever, 2005).

Codron Jean-Marie, Lucie Siriex and Thomas Reardon, 'Social and environmental attributes of food products in an emerging mass market: Challenges of signalling and consumer perception with European illustrations', *Agriculture and Human Values*, Vol. 23 (2006) 283–97.

Datamonitor, *Global Food Retail: Industry Profile*, Reference code 0199–2058 (2006).

Deere, Carmen D., *The Feminization of Agriculture? Economic Restructuring in Rural Latin America*, Occasional Paper No. 1 (Geneva: UNRISD, 2005).

Dolan, Catherine S., 'Benevolent intent? The development encounter in Kenya's horticulture industry', *Journal of Asian and African Studies*, Vol. 40 (2005) 411–37.

Dryzek, John, 'Green reason: Communicative ethics and the biosphere', *Environmental Ethics*, Vol. 12 (1990) 195–210.

DSN (Drug Store News), Retailing Today, *Retailers Must Double Efforts to Keep Washington's Attention*, 25 February (2002). www.retailingtoday.com (accessed on 1 October 2007).

Edwards, Jim and Sonia Reyes, 'Big food lobbies FDA on "low-carb" ruling', *Brandweek*, 10644318, Vol. 45, Issue 37, 18 October (2004). http://web.ebscohost.com (accessed on 21 June 2007).

FAO (Food and Agriculture Organization of the United Nations), *Food Safety Certification: Report* (Rome: FAO, 2006a).

——, *Farm Investment Helps Slow Migration*, FAO Newsroom (Rome: FAO, 2006b). www.fao.rog/newsroon/en/news/2006/1000313/index.html (accessed on 3 October 2007).

——, *Trade Reforms and Food Security: Conceptualising the Linkages* (Rome: FAO, 2003).

Fuchs, Doris, 'Transnational corporations and global governance: The effectiveness of private governance'. In Stefan Schirm (ed.), *Globalization. State of the Art of Research and Perspectives* (London: Routledge, 2006).

——, *Understanding Business Power in Global Governance* (Baden-Baden: NOMOS, 2005a).

——, 'Commanding heights? The strength and fragility of business power in global politics', *Millennium*, Vol. 33, No. 3 (2005b) 771–803.

Fuchs, Doris and Agni Kalfagianni, 'Private authority in the food chain: Implications for sustainability and democratic legitimacy'. In Tony Porter and Karsten Ronit (eds),

The Challenges of Global Business Authority: Democratic Renewal, Stalement or Decay? (New York: SUNY Press, forthcoming).

Fuchs, Doris, Agni Kalfagianni and Maarten Arentsen, 'Retail power, private standards and sustainability in the global food system'. In Jennifer Clapp and Doris Fuchs (eds), *Agro-Food Corporations, Global Governance and Sustainability* (Boston, MA: MIT Press, forthcoming).

Gibson, Robert (ed.), *Voluntary Initiatives* (Peterborough: Broadview Press, 1999).

Greven, Thomas, 'Private, Staatliche und Überstaatliche Interventionen zur Verankerung von Arbeitnehmerrechten'. In Hans Bass and Steffen Melchers (eds), *Neue Instrumente zur Sozialen und Ökologischen Gestaltung der Globalisierung: Codes of Conduct, Sozialklauseln, nachhaltige Investmentfonds* (Münster/Hamburg/Berlin: Lit-Verlag, 2004).

Hatanaka, Maki, Carmen Bain and Lawrence Busch, 'Third party certification in the global agrifood system', *Food Policy*, Vol. 30 (2005) 354–69.

Haufler, Virigina, *A Public Role for the Private Sector* (Washington, DC: Carnegie Endowment for International Peace, 2001).

Healthmatters, 'Food industry is lobbying hard to head off regulation', *Healthmatters*, Vol. 56, No. 5 (2004) 5.

IFAD (International Fund for Agricultural Development), *Rural Poverty Report 2001: The Challenge of Ending Rural Poverty* (Oxford: Oxford University Press, 2001).

Jaffee, Steven and Spencer Henson, *Standards and Agro-Food Exports from Developing Countries: Rebalancing the Debate*, Policy Research Paper No. 3348 (Washington, DC: World Bank, 2004).

Jones, Eluned and L.D. Hill, 'Re-engineering marketing policies in food and agriculture: Issues and alternatives for grain grading policies'. In Daniel I. Padberg (ed.), *Re-Engineering Marketing Policies for Food and Agriculture* (College Station, TX: Food and Agricultural Marketing Consortium, Department of Agricultural Economics, Texas A&M University, 1994).

Josling, Tim, 'The impact of food industry globalization on agricultural trade policy'. In C.B. Moss, G.C. Rausser, A. Schmitz, T.G. Taylor and D. Zilberman (eds), *Agricultural Globalisation, Trade and the Environment* (Boston, MA: Kluwer Academic Publishers, 2002).

King, Andrew and Michael Lenox, 'Industry self-regulation without sanctions', *Academy of Management Journal*, Vol. 43, No. 4 (2000) 698–716.

Konefal, Jason, Michael Mascarenhas and Maki Hatanaka, 'Governance in the global agro-food system: Backlighting the role of transnational supermarket chains', *Agriculture and Human Values*, Vol. 22 (2005) 291–302.

Lang, Tim, 'Food industrialisation and food power: Implications for food governance', *Development Policy Review*, Vol. 21, Nos 5–6 (2003) 555–68.

Lines, Tom, Gonzalo Fanjul, Penny Fowler and Celine Charveriat, *The Rural Poverty Trap: Why Agricultural Trade Rules Need to Change and What UNCTAD XI Could Do about It*, Oxfam Briefing Paper No. 59 (Oxford: Oxfam International, 2004).

Marquez, Ivan, 'Development ethics and the ethics of development', *World Futures*, Vol. 61 (2005) 307–16.

Mazzocco, Michael A., 'HACCP as a business management tool', *American Journal of Agricultural Economics*, Vol. 78 (1996) 770–4.

McGrew, Anthony, 'Models of transnational democracy'. In David Held and Anthony McGrew (eds), *The Global Transformations Reader* (Cambridge: Polity Press, 2003).

McMichael, Philipp, *Global Development and the Corporate Food Regime*, paper presented at the Symposium on New Directions in the Sociology of Global Development, XI World Congress of Rural Sociology, 25–30 July (2004).

Mingione, Enzo and Enrico Pugliese, 'Rural subsistence, migration, urbanisation and the new food regime'. In Alessandro Bonnano, Lawrence Busch, William Friedland, Lourdes Gouveia and Enzo Mingione (eds), *From Columbus to ConAgra: The Globalisation of Agriculture and Food* (Lawrence, Kansas: University Press of Kansas, 1994).

OECD (Organisation for Economic Co-operation and Development), *Competition and Regulation in Agriculture: Monopsony Buying and Joint Selling* (Paris: OECD, 2006).

Pearson, Ruth, 'Beyond women workers: Gendering CSR', *Third World Quarterly*, Vol. 28, No. 4 (2007) 731–49.

Prieto-Carrón, Marina, 'Corporate social responsibility in Latin America: Chiquita, women banana workers and structural inequalities', *Journal of Corporate Citizenship*, Vol. 21 (2006) 1–10.

Reardon, Thomas, Jean-Marie Codron, Lawrence Busch, James Bingen and Craig Harris, 'Global change in agrifood grades and standards: Agribusiness strategic responses in developing countries', *International Food and Agribusiness Management Review*, Vol. 2, No. 3 (2001) 421–35.

Reardon, Thomas and Elizabeth Farina, 'The rise of private food quality and safety standards: Illustrations from Brazil', *International Food and Agribusiness Management Review*, Vol. 4, No. 4 (2002) 413–21.

Reardon, Thomas, Peter Timmer and Julio Berdegue, *The Rapid Rise of Supermarkets in Developing Countries: Induced Organisational, Institutional and Technological Change in Agrifood Systems*, paper presented at the Meetings of the International Society for New Institutional Economics, Tucson, Arizona, September (2004).

Sabatini, Christopher and Eric Farnsworth, 'The urgent need for labor law reform', *Journal of Democracy*, Vol. 17, No. 4 (2006) 50–63.

Schaller, Susanne, *The Democratic Legitimacy of Private Governance: An Analysis of the Ethical Trading Initiative*, INEF Report 91/2007 (Duisburg: Institute for Development and Peace, University of Duisburg-Essen, 2007).

Scharpf, Fritz W., *Problem Solving Effectiveness and Democratic Accountability in the EU*, MPIfG Working Paper 03/1 (Cologne: Max Planck Institute for the Study of Societies, 2003).

Smith, Graham, *Deliberative Democracy and the Environment* (London: Routledge, 2003).

Smith, Sally and Stephanie Barrientos, 'Fair trade and ethical trade: Are there moves towards convergence?', *Sustainable Development*, Vol. 13 (2005) 190–8.

Tansey, Geoff and Tony Worsley, *The Food System: A Guide* (London: Earthscan, 1995).

Utting, Peter, *Regulating for Social Development: The Potential and Limits of Corporate Responsibility and Accountability*, paper presented at the Workshop on Fair Trade, Corporate Accountability and Beyond: Experiments in 'Globalising Justice', Melbourne, 19–20 December (2007).

Utting, Peter and Jennifer Clapp (eds), *Corporate Accountability and Sustainable Development* (New Delhi: Oxford University Press, 2008).

van der Grijp, Nicolien, Terry Marsden and Josefa S.B. Cavalcanti, 'European retailers as agents of change towards sustainability: The case of fruit production in Brazil', *Environmental Sciences*, Vol. 2, No. 4 (2005) 445–60.

von Mirbach, Martin, 'Demanding good wood'. In Robert Gibson (ed.), *Voluntary Initiatives* (Peterborough: Broadview Press, 1999).

Wang, Zhigang, Yanna Mao and Fred Gale, 'Chinese consumer demand for food safety attributes in milk products', *Food Policy*, Vol. 33, No. 1 (2008) 27–36.

Washington Post Foreign Service, *In Rural Argentina, the Legacy of Migration*, Friday 14 September (2007). www.washingtonpost.com (accessed on 1 October 2007).

Wolf, Klaus D., 'Governance: Concepts'. In Jürgen Grote and Bernard Gbiki (eds), *Participatory Governance: Political and Societal Implications* (Opladen: Leske+Budrich, 2002).

Young, Iris M., *Inclusion and Democracy* (Oxford: Oxford University Press, 2000).

10
Spaces of Contestation: The Governance of Industry's Environmental Performance in Durban, South Africa

James Van Alstine

Introduction

Through liberalization and globalization, transnational corporations (TNCs) are arguably the most important actors in the global economy. In the last two decades there has been a move towards TNC and host country cooperation and industry self-regulation.[1] Civil society opposition, however, has emerged at multiple scales, concerned that there cannot be corporate responsibility without accountability.[2] While the case can be made for increased recognition of TNCs' responsibilities towards the countries in which they operate, how TNCs are governed in developing countries is a relatively understudied area. This chapter seeks to contribute to this area of inquiry by exploring how industry's performance in the field of environmental health has evolved in a South African context.

Studies on the governance of corporate environmentalism have focused on factors that are both internal (Prakash 2000) and external (Hoffman 2001) to the firm. Previous work often fails to recognize the complexity and interaction between international, home and host country governance mechanisms. Often analysis is limited to one type of governance structure, such as international norms and standards or self-regulatory initiatives (for example, Christmann and Taylor 2006; King and Lenox 2000), therefore limiting the ability to rigorously explain changes in local corporate behaviour (Gouldson and Sullivan 2007). Corporate environmentalism drivers have been examined in advanced industrialized countries (see, for example, Hoffman 1999; Kagan et al. 2003), but beyond describing and prescribing corporate environmental behaviour (Utting 2002), comparatively little analytical research has taken place on its evolution in developing country contexts.[3]

Since democratization the government has attached a high priority to capital accumulation and lacked capacity to implement social and environmental policy, while civil society has remained fragmented.[4] Indeed, at the turn of this century South African air pollution legislation could be compared to that of the United States in the early 1970s (Lents and Nikkila 2000: 4), yet a number of examples can be cited where industry has taken significant steps to improve its social and environmental performance beyond compliance with government regulations (NBI 2008; SAPIA 2007). This chapter seeks to identify new governance structures within multiscale, multi-actor spaces of contestation that have emerged to discipline business and promote corporate environmental behaviour conducive to inclusive development. Focusing in particular on the issue of industrial air pollution, it explores how and why the environmental performance of two oil refineries in Durban, South Africa has changed.

The chapter begins by considering the environmental governance of firms and constructing a theoretical framework using concepts from institutional and organizational theory. Next, the history of the South African fuel oil industry, post-apartheid government strategies and the local context is discussed in order to understand how these factors might impact corporate environmental performance. The environmental performance of the Engen and SAPREF fuel oil refineries in South Durban is then analysed. The role of parent company influence, contestation and governance structures are examined in an in-depth case study which analyses how and why the issue areas of environmental and public health have been constructed in the South Durban Basin since democratization.

The analysis highlights how spaces of multiscale governance and place-based civil society activism have shaped and constrained the behaviour of TNCs. In a nascent and transitioning democracy it is found that a progression may occur from the normative to regulative institutions as government builds capacity and civil society demands accountability from both the private and public sectors. The chapter concludes by summing up the key findings and reflecting on their implications for activism and policy.

Explaining corporate environmental behaviour

The environmental governance of corporations from the 'inside' and the 'outside' is evolving constantly (Brown et al. 1993; Howes et al. 1997). The term environmental governance is being used to signify a range of internal and external hard and soft rules, such as laws, regulations, policies, practices and social understandings, which shape and constrain corporate behaviour. Some scholars highlight how internal factors to the firm, such as unique resources, strategies and structures, may influence heterogeneous corporate behaviour,[5] whereas others highlight how external institutional pressures may lead to homogenous corporate behaviour (DiMaggio and Powell 1991; Hoffman 1999). Few have attempted to incorporate both strategy and institutional analysis into a more holistic account of changing corporate environmental behaviour (Bansal 2005). One of the primary interests in this study is the relationship between the macro- and the micro-levels of analysis, that is, how social structures and processes impact organizational behaviour and how organizations in turn affect their structural environment. Within this analysis, both institutional and strategic factors are thereby considered.

The diffusion of informal and formal rules to govern corporate environmental performance occurs at multiple spatial scales. Indeed, there has been increasing recognition that environmental governance may be large-scale, small-scale and cross-scale (Adger et al. 2003; Ostrom et al. 2002). 'Politics of scale' debates have permeated multiple disciplines that study human–environment interaction in recent years (Bulkeley 2005; Eckerberg and Joas 2004). Governance structures often do not fall neatly within boundaries. They may be multidirectional; an organization not only reacts but interacts with its external environment (Hoffman 2001).

The way in which corporate actors make decisions at the local level is determined by a combination of rules, norms and beliefs that permeate through the multiple levels of governance. From a TNC perspective, a distinction can be drawn between home and host country operations (Delmas and Toffel 2004). For example, Shell considers itself to be a 'Group' of companies, which operate in more than 110 countries worldwide. But how corporate-level policies and practices impact on site-level processes and outcomes (Gouldson and Sullivan 2007), and how TNCs operate in multiple and sometimes conflicting organizational fields (Westney 1993) are poorly understood.

Distilled from the work of institutional and organizational theorists, three sets of factors shape and constrain organizational behaviour.[6] At the macro level the *organizational field* is conceptualized as a discursive space where all relevant actors partake in the contestation of an issue area (Hoffman and Ventresca 2002; Powell and DiMaggio 1991). This is the primary theatre for the interplay of power dynamics. Some scholars have been critical of how business seeks to accommodate stakeholder concerns in order to legitimize their positions of power in society.[7] The case study that follows discusses how competing actors wield power to shape the discursive space, and channel the process of institutionalization.

At the meso level *institutional dimensions* are the formal and informal rules that shape and constrain corporate behaviour. Within this context institutions set the 'rules of the game' and organizations are the 'players of the game' (North 1990). Institutions, it is posited, originate within the firm's business, economic, political and social networks that constitute its organizational field (Hoffman and Ventresca 2002). These governance structures are observable through changing regulative, normative and cognitive institutions (that is, rules, norms and beliefs) (Scott 2001). The analysis pays close attention to how various forms of institutions and their mechanisms for change have shaped and constrained corporate behaviour in the field of social and environmental performance in South Durban over time.

Finally at the micro level is *organizational legitimacy*, or how well an entity fits its legitimating environment and by what means and strategies it seeks to do so (Suchman 1995). The legitimating environment of a TNC is, however, highly complex (Westney 1993). Given Engen and SAPREF are both subsidiaries of parent companies, and face internal and external legitimacy risks (Kostova and Zaheer 1999). Externally, they both have host community, host government, home country and international stakeholders that may place competing demands on them. There may be rival pressures between the internal and external legitimacy demands, as well as lack of consistency between home country corporate leadership and strategy to host country local leadership and operational behaviour (Wheeler et al. 2002: 312). Here attention is given to how the refineries use strategies to gain, maintain and repair legitimacy (Suchman 1995). For example, fuel oil refineries in South Africa must maintain external legitimacy at the local, provincial, national and international levels, and internal legitimacy must be maintained with local employees and the headquarters of parent companies.

As Suchman (1995: 577) summarizes: 'Because real-world organizations face both strategic operational challenges and institutional constitutive pressures, it is important to incorporate this duality into a larger picture that highlights both the ways in which legitimacy acts like a manipulable resource and the ways in which it acts like a taken-for-granted belief system.' Thus the analysis uses document, discourse and in-depth interview analysis to identify modes of governance, the role of power, mechanisms of institutional change and corporate legitimation strategies within the South African field of environmental health and industrial air pollution.[8]

The South African context

Today's South African liquid fuels industry is in a process of transition from an industry that served the apartheid era of secrecy and boycotts to one that is more in line with the democratic and economic needs of South Africa. As the South African Petroleum Industry Association's (SAPIA) 1996 Annual Report highlights (p. 11):

> Past policy on oil supplies was directed at self sufficiency, self protection and secrecy. South Africa now fortunately has new priorities – based on reconstruction and development, and attracting new investments. Within this miraculous change, the petroleum industry as a whole must undergo its own transformation.

The history of the fuel oil industry sets the context for its post-apartheid environmental legitimacy challenges.

The liquid fuels industry

The oil industry was established in South Africa in 1884 when the first oil company was founded in Cape Town to import refined products (Mbendi 2007). Given the apartheid regime's aim of self-sufficiency, 'the early reliance upon imports set the basis for subsidization and support for locally refined or manufactured liquid fuels' (Task Team 2006: 41). Four fuel oil refineries were established within two decades: Genref in 1954 by Mobil in South Durban, which is now operated by Engen; SAPREF in 1964 by Shell and British Petroleum (BP) also in South Durban; Calref in 1966 by Caltex in the northern suburbs of Cape Town, which is now operated by Chevron; and Natref in 1971/72 by Sasol and Total in Sasolburg.

The history of the liquid fuels industry in South Africa goes hand in hand with that of the synthetic fuel programme. Given trade sanctions and a policy of economic nationalism, the apartheid government sought energy security through the development of a synthetic fuel programme using technology from pre-Second World War Germany and the launch of the parastatal company Sasol in 1951 (Beinart 2001: 176). The apartheid government gave primacy to Sasol (now privatized) and the synthetic fuels industry in order to ensure energy security under trade sanctions. It is alleged that this political and economic uncertainty led to inadequate investment by the oil companies in refinery maintenance (Task Team 2006: 43).

This background provides an important context for today's liquid fuels industry; as a result of political and economic influences, it is marked by a unique regulatory framework and a significant degree of government involvement (DME 1998). The downstream oil and gas sector in South Africa has survived upon a complex set of government incentives and regulations that, since democratization, have slowly moved towards market liberalization. A veil of secrecy, limited stakeholder engagement and underinvestment at the crude oil refineries characterized the pre-1994 industry. After democratization, the foundations were set for the environmental governance of industry, but the implementation and enforcement of regulation has taken time.

Environment versus development

As apartheid was dismantled, South Africa experienced an extraordinary transition to non-racial, multiparty democracy. Negotiations, elections and reconstruction unleashed a new politics in 1994 (Beinart 2001). In 1996, the African National Congress's (ANC) pro-poor Reconstruction and Development Programme (RDP) was displaced by the neoliberal Growth, Employment and Redistribution (GEAR) policies. Environmental analysts warned early on that there may be trade-offs between protecting the environment and enhancing social and economic development in post-apartheid South Africa (Cock and Koch 1991; UNDP 2003: 128), and in fact GEAR prioritized the goals of industrial development and economic growth over environmental concerns (GEAR 1996: appendix 11; UNDP 2003: 128).

Given the apartheid legacy and the post-apartheid prioritization of economic growth and social delivery, environmental protection was limited in the new South Africa. In the late 1990s the field of environmental and air pollution management lacked formal authority: air pollution laws were based upon 1965 legislation and government regulators lacked capacity to enforce existing permits (Acutt et al. 2004; Lund-Thomsen 2005). Yet the foundation for path-breaking environmental regulation, local-level governance and citizen participation in environmental decision making was enshrined in the 1996 South African Constitution, which guarantees a citizen's 'right to an environment that is not harmful to their health or well-being' (Republic of South Africa 1996: 1251–2).

The framework legislation for environmental governance in South Africa is provided by the National Environmental Management Act (NEMA), which was promulgated in 1998. In accordance with the Constitution, provincial and local spheres of government also have responsibilities for creating laws and implementing national legislation. As discussed in the case study below, municipal government has had significant influence on the governance of transnational capital. There have been ongoing efforts to develop a coherent body of environmental laws related to environmental management. In particular, an environmental management inspectorate, known as the 'Green Scorpions', was created in 2003 to enforce environmental legislation and the Air Quality Management Act (AQMA) promulgated in 2005 (SA DEAT 2004: 60–1; National Treasury, Republic of South Africa 2007).

Although these foundations are promising, environmental protection is faced with a number of challenges in South Africa. The conflict between environment and development is exemplified by the resistance to environmental impact assessment (EIA) regulation from national and provincial politicians, which resulted in the streamlining of EIA regulations in 2006. In addition, much environmental management legislation is still being developed and implemented. Although the environmental inspectorate was established in 2003, until laws have been promulgated and implemented, there will be a lack of strong sanctions to enforce compliance. The apartheid legacy has also left the shadow of a fragmented, outdated, and weakly enforced legislative framework governing environmental management, and the rapid regulatory reform process has been challenged by a lack of technical expertise and institutional memory within the Department of Environmental Affairs and Tourism's (DEAT) staff (Lund-Thomsen 2005; SA DEAT 2006). In sum, although it has made noteworthy strides at the national level, South Africa has significant organizational, material, political and institutional hurdles to overcome in its efforts to manage the impacts of industrial development. Highlighting the ongoing tension between environment and development in the new South Africa, one KwaZulu Natal provincial government employee said, 'We have been charged to do developmental environmental management.'[9]

The South Durban Basin

Durban provides an exceptional case given the strategic priority placed upon embedded transnational capital in South Durban's industrial basin. The subjects of the study are two coastal fuel oil refineries with the following characteristics:[10] SAPREF a 50/50 joint venture between Shell and BP but operated by Shell; and Engen, 80 per cent owned by PETRONAS, the Malaysian national oil company, and 20 per cent owned by Worldwide African Investment Holdings Ltd., a major black South African investment group. The refineries were built over 40 years ago.

The South Durban Basin is bordered by two high-lying ridges south of the port city of Durban. South Durban is the second largest industrial area in South Africa and, as the economic hub of KwaZulu-Natal, contributes approximately 8 per cent of the gross national product (GNP). Engen and SAPREF are both highly complex refineries. SAPREF has an output capacity of 180,000 barrels of crude oil per day, and Engen's output capacity is 150,000 barrels per day, which is approximately 60 per cent of South Africa's liquid fuel oil refining capacity. Also located in this relatively small area are Africa's largest chemical storage facility, a Mondi paper mill, an international airport, a sewage treatment plant, a busy freeway, and over 180 smokestack industries (Wiley et al. 2002). In addition, the flight paths for the airport limit the smokestack heights, preventing the proper dispersion of emissions from the refineries. It is not surprising that the Basin is recognized as one of the country's pollution hotspots.

Many of the issues relating to the contestation of corporate environmental performance in South Durban's industrial district are a direct consequence of the apartheid-planning regime. In the 1950s, land was made available for industrial development and the refineries were built. Under the apartheid government's Group Areas Act, land adjacent to the refineries was subsequently set aside for residential developments to house African, Coloured, and Asian populations. The two refineries are located a few kilometres apart, but Engen has closer proximity to communities. By locating relatively deprived communities next to the refineries, apartheid planning provided a basis for many of the issues relating to perceived environmental injustices that are apparent in the area today. Under the apartheid regime, opportunities for local community members to access information, participate in decision making or even express dissent were almost entirely absent. The legacy of plant underinvestment and unjust urban planning has made South Durban a test case for environmental justice activists (Wiley et al. 2002). Within South Africa's new democracy new political space was created for the previously excluded majority (Wiley et al. 2002).

Organizational behaviour

Society's expectations regarding what constitutes legitimate organizational behaviour in post-apartheid South Africa evolved in context-specific ways. Shell's Social Performance Review of SAPREF in 2002 summarized the challenges: 'The major implication for South African industrial facilities such as SAPREF is that they can no longer rely on their pre-1994 relationship with government for their license to operate, but must instead proactively engage with a range of other stakeholders' (Shell 2003: 12). Within this dynamic host country and community context Engen and SAPREF have made efforts to improve their environmental performance.

Corporate environmental performance

Corporate environmental performance is a discretionary activity that varies by industry sector, company and operating context. To explain how and why corporate environmentalism has evolved in post-apartheid South Africa, this study investigates how the environmental performance at two South African fuel oil refineries has changed, and how and why each refinery's progress has differed. Corporate behaviour can be assessed in terms of substantive or symbolic commitments to improve environmental performance (Mason 2005: 146). A variety of internal and external processes and outcomes can be evaluated to observe how the environmental performance of firms has changed over time (Ilinitch et al. 1998). For example, categories include organizational processes, compliance with targets, laws and regulations, stakeholder relations and environmental impacts. Indicators for these categories include the adoption of environmental management systems, plant upgrades, fines and penalties, publication of environmental reports and data, and actual emissions levels and incidents.

It is important to recognize, however, the limitations of this typology; for example, internal regulatory compliance may be influenced by external factors, such as the threat of regulation. In addition, internal processes such as environmental management systems may influence reductions in environmental emissions and public access to environmental data. Although some studies have narrowed the definition of corporate environmentalism to the examination of 'beyond compliance' corporate policies (for example, Prakash 2000), here the definition is kept broader to include both processes and outcomes in order to see the changing dimensions of corporate environmental performance over time. In developing country contexts, where regulation may be nonexistent or weakly enforced, it is relevant to maintain a broader definition of corporate environmentalism.

Table 10.1 details Engen and SAPREF's corporate environmental performance with a focus on air emission reductions over time.[11] The timing and substance of these initiatives are significant. On internal processes, the substance of SAPREF's environmental performance improvements appears

Table 10.1   Engen and SAPREF's corporate environmental performance

	Engen	SAPREF
Internal processes	1999: STOP safety system 2003: Risk Assessment Programme for underground storage facilities 2004: Implementing integrated health, safety, environment and product quality management system 2005: 'Great Days' programme – staff incentives tied to refinery performance 2006: Implementing ISO 14001 2006: Implementing Global Reliability System 2006: Implementing Process Safety Management 2006: Incident reporting via SiteSafe	2000: ISO 14001 certified 2000: Performance incentive scheme 2002: Shell Performance Review 2004: Near miss and learning event reporting 2004: Hearts and Mind behavioural safety approach 2004: Tip-offs initiative 2005: Transfer line risk management system 2005: Hazards and effects management process 2006: Business Improvement Review
Internal outcomes	1993: New sulphur recovery complex commissioned 1999: Volatile organic compound (VOC) survey 2001: Switch to gas from heavy fuel oil for sulphur dioxide (SO_2) reductions 2002: SO_2 and VOC reduction upgrade, R109m 2003: Refinery safety record 2004: Nitrogen oxide (NOx) and particulates reduction projects, R125m 2005: Acquired five-year schedule trade permit from local government 2005: Fined R10,000 for SO_2 exceedances	1995: VOC reduction project 1998: Switch to gas from heavy fuel oil for SO_2 reductions 2001 onwards: Health, Safety, and Environment (HSE) performance targets (published) 2002: SO_2 reduction upgrade, R350m 2002: Particulates reduction upgrade, R27m 2002: New flare pilots R4.7m 2005: VOC leak detection programme initiated 2006: Acquired five-year schedule trade permit from local government
External processes	1995: Engaged proactively with communities 1998: Established Good Neighbour Agreement (GNA) with communities 2002: Stakeholder assessment 2003: Began publishing Sustainability Report 2004: Began reporting in accordance with the Global Reporting Initiative 2004: Community Liaison Forum established	2001: Began publishing stakeholder reports 2003: Stakeholder engagement plan 2003: Began publishing online emissions data 2003: Community Liaison Forum established 2003: Community survey 2004: Increased refinery visits 2004: Began reporting in accordance with the Global Reporting Initiative
External outcomes	Since 1998: Reduction of SO_2 by 65% Since 1999: Reduction of VOCs by 67% History of plant upsets and incidents	Since 1995: Reduction of SO_2 by 60% Since 1999: Reduction of VOCs by almost 35% 2005: Replacing 7 product transfer pipelines, R340m History of plant upsets and incidents

Note: 1 rand (R) = \$0.1016 (October 2008).
Sources: Challenor (1999); Engen (2004, 2005, 2006, 2007b); SAPREF (2004, 2005, 2006, 2007); Shell (2003).

to be more substantive. Through parent company pressure, SAPREF became ISO (International Organization for Standardization) 14001 certified early on and was recognized as a hotspot area. SAPREF's increase in safety and reliability management processes coincided with the arrival of a new managing director, Wayne Pearce, in 2004. Engen has recently taken noteworthy steps in improving its safety, reliability and environmental processes.

In respect of internal outcomes, both plants have made substantive environmental upgrades, in particular in relation to SO_2, particulate and VOC emissions. As will be discussed, community and regulatory pressure centred around SO_2 reductions at first, whereas more recently VOCs have been targeted. Although Engen (2006: 21) claims it works towards environmental performance targets, these yearly goals are not always reported. In contrast, SAPREF's stakeholder reports quite clearly layout intended environmental goals and outcomes. Both refineries have acquired their five-year schedule trade permit from the local government (Engen in 2005 and SAPREF in 2006), however in 2005 Engen was fined R10,000 for exceeding SO_2 emissions.

In respect of external processes, Engen and SAPREF differ significantly. From the mid-1990s, Engen engaged proactively with local stakeholders and established a landmark GNA with the surrounding communities in 1998. SAPREF, on the other hand, did not openly engage with community stakeholders until 2000. As will be discussed, Engen's efforts to renew its GNA in 2003 failed and the legacy of mistrust persists, although its external reporting efforts did increase. SAPREF became more strategic with its external communication processes from 2001 to 2004, and has made significant strides towards repairing its local social and environmental legitimacy. Regarding external outcomes, both refineries have made substantive reductions in SO_2 and VOC emissions. However, SAPREF and Engen have continued to have a steady rate of fires and spills since 2001 (Engen 2006; SAPREF 2006). Though most of these incidents are considered minor, some have potential health impacts and are highly visible to local communities, exacerbating lack of trust in plant integrity and management. Therefore, as will be discussed under the section on 'Organizational field dynamics in the South Durban Basin', the refineries engage in a continual process of legitimating their environmental performance within host communities.

Parent company influence

Engen and SAPREF may also encounter internal parent company legitimacy pressures (Kostova and Roth 2002). Strength and style of parent–subsidiary oversight may be a significant factor in influencing the environmental performance of refineries (Rosenzweig and Singh 1991). Clearly there are wide differences between PETRONAS and Shell, such as size, revenues, ownership structure, culture and home country characteristics. Although it is beyond the scope of this analysis to fully evaluate how subsidiary culture and practices is influenced by the parent company, some relevant observations can be made.

Although PETRONAS published its first sustainability report in 2007, the report has limited information on environmental and social performance, and no statements could be found on its health, safety and environment (HSE) influence in subsidiaries and joint ventures. PETRONAS does highlight the implementation of a Group HSE Management system and Corporate Sustainability Framework, and reports aggregate environmental indicators on incidences of emissions to air, effluent discharge and waste management (PETRONAS 2007). Shell has been producing sustainability reports since 1997 and, on parent–subsidiary relations, stresses the application of its policies and procedures Control Framework, which include General Business Principles and Code of Conduct, and HSE standards to all companies and joint ventures where it has a controlling interest (Shell 2007). However, in Shell's 2007 sustainability report there is little detail about how its social and environmental principles are applied between sites throughout its operations.

Interestingly, PETRONAS reported that air emissions incidents had jumped from two in 2006 to 196 in 2007 'largely due to the introduction of more stringent air quality regulations in Durban, South Africa where our refinery is located' (PETRONAS 2007: 5). From this statement, it can be inferred that PETRONAS is focused on compliance, as a reported 'incident' is a beyond compliance event as opposed to a beyond internal standard or target occurrence. Environmental and operational oversight appears to be limited within PETRONAS as its Malaysian refineries have been ISO14001 certified, whereas Engen has yet to achieve this goal. There may also be opportunities for PETRONAS to learn from Engen, especially with regards to sustainability reporting, as Engen has been producing comprehensive reports since 2003. Shell requires external certification of HSE management systems (for example, ISO14001 or Eco-Management and Audit Scheme/EMAS) for all major installations, and all of its businesses must establish and implement a Stakeholder Engagement Plan, a Social Performance Plan and Social Performance Reviews (Shell 2006a). Specific issue and location reports are chosen on the basis of having the highest impact on their reputation and financial performance; therefore not all of Shell's companies and joint ventures report at the site level (Shell 2006b).

Not surprisingly, in contrast to PETRONAS, Shell participates in, or pledges support for, international corporate responsibility norm-making initiatives, such as the Extractive Industries Transparency Initiative (EITI), the Global Compact, the Organisation for Economic Co-operation and Development (OECD) Guidelines for Multinational Enterprises, and the Voluntary Principles on Security and Human Rights. A recent Transparency International report evaluating the upstream revenue transparency of 42 leading national and international oil and gas companies found that Shell was a high performer and PETRONAS a low performer abroad (Transparency International 2008).

These cases, in particular that of SAPREF, illustrate how the development of parent company policies and practices can exert pressure on the environmental and social performance of subsidiaries. But is such performance more influenced by internal strategy and parent company pressure or by external organizational field and governance dynamics?

Organizational field dynamics in the South Durban Basin

An organization may participate in multiple fields. For example, an oil refinery may participate in fields related to maintaining its economic, social and environmental legitimacy. In the dynamic and often rapidly changing contexts of emerging economies, fields might evolve quickly and in surprising ways. Multiple actors engage in these spaces of contestation to pursue their interests, which result in socially constructed outcomes. To illustrate how the field of environmental and public health related to the oil refineries in the South Durban Basin has been structured, this section begins with a high-level analysis of how public interest has evolved, and then utilizes a multiscale, multi-actor framework to spatialize the organizational field, that is, the relationships between actors and issues. The discussion highlights the contestation of the organizational field, the evolution of institutional dimensions, and Engen and SAPREF's legitimation strategies. A growing body of academic and non-governmental organization (NGO) research has been pursued within the field of corporate environmentalism, sustainable development, and the oil and gas sector within South Africa, paving the way for this study.[12]

Public interest in Engen and SAPREF

A starting point for this analysis is to consider how the public's interest in Engen and SAPREF has changed over time. Newspaper article searches were analysed yearly from 1995 to 2006 and 461 articles were categorized (see Figure 10.1). Articles were selected using keyword searches based upon the refinery names.[13] All articles found in the keyword searches were used in the analysis to guard against purposeful sampling strategy biases, and a variety of daily and weekly newspapers from national and international news sources were chosen to minimize the selection and description biases of news agencies (Barranco and Wisler 1999; Earl et al. 2004). Within the context of South Africa's post-apartheid media reform (Barnett 2003), it is assumed that the newspapers will report on the issues of greatest social concern.[14] The newspaper data are triangulated with data from in-depth interviews and other documents so that accuracy and content of issue areas are to some degree verified.

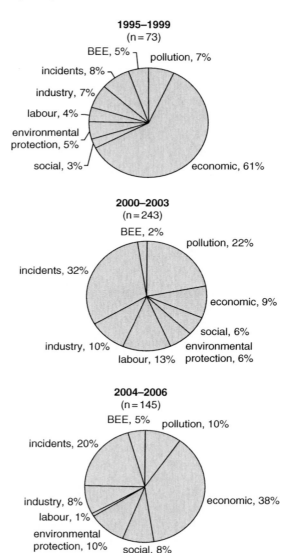

Figure 10.1   SAPREF and Engen refinery newspaper analysis

Figure 10.1 demonstrates the evolution of public interest related to the refineries. Between 1995 and 1999, public concern was dominated by economic interests. Pollution, incidents and environmental protection represented only 20 per cent of the articles published on SAPREF and Engen compared to 61 per cent of articles on economic issues. And during this period there was a relatively low volume of newspaper articles published on the refineries compared to later years. From 2000 to 2003 articles on pollution, incidents, and environmental protection increased to 60 per cent and articles on economic issues dropped to just 9 per cent of the total sample. The volume of articles published per year on the refineries quadrupled from the late 1990s to the early 2000s.[15]

From 2004 to 2006 articles on pollution, incidents, and environmental protection and economic issues were split quite evenly – at 40 and 38 per cent, respectively. The number of articles published per year showed a slight decline. Environmental protection articles increased slightly from previous years, and articles on pollution and incidents were down somewhat. During this period articles pertaining to social issues, such as social investment initiatives, rose in frequency from 3 to 8 per cent. The subject of Black Economic Empowerment (BEE), the redistribution of capital to historically disadvantaged South Africans, occurred between 2 and 5 per cent of the time. The industry category included upgrades and other initiatives that the refineries were engaging in and ranged between 7 and 10 per cent, and articles related to labour were relatively small percentages, except in 2000 to 2003; a worker dispute at Engen in 2001 increased the average to 13 per cent for this period. As will be discussed, a variety of civil society engagement strategies, refinery incidents and external events raised the profile of the HSE issue area.

This analysis demonstrates that post-2000 the public took a keen interest in environmental and public health concerns in the South Durban Basin. To understand how and why these issue areas have evolved and to recognize mechanisms of institutional change, the organizational field dynamics are now explored.

1995–99: Emerging issues and actors

Figure 10.2 demonstrates that in the mid- to late 1990s the organizational field of industrial pollution became fragmented. From 1995 to 1999, articles about SAPREF's proposed expansion plans, Engen's equity purchase by PETRONAS, and deregulation of the refining and retail markets appeared relatively frequently. During this time there was increasing concern about the economic sustainability of the industry. The Asian economic crisis stymied the planned refinery expansion at SAPREF, and although there were discussions about an Engen–Sasol merger, this did not take place. This era of low margins and market uncertainty may have slowed development of the petrochemical industry in the Basin and allowed civil society's interest in environmental health-related issues to mature.

President Mandela's visit to open an Engen refinery upgrade in 1995 marked the rise of a new form of post-apartheid activism that united white, African, Coloured and Indian communities in the Basin. President Mandela

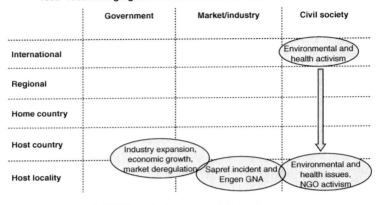

1995–1999 Emerging issues and actors in the South Durban Basin

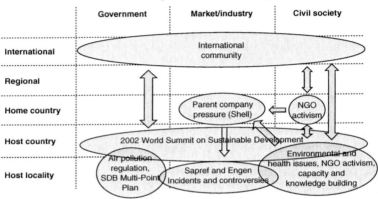

2000–2003 Knowledge wars and discursive power

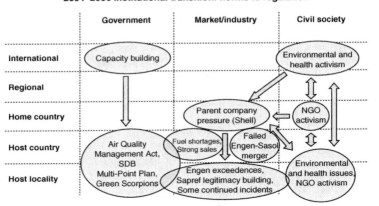

2004–2006 Institutional transition: norms to regulation

Figure 10.2 Organizational field dynamics in the South Durban Basin (SDB)

took notice of protestors outside the refinery gate, and personally engaged in discussions with community leaders, refinery managers and local government representatives to resolve the community concerns about high levels of air pollution in the Basin. In 1996 the South Durban Community Environmental Alliance (SDCEA) was founded through the efforts of local leaders to unite communities using the rhetoric of environmental justice to fight industrial polluters. In the late 1990s international networks were being built with activists and environmental health specialists. The norms of what industry's contribution to society should be were changing. As discussed, Engen engaged in a process of communication and negotiation with local stakeholders and established a GNA. Although SAPREF did not seek to repair external legitimacy through communications at this point, it did come under internal scrutiny after a 1998 explosion at the refinery.

Also in 1998, Bobby Peek, one of SDCEA's founders, brought international recognition and legitimacy to the new post-apartheid pollution struggle by winning the prestigious Goldman Environmental Prize. In 1999 Peek founded Groundwork, a South African NGO dedicated to environmental justice struggles. Civil society also took aim at government's promotion of industrial development. In 1997 Durban's municipal government undertook a Strategic Environmental Assessment (SEA) aimed to guide future development of the South Durban Basin according to sustainable development criteria. Given the findings of the SEA, that future industrial development could result in the loss of existing residential areas, tensions between municipal government and local communities undermined the impact of the study (Roberts and Diederichs 2002).

In this early stage, the economic growth imperative promoted by the ANC encountered opposition from community-based activism. Using the discourse of environmental rights, legitimated by the Constitution, opposition to perceived industrial development and pollution injustices flourished in the Basin. Regulative and normative institutions to mitigate pollution and protect environmental health were weak. Engen's circumstances in 1995 were very different to SAPREF's. Engen was independent and the refinery was in closer proximity to the community.[16] Events, activism and internal champions propelled Engen into seeking to repair its legitimacy. It would take SAPREF, on the other hand, five more years to follow suit.

2000–03: Knowledge wars and discursive power

From 2000 to 2003 community-based activism was propelled by international events and industrial incidents. Capacity building and resources obtained through international networks enabled civil society to wield discursive power. As demonstrated by the increase in press coverage, the organizational field became structured around environmental health issues. A form of multiscalar regulation had evolved where Friends of the Earth International (FoEI) networked NGOs engaged Shell within its home country and Shell subsidiaries within their host countries. Stakeholders wielded normative pressure to mitigate industrial pollution in the Basin. Key events such as a journalist's investigation into cancer in the Basin in 2000, a 2002 health study, the World Summit on Sustainable Development (WSSD) hosted in Johannesburg in 2002, and a report by SDCEA helped to push the momentum forward rapidly.[17] During this time period what can be termed 'knowledge wars' ignited. Air pollution became contested and constructed from the bottom up. Forms of relational and knowledge-based power characterized the organizational field (Hajer 1995: 49; Litfin 1994: 18). Public perception was formed by 'civic science', the 'changing relationship between science, expert knowledge, and citizens in democratic societies' (Bäckstrand 2003: 24). Networked to NGOs in the United States, Groundwork utilized the 'Bucket Brigade' community air sampling technique to highlight the presence of cancer causing VOCs, such as Benzene. Activists and the media were able to construct knowledge around the issue area of air pollution and environmental health such that government and industrial facilities could not turn a blind eye.

The next few years were marked by institutional strengthening, the internationalization of NGO networks, and continued community–industry mistrust. First in 2000, spurred by civil society pressure, the national government launched the Multi-Point Plan (MPP), a multistakeholder air pollution management initiative in the Basin, co-funded by industry in South Durban, government and international organizations.[18] The MPP was successful in reducing SO_2 emissions by 40 per cent from 2000 to 2005 (SA DEAT 2007). The multistakeholder forum consists of members from national government, provincial government, Durban municipality, industry, communities and organized labour (Nhlapo 2001). The MPP aims to reduce air pollution to meet health-based air quality standards, to improve air pollution management at local government level and to enhance the quality of life for the local community (SA DEAT 2007). Key components of the MPP include establishing an air quality management system, phasing out dirty fuels, implementing a health risk assessment and an epidemiological study.

In response to the MPP regulatory framework Engen and SAPREF began to make substantive improvements in environmental performance improvements. Although Engen made unsuccessful attempts to negotiate another GNA in 2003, the refinery managers felt the process had run its course, given that rules and legislation had largely caught up with societal expectations (Engen 2007a). Activists believed that Engen had not delivered on the first agreement and did not want to legitimize their underperformance with another agreement. Engen became increasingly frustrated with SDCEA as all attempts to expand production were vehemently opposed, although Engen's expansion plans were eventually approved in 2003.

In 2000, SAPREF's general manager appeared to have a 'road to Damascus' moment when he acknowledged the need to talk to community stakeholders.[19] However, this was perhaps a decade too late, given the level of mistrust that had built up. In 2000 SAPREF admitted that it had under-reported SO_2 emissions by up to 12 tons per day since 1995. SAPREF also had a major incident in 2001; an underground pipeline leaked over one million litres of petrol into the soil and groundwater under several homes in the local community of Wentworth. Remediation efforts were still ongoing at the time of writing in 2008. Thus, in 2002, when SAPREF commissioned its new sulphur recovery unit to reduce the level of SO_2 emissions, it was greeted with scepticism by community activists. In fact, there was a public debate between Bobby Peek and Richard Parkes, General Manager of SAPREF, regarding leak remediation and whether to repair or replace SAPREF's pipelines (Parkes 2002; Peek 2002). In addition, SDCEA failed to establish an environmental performance agreement with SAPREF. As one academic explained, SAPREF was the least willing to talk and to provide the information necessary for negotiation.[20] Cross-scale parent company pressure also took place. Peek and D'Sa in 2003, with other FoEI representatives, became shareholders of Shell so that they could participate in Shell's annual general meeting (AGM) and voice their concerns (Groundwork 2003).

Between 2000 and 2003 the organizational field of environmental health in the Basin became unleashed. The discursive strategies and power of community-based activists caused significant internal and external legitimacy risks, particularly for SAPREF. Norms, ideas and understandings related to SO_2 and VOC emissions within the Basin impelled both government and industry to act. Both refineries demonstrated some substantive internal and external outcomes during this period in efforts to gain and/or repair legitimacy at the local level. Distinct between the two firms is the level of parent company pressure. SAPREF focused on internal processes during this time period that were initiated by Shell International, whereas PETRONAS appeared to take a hands-off approach, and it is not apparent that Engen made substantial management system improvements.

2004–06: Institutional transition: norms to regulation

By 2006 the organizational field had evolved remarkably. Increased collective understanding of industrial air pollution in the Basin was achieved. A transition from normative to regulative institutions was made as the government actively built capacity both legislatively and through human resource development. The organizational field shifted from being dominated by contestation and civil society activism to being comprised of regulatory action, for example: in 2003 DEAT launched the 'Green Scorpions', a team of environment management inspectors, to build environmental law enforcement capacity; the AQMA promulgated in 2005 replacing the out-dated 1965 legislation; Engen became the first facility in South Durban to receive its revised municipal government scheduled trade permit in 2005; and the outcomes of the MPP health study were made public in 2006.

Durban in fact became the learning case for the implementation of the AQMA. The MPP and the new pollution permits that Engen and SAPREF adopted (SAPREF received its revised permit in 2006) set the benchmark against which other pollution hotspots are judged. As part of the outcomes of the MPP, air emissions data went online in 2004, allowing actors from the local to global to hold industry and government to account. Cross-national institutionalization of best practice norms was apparent as Norwegian experts helped implement the air quality monitoring programme by training per-mitting officers and analysing emissions data. Local government was able to build capacity and implement a credible air monitoring system in order to function successfully as regulators. However, creativity was also needed. Dur-ban's health department cleverly adapted local by-laws to hold the refineries to account through the permitting process in lieu of a functioning top-down regulatory regime.

Activists continued to put pressure on Shell International and, in 2005, FoEI community representatives, including SDCEA's Chairman Desmond D'Sa, met with Shell's CEO Jeroen van der Veer, who agreed to a direct line of communication from Shell's fenceline communities to the highest level of decision making within Shell (FoEI 2005), although more recent corres-pondence with Shell representatives suggests that this linkage has not been continued.[21] Regardless, the level of sophistication of this multiscale activism is noteworthy. Equally interesting is the lack of engagement of activists with PETRONAS, Engen's parent company. Indeed as Desmond D'Sa remarked, 'We are putting together a huge campaign against Engen, in South Africa not in Malaysia. The Malaysians just won't listen to us. So we will campaign in South Africa.'[22]

With the tightening of industry regulation, Engen has experienced difficul-ties. As discussed under the section on 'Organizational behaviour', Engen was fined R10,000 in 2005 for exceeding its SO_2 pollution permit requirements. Although a relatively small sum, SDCEA was pleased as it set the precedence for future legal action. SAPREF, in particular, appears to have acquiesced to community demands. There was considerable disagreement between local communities and SAPREF over action to be taken as a result of the 2001 petrol leak. Local government had commissioned a pipeline inspection report that was completed in 2004. SAPREF initially said it would conduct selective repairs of its pipelines, but in late 2005 it replaced the seven supply lines instead. NGOs claimed victory, but SAPREF insisted that it was a business decision.[23] Undermining legitimacy building by both Engen and SAPREF were a variety of incidents between 2004 and 2006, such as flaring incidents, gas and oil leaks, and fires (Engen 2007a; SAPREF 2006).

From 2004 to 2006, governance in the Basin became much more orderly. Industrial point polluters had to maintain both regulative and normative legitimacy. In this process community-based organizations such as SDCEA became disempowered. A legitimate local regulatory system now existed, thus

SDCEA would have to adapt its strategy to participate meaningfully within a more structured organizational field. Facing external legitimacy risks when seeking to expand, Engen initially focused on external processes through increased stakeholder engagement, but eventually began to implement a number of internal processes, such as ISO14001 and a Global Reliability System in 2006. SAPREF doubled its focus on internal and external processes, coinciding with the arrival of a new managing director, which has led to substantive outcomes, such as initiating a VOC leak detection programme and agreeing to replace its pipelines.

Implications and conclusions

The way in which the governance of industrial air pollution in South Durban has evolved has been labelled the 'Durban model' by those seeking to replicate its successes.[24] This is a complex story about civil society activism, government capacity building and parent–subsidiary company relations. The research highlights how place-based civil society activism within spaces of multiscale governance have shaped and constrained multinational corporate behaviour.

Mechanisms of institutional change include civil society pressure, the media, and high-profile events and incidents. Enabled through the media, community-based activism has driven improvement in private sector environmental performance and municipal government air quality monitoring, regulation and enforcement in South Durban. Events and industry incidents, such as President Mandela's visit to Engen in 1995, SAPREF's pipeline leak in 2001 and the World Summit on Sustainable Development, focused national and international attention on pollution in the South Durban Basin. Accelerating the process of institutional change, international actors have built capacity within civil society and municipal government, individuals have emerged as social and environmental performance leaders within their companies, and parent companies have taken selective interest in subsidiary environmental performance.

A fundamental mismatch between industry's expert and technocratic rationality, the government's conciliatory and bureaucratic rationality, and communities' rights-based rationality is apparent. Initiatives such as Durban's SEA in the late 1990s failed to produce the desired results. As an industry insider summarized: 'It's a question of trust. Clearly when you set out on these discussions with two sets of opposing sides it takes a long time to build that trust.'[25] South Durban's MPP was spearheaded after civil society did not legitimize the SEA processes.

The MPP is an example of a multistakeholder initiative that has gained the levels of trust needed to become legitimate in the eyes of industry, government and communities. A consensual process from the start ensured support for the project scope and methodology, thus resulting in an effective regulatory framework that would be the test case for implementation of the AQMA (Chetty 2007). Key success factors include: political commitment from all spheres of government; the use of scientific quantification with multistakeholder input and third party data verification; participatory decision making that supported a 'social compact' building process; and capacity building at the local level (Chetty 2007). Though initiated at the local level, international linkages have enabled its success. International organizations have contributed funding and capacity building for the development and implementation of the MPP.[26] However, there is opportunity for more research to examine how the stakeholders participating in the MPP have both influenced and been influenced by the initiative.

Although the MPP may have achieved collective action around the issue of air pollution in the Basin, SDCEA is still very much at odds with the two oil refineries. Part of the issue is that industry in South Durban feels that SDCEA continually moves the goalposts, and that all stakeholders, including community activists, need to be accountable. This type of multidirectional accountability is drafted into the MPP, but was missing in Engen's GNA, thus negotiations to renew it broke down. However, a question does remain with regards to the representation of SDCEA. For example, some question community democracy in the Basin as post-apartheid activists, such as Peek and D'Sa achieve iconic status through the use of the media. This questions whether or not environmental justice activism is in fact a cohesive social movement representing community consensus, or is driven by fragmented ideology lacking the legitimacy to create cultural change at the local level (Cock 2004). It is difficult to imagine how 'inclusive' the development path will be in South Durban, with such polarized opposition from SDCEA. Thus SDCEA, as the pollution struggle moves within government's remit, may need to reconnect with its constituency in order to recreate its mission and legitimacy in the Basin.

The differences between Engen and SAPREF's environmental performance improvement strategies have been highlighted. It is clear that the role of an actively engaged parent company is significant. Engen attempted to repair its legitimacy first, but has perhaps been constrained by resources or lack of parent company interest. SAPREF began actively participating in the field quite late comparatively, but has had significant parent company interest and oversight. It is recommended that industry actively and openly participates in the construction of a nascent organizational field like environmental protection. Yet it must do so ready to share power and understanding the issue area in order to obtain trust from local stakeholders. Given the incidents that continue to plague the fuel oil industry, this will be an uphill challenge. An area for further research is to investigate the influence and role of parent companies in governing their subsidiaries' environmental and social performance.

While the fuel oil industry has made progress in terms of levelling the playing field between the independents and former state-owned companies, more is needed on the environmental front. Clearly there is no consensus within the industry. This analysis has been limited to Engen and SAPREF, perhaps the leaders in terms of environmental performance in South Africa. In fact, Durban may be unique and potentially an uncompetitive location to do business due to more strict local environmental standards. More transparent and comparative work between Sasolburg, Secunda, Cape Town and Durban is needed to highlight gaps so that all stakeholders can become accountable in assuring a clean and healthy environment. Although constrained as a membership organization, the South African Petroleum Industry Association (SAPIA) could take a more proactive role through publishing comparative refinery statistics in their annual reports, and strongly suggesting that all refineries establish websites and stakeholder reports that communicate their sustainable development progress.

Post-apartheid activism has helped fragment the legacy of industry–government collusion and secrecy. Spaces for what constitutes new frames of legitimate corporate environmental performance have evolved. The rhetoric of environmental justice is particularly effective in the context of South Africa's new constitution, but environmental justice or 'protest' activism, achieved through use of media, may not have consensus to create long-term cultural change at the community level. This analysis aims to provide state and non-state actors, both within South Africa and abroad, with a learning tool of how greater sensitivity needs to be given to context specific solutions in order to mitigate business–society conflicts, and thus contribute to environmental and social well-being.

Notes

1. Brown et al. (1993); Glasbergen (1998); Levy and Newell (2005).
2. Bendell (2004); FoEI (2002, 2006); O'Rourke (2004).
3. Christmann (2004), Garcia-Johnson (2000) and Perkins (2007) are notable exceptions.
4. Acutt et al. (2004); Lund-Thomsen (2005); Marais (2001).
5. Aragón-Correa (1998); Russo and Fouts (1997); Sharma and Vredenburg (1998).
6. Hoffman (1999, 2001); Kostova and Zaheer (1999); Meyer and Rowan (1977); Powell and DiMaggio (1991); Scott (2001).
7. Hamann and Acutt (2003); Idemudia (2007); Levy and Newell (2002); Utting (2000).
8. Primary and secondary data sources were used, including 61 key informant semi-structured interviews, newspaper articles, corporate and industry association reports and government documents. Interviews were conducted in 2004 and 2006.
9. Interview, Director, KwaZulu-Natal Department of Agriculture and Environmental Affairs, 7 April 2006.
10. Mbendi (2007); OGJ (2003); SAPIA (2005).

11. This data is self-reported by Engen and SAPREF, but their corporate reports have been verified by external consultants. The data are also scrutinized by local NGOs, so the trends found by categorizing the data are believed to be reliable.
12. See, for example, Acutt (2003); Acutt et al. (2004); Barnett and Scott (2007); Groundwork (2006); Lund-Thomsen (2005); Nurick and Johnson (1998); Patel (2000); SDCEA-DN (2003); Wiley et al. (2002).
13. Searches were made on a number of different keywords including 'SAPREF', 'Engen, Durban', 'Engen refinery', and 'Enref'. A variety of South African and international sources were used including: Sabinet's South African media search, a South African online information portal; Independent Online's news search, which represents a variety of local and national papers; and LexisNexis' all English-language news search engine.
14. However, it is possible that Durban has more proactive investigative journalism than other South African communities, and thus is more supportive of community activists.
15. There was an average of almost 15 articles published per year from 1995 to 1999, almost 62 articles per year from 2000 to 2003, and just over 48 articles per year from 2004 to 2006.
16. PETRONAS purchased equity in Engen in 1996.
17. Carnie (2000, 2002); Fatah (2002); Ismail (2002); SDCEA-DN (2003).
18. The total MPP budget was R29.8m with a R10m contribution from industry (SA DEAT, 2007); large point-polluters funded the initiative on a sliding scale based upon their contribution to pollution in the Basin (interview, Programme Manager for Multi-Point Plan, eThekwini (Durban) Municipality, 30 March 2006).
19. Interview, Former Shell Vice President of External Affairs, 23 March 2006.
20. Interview, Professor, Peninsula Technicon, Cape Town, 9 September 2006.
21. Interview, Director, Shell Social Performance Management Unit, 26 February 2007.
22. Interview, Chairman, South Durban Community Environmental Alliance (SDCEA), 10 April 2006.
23. Interview, Sustainability Manager, SAPREF, 12 September 2006.
24. Interview, Chairman, South Durban Community Environmental Alliance (SDCEA), 10 April 2006.
25. Interview, Environmental Manager, South Africa Petroleum Industry Association (SAPIA), 11 September 2006.
26. The Norwegian Agency for Development Cooperation (NORAD), the United States Agency for International Development (USAID) and the Danish International Development Assistance (Danida) have all contributed funding. Interestingly, Danida has also been one of SDCEA's funders. The Norwegian Institute for Air Research (NILU) and the Canadian Sustainability Cities Initiative have helped build capacity within local government, and the University of Michigan partici- pated in the health risk assessment and epidemiological study.

References

Acutt, Nicola J., *Perspectives on Corporate Responsibility: The South African Experience with Voluntary Initiatives* (Norwich: University of East Anglia, 2003).
Acutt, Nicola J., Veronica Medina-Ross and Tim O'Riordan, 'Perspectives on corporate social responsibility in the chemical sector: A comparative analysis of the Mexican and South African cases', *Natural Resources Forum*, Vol. 28 (2004) 302–16.

Adger, Neil W., Katrina Brown, Jenny Fairbrass, Andrew Jordan, Jouni Paavola, Sergio Rosendo and Gill Seyfang, 'Governance for sustainability: Towards a "thick" analysis of environmental decisionmaking', *Environment and Planning A*, Vol. 35(6), June (2003) 1095–110.

Aragón-Correa, J.A., 'Strategic proactivity and firm approach to the natural environment', *Academy of Management Journal*, Vol. 41, No 5 (1998) 556–67.

Bäckstrand, Karin, 'Civic science for sustainability: Reframing the role of experts, policy-makers and citizens in environmental governance', *Global Environmental Politics*, Vol. 3, No. 4 (2003) 24–40.

Bansal, Partima, 'Evolving sustainably: A longitudinal study of corporate sustainable development', *Strategic Management Journal*, Vol. 26 (2005) 197–218.

Barnett, Clive, 'Media transformation and new practices of citizenship: The example of environmental activism in post-apartheid Durban', *Transformation*, Vol. 51 (2003) 1–24.

Barnett, Clive and Dianne Scott, 'Spaces of opposition: Activism and deliberation in post-apartheid environmental politics', *Environment and Planning A*, Vol. 39 (2007) 2612–31.

Barranco, José and Dominique Wisler, 'Validity and systematicity of newspaper data in event analysis', *European Sociological Review*, Vol. 15, No. 3 (1999) 301–22.

Beinart, William, *Twentieth-Century South Africa* (Oxford: Oxford University Press, 2001).

Bendell, Jem, *Barricades and Boardrooms: A Contemporary History of the Corporate Accountability Movement*, Programme on Technology, Business and Society, Paper No. 13 (Geneva: UNRISD, 2004).

Brown, Halina Szejnwald, Patrick Derr, Ortwin Renn and Allen L. White, *Corporate Environmentalism in a Global Economy: Societal Values in International Technology Transfer* (Westport, CT: Quorum Books, 1993).

Bulkeley, Harriet, 'Reconfiguring environmental governance: Towards a politics of scales and networks', *Political Geography*, Vol. 24, No. 8 (2005) 875–1014.

Carnie, Tony, 'Disease stalks Merebank kids, study finds', *Independent Online (IOL)*, 28 February (2002). www.iol.co.za/index.php?set_id=1&click_id=13&art_id= ct20020228211611476W200895 (accessed on 15 December 2008).

——, 'Durban cancer cluster "not a fluke" – expert', *Independent Online (IOL)*, 10 September (2000). www.iol.co.za/index.php?set_id=1&click_id=13&art_id= ct20000910215512895S320884 (accessed on 15 December 2008).

Challenor, Martin, 'Historic Durban environmental deal reached', *The Daily News*, 7 December (1999) 11.

Chetty, Siva, *Processes That Led to a Dramatic Reduction in SO_2 in the South Durban Basin*, eThekwini Municipality (Durban: Pollution Control Support, eThekwini Health, 2007).

Christmann, Petra, 'Multinational companies and the natural environment: Determinants of global environmental policy standardization', *Academy of Management Journal*, Vol. 47, No. 5 (2004) 747–60.

Christmann, Petra and Glenn Taylor, 'Firm self-regulation through international certifiable standards: Determinants of symbolic versus substantive implementation', *Journal of International Business Studies*, Vol. 37 (2006) 863–78.

Cock, Jacklyn, *Connecting the Red, Brown and Green: The Environmental Justice Movement in South Africa* (Durban: University of KwaZulu-Natal (UKZN), Centre for Civil Society, 2004).

Cock, Jacklyn and Eddie Koch, *Going Green: People, Politics and the Environment in South Africa* (Cape Town: Oxford University Press, 1991).

Delmas, Magali and Michael W. Toffel, 'Stakeholders and environmental management practices: An institutional framework', *Business Strategy and the Environment*, Vol. 13 (2004) 209–22.

DiMaggio, Paul and Walter W. Powell, 'The iron cage revisited: Institutional isomorphism and collective rationality in organizational fields'. In Walter W. Powell and Paul DiMaggio (eds), *The New Institutionalism in Organizational Analysis* (Chicago, IL: The University of Chicago Press, 1991).

DME (Department of Minerals and Energy, Republic of South Africa), *White Paper on the Energy Policy of the Republic of South Africa*, December (Pretoria: Department of Minerals and Energy, 1998).

Earl, Jennifer, Andrew Martin, John D. McCarthy and Sarah A. Soule, 'The use of newspaper data in the study of collective action', *Annual Review of Sociology*, Vol. 30 (2004) 65–80.

Eckerberg, Katarina and Marko Joas, 'Multi-level environmental governance: A concept under stress?', *Local Environment*, Vol. 9(5) (2004) 405–12.

Engen, *Engen Sustainability Report* (Cape Town: Engen Ltd., 2007a).

——, *A History of Success* (2007b). www.engen.co.za (accessed on 27 September 2007).

——, *Engen Limited Sustainability Report 2006* (Cape Town: Engen Ltd., 2006).

——, *Engen Limited Sustainability Report 2005* (Cape Town: Engen Ltd., 2005).

——, *Engen Petroleum Limited Sustainability Report 2004* (Cape Town: Engen Petroleum Ltd., 2004).

Fatah, Sonya, 'The environment's rich dad, poor dad scenario', *Business Day*, 14 August (2002). www.businessday.co.za/Articles/TarkArticle.aspx?ID=584572 (accessed on 16 September 2008).

FoEI (Friends of the Earth International), *Corporate Campaigns: Case Study on Shell* (2006). www.foe.co.uk/campaigns/corporates/case_studies/shell/index.html (accessed on 26 March 2006).

——, *Shell Fenceline Communities: Shell CEO Must Deliver on His Promises*, Press Release, 8 December (2005). www.corribsos.com/index.php?id=493 (accessed on 15 December 2008).

——, *Towards Binding Corporate Accountability* (2002). www.foei.org/corporates/towards.html (accessed on 14 March 2006).

Garcia-Johnson, Ronie, *Exporting Environmentalism: U.S. Multinational Chemical Corporations in Brazil and Mexico* (Cambridge, MA: MIT Press, 2000).

GEAR (Growth, Employment and Redistribution), *Growth, Employment and Redistribution: A Macroeconomic Strategy* (Pretoria: Department of Finance, 1996).

Glasbergen, P., *Co-operative Environmental Governance: Public-Private Agreements as a Policy Strategy* (Dordrecht/London: Kluwer Academic, 1998).

Gouldson, Andy and Rory Sullivan, 'Corporate environmentalism: Tracing the links between policies and performance using corporate reports and public registers', *Business Strategy and the Environment*, Vol. 16, Nos I–II (2007) 1–11.

Groundwork, *Groundwork website* (2006). www.groundwork.org.za/default.asp (accessed on 20 March 2007).

——, *Press Release: Communities Attend Royal Dutch Shell's AGs in London/The Hague and Raise Their Concerns* (2003). www.groundwork.org.za/Press%20Releases/pr_shell_agm.htm (accessed on 3 January 2007).

Hajer, Maarten A., *The Politics of Environmental Discourse: Ecological Modernization and the Policy Process* (Oxford: Clarendon Press, 1995).

Hamann, Ralph and Nicola Acutt, 'How should civil society (and the government) respond to "corporate social responsibility"? A critique of business motivations and the potential of partnerships', *Development Southern Africa*, Vol. 20, No. 2 (2003) 255–70.

Hoffman, Andrew J., 'Linking organizational and field-level analyses', *Organization & Environment*, Vol. 14, No. 2 (2001) 133–56.

——, 'Institutional evolution and change: Environmentalism and the U.S. chemical industry', *The Academy of Management Journal*, Vol. 42, No. 4 (1999) 351–71.

Hoffman, Andrew J. and Marc J. Ventresca, *Organizations, Policy and the Natural Environment: Institutional and Strategic Perspectives* (Palo Alto, CA: Stanford University Press, 2002).

Howes, Rupert, J. Skea and Bob Whelan, *Clean and Competitive? Motivating Environmental Performance in Industry* (London: Earthscan, 1997).

Idemudia, Uwafiokun, *Corporate Partnerships and Community Development in the Nigerian Oil Industry*, Programme on Markets, Business and Regulation, Paper No. 2 (Geneva: UNRISD, 2007).

Ilinitch, A.Y., N.S. Soderstrom and T.E. Thomas, 'Measuring corporate environmental performance', *Journal of Accounting and Public Policy*, Vol. 17 (1998) 383–408.

Ismail, Farhana, 'Greenpeace activists storm refinery', *Independent Online (IOL)*, 4 September (2002). www.iol.co.za/index.php?set_id=1&click_id=13&art_id=ct20020904125554950G652384 (accessed on 15 December 2008).

Kagan, R.A., N. Gunningham and D. Thornton, 'Explaining corporate environmental performance: How does regulation matter?', *Law & Society Review*, Vol. 37, No. 1 (2003) 51–90.

King, Andrew A. and Michael J. Lenox, 'Industry self-regulation without sanctions: The chemical industry's responsible care program', *The Academy of Management Review*, Vol. 43, No.4 (2000) 698–716.

Kostova, Tatiana and Kendall Roth, 'Adoption of an organizational practice by subsidiaries of multinational corporations: Institutional and relational effects', *Academy of Management Journal*, Vol. 45, No. 1 (2002) 215–33.

Kostova, Tatiana and Srilata Zaheer, 'Organizational legitimacy under conditions of complexity: The case of the multinational enterprise', *Academy of Management Review*, Vol. 24, No. 1 (1999) 64–81.

Lents, James M. and Nick Nikkila, *South African Air Quality Related Findings and Recommendations* (Rancho Cucamonga, CA: Global Sustainable Systems Research/ GSSR, 2000). www.rmef.co.za/home/server/air_quality/lents_report/lent_report_air_quality.html (accessed on 15 December 2008).

Levy, David L. and Peter Newell, *The Business of Global Environmental Governance* (Cambridge, MA: MIT Press, 2005).

——, 'Business strategy and international environmental governance: Toward a neo-Gramscian synthesis', *Global Environmental Politics*, Vol. 2, No. 4 (2002) 84–101.

Litfin, Karent T., *Ozone Discourses: Science and Politics in Global Environmental Cooperation* (New York: Columbia University Press, 1994).

Lund-Thomsen, Peter, 'Corporate accountability in South Africa: The role of community mobilizing in environmental governance', *International Affairs*, Vol. 81, No.3 (2005) 619–33.

Marais, Hein, *South Africa Limits to Change: The Political Economy of Transition* (Cape Town: UCT Press, 2001).

Mason, Michael, *The New Accountability: Environmental Responsibility across Borders* (London: Earthscan, 2005).

Mbendi. *South Africa: Oil and Gas Overview* (2007). www.mbendi.co.za/indy/oilg/af/sa/p0005.htm (accessed on 17 February 2007).

Meyer, John W. and Brian Rowan, 'Institutionalized organizations: Formal structure as myth and ceremony', *The American Journal of Sociology*, Vol. 83, No. 2 (1977) 340–63.

NBI (National Business Initiative), *National Business Initiative website* (2008). www.nbi.org.za (accessed on 26 March 2008).

Nhlapo, Phumi, 'Forum slings mud at state on industrial clean-up plan', *Sunday Tribune*, 29 July (2001) 3.

North, Douglass C., *Institutions, Institutional Change and Economic Performance* (Cambridge: Cambridge University Press, 1990).

Nurick, Robert and Victoria Johnson, 'Toward community based indicators for monitoring quality of life and the impact of industry in south Durban', *Environment and Urbanization*, Vol. 10, No. 1 (1998) 233–50.

OGJ (Oil & Gas Journal), 'Worldwide refining survey', Vol. 101, No. 49 (2003).

O'Rourke, D., *Community-Based Regulation: Balancing Development and Environment in Vietnam* (Cambridge, MA: MIT Press, 2004).

Ostrom, Elinor, T. Dietz, N. Dolsak, P. Stern, S. Sonich and E. Weber (eds), *The Drama of the Commons* (Washington, DC: National Academy Press, 2002).

Parkes, Richard, 'Criticism absurd and unfounded', *Daily News*, 29 January (2002) 13.

Patel, Zarina, 'Rethinking sustainable development in the post-apartheid reconstruction of South African cities', *Local Environment*, Vol. 5, No. 4 (2000) 383–99.

Peek, Bobby, 'Sapref: What about accountability?', *Daily News*, 8 January (2002) 6.

Perkins, Richard, 'Globalizing corporate environmentalism? Convergence and heterogeneity in Indian industry', *Studies in Comparative International Development*, Vol. 42, Nos 3–4 (2007) 279–309.

PETRONAS (Petroliam Nasional Berhad), *Petronas Group Sustainability Report 2007* (Kuala Lumpur: PETRONAS, 2007).

Powell, Walter W. and Paul DiMaggio, *The New Institutionalism in Organizational Analysis* (Chicago, IL: University of Chicago Press, 1991).

Prakash, Aseem, *Greening the Firm: The Politics of Corporate Environmentalism* (Cambridge, UK/New York: Cambridge University Press, 2000).

Republic of South Africa, *Constitution of the Republic of South Africa No. 108 of 1996* (Pretoria: Republic of South Africa, 1996).

Republic of South Africa, National Treasury, *National Budget 2007: National Medium Term Expenditure Estimates – Environmental Affairs and Tourism* (Pretoria: National Treasury, 2007). www.treasury.gov.za/documents/national%20budget/2007/ene/Default.aspx (accessed on 15 December 2008).

Roberts, Debra and Nicci Diederichs, 'Durban's local Agenda 21 programme: Tackling sustainable development in a post-apartheid city', *Environment & Urbanization*, Vol. 14, No. 1 (2002) 189–201.

Rosenzweig, Philip M. and Jitendra V. Singh, 'Organizational environments and the multinational enterprise', *Academy of Management Review*, Vol. 16, No. 2 (1991) 340–61.

Russo, Michael V. and Paul A. Fouts, 'A resource-based perspective on corporate environmental performance and profitability', *The Academy of Management Journal*, Vol. 40, No. 3 (1997) 534–59.

SA DEAT (South Africa Department of Environmental Affairs and Tourism), *South Durban Basin Multi-Point Plan: Case Study Report* (Pretoria: DEAT, 2007).

——, *DEAT Strategic Plan: 1 April 2005 to 31 March 2010* (Pretoria: DEAT, 2006).

——, *10 Year Review: Department of Environmental Affairs and Tourism* (Pretoria: DEAT, 2004).

SAPIA (South African Petroleum Industry Association), *SAPIA website* (2007). www.sapia.org.za/index.htm (accessed on 15 September 2007).

——, *SAPIA Annual Report 2005* (Cape Town: SAPIA, 2005).

——, *SAPIA Annual Report 1996* (Cape Town: SAPIA, 1996).

SAPREF (South African Petroleum Refineries), SAPREF website (2007). www.sapref.com/profile.htm (accessed on 1 January 2007).

——, *Sustainability in Focus* (Durban: SAPREF, 2006).

——, *Sustainability in Focus* (Durban: SAPREF, 2005).

——, *Towards Sustainability 2004* (Durban: SAPREF, 2004).

Scott, W. Richard, *Institutions and Organizations* (Thousand Oaks, CA: Sage, 2001).

SDCEA-DN (South Durban Community Environmental Alliance), *Comparison of Refineries in Denmark and South Durban in an Environmental and Societal Context: A 2002 Snapshot* (South Durban: SDCEA-DN, 2003).

Sharma, Sanjay and Harrie Vredenburg, 'Proactive corporate environmental strategy and the development of competitively valuable organizational capabilities', *Strategic Management Journal*, Vol. 19 (1998) 729–53.

Shell, *Responsible Energy: The Shell Sustainability Report 2007* (London: Royal Dutch Shell plc, 2007).

——, *Shell's Approach to Interacting with Communities* (2006a). www.shell.com (accessed on 26 March 2006).

——, *Shell's Approach to Reporting* (2006b). www.shell.com (accessed on 26 March 2006).

——, *2002 Social Performance Review: SAPREF Refinery, Durban, South Africa* (Durban: SAPREF, 2003).

Suchman, Mark, 'Managing legitimacy: Strategic and institutional approaches', *Academy of Management Review*, Vol. 20 (1995) 571–610.

Task Team, *Possible Reforms to the Fiscal Regime Applicable to Windfall Profits in South Africa's Liquid Fuel Energy Sector, with Particular Reference to the Synthetic Fuel Industry: A Discussion Document for Public Comment*, report by the Task Team appointed by the Minister of Finance, Republic of South Africa, Pretoria, 20 July (2006).

Transparency International, *Promoting Revenue Transparency* (Berlin: Transparency International, 2008).

UNDP (United Nations Development Programme), *South Africa Human Development Report 2003* (Cape Town: Oxford University Press, 2003).

Utting, Peter, *The Greening of Business in Developing Countries: Rhetoric, Reality and Prospects* (London: Zed Books, 2002).

——, *Business Responsibility for Sustainable Development*, Occasional Paper No. 2 (Geneva: UNRISD, 2000).

Westney, Eleanor D. 'Institutionalization theory and the multinational corporation'. In Sumantra Ghoshal and Eleanor D. Westney (eds), *Organization Theory and the Multinational Corporation* (New York: St. Martin's Press, 1993).

Wheeler, David, Heike Fabig and Richard Boele, 'Paradoxes and dilemmas for stakeholder responsive firms in the extractive sector: Lessons from the case of Shell and the Ogoni', *Journal of Business Ethics*, Vol. 39 (2002) 297–318.

Wiley, D., C. Root and S. Peek, 'Contesting the urban industrial environment in South Durban in a period of democratisation and globalisation'. In Bill Freund and Vishnu Padayachee (eds), *(D)urban Vortex: South African City in Transition* (Pietermaritzburg: University of Natal Press, 2002).

11
Challenging Governance in Global Commodity Chains: The Case of Transnational Activist Campaigns for Better Work Conditions

Florence Palpacuer[1]

The coordination or 'functional integration' of complementary activities across locations constitutes a distinctive feature of globalization in contemporary capitalism (Dicken 1998). In industries such as apparel, electronics and automobiles, it has led to the emergence of 'Global Commodity Chains' (GCCs) governed by large lead firms that retain direct control over marketing and design activities in Northern markets while arranging for the manufacture of their products in complex transnational networks spanning Southern countries. Although mainstream economists continue to think of globalization in terms of international competition, seeing the surge of manufacturing imports in mature markets as resulting from the superior cost advantage of Southern producers, a GCC perspective emphasizes that the globalization of production has been driven primarily by large firms in the North taking advantage of information and communication technologies, transport deregulation, trade liberalization, and an abundant labour supply in the South to reorganize production across countries and world macroregions in order to lower cost, increase flexibility, and build up scale (Gereffi 1994).

At the manufacturing end of GCCs, activities spread to an ever-wider range of countries and trade liberalization enhanced competition among both producers and workers, contributing to depress labour standards on a world scale. Concurrently, power concentration strongly increased at the 'top' of global chains due to massive industry consolidation in both retailing and global branding, while growing pressures were exerted to extract rents out of these chains on the part of a financial sphere comprising lead firms' top management and major institutional shareholders.[2] During the 1990s, such increased inequalities and continuous deterioration of working conditions at the base of GCCs prompted the emergence of a 'corporate accountability movement' composed of transnational networks of social movement organizations (SMOs) and trade unions seeking to improve social conditions by empowering workers and re-establishing the social responsibility of profit-accumulating firms at the top of GCCs.[3]

This chapter aims to assess the significance of such networks in their attempts to build new forms of social regulation in GCCs. The first section highlights key organizational and strategic characteristics of activist networks, drawing on two campaign cases involving the Matamoros factory (Mexico) in 2003 and the Hermosa manufacturing facility (El Salvador) in 2006. The second section compares three ways in which the emergence of these networks has – or has not – been acknowledged in the governance debate by referring to decision systems and power relations that shape resource allocation processes in firms and GCCs, and how they should be organized in order to contribute to improve social welfare in the world economy. Underlining the limitations of both shareholder and stakeholder views of governance, the third section discusses the significance of transnational activist campaigns from an institutional perspective in order to show how these campaigns can be perceived as a new mode of regulation of the global economy.

Transnational activist campaigns in the clothing industry

Over the course of the 1990s, the global clothing industry witnessed the emergence of activist networks organized around the Clean Clothes Campaign (CCC) in Europe, the Maquila Solidarity Network (MSN) in Canada and Mexico, and a more fragmented base of activist organizations in the United States (US) including the United Students against Sweatshops (USAS), the National Labour Committee (NLC), and the Campaign for Labor Rights (CLR), among others. These coalitions brought together a mosaic of community groups acting for the defence of human rights, women, consumers, immigrants, workers, as well as religious groups, student groups, teacher associations and, in some cases, lawyers and political organizations. The rise of this 'anti-sweatshop movement' in the clothing sector has been well documented with reference to the United States,[4] and is part of a broader 'globalization from below' by which counter-hegemonic groups have developed forms of 'transnationally organized resistance' against the unequal exchanges produced or intensified by economic globalization (Sousa Santos and Rodríguez-Garavito 2005; Sousa Santos 2006). In characterizing the varied forms and dynamics that such organized resistance might take, della Porta and Tarrow (2005: 7) stress the long-term, intense interactions observed in transnational collective actions defined as 'coordinated international campaigns on the part of networks of activists against international actors, other states, or international institutions'. Against this background, this chapter will focus on two campaign cases in the clothing sector. It shall highlight some key organizational characteristics of activist networks in the global apparel chain, and identify a number of changes in the ways in which these campaigns have been handled over time, both by activist groups and the global companies they target.

Transnational activist networks in action

The activist campaign organized against Puma in 2003 involved women workers from Matamoros Garments, a factory in Mexico assembling Puma products destined for the American market.[5] On 13 January, these Mexican workers had gone on strike to denounce conditions of forced overtime, unpaid wages, verbal abuse, persistent health and safety violations, and denial of freedom to create an independent local labour union. Frequently encountered in the global apparel industry, such conditions were contrary to the principles established in Puma's code of conduct. When Matamoros garment workers went on strike, they formed an independent local union, the Sindicato Independiente de Trabajadores de la Empresa Matamoros Garment (SITEMAG/Independent Union of Matamoros Garment Workers), and joined the Centro de Apoyo al Trabajador (CAT/Workers Support Centre), formed in 2001 that called upon a variety of foreign SMOs including USAS, Mexico Solidarity Network and the CLR in the United States, MSN in Canada, No Sweat in the United Kingdom (UK) and the CCC in Germany, thus establishing global connections in support of local workers. The campaign involved several types of operations on the part of SMOs. In Germany, CCC and representatives of Matamoros workers held press conferences and met with Puma representatives. In the United States, Sweatshop Watch launched an email campaign making sample letters available and asking members of its mailing list and website visitors to write to Puma's Director of Social and Environmental Affairs. Letters were also sent to the Mexican government and embassies over the world, asking for the recognition of Matamoros workers' independent local union. In addition, No Sweat organized picketing in front of Puma stores in a dozen cities in the United Kingdom on Women's Day, 8 March 2003.

These actions involved a network of SMOs across North America, Europe and Latin America that closely matched the geography of the portion of Puma's production chain involved in the campaign, including headquarters in Germany, where the company's product development, branding and social affairs were located, subcontracting in Mexico, and a sourcing agent in the United States. The ways in which Puma responded to the campaign revealed a learning curve pattern in interacting with SMOs. The first response from Puma was to deal with a situation of labour unrest by cutting orders and ending work with Matamoros. Under subsequent SMO pressures, Puma returned to the factory but provided a second response based on denial: three staff members were sent to Mexico and filmed workers declaring that employment and work conditions were fine at Matamoros. The CAT and SITEMAG immediately contradicted these opinions and the video was never displayed to the public.

The case came to an abrupt end in Mexico when the Matamoros factory closed down in March 2003, officially for technical reasons. It had some influence on Puma's social policy, however, prompting the sportswear brand to join the Fair Labor Association (FLA), the main US-based organization involved in monitoring work conditions at suppliers' factories in the apparel industry.[6] In May 2004, SMOs from Mexico, Canada and the United States also made a public communication to the Canadian government under the North American Free Trade Agreement's (NAFTA) labour provision.[7] In May 2005, having reviewed extensive evidence, the Canadian government launched a complaint against Mexico on the issue of freedom to organize independent unions. The Puma-Matamoros campaign thus served to engage Puma towards greater corporate accountability, to draw public attention in the North on working conditions in apparel factories worldwide, and to put to work the regional institutional framework for labour rights in North America.

The Hermosa campaign was launched a few years later, at the end of 2005, in support of a group of women garment workers in El Salvador who demanded the payment of due wages, social security coverage and severance payment after their factory, Hermosa Manufacturing, was closed down by its owner in May of the same year.[8] While the owner subsequently rehired part of the workforce in a new factory, 63 workers who had been involved in forming a union (STITTAS) at Hermosa in April 2005 failed to find another job in the area. Some were experiencing critical living and health conditions while lacking access to health insurance. Initiated in Germany under the 'Urgent Appeal' system under which local workers can mobilize CCC campaigning capacity, the campaign spread to other European countries through the CCC network and was relayed by USAS and MSN in North America.

Some of the tactics used in the Hermosa campaign to support demands of former Hermosa workers were similar to those utilized in the Matamoros case. Sample letters, for example, were made available on SMO websites to be sent both to Salvadorian authorities and representatives of various retail and brand companies identified as having sourced products from Hermosa in recent years. The campaign was especially active in Germany, where a trip was organized for a representative of the workers to give public and press conferences, meet with German representatives of the International Textile, Garment and Leather Workers Federation (ITGLWF), and corporate social responsibility (CSR) representatives at Adidas, one of the brands targeted by the campaign. Capitalizing on the fact that the world football championship was being hosted in Germany during the Spring of 2006, CCC Germany mobilized various German activist and faith groups to organize a number of events at Adidas' annual shareholder meeting. For instance, members of Jugend Aktion für Natur- und Umweltschutz Niedersachsen (JANUN/Youth Action Network for Nature Conservation and Environmental Protection) delayed the meeting by playing football at the entrance of the building, made a shareholder statement asking Adidas for more socially responsible corporate behaviour, and performed street theatre while distributing campaign leaflets.

Building up collective dynamics

Despite a number of similarities with Matamoros, the Hermosa case illustrates some evolution in the manner in which transnational activist networks organized campaigns and how companies responded to them. Crucial in this regard are forms of institutionalization by which campaign processes become more formalized and collective. Campaigning groups evolved from targeting a specific company towards the joint targeting of several brands at the international level, seeking to reach a sort of economy of scale and promote collective dynamics across firms targeted by a campaign, as had occurred in broader thematic campaigns such as Play Fair at the Olympics (Merk 2005). Companies involved in the Hermosa case included Wal-Mart, Russell Athletic, Nike, Pentland, Reebok, Adidas and Puma, a mix of 'buyers' including both companies that campaign groups had already worked with, such as Nike or Puma, and others considered important to target, such as Wal-Mart. The quick identification and simultaneous targeting of several brands at the transnational level was made possible both by the trust-based relations developed between campaign groups of various regions over time, and by the use of the Internet, speeding up the deployment of a campaign from about 18 months at the end of the 1980s to a few weeks.[9]

On the companies' side, the FLA had established in 2002 a 'third-party complaint mechanism' that allowed any person to report on a situation of non-compliance with the association's code of conduct in factories producing for FLA affiliates, on behalf of factory workers. This provided a procedure for addressing issues related to the application of codes of conduct on a collective, rather than individual firm, basis. A complaint was filed by CCC Germany in late 2005 regarding problems at Hermosa, including alleged violations of freedom of association, failure to pay wages, severance and other legal benefits due to the workers, and failure to provide alternative employment. This case was especially sensitive as it revealed weaknesses in the control system that companies had established on the basis of regular audits of code compliance at their suppliers' factories. Ongoing code violations, such as failing to make pension fund payments, had gone unnoticed through several audits of code compliance at Hermosa over the years preceding closure.

Targeted companies reacted by denying or minimizing their sourcing activities with Hermosa, an initial response identified as typical by campaign organizers – and specified, with suggestions of appropriate response, in a CCC campaigning manual (see also Merk 2005). As a second step, within the context of the FLA complaint procedure, brand affiliates – primarily Adidas, Nike and Russell – started to investigate the case and put pressure both on the Salvadorian government and on their suppliers in El Salvador to meet workers' demands and help them get re-employed. Being simultaneously targeted encouraged brand firms to construct collective responses to the crisis, and the FLA served as a forum for frequent informal discussions as the campaign proceeded.[10] In February 2006, the FLA launched 'step 3' of its complaint procedure involving an external expert assessment of the case, eventually leading to the release of an interim report in August of the same year. Investigations led by the brands revealed that government officials had been aware that Hermosa did not pay retirement and social security contributions during the period 1996–2005 but had continued to issue social security certificates to workers without informing them. Brand actions towards the Salvadorian authorities as well as local suppliers did not produce successful outcomes in terms of the re-employment of former Hermosa workers. 'The buyers told us that they were unwilling to pressure [their] suppliers to give ex-Hermosa workers priority hiring ... because they did not believe that they have the right to tell another company whom to hire', observed the MSN (2007a: 9) in a detailed report on the Hermosa case.

By the end of 2006, in the face of continuing campaign pressures and persisting failure to improve the condition of unemployed ex-Hermosa workers, the FLA set up a fund on the basis of donations from brand affiliates. According to MSN (2007a), this initiative came out of discussions between the German CCC, CCC International, Adidas and the FLA. Initially geared towards more sustainable forms of support, such as microcredit, the initiative evolved towards an emergency response to the critical living conditions reached by local workers. Between December 2006 and February 2007, a collected sum of $36,000[11] was distributed through a Salvadorian SMO to unemployed former Hermosa workers. Although the fund was positively received, it also acted as a catalyst to reveal divergences among actors involved with regard to the scope of brand corporate responsibility and the forms that it should take. FLA companies viewed the fund as a charity act independent of the wages, benefits and severance payments due to the workers, an estimated sum of $825,000. The fear of setting a precedent that would contribute to establish their responsibility for the payment of workers' wages at suppliers' factories prevented a number of brands from donating to the fund or induced them to minimize their donation, thus contributing to explain the relatively low amount of $36,000 accumulated in the fund, when the FLA had anticipated a total of $100,000. Some buyers expressed their reluctance in anonymous interviews conducted by the MSN (2007a: 14): 'it doesn't fit with how we prioritize where to put our resources', 'there was a lack of enthusiasm precisely because it was seen as compensation to the workers', 'we can't respond like this. It's unmanageable, it's unfair ... it's letting the people who are responsible, the owners and the government, off the hook'. On the other hand, former unionized workers believed that brand companies should compensate them for the full amount owed by Hermosa. Local SMOs, international campaign groups as well as the international union, all emphasized that the fund was insufficient and relayed workers' demand for further contributions. Arguments included that the German CCC had been signalling problems with the Hermosa factory that were left unaddressed by global buyers since 2000, and that buyers could create a fund for compensation as a form of advance payment and pursue legal actions to obtain compensation afterwards. The fund was also compared to similar initiatives that had yielded greater results for the workers in the past (see MSN 2007a: 28).

The situation of local workers thus remained critical and on that account, as in the Matamoros case, the campaign failed to reach its initial objectives. On other aspects, however, it produced successful outcomes at the local level. One involved the trial of Hermosa's owner held in El Salvador during the second half of 2006 for the failed payment of retirement and social security contributions. Induced by campaign pressures, according to a German CCC representative, the trial was the first of its kind in the country and contributed to a stricter compliance approach by the Salvadorian government (Bureau of Democracy, Human Rights and Labor, Embassy of the United States, El Salvador, 2008). Another positive outcome at the local level lay in workers' empowerment. Through the campaign, the group of struggling workers learned to build both local and international alliances for the defence of their rights, using Internet connections, participating in various kinds of meetings and negotiation, and receiving support from a coalition of about a dozen local SMOs acting for the defence of women and workers' rights in El Salvador. The financial aid that they managed to obtain, however limited, provided a symbolic recognition of the legitimacy of their demands and of the steps taken to get them heard and answered at the international level.

Normative views of governance in GCCs: Situating transnational campaigns?

Beyond the reactions of individual companies to particular campaigns, a variety of ideological responses to the rise of transnational campaigns can be observed in the governance debate addressing the social consequences of globalization. Normative discussions of governance in academic and policy circles have revolved around three perspectives conveying distinct representations of the nature of the firm, the role of public institutions and the ways in which economic activities can be made to improve social welfare, while offering contrasted views of the significance and desirability of transnational activism.[12]

Shareholder versus stakeholder views of GCC governance

The debate on corporate governance has mainly opposed 'shareholder' and 'stakeholder' perspectives on the running of large corporations. The shareholder approach draws on property rights theory (Alchian and Demsetz 1972) and agency theory (Fama and Jensen 1983; Jensen 2000) to give primacy to ownership in the appropriation of wealth generated by large corporations. It also builds on transaction cost theory (Williamson 1975, 1985) to define the firm as a 'nexus of contracts', that is, a sum of bilateral contracts between individuals making opportunistic and – limitedly – rational decisions. According to this view, the market provides, or should provide, the best regulatory mechanism for maximizing shareholder value, and state intervention should be restricted to ensuring the efficient operation of markets in the spheres of corporate ownership and management (Jensen 2000). A central claim of the shareholder view and a major foundation for its social legitimacy lie in the idea that maximizing shareholder value can provide the best avenue for maximizing the performance of the economy as a whole, and thereby improving social welfare. Relying on a doctrine of methodological individualism, this view promotes a conception of the firm that excludes all forms of collective action and ignores power imbalances and conflicting interests between various social groups contributing to a firm's activity, including shareholders, employers, clients and suppliers.

On the social side, a market-based view holds that institutional arrangements built on principles other than free competition are potentially detrimental to both economic performance and social welfare. Unions, for instance, are seen as monopolies aiming to control production and increase costs, offering 'unfair' advantages to their members at the expense of consumers, other workers, and, ultimately, the whole society (Simons 1944; Friedman 1962). Likewise, any attempt by firms to collectively address issues of working conditions at their suppliers would be contrary to the principles of free competition and fall under anti-trust laws, as implied in buyers' resistance to acknowledge responsibility for severance payments due to laid-off workers in the Hermosa case and, more broadly, for work conditions at their suppliers' factories. Consequently, objectives pursued by both activist SMOs and labour unions are not seen as legitimate under a shareholder governance system. Corrective actions that impede market forces are seen as undesirable social policies.

A corresponding, if softer, view of the role of markets in GCC governance can be found in a typology developed by Gereffi et al. (2005) where GCCs governed by the market are seen as presenting the lowest degree of power asymmetry in interfirm relationships. Like the firm itself, under specific conditions of exchange codification, a GCC defined as a 'nexus of contracts' could thus presumably provide a desirable model to promote social welfare. GCC writers do not explicitly endorse a market view, however, and consider that other arrangements such as close, socially embedded interfirm working relationships could prove just as effective on a contingent basis.

In line with such a socially embedded perspective, the stakeholder view arose in reaction to core assumptions of the shareholder approach, claiming that a focus on shareholder value was not only unfair from an ethical point of view but also detrimental to corporate performance (Freeman 1984; Post et al. 2002). Inspired by the human relations school, it emphasized the corporate benefits to be derived from investing in relationships with a broad set of constituents: 'Individuals well endowed with economic and social capabilities will be more productive; companies which draw on the experience of all of their stakeholders will be more efficient' (Kelly et al. 1997: 244). Much of the surging interest in participative management and cooperative interfirm linkages during the early to mid-1990s relied on similar premises. Sociologists emphasized the role of trust in allowing for flexible, open-ended interfirm relations seen as more conducive to innovation than arm's length market relations,[13] as did the burgeoning literature promoting industrial clusters as a new route for economic development (Pyke et al. 1990; Nadvi and Schmitz 1994). Attempts to incorporate such notions in GCC analysis were also made by taking into account the formation of transnational production linkages within local industrial systems (Humphrey and Schmitz 2002; Palpacuer and Parisotto 2003).

Ethical considerations promoting cooperative behaviours within and between firms reappeared in a more recent form in the managerial literature on CSR, arguing that stakeholder-oriented governance could simultaneously boost economic performance and improve social welfare. Corporations would thus act on the basis of 'enlightened self-interest' when adopting codes of conduct, for instance, by realizing that the value of their products depended on consumers' perception of their endorsement of a socially responsible behaviour with suppliers (O'Higgins 2003: 52–64). The stakeholder view suggests that balancing social and economic considerations in the governance of the corporation could and should be done primarily on the basis of 'voluntary individual action' (Brabet 2004; Utting 2005b). When members of this school prescribed governance reform (for instance, Blair 1995), they did so with considerable caution, emphasizing that existing forms of regulation should presumably be sufficient for stakeholder-oriented governance to spontaneously emerge from the decision-making pattern of individuals running the corporation. As pointed out by O'Sullivan (2000: 59), such policy orientations maintained 'the neo-classical assumptions that resource allocation is individual and optimal'. Although claiming to take into account a variety of interests in the running of the corporation, the stakeholder view has thus persistently overlooked the role of power relations in shaping the distribution of wealth among actors involved in transnational production processes, and the need to introduce collective rules, beyond individual decisions, to alleviate inequalities in wealth distribution in GCCs. Within the context of multistakeholder initiatives (MSIs) launched by firms to promote social standards on a collective – rather than individual – basis, such as the FLA, proponents of CSR have adopted a critical stance vis-à-vis public regulation, preferring a 'naming and praising' approach that engages companies in 'social learning' to the 'naming and shaming' strategies of campaign groups and their focus on demanding accountability (Utting 2002: 27). Reflecting broadly on CSR, Utting (2005a: 23) concluded that

> at best, [it] can contribute to raising awareness of certain social and environmental problems and serve to caution against blind faith in both market forces and state regulatory capacity.... At worst, CSR involves a transfer of regulatory authority to largely unaccountable agents and renders more palatable a model of capitalism that generates or reinforces widespread social exclusion, inequality and environmental degradation.

An institutional view of GCC governance

In light of the failure of shareholder and stakeholder perspectives to address issues of power relations and raising inequalities in GCCs, a third approach can be devised by building on the core analytical premises of early institutional theory, shared by subsequent research in French regulation theory, to explore new institutional developments aiming to improve the welfare of deprived social groups at the base of global chains. A distinctive feature of institutional analysis, as defined by early labour market theorists, was to see individual action as embedded in collective dynamics by which norms and rules were developed and sustained in society and the economy (Kerr 1950; Cain 1976). Such dynamics contributed to shape opportunities and constraints faced by individuals belonging to diverse social groups and generated inequalities in their capacity to access resources such as education and well-paid jobs in the labour market. An institutional perspective on market dynamics thus called for public policy aimed at alleviating such inequalities (see, for instance, Doeringer and Piore 1971), insofar as social cohesion and social welfare were not seen as spontaneously resulting from economic performance, itself optimally produced by market forces. Sharing such a core tenet of the old American institutionalism, the French regulation school went a step further by arguing that capitalism could not perpetuate itself without institutions that channelled the forces of competition and produced stable forms of wealth redistribution. Key economic conditions and institutions were identified that allowed for a 'virtuous circle' of wealth generation and redistribution to develop in industrialized countries under the Fordist system of the post-Second World War period (see Boyer 1987, 1996; Boyer and Durand 1997).

A central redistributive mechanism of that time laid in labour laws and collective bargaining systems by which the employment relation could simultaneously mobilize labour forces for production purposes and fuel market growth on the basis of regular wage increases (Grahl and Teague 2000). Along similar lines, radical labour economists and historians have analysed how a combination of social struggle on the part of workers and economic interest of large corporations allowed for such institutions to progressively build up and stabilize the Fordist system in the United States (Gordon et al. 1982; Jacoby 1985, 1991). Labour laws and collective bargaining systems provided the type of 'institutional order' or 'public process', in the words of organizational sociologist Philip Selznick (1969), that offered 'a setting for ordered controversy and accommodation, whereby the opportunity and capacity for legitimate self-assertion [of a variety of interests involved in the production process] could be guaranteed' (cited in Perrow 1986: 114).

For the sake of further comparisons with contemporary forms of social struggles and attempts to 'regulate' – in the French school sense of allowing for the social production and reproduction of – GCCs, several important characteristics of the Selznickian 'institutional order' established through state policy and collective bargaining systems during the Fordist period should be emphasized. First, these institutions emerged out of a process of conflict and confrontation allowing for the expression, recognition and organized convergence of a variety of interests in society and the economy. Conflicts could thus be seen as playing an instrumental role in the formation of an institutional context that allowed for the 'legitimate self-assertion' of diverse interests and the reach of a consensus among actors involved. At the local level, scholars interested in the institutional dynamics of industrial districts similarly pointed out that 'trust relations . . . seem more a consequence than a pre-condition of practical cooperation among local actors, and social consensus less an antithesis of conflict than an outcome of its successful resolution' (Zeitlin 1992: 287). Similarly, Fordist institutions were built on the principle of democratic representation, either in the form of elected workers representatives in collective bargaining systems, or as citizens' representation in the vote of national labour laws.

Second, the set of rules embodied into Fordist institutions had a binding character that restricted the freedom of action of all actors involved. Perrow (1986) emphasized that formal rules could effectively protect workers against arbitrary managerial decisions, an argument long-established in institutional and radical labour market theories (Doeringer and Piore 1971; Gordon et al. 1982). Such a regulatory system did not – and this comes as a major difference with the stakeholder view – rely on the voluntary action of individual agents or corporations. Translated in terms of corporate governance, this perspective implies that stakeholder participation becomes institutionalized so that, for instance, 'employees' role in governance is not at the discretion of any other group in the economy (such as shareholders)' (O'Sullivan 2003: 21). Finally, the scope of application of Fordist rules roughly matched the perimeter of corporations' economic activities. As such, it provided an effective scheme for stabilizing the workforce and employment relations, thus serving corporate management objectives to standardize work practices in order to boost productivity in the context of mass production systems. It also allowed for a 'virtuous cycle' to develop by establishing a link between wages, purchasing power and market growth.

Such a perspective highlights a major consequence of the rise of GCCs in deploying production systems across a wide variety of local or national institutional systems that remain largely disconnected and of highly unequal redistributive capacities. Having differentiated spaces of production and consumption in global chains, lead firms no longer faced obligations or incentives to promote regular collective wage increases in their production system, and they stopped doing so during the 1980s and 1990s by adopting individualized compensation schemes and/or subcontracting work to employers and places where Fordist counterpowers, that is, the state and labour union, were weakly organized or non-existent (Bonacich and Appelbaum 2000; Capelli 1999). While economic decisions became increasingly centralized in global management systems, societies remained organized – and redistributive institutions continued to operate – on a national basis. As a result, the capacity of Fordist counterpowers to channel economic forces towards the reinforcement of social cohesion within countries deeply weakened. Remaining anchored in national systems, binding rules no longer cover the production activities of global firms. Tightly regulated systems providing for high wages and social protection competed against loosely regulated, lower-wage locations within GCCs, in what could be called a 'vicious cycle' of global downward competitive pressures on wages and working conditions. The growing financialization of corporate governance at the top of GCCs thus concurred with the demise of older modes of governance promoting the employment relation, rather than ownership, as a primary vehicle for wealth redistribution in society. The International Labour Organization (ILO) repeatedly pointed to the social imbalances generated by such a shift where 'market opening measures and financial and economic considerations predominate over social ones . . . [so that] . . . workers and the poor have no voice in this governance process' (ILO 2004: xi).

Against this backdrop, the emergence of new social movements aiming to recreate some mode of regulation at the global level takes on a distinct significance. While a shareholder view negates the very legitimacy of campaign and labour organizations, and a firm-centred stakeholder view continues to place power in the hands of lead firms in GCCs that accommodated social critics through CSR tools and discourses, an institutional view rooted in French regulation theory holds that the sharing of decision-making capacities with strong labour counterpowers is not only legitimate but also necessary in order to ensure the very sustainability of global production systems. As such, it fits nicely into recent neo-Gramscian analysis of global production that make explicit the mechanisms by which a dominant elite manages to establish and sustain hegemony over subordinate groups in GCCs (Levy 2008). In Gramsci's view, hegemony operates not only by the identification of dominant groups' interests with the common interest – as sophisticatedly done in the shareholder view – and the diffusion of an ideology of mutuality of interests – as conveyed in CSR discourses – but also by political and material compromises that accommodate subordinate groups to some degree (1971, in Levy 2008: 20–1). Transnational activist networks can thus be seen as embodying social struggles over the building of some forms of consensual processes leading to some political and material compromises within the context of GCCs.

Building a new 'institutional order'?

In line with an institutional view of governance, contemporary activist campaigns forming the 'corporate accountability movement' – as framed by, among others, Utting (2005a), Bendell (2004) and Newell (2002) – in the global clothing chain will be discussed. Particular attention is paid to European and Canadian SMOs and two similarities that these movements exhibit with the formative stages of counterpower organizing in the Fordist era: the search for a coincidence of social and economic dynamics, and the role of conflicts in the construction of a system of binding rules.

Towards a coincidence of social and economic dynamics in GCCs

Traditional counterpowers in the form of the state and labour unions were established in national boundaries that matched the geographical scope of production systems in the Fordist era, and focused on production capabilities as key sources of profits in large firms' economic activities. By contrast, contemporary campaigns share some central features of GCCs and have adapted to some core foundations of their economic and financial power. Inter-organizational linkages allow for the quick build-up of alliances on a campaign basis, matching the agility that global firms gained for themselves through transnational vertical disintegration. While states and labour unions face the limits of operating mainly within the framework of a national mandate – although a number of global union federations have actively promoted international framework agreements with multinationals in recent years (Riisgaard 2005) – activist networks have developed a transnational scope of action and collaborate to establish social and cognitive linkages between production workers in the South and consumers in the North. In Levy's (2008: 31) view, 'the political sustainability of GPNs [global production networks] depends, in part, on the insulating effect of distance between conditions of production and consumption' so that 'activists have used these insights in their attempts to build discursive and organizational connections across the barriers of distance to highlight the contradictions within GPNs'. Such linkages can be seen as providing a foundation for further institutional developments at the transnational level by forming a common frame of reference and values for new rule-building activities in GCCs.

The organization of 'exposure trips' by activist groups provides one vehicle for doing so, either in a South–North orientation, when Southern workers come to Western markets, give press conferences and meet with corporate representatives as they did during the Matamoros and Hermosa campaigns, or in a North–South direction, as done for instance by Women in Informal Employment: Globalizing and Organizing (WIEGO), a network of Southern women workers' groups formed in 1997, when getting mainstream economists from Anglo-Saxon countries to visit informal workers in India (Chen et al. 2004). Southern and Northern SMOs also devised 'creation actions' based on theatre, exhibitions and fashion shows aiming to raise both worker and consumer awareness of the social and economic dimensions of globalization. For instance, the CAT, involved in the Matamoros campaign in Mexico, brings theatre plays to communities where *maquila* workers live in order to help them deal with issues of workplace struggles and harassment ('The Other King Kong Story'), union organizing ('The Machine') or women's conditions ('The Capital M in Mujer is not for Macho!') (Ascoly and Finney 2005). JANUN, a German youth organization involved in the Hermosa campaign, organizes walking tours for school classes in city centres, stopping in front of clothing and sports goods stores to tell stories about social and environmental issues at various stages of GCCs for these products and brands appreciated by the youth.[14]

While counterpowers historically focused on factories as places of social struggle, activist networks have shifted towards end-markets to reach the core profit-generating capabilities of GCC leaders, such as branding, marketing and other product differentiation investments. The founder of a clothing campaign group recalled, in relation to the first campaign launched by this organization: 'We didn't understand until then the power of the brand, and the fact that you could influence a company because of its brand sensitivity and vulnerability.' Contemporary activist campaigns seek to multiply 'pressure points' by combining actions at shareholder meetings, retail stores, jazz festivals, and so on. In both Europe and Canada, activist SMOs aim to target several buyers and get them to work together in a campaign, or to group demands around a common theme or area in order to amplify campaigns beyond the level of individual brands. This broadening of campaign perspectives is made possible by the dynamic learning pattern developed in relationships between SMOs and global buyers over the 1990s and early 2000s. As noted in an assessment report of the 'Urgent Appeal' system by which the CCC handles demands for international support: 'Nowadays, most of the cases taken up by the CCC are no longer about establishing [brand] responsibility but about trying to solve the problem in the workplace and develop, if possible, policies to prevent future violations. This is more complex for the CCC, whose strategy since 2003 includes working to bring brands together to collectively pressure their shared suppliers to resolve violations' (Dent 2005: 13).

Activist SMOs have also increasingly focused on the 'root causes' of labour abuses that relate to lead firms' sourcing policies. Self-evident for campaigners, the link between sourcing practices and working conditions at suppliers' factories had become somehow blurred by the creation of CSR departments within large firms, in charge of interacting with campaigners and developing codes of conduct procedures independently of corporate sourcing departments and demands made on suppliers in terms of price, quality and delivery. The consequences on workers' wages and working hours of continuously declining prices and delivery times imposed by lead firms on suppliers have been made explicit in several reports from SMOs and MSIs, such as the United Kingdom-based Ethical Trading Initiative (ETI) (Barrientos and Smith 2006). 'Perverse patterns' of labour market flexibilization, subcontracting, and growing concentration of economic power in large corporations have been questioned and greater 'political coherence' demanded between firms' CSR policies and the economic rationale of their global sourcing policies (Utting 2005a: 7–12).

As recommended in the managerial literature on interfirm networks (Jarillo 1993; Miles and Snow 1994), activist campaigns build on long-term, trust-based relationships both at the global level, when coordinating transnational action, and at the local level, in their home country. On a global scale, the issue of trust is particularly important with regard to the reliability of information gathered on a case by various partners, because statements regarding a given work situation engage the credibility of SMOs' claims and actions, while being continuously disputed by companies and other actors targeted by campaigns.[15] At the local level in the North, activist coalitions such as the MSN and the CCC maintain a small staff in each country but rely on relationships with large, long-standing national SMOs including faith, labour, feminist and teachers' organizations to leverage resources and build up scale. For instance, Ethique sur l'Etiquette (ESE), a French member of CCC, is supported by the Catholic Committee against Hunger and for Development (CCFD) and the Confédération Française Démocratique du Travail (CFDT/French Democratic Confederation of Labour), among others. In the United Kingdom, Labour Behind the Label (LBL) works with Christian Aid, Oxfam and Women Working Worldwide (WWW). In Canada, MSN acts as the secretariat of the Ethical Trading Action Group (ETAG), a coalition that includes church, teachers, and labour organizations, as well as Oxfam. Open, flexible relationships are a core operating principle of these networks both within and across countries. 'It's not a military structure, people get into a campaign based on their own interest', mentioned an MSN staff member. The CCC also developed as a 'very open, structurally loose and non-hierarchical network in which every national coalition of partner organizations has, for example, to pay its own way' (Zeldenrust, cited in Ascoly and Finney 2005: 53).

In the South, 'historical partners' play a central role in bringing new cases of labour abuses to the attention of Northern SMOs. 'We're more likely to take on a campaign if we get approached by a group we've developed a historical relationship with', comments an MSN coordinator. At CCC, the objective to develop long-term relationships with workers' groups in the South is given explicit pre-eminence over short-term opportunities for campaigning against large brands in the North. Because local workers bear major risks in terms of retaliation – including death threats on them and their families – campaigns are launched and pursued according to their decision.[16] Continuous interactions between Northern and Southern organizations are also conducive to capacity-building dynamics. For instance, a successful campaign targeting Nike and Reebok in 2001 in support of workers' organizing efforts at the Kukdong factory in Mexico played a major role in the formation of the CAT, a local workers' group that became involved in subsequent campaigns such as Matamoros. In El Salvador, relationships developed between CCC Germany and local SMOs such as Las Melindas also proved instrumental in launching the Hermosa campaign. A widely publicized campaign against The Gap regarding working conditions at Mandarin International in El Salvador led to the formation of the Grupo de Monitoreo Independiente de El Salvador (GMIES/Independent Monitoring Group of El Salvador), a local monitoring organization now accredited as an FLA code monitor and recruited by Adidas on the Hermosa case. The formation of sustained transnational linkages among activist organizations during the 1990s thus matches the structure of production in GCCs, and activist pressures are exerted on the main profit-generating mechanisms of this structure. If a new coincidence between social and economic dynamics can be seen to emerge here, a new mode of regulation is far from established insofar as transnational counterpower networks are not covering the full scope of global production, nor even a significant portion of it, so that a vast majority of workers remain unorganized and labour rights violations are persistently widespread in the labour-intensive segments of GCCs.

The role of conflict in rule-building processes

Other similarities between contemporary campaigns and the social dynamics observed in the formative stages of the Fordist period can be seen in the adoption of a confrontational attitude vis-à-vis large corporations, aimed at promoting a Selznickian 'legitimate self-assertion' of production workers in GCCs (Bonacich and Appelbaum 2000; Sum and Pun 2005). As a consequence, classic dilemmas historically faced by labour unions in terms of arbitration between confrontational and cooperative attitudes vis-à-vis corporations have arisen in global counterpower networks as well (Utting 2005a). In both Canada and Europe, major activist SMOs have agreed, as campaigns became more institutionalized, to contact brand companies and ask for corrective action at a supplier's factory before launching a public campaign on behalf of abused workers. In some cases, delays between initial contacts made with the brand and the launch of a campaign can extend up to a year.[17] Partly as a result of such forms of cooperation, 30 to 40 per cent of demands made by local worker groups for international actions within the context of CCC Urgent Appeal system do not lead to a public campaign.[18] 'You can't just attack, you have to be willing to talk', 'the idea is, oppose and propose at the same time, you cannot oppose if you don't propose', explained leading activists in these SMO networks. As a result, campaign SMOs have become increasingly absorbed in dealing with responses to social pressures that corporations have constructed in the form of codes of conducts and audits of code compliance, either in industry associations or in MSIs where collective codes have been launched under governance systems including firms, some activist and/or non-activist civil society organizations and/or labour unions, producing a diverse and shifting array of institutional arrangements within the global clothing industry.[19] Local projects involving multiple stakeholders have also multiplied in recent years, including the Joint Initiative on Corporate Accountability and Workers' Rights (JO-IN) launched in Turkey in 2004 by several major MSIs and the CCC to test best practices in codes of conduct (MSN 2007b).

Corporate and MSI codes of conduct have been either praised as efficient substitutes for declining or inexistent forms of Fordist regulation, in keeping with a stakeholder view of corporate governance, or criticized for favouring the development of a managerial 'audit culture' that remains largely disconnected from actual work conditions and labour issues at supplier factories, in line with core assumptions of an institutional perspective (O'Rourke 2006; Sum and Pun 2005). Both activist SMOs and international labour unions have indeed pointed out that the social auditing of codes was 'not sustainable [and] need[ed] to be replaced by a mature system of industrial relations based on social dialogue where representatives of management and workers become daily monitors of workplace situations' (Secretary General of the ITGLWF, in MSN 2007b: 22–3; see also CCC 2005). Accordingly, MSI codes are seen as responding to 'a need for temporary or transitory institutions that are going to experiment with different ways of enforcement or implementation of labour standards.... I think it sort of lays the ground for other forms of regulations that could come later', reflects a MSN leader. Likewise, in the words of a CCC representative: 'we support the development of MSIs because we believe that in the short term they could do a better job to help workers than governments could do, while at the same time we recognize that in the long term it has to be included into more accountability or a sort of regulatory framework.... To us, the MSIs are really a second-best solution.'[20] Echoing historical divisions within the union movement, such an opinion is not shared by more radical campaign groups: 'Most of the US groups would say that they do not accept that. Their focus is almost entirely on factory-by-factory worker organizing. That's the only thing they see as legitimate.'[21]

The idea of involving the ILO to build up more robust institutional arrangements in the long run was mentioned by representatives of SMOs in both Europe and Canada. 'Today if the ILO came forward with a good document saying "we want to set up an official mechanism specifically for the garment industry to promote freedom of association and deal with complaints", happily the whole anti-sweatshop movement would push, like, the top-20 brands into it, and I think on the European side a lot of brands would almost breath easy because they'd think "at least I'm spared the 50 different codes and 60 different initiatives and a lot of campaign trouble"', commented a leading CCC representative. Indeed, a momentum was identified among the most progressive brands for more collective forms of regulation: 'I think there's a transition taking place, everyone is searching for ways to regulate the industry, even the companies are, really. Companies that have been under the scan and been further than the other ones would like a level playing field. They want to see other companies pulled into the loop.'[22] Accordingly, the balance between conflicts and cooperation maintained by major activist SMOs in Europe and Canada aims at building more constraining forms of social regulation in GCCs in the future. More generally, the corporate accountability movement emphasizes the need for binding rules, including firms' obligation to answer to different stakeholders as well as elements of enforceability linking compliance failures to some sort of penalty (Newell 2002; Utting 2005a).

The issue of conflict and cooperation involves SMO relationships not only with global brands but also – in more subtle ways – with labour unions. 'Quite apart from our relations to the MSIs, we are in the dynamics of conflict between unions and SMOs everyday, all the time.... We take that with us, with every case that we do', comments an activist leader. Likewise, the literature underlined that a variety of cases could be observed where SMOs acted either as confronting or supporting unions at the local level (O'Rourke 2006; Utting 2005a). The campaigns under study revealed a more complex pattern. On the one hand, activist SMOs in Europe and Canada are primarily geared towards improving work conditions and supporting workers' empowerment through organizing. MSN defines itself on its webpage as 'a labour and women's rights organization that supports the efforts of workers in global supply chains to win improved wages and working conditions and a better quality of life.' Likewise, CCC aims 'to improve working conditions and empower workers in the global apparel industry, in order to end the oppression, exploitation and abuse of workers in this industry, most of whom are women.' Both organizations have a strong representation of labour unions in their membership base in various countries, and in some places the CCC office is hosted by a labour union. The lack of freedom of association and obstacles to workers' organizing efforts came up in 75 per cent of campaign cases launched by the CCC between 1999 and 2003 under its Urgent Appeal system (Dent 2005). SMOs, therefore, are using campaigns to promote the diffusion of core demands of labour unions committed to the defence of workers' rights in the global clothing industry.

On the other hand, some campaign cases have exposed the drawbacks of labour unions that do not adequately represent workers' interests, a situation typical of a number of production countries such as Mexico and El Salvador. 'We have a mandate to bring change in unions as well', commented a CCC representative. Activists point out some general limitations of traditional labour unions: 'the old structure of labour organizing cannot operate globally; it cannot deal with the regulation gap that developed when companies started to go global and to subcontract.' The specialization of trade unions by country and industry makes interconnections difficult during campaigns and creates conditions for the emergence of conflicting interests, as happened when a labour union specialized in chemicals and historically established at Puma in Germany sided with the firm's CSR department against SMOs and the local Mexican independent garment union during the Matamoros campaign.[23] In such situations, campaigns are revealing tensions internal to the international union movement, itself trapped by the conflict versus cooperation dilemma with large corporations. Some unions opting for cooperative relations in a given context might find themselves hostile to grassroots unions' activist initiatives in other contexts, as illustrated by Cumbers et al. (2008) in their case study of the International Chemical, Energy, Mining and General Workers Federation (ICEM). In other cases, a lack of coordination might hamper relationships between transnational SMO networks and international trade union federations. In the Hermosa campaign, for instance, when negotiations around the setting up of a fund were already well advanced between FLA brands, the CCC, local SMOs and Hermosa workers, the ITGLWF stepped in and called for a brand meeting for similar purposes. Only Wal-Mart – that had remained unresponsive to previous calls from SMOs during the campaign – agreed to participate.[24] Some SMO representatives also pointed to a 'generation gap' between activists and labour unions, as well as a gender issue: 'In the labour movement as a whole I believe we're still stuck in an old-fashioned organizing model that doesn't answer to the needs, including the organizing needs, of women workers' (Zeldenrust, cited in Ascoly and Finney 2005: 53). Activist SMOs can thus be seen to play a role not only in bringing changes in subcontracting and employment practices in GCCs but also in the ways in which the union movement itself responds to the challenges of the 'global factory' (Fuentes and Ehrenreich 1983).

Concluding remarks

Over the course of the 1990s, in the various end-markets of Europe and North America, new SMOs have emerged to promote improvements in the working conditions of women garment workers in Southern producing countries. Campaigning played a central role in the foundation of these SMOs – the 1989 C&A campaign and the 1994 campaign against The Gap have respectively become founding myths in the history of the CCC and MSN – and continues to provide the main lever by which these SMOs can make their voice heard in discussions with global brands and more collaborative initiatives such as the MSIs. As shown in this chapter, activist SMOs dedicated to the global clothing industry have gained leverage and scaled up their activities by adopting a network form of organization mirroring the organizational strategies by which major lead firms have reconfigured their production chain on a global scale.

This corporate accountability movement has been framed as illegitimate and potentially harmful in a shareholder view of GCC governance, and as inadequate in its conflict dimension along a firm-centred stakeholder view. From an institutional perspective, because such a movement is searching for new forms of coincidence between networks of countervailing power and corporate networks, while combining conflicts and negotiation in the exercise of such power, it could be perceived as contributing to a new mode of regulation in the global economy. A strong engagement from governments, possibly channelled by the ILO, but going much further in terms of actual enforcement capacity, will nevertheless be needed for such initiatives to lead to the construction of a true mode of regulation in the French Regulation theory sense of the term. In the meantime, workers by the hundreds of millions will continue to work under oppressive conditions, including long hours, poor wages, health problems, sexual harassment and union repression in GCCs. Looking at the road ahead, whether GCCs can actually be regulated in the sense of being made to actually upgrade rather than downgrade social (and environmental) conditions, or whether addressing these issues will require deep reconfigurations of production and consumption, remains an open question.

Notes

1. I wish to thank an anonymous reviewer for very useful comments, as well as the people in social movement organizations (SMOs) and multistakeholder initiatives (MSIs) interviewed for this research, for their openness and availability.
2. Gibbon (2002); Gibbon and Ponte (2005); Palpacuer et al. (2005).
3. Newell (2002); Bendell (2004); Utting (2005a).
4. Bonacich and Appelbaum (2000); Bender and Greenwald (2003); Esbenshade (2004).
5. Information on the Matamoros case has been collected by the author from the websites of SMOs involved in the campaign, including www.sweatshopwatch.org, www.nosweat.org.uk, www.maquilasolidarity.org, as well as email exchanges with a Puma Social and Environmental Affairs representative.
6. The FLA was established in the late 1990s as a successor body to the White House Apparel Industry Partnership.
7. The North American Agreement on Labour Cooperation (NAALC) includes 11 labour principles such as freedom of association, discrimination, and minimum wage.
8. The Hermosa case was documented using campaign groups' websites, interviews at CCC International Secretariat, CCC Germany, MSN, and the FLA, and the detailed and extensive report produced by MSN (2007a) on the Hermosa case for the FLA.
9. Interview with CCC International secretariat, Amsterdam, April 2007.
10. FLA interview, Geneva, May 2007.

11. All references to $ are to US dollars.
12. I have elaborated elsewhere on these three views to highlight how they link up to various schools of thoughts in organizational theory (Palpacuer 2006), and how the link can be made between corporate-level and chain-level governance (Palpacuer 2008).
13. Powell (1990); Sako (1992); Uzzi (1997).
14. JANUN interview, Germany, November 2007.
15. For instance, controversies typically arise regarding when a company started and/or ended sourcing from a given supplier.
16. Interview with CCC International Secretariat, Amsterdam, April 2007.
17. Admittedly, longer delays also stem from the preparation time required by the increasingly collective dimension of campaigns that now simultaneously target several brands.
18. CCC interview, International Secretariat, Amsterdam, April 2007.
19. Gereffi et al. (2001); O'Rourke (2003); Utting (2002).
20. CCC interview, International Secretariat, Amsterdam, April 2007.
21. MSN interview, June 2007.
22. MSN interview, June 2007.
23. CCC Germany, interview, April 2007.
24. Interviews with FLA (May 2007) and CCC representatives (April 2007).

References

Alchian, Armen and Harold Demsetz, 'Production, information costs, and economic organization', *American Economic Review*, Vol. 62, No. 5 (1972) 777–95.

Ascoly, Nina and Chantal Finney, *Made by Women: Gender, the Global Garment Industry and the Movement for Women Workers' Rights* (Amsterdam: Clean Clothes Campaign, 2005).

Barrientos, Stephanie and Sally Smith, *The ETI Code of Labour Practice: Do Workers Really Benefit?* (Brighton: Institute for Development Studies (IDS), University of Sussex, 2006).

Bendell, J., *Barricades and Boardrooms: A Contemporary History of the Corporate Accountability Movement*, Programme on Technology, Business and Society, Paper No. 13 (Geneva: UNRISD, 2004).

Bender, Daniel E. and Richard A. Greenwald, *Sweatshop USA: The American Sweatshop in Historical and Global Perspective* (New York: Routledge, 2003).

Blair, Margaret, *Ownership and Control* (Washington, DC: Brookings, 1995).

Bonacich, Edna and Richard Appelbaum, *Behind the Label: Inequality in the Los Angeles Apparel Industry* (Berkeley, CA: University of California Press, 2000).

Boyer, Robert, *The Seven Paradoxes of Capitalism or Is a Theory of Modern Economies Still Possible?*, Working Paper No. 9620 (Paris: CEPREMAP, 1996).

——, *La Théorie de la Régulation: Une Analyse Critique* (Paris: La Découverte, 1987).

Boyer, Robert and Jean-Pierre Durand, *After Fordism* (London: Macmillan Press, 1997).

Brabet, Julienne, 'Responsabilité sociale et gouvernance de l'entreprise'. In Jacques Igalens (ed.), *Tous Responsables* (Paris: Editions d'Organisation, 2004).

Bureau of Democracy, Human Rights and Labor, Embassy of the United States, El Salvador, *Human Rights Report: El Salvador*, San Salvador, 6 March (2007). http://sansalvador.usembassy.gov/news/2007/reports/hr/elsalvador.html (accessed in November 2008).

Cain, Glen, 'The challenges of segmented labour market theories to orthodox theories', *Journal of Economic Literature*, Vol. 14, December (1976) 1215–57.

Capelli, P., *The New Deal at Work: Managing the Market-Driven Workforce* (London: Harvard Business School Press, 1999).

CCC (Clean Clothes Campaign), *Looking for a Quick Fix: How Weak Social Auditing is Keeping Workers in Sweatshops*, Collective report (Amsterdam: CCC, 2005).

Chen, Martha, Renana Jhabvala, Ravi Kanbur, Nidhi Mirani and Karl Osner, *Reality and Analysis: Personal and Technical Reflections on the Working Lives of Six Women* (Gujarat: Cornell-SEWA-WIEGO Exposure and Dialogue Program, 2004).

Cumbers, Andrew, Corinne Nativel and Paul Routledge, 'Labour agency and union positionalities in global production networks', *Journal of Economic Geography*, Vol. 8, No. 3 (2008) 369–88.

della Porta, Donnatella and Sydney Tarrow, *Transnational Protest and Global Activism* (Lanham, MD: Rowman & Littlefield, 2005).

Dent, Kelly, *Urgent Appeals Impact Assessment Study* (Amsterdam: CCC, 2005).

Dicken, Peter, *Global Shift: The Internationalisation of Economic Activity*, 3rd edition (New York: The Guildford Press, 1998).

Doeringer, Peter and Michal Piore, *Internal Labour Markets and Manpower Analysis* (Armonk, NY: M.E. Sharpe, 1971).

Esbenshade, Jill, *Monitoring Sweatshops: Workers, Consumers and the Global Apparel Industry* (Philadelphia, PA: Temple University Press, 2004).

Fama, Eugène and Michael Jensen, 'Agency problems and residual claims', *Journal of Law and Economics*, Vol. 26 (1983) 327–49.

Freeman, Edward, *Stakeholder Management: A Strategic Approach* (Boston, MA: Pitman, 1984).

Friedman, Milton, *Capitalism and Freedom* (Chicago, IL: University of Chicago, 1962).

Fuentes, Annette and Barbara Ehrenreich, *Women in the Global Factory* (Boston, MA: South End Press, 1983).

Gereffi, Gary, 'The organization of buyer-driven global commodity chains: How US retailers shape overseas production networks'. In Gary Gereffi and Miguel Korzeniewicz (eds), *Commodity Chains and Global Capitalism* (Westport, CT: Greenwood Press, 1994).

Gereffi, Gary, Ronie Garcia-Johnson and Erika Sasser, 'The NGO–industrial complex', *Foreign Policy*, July–August (2001) 55–65.

Gereffi, Gary, John Humphrey and Tim Sturgeon, 'The governance of global value chains', *Review of International Political Economy*, Vol. 12, No. 1, February (2005) 78–104.

Gibbon, Peter, 'At the cutting edge? Financialisation and UK clothing retailers' global sourcing patterns and practices', *Competition & Change*, Vol. 6, No. 3 (2002) 289–308.

Gibbon, Peter and Stephano Ponte, *Trading Down; Africa, Value Chains, and the Global Economy* (Philadelphia, PA: Temple University Press, 2005).

Gordon, David M., Richard Edwards and Michael Reich, *Segmented Work, Divided Workers* (Cambridge: Cambridge University Press, 1982).

Grahl, John and Paul Teague, 'The Regulation School, the employment relation and financialization', *Economy & Society*, Vol. 29, No. 1 (2000) 160–78.

Humphrey, J. and H. Schmitz, 'How does insertion in global value chains affect upgrading in industrial clusters?', *Regional Studies*, Vol. 36, No. 9 (2002) 1017–27.

ILO (International Labour Organization), *A Fair Globalization: Creating Opportunities for All*, report of the World Commission on the Social Dimension of Globalization (Geneva: ILO, 2004).

Jacoby, Stanford M., *Masters to Managers: Historical and Comparative Perspectives on American Employers* (New York: Columbia University Press, 1991).

——, *Employing Bureaucracy* (New York: Columbia University Press, 1985).

Jarillo, Carlos, *Strategic Networks: Creating Borderless Organization* (Oxford: Butterworth Heinemann, 1993).

Jensen, Michael, *A Theory of the Firm* (Boston, MA: Harvard University Press, 2000).

Kelly, Gavin, Dominic Kelly and Andrew Gamble, *Stakeholder Capitalism* (Basingstoke: Macmillan, 1997).

Kerr, Clark, 'Labour markets: Their character and consequences', *American Economic Review*, Vol. 40, May (1950) 278–91.

Levy, David, 'Political contestation in global production networks', *Academy of Management Review*, Vol. 33, No.4, October (2008) 943–63.

Merk, Jeroen, *The Play Fair at the Olympics Campaign: An Evaluation of the Company Responses* (Amsterdam: CCC, 2005).

Miles, Raymond E. and Charles C. Snow, *Fit, Failure and the Hall of Fame: How Companies Succeed or Fail* (New York: Free Press, 1994).

MSN (Maquila Solidarity Network), *Emergency Assistance, Redress and Prevention in the Hermosa Manufacturing Case*, report prepared for the Fair Labour Association (Toronto: Maquila Solidarity Network, 2007a).

——, *Heightened Global Competition Tests the Limits of CSR Initiatives*, MSN Codes Memo No. 21, February (2007b).

Nadvi, Khalid and Hubert Schmitz, *Industrial Clusters in Less Developed Countries: Review of Experiences and Research Agenda*, Discussion Paper No. 339 (Brighton: IDS, University of Sussex, 1994).

Newell, Peter, 'From responsibility to citizenship: Corporate accountability for development', *IDS Bulletin*, Vol. 33, No. 2 (2002) 91–100.

O'Higgins, Eleanor R.E., 'Global strategies: Contradictions and consequences', *Corporate Governance*, Vol. 3, No. 3 (2003) 52–66.

O'Rourke, Dana, 'Multi-stakeholder regulation: Privatizing or socializing global labour standards?', *Competition and Change*, Vol. 34, No. 5 (2006) 899–918.

——, 'Outsourcing regulation: Analyzing nongovernmental systems of labour standards and monitoring', *The Policy Studies Journal*, Vol. 31, No. 1 (2003) 1–29.

O'Sullivan, Mary, 'Employees and corporate governance'. In Peter K. Cornelius and Bruce Kogut (eds), *Corporate Governance and Capital Flows in a Global Economy* (New York: Oxford University Press, 2003).

——, *Contests for Corporate Control* (Oxford: Oxford University Press, 2000).

Palpacuer, Florence, 'Bringing the social context back in: Governance and wealth distribution in global commodity chains', *Economy and Society*, Vol. 37, No. 3, August (2008) 393–419.

——, 'Globalization and corporate governance: Issues for management researchers', *Society and Business Review*, Vol. 1, No. 1 (2006) 45–61.

Palpacuer, Florence, Peter Gibbon and Lotte Thompsen, 'New challenges for developing country suppliers in global clothing chains: A comparative European perspective', *World Development*, Vol. 33, No. 3, March (2005) 409–30.

Palpacuer, Florence and Aurelio Parisotto, 'Global production and local jobs: Can global production networks be used as levers for local development?', *Global Networks: A Journal of Transnational Affairs*, Vol. 3, No. 2, April (2003) 97–120.

Perrow, Charles, *Complex Organizations* (Glenview, IL: Scott, Foresman and Co., 1986).

Post, Jim E., Lee E. Preston and Sybille Sachs, *Redefining the Corporation: Stakeholder Management and Organizational Wealth* (Palo Alto, CA: Stanford University Press, 2002).

Powell, Walter W. 'Neither market nor hierarchy: Network forms of organization'. In Barry M. Straw and Larry L. Cummings (eds), *Research in Organizational Behavior*, Vol. 12 (1990) 295–336.

Pyke, Frank, Giacomo Becattini and Werner Sengenberger, *Industrial Districts and Inter-Firm Co-operation in Italy* (Geneva: International Institute for Labour Studies, ILO, 1990).

Riisgaard, Lone, 'International framework agreements: A new model for securing workers rights?', *Industrial Relations: A Journal of Economy and Society*, Vol. 44, No. 4 (2005) 707–37.

Sako, Mari, *Prices, Quality and Trust: Inter-Firm Relations in Britain and Japan* (Oxford: Oxford University Press, 1992).

Selznick, Philip, *Law, Society and Industrial Justice* (New York: Russell Sage Foundation, 1969).

Simons, Herbert, 'Some reflections on syndicalism', *The Journal of Political Economy*, Vol. 52, No. 1, March (1944) 1–25.

Sousa Santos, Buenaventura, 'Globalizations', *Theory, Culture & Society*, Vol. 23, No. 2 (2006) 393–412.

Sousa Santos, Buenaventura and Cézar Rodriguez-Garavito, *Law and Globalization from Below: Towards a Cosmopolitan Legality* (Cambridge: Cambridge University Press, 2005).

Sum, Ngai-Ling and Ngai Pun, 'Globalization and paradoxes of ethical transnational production: Code of conduct in a Chinese workplace', *Competition and Change*, Vol. 9, No. 2 (2005) 181–200.

Utting, Peter, *Rethinking Business Regulation: From Self-Regulation to Social Control*, Programme on Technology, Business and Society, Paper No. 15 (Geneva: UNRISD, 2005a).

——, 'Corporate responsibility and the movement of business', *Development in Practice*, Vol. 15, Nos 3/4 (2005b) 375–88.

——, 'Regulating business via multistakeholder initiatives: A preliminary assessment'. In NGLS and UNRISD (eds), *Voluntary Approaches to Corporate Responsibility: Readings and a Resource Guide* (Geneva: NGLS and UNRISD, 2002).

Uzzi, B., 'Social structure and competition in interfirm networks: The paradox of embeddedness', *Administrative Science Quarterly*, Vol. 42, No. 1 (1997) 35–67.

Williamson, Oliver E., *The Economic Institutions of Capitalism: Firms, Markets and Relational Contracting* (New York: The Free Press, 1985).

——, *Markets and Hierarchies: Analysis and Antitrust Implications* (New York: The Free Press, 1975).

Zeitlin, Jonathon, 'Industrial district and local economic regeneration: Overview and comment'. In Frank Pyke and Werner Sengenberger (eds), *Industrial Districts and Inter-Firm Co-operation in Italy* (Geneva: International Institute for Labour Studies, ILO, 1992).

Index